Lecture Notes in Computer Science 2603

Edited by G. Goos, J. Hartmanis, and J. van Leeuwen

Springer
Berlin
Heidelberg
New York
Barcelona
Hong Kong
London
Milan
Paris
Tokyo

Alessandro Garcia   Carlos Lucena
Franco Zambonelli   Andrea Omicini
Jaelson Castro (Eds.)

Software Engineering for Large-Scale Multi-Agent Systems

Research Issues and Practical Applications

Springer

Series Editors

Gerhard Goos, Karlsruhe University, Germany
Juris Hartmanis, Cornell University, NY, USA
Jan van Leeuwen, Utrecht University, The Netherlands

Volume Editors

Alessandro Garcia
Carlos Lucena
Pontifícia Universidade Católica do Rio de Janeiro - PUC-Rio
Rua Marquês de São Vicente, 225, Ed. Pe. Leonel Franca
22453-900 Rio de Janeiro, Brazil
E-mail: {afgarcia,lucena}@inf.puc-rio.br

Franco Zambonelli
Università di Modena e Reggio Emilia
Dipartimento di Scienze e Metodi dell'Ingegneria
Via Allegri 13, 42100 Reggio Emilia, Italy
E-mail: franco.zambonelli@unimo.it

Andrea Omicini
Università di Bologna, Dipartimento di Elettronica, Informatica e Sistemistica (DEIS)
Via Rasi e Spinelli, 176, 47023 Cesena (FC), Italy
E-mail: aomicini@deis.unibo.it

Jaelson Castro
Universidade Federal de Pernambuco, Centro de Informática
Av. Prof. Luiz Freire S/N, 50732-970 Recife PE, Brazil
E-mail: jbc@cin.ufpe.br

Cataloging-in-Publication Data applied for

A catalog record for this book is available from the Library of Congress.

Bibliographic information published by Die Deutsche Bibliothek.
Die Deutsche Bibliothek lists this publication in the Deutsche Nationalbibliografie;
detailed bibliographic data is available in the Internet at <http://dnb.ddb.de>.

CR Subject Classification (1998): D.2, I.2.11, C.2.4, D.1.3, H.5.3

ISSN 0302-9743
ISBN 3-540-08772-9 Springer-Verlag Berlin Heidelberg New York

Springer-Verlag Berlin Heidelberg New York
a member of BertelsmannSpringer Science+Business Media GmbH

http://www.springer.de

© Springer-Verlag Berlin Heidelberg 2003
Printed in Germany

Typesetting: Camera-ready by author, data conversion by PTP-Berlin GmbH
Printed on acid-free paper   SPIN: 10872742   06/3142   5 4 3 2 1 0

Preface

Over the past few years, Object-Oriented Software Engineering has proven to be a powerful paradigm for supporting the development of high-quality software systems. However, we are now faced with the task of engineering large-scale systems composed of pervasive software components that move across and adapt to non-deterministic and open environments, like the Internet, in order to achieve system goals through the coordination of autonomously distributed specialized services. This need for autonomous and pervasive components has spurred the revitalization of the notions and properties associated with software agents and Multi-Agent Systems (MASs). The MAS concepts are being explored to cover most of the software development lifecycle from conceptual modeling and requirements specifications to architectural definition, design and implementation.

MASs and their underlying theories provide more natural support for properties such as autonomy, mobility, environment heterogeneity, organization, openness, and intelligence. As a consequence, agent-based systems are likely to provide new insights into the complexity of developing and maintaining modern software. However, developing robust large-scale agent-based systems will require new software engineering approaches. There are currently many methods and techniques for working with individual agents or systems built using only few agents. Unfortunately, agent-based software engineering is still in its infancy and existing software engineering approaches are unable to cope with large MASs.

MAS features are now being applied to the development of large industrial systems, where such systems involve hundreds, or perhaps thousands of agents. There is a pressing need for software engineering techniques that allow the peculiarities of these systems to be effectively managed, and for methods to guide the process of MAS development. Without adequate development techniques and methods, such systems will not be sufficiently dependable, robust, trustworthy, and extensible. In addition agent-based systems will be difficult to comprehend, and their components will not likely be reusable.

The complexity associated with large MASs is not straightforward. When a huge number of agents interact over heterogeneous environments, various phenomena occur that are not as easy to explain as when only a few agents are working together. As the multiple software agents become highly collaborative and operate in networked environments, they must be context-aware and deal with environment uncertainty. It makes their coordination and management more difficult and increases the likelihood of the occurrence of exceptional situations, such as security holes, privacy violations, and unexpected global effects. Moreover, as users and software engineers delegate more autonomy to their MASs, and put more trust in their results, new concerns arise in real-life applications. However, many existing agent-oriented solutions are far from ideal; in practice, the systems are often built in an ad hoc manner, are error-prone, not scalable, not dynamic, and not generally applicable to large-scale environments. Commercial success for MAS applications will require scalable solutions based on software engineering approaches in order to ensure effective deployment and to enable reuse.

Today topics related to MASs appear in a wide variety of conference proceedings and journals. However, the research efforts in terms of software engineering for large MASs tend to be scattered in the literature and do not appear as a coherent research topic worth pursuing for its own importance. The papers selected for this book represent one of the first efforts at compiling lessons learned from the application of MAS notions to realistic large-scale software systems. The research presented in this volume illustrates the broad range of software engineering approaches that are being used to cope with the complexity of such systems and to promote the construction of dependable MASs with reusable components. Further, the power of agent-based software engineering is demonstrated through examples that are representative of real-world applications. They describe experiences and techniques associated with large MASs in a variety of problem domains that include network monitoring, e-commerce, Web services, healthcare, and traffic management. The authors have chosen these particular problem domains because they encompass significant kinds of complex problems faced by software engineers practicing in the MAS domain.

Given the comprehensive selection of case studies and software engineering solutions for MAS applications, this book provides a valuable resource for a vast audience of readers. The intended primary audience for this book includes researchers and practitioners who are interested in the progress of software engineering for MASs (especially large, complex systems), individuals interested in understanding the interplay between agents and objects in software development, and those interested in experimental results from MAS applications. Practicing software engineers involved with particular aspects of MASs may find it interesting to learn about experiences in using software engineering approaches to build real systems. A number of chapters in the book discuss the development of MASs from requirements and architecture specifications to implementation. One key contribution of this volume is the description of fresh approaches to reasoning about complex MASs.

This book brings together a collection of 17 papers addressing a wide range of issues in software engineering for large-scale MASs, reflecting the importance of agent properties in today's software systems. The papers presented describe recent developments on specific issues and practical experience. The research issues addressed consist of: (i) a modeling framework, (ii) integration of agent abstractions with other software engineering abstractions and techniques (such as objects, roles, components, aspects, reflection, and patterns), (iii) innovative approaches for coordination and mobility, and (iv) approaches to meeting quality attributes for large-scale MASs, such as dependability, scalability, reusability, and maintainability. At the end of each chapter, the reader will find a list of interesting references for further reading. The book is organized into six parts that deal with topics related to: (i) Software Engineering Foundations, (ii) Requirements Engineering and Software

Architecture, (iii) Coordination and Mobility, (iv) Reuse, (v) Dependability, and (vi) Empirical Studies and Applications.

Software Engineering Foundations. The first part of the book focuses on foundations for the development of large agent-based systems. The paper by Silva et al. presents a conceptual framework for modeling large-scale MASs. It identifies abstractions for agent-based software engineering in the light of classical abstractions of object-oriented software engineering. The framework ontology allows for the characterization of large-scale software systems as organizations of agents, objects, and their common and distinguished abstractions. The paper by Odell et al. examines how the notion of role might be used to design complex agent systems. Its authors use social and organizational systems theory as a source of inspiration.

Requirements Engineering and Software Architecture. The second part comprises three papers that propose approaches to define requirements and software architectures for agent-oriented systems, and discuss traceability among the artifacts produced in the early stages of MAS development. The paper by Cysneiros and Yu presents a requirements-engineering methodology based on agent concepts such as autonomy, intentionality, and sociality. The proposed methodology complements and extends the *i** modeling framework. The paper by Castro et al. argues that requirements traceability is essential for the development of complex MASs, although it is not currently supported by any of the existing agent-oriented methodologies. Its authors present a framework that extends the Tropos methodology to encompass requirements traceability. The paper by Silva et al. motivates the use of the Reflective Blackboard pattern in the architectural design stage of large-scale MAS development. The proposed pattern provides, early in the architecture definition, the context in which more detailed decisions related to system-level properties, such as coordination, mobility, security, and fault tolerance, can be made in the later stages of large MAS development.

Coordination and Mobility. The papers in the third part provide solutions for dealing with coordination and mobility problems in complex MASs. The paper by Roman et al. extends the notion of declarative specifications and provides the mechanisms needed to access the specified resources despite rapid changes in the environment caused by the mobility of hosts, migration of software agents, and changes in connectivity. The paper by Mamei and Mahan focuses on the problem of engineering the respective movements' coordination of huge numbers of agents. It proposes an approach that takes inspiration from the laws of physics. The authors' idea is to have the movements of agents driven by abstract force fields, generated by the agents themselves and propagated via some infrastructure or by the agents in an ad hoc way. The paper by Gustavsson and Fredriksson argues that large MASs emphasize the notion of coordinated behavior and openness, and hence methodological approaches to such systems would benefit from a holistic and context-sensitive framework, i.e., a framework for information ecosystems. According to the authors, the proposed framework allows explicit addressing of important systemic properties of large MASs, such as coordination, trustworthiness, adaptation, and robustness.

Reuse. The fourth part of the book is composed of two papers that are concerned with reusability issues in MASs. The paper by Holvoet and Steegmans first overviews possible ways of reuse in agent-based systems and then presents the MASORG approach to improving MAS reusability. The proposal is largely inspired by three pillars of today's software engineering practice and research, namely separation of concerns, design patterns, and frameworks. In their paper, Pace et al. discuss a CASE environment, called Smartweaver, for supporting the development of aspect-oriented MASs. Smartweaver promotes the reuse of MASs by capturing and keeping agency properties separated from the basic agent functionalities based on concepts from the aspect-oriented paradigm. The paper by Griss discusses the interplay between software components and agents, and how the use of software agents can improve significantly software reuse.

Dependability. The papers in the fifth part focus on dependability issues in the development of complex MASs. The paper by Guessoum et al. presents a role-centric approach to evaluating the criticality of software agents and improving their dependability in terms of reliability and availability. The agent criticality is used to replicate agents in order to maximize their dependability based on available resources. The paper by Huhns et al. describes how agent-oriented software engineering can be used to achieve robust large software systems. It also speculates on the implications of multiagent-based redundancy for software development.

Empirical Studies and Applications. The last part is concerned with applications, practical problems, and experience in engineering real-world MASs. The paper by Zambonelli et al. reports about an experiment where the behavior observed in dissipative cellular automata resulted in stable macro-level global structures emerging from local interactions among cells. Since dissipative cellular automata exhibit some characteristics of open multi-agent systems, they argue that similar sorts of macro-level behaviors are likely to emerge in MASs and need to be studied, controlled, and fruitfully exploited. They describe some results of a preliminary set of experiments. In their paper, Sycara et al. identify challenges that confront large-MAS designers and claim that these challenges can be successfully addressed by agent-based software engineering based on their vast experience in developing complex MASs. The paper by Tripathi et al. presents their experiences with the development of a MAS for network monitoring. The major challenges in this system were dealing with security problems, the coordination of a huge number of agents to achieve monitoring functions, and fault recovery. The paper by Alencar et al. proposes a declarative agent-based approach to orchestrate and monitor data consistency and business processing. It also describes the current system implementation and applications in which the proposed approach has been applied.

The motivation for the production of this book was the *1st International Workshop on Software Engineering for Large-Scale Multi-Agent Systems* (SELMAS

2002)[1], organized in association with the 24th International Conference on Software Engineering, held in Orlando, Florida, USA, in May 2002. SELMAS 2002 was our first attempt to put together software engineering practitioners and researchers to discuss the multifaceted issues that emerge when using MASs to engineer complex systems. Later the organizers decided to extend the workshop scope covered by the present book. For that purpose they invited several workshop participants to prepare chapters for this book based on their original position papers, and also extended an invitation to a number of other leading researchers in the area to submit additional chapters. After an extensive reviewing process, involving more than 70 reviewers, we selected the papers that appear in this volume.

We are confident that this book will be very useful to the software engineering community, by providing many original and distinct views on such an important interdisciplinary topic, and by contributing to the development of an understanding and crossfertilization among individuals in this research area. It is only natural that the choice of contributors to this book reflects the personal views of the book editors. We raise this point only to suggest that despite the volume of papers and work on software engineering for large-scale MASs, there are still many interesting challenges to be explored. The contributions that can be found in this book are only the beginning. Our thanks go to all the authors, whose work made this book possible. Many of them also helped during the reviewing process. We would like to thank Alfred Hofmann of Springer-Verlag and Juris Hartmanis, LNCS series editor, for recognizing the importance of publishing this book. In addition, we would like to thank the members of the Program Committee who invested many hours reviewing the submitted papers. Also we acknowledge the support and cooperation from Rosa Pinto and Andréa Castor (CIn-UFPE) and the SoC+Agents and TecComm teams (PUC-Rio) which helped us in the preparation of this volume.

January 2003

Alessandro Garcia
Carlos Lucena
Franco Zambonelli
Andrea Omicini
Jaelson Castro

---

1 Garcia, A., Lucena, C.: Software Engineering for Large-Scale Multi-Agent Systems - SELMAS 2002 (Workshop Report). ACM Software Engineering Notes, Vol. 27, No. 5, September 2002, pp. 82–88.

2002)[1], organized in association with the 24th International Conference on Software Engineering, held in Orlando, Florida, USA, in May 2002. SELMAS 2002 was our first attempt to put together software engineering practitioners and researchers to discuss the multifaceted issues that emerge when using MASs to engineer complex systems. Later the organizers decided to extend the workshop scope covered by the present book. For that purpose they invited several workshop participants to prepare chapters for this book based on their original position papers, and also extended an invitation to a number of other leading researchers in the area to submit additional chapters. After an extensive reviewing process, involving more than 70 reviewers, we selected the papers that appear in this volume.

We are confident that this book will be very useful to the software engineering community, by providing many original and distinct views on such an important interdisciplinary topic, and by contributing to the development of an understanding and crossfertilization among individuals in this research area. It is only natural that the choice of contributors to this book reflects the personal views of the book editors. We raise this point only to suggest that despite the volume of papers and work on software engineering for large-scale MASs, there are still many interesting challenges to be explored. The contributions that can be found in this book are only the beginning. Our thanks go to all the authors, whose work made this book possible. Many of them also helped during the reviewing process. We would like to thank Alfred Hofmann of Springer-Verlag and Juris Hartmanis, LNCS series editor, for recognizing the importance of publishing this book. In addition, we would like to thank the members of the Program Committee who invested many hours reviewing the submitted papers. Also we acknowledge the support and cooperation from Rosa Pinto and Andréa Castor (CIn-UFPE) and the SoC+Agents and TecComm teams (PUC-Rio) which helped us in the preparation of this volume.

January 2003

Alessandro Garcia
Carlos Lucena
Franco Zambonelli
Andrea Omicini
Jaelson Castro

---

1 Garcia, A., Lucena, C.: Software Engineering for Large-Scale Multi-Agent Systems - SELMAS 2002 (Workshop Report). ACM Software Engineering Notes, Vol. 27, No. 5, September 2002, pp. 82–88.

Evaluation and Program Committee

Table of Contents

Software Engineering Foundations

Requirements Engineering and Software Architecture

Coordination and Mobility

Reuse

Dependability

Empirical Studies and Applications

Taming Agents and Objects in Software Engineering

Viviane Silva[1], Alessandro Garcia[1], Anarosa Brandão[1], Christina Chavez[2],
Carlos Lucena[1], and Paulo Alencar[3]

[1] PUC-Rio, Computer Science Department, SoC+Agent Group,
Rua Marques de São Vicente, 225 - 22453-900, Rio de Janeiro, RJ, Brazil
{viviane, afgarcia, anarosa, lucena}@inf.puc-rio.br

[2] UFBA, Computer Science Department
Av. Ademar de Barros, s/n – 40170-110, Salvador, BA, Brazil
flach@ufba.br

[3] University of Waterloo, Computer Science Department, Computer Systems Group
Waterloo, Ontario, N2L 3G1 Canada
palencar@csg.uwaterloo.ca

Abstract. Agent-based software engineering has been proposed in addition to
object-oriented software engineering as a means of mastering the complexity
associated with the development of large-scale distributed systems. However,
there is still a poor understanding of the interplay between the notions of agents
and objects from a software engineering perspective. Moreover, the many facets
of agent-based software engineering are rarely used in the various phases of the
software development lifecycle because of the lack of a comprehensive
framework to provide the software designers with a clear understanding of the
use of these two key abstractions. In this context, this paper presents TAO, an
evolving innovative conceptual framework based on agent and object
abstractions, which are the foundations for modeling large-scale software
systems. The conceptual framework allows for the characterization of large-
scale software systems as organizations of passive components, the objects, and
autonomous components, the agents, with each of these elements playing roles
to interact with each other and to coordinate their actions in order to fulfill
system goals.

1 Introduction

With the advances in Internet technologies 24, 50, 67, software systems are
undergoing a transition from monolithic architectures based on passive components
into open and distributed architectures composed of organizations of autonomous
components, that operate and move across different environments in order to achieve
their goals in a coordinated way 47, 69, 77. Object-oriented software engineering 5,
6, 46, 60 has succeeded to support the development of high-quality software systems,
but the complexity raised in this architectural transition is no longer affordable in
terms of its abstractions, modeling languages, and methodologies 19, 20, 36, 44, 56,
66, 75. The limitations of the object paradigm has spurred research on agent-based
software engineering 32, 33, 34 as an additional approach to the development of

A. Garcia et al. (Eds.): SELMAS 2002, LNCS 2603, pp. 1–26, 2003.

large-scale systems from their conceptual modeling 10, 68, 71 to their computational modeling 18, 21, 55 .

While the object abstraction is fundamentally applied to model resources or passive components, the agent abstraction is naturally tailored to represent autonomous components in the software system. The notion of multi-agent systems (MASs) 64 and the underlying theories associated with their many properties bring with them more natural support for autonomy, coordination, mobility, organization, openness, and intelligence. In this context, the discipline of Software Engineering is trying to understand how the lessons learned from the application of these agent theories in Artificial Intelligence can be used to overcome the limitations of object-oriented software engineering and lead to a mastery of the complexity of modern software. The successful and widespread deployment of large-scale MASs requires a unifying set of central abstractions to support modeling languages and respective methodologies for an agent and object-centric software engineering. However, there is still a poor understanding of the interplay between the agent and object notions from a software engineering perspective.

As is the case with any new software engineering paradigm, researchers are beginning to strive to formulate the methodologies that guide the process of constructing MASs 27, 39, 42, 57, 71 . Many, such as Agent UML 54 and MAS-CommonKADS 26 , are extensions of previous object-oriented methodologies and languages, while others, such as the AAII methodology 39 , are extensions of knowledge engineering methodologies. Existing methodologies propose very distinct and varying sets of abstractions suitable for different domains. Each methodology has incorporated its own abstractions for conceptual and computational modeling, and there is no agreement about a common group of abstractions that can be used across different methodologies. As a consequence, it is very difficult to understand the interplay between agents and objects from a software engineering perspective, and the real contributions of agents in the construction of large-scale systems. The many facets of agent and object-based software engineering are still rarely used in the various phases of the software lifecycle because of the lack of a comprehensive framework 19, 72 .

In this context, this paper presents TAO (Taming Agents and Objects conceptual framework), whose goal is to provide the foundations for agent and object-based software engineering. This paper is not a survey of existing concepts used by methods, languages and methodologies for MAS but a definition of an ontology that defines the essential concepts, or abstractions, for developing MASs. The benefit of having a conceptual framework is to provide support for developing new methodologies, methods and languages based on the essential concepts defined and related in the framework. Each concept is viewed as candidate abstraction for modeling languages, methodologies and support environments to be applied in different phases of the MAS development. We classify the abstractions used to establish our ontology into three categories: (i) fundamental abstractions, (ii) grouping abstractions, and (iii) environment abstractions.

TAO can be tailored to different domains since its basic ontology can be extended to accommodate new abstractions for new domains. TAO enables different research teams to compare and discuss their formulations based on the unified terminology of the proposed foundations. The remainder of this paper is organized as follows. Section 2 presents the conceptual framework and a brief view of the abstractions and their relationships. Section 2 also describes example used in the paper in order to illustrate our definitions. A definition of the fundamental, environment and grouping abstractions are presented in Sections 3, 4 and 5 and the relationships between those abstractions are introduced and defined in Section 6. Section 7 provides an overview on how the templates used throughout the paper should be formalized. Section 8 reviews some related work and Section 9 discusses some future directions for research in this area. Finally, Section 10 presents the conclusions of our work.

2 The Conceptual Framework

2.1 The Role of the Conceptual Framework

A conceptual framework is critical for both the problem understanding (conceptual modeling) and the solution proposal (computational modeling) of any development project as software systems become more complex 11 . The purpose of conceptual models is to provide an understanding of the domain describing the problem. Conceptual models describe the problem raised by the user and to be solved by the software system 11 . In order to produce a solution, computational models may be generated based on conceptual models. Computational models are used to describe the form of the software system that solves the problem. A computational model is the definition of a software product, and is the output of requirement specification and design activities 11 . Fig. 1 shows a four-layer picture that illustrates the role of the conceptual framework using the metadata architecture MOF 53 for a simple example. Although computational models do not appear in Fig. 1 these models are generated at the domain model layer.

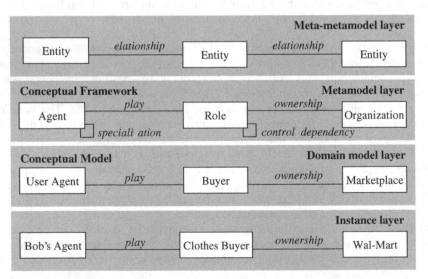

Fig. 1. The role of the conceptual framework using OMG-MOF 53

The four MOF layers are: meta-metamodel layer, metamodel layer, domain model layer and instance layer. The meta-metamodel layer is comprised of the description of the structure and semantics of meta-metadata. In this paper, we use the ER model (Entity-Relationship model) 13 to describe the entity and relationship meta-metadata that appear in this layer. The entity and relationship meta-metadata provide the basic definition that describes the different entities and relationships instances that appear in the metamodel layer.

Our work is concentrated in the metamodel layer (conceptual framework) which we use to define the conceptual framework TAO developed for the MAS domain. TAO defines the set of metadata, i.e. entity instances and relationship instances that must appear on the metamodel layer level. The framework defines a total of 6 entity instances such as agents, roles and organizations and a total of 8 relationship instances such as play, control and owner (Fig. 1).

The main role of TAO is to provide a unified conceptual framework to understand distinct abstractions and their relationships in order to support the development of large-scale MASs. The proposed framework elicits an ontology that connects consolidated abstractions, such as objects and classes, and "emergent" abstractions, such as agents, roles and organizations, which are the foundations for agent and object-based software engineering. TAO presents the definition of each abstraction as a concept of its ontology, and makes provision for relationships between them.

In contrast with the metamodel layer, which is domain independent, the domain model layer (conceptual model) depicts the data specific to the application domain. The metadata at the metamodel layer are instantiated into data through domain models using the domain information. Entities and relationship instances defined in the metamodel layer are used in the domain model layer according to the domain information defining the conceptual model. The conceptual model is an instance of the conceptual framework based on domain information. The example presented in Fig. 1 shows a partial domain model where the metadata *Agent,* *ole* and *rgani ation* are instantiated as *ser Agent, Buyer* and *Marketplace,* respectively and the relationships *play* and *owner* are selected from the set of relationship instances defined in the metamodel layer by the conceptual framework. Recall that those entities and relationships are used according to the domain information.

In order to create domain models, modeling languages, methodologies and methods such as 27, 39, 42, 54, 57, 71 are needed. Modeling languages are used to provide a common language that elicits the meaning of each data element described in the conceptual model. Methods and methodologies are used to guide and help the designer in the creation of domain models.

The instance (information) layer characterizes the possible domain model occurrences. This layer describes the specific instances of the domain model data that may occur during the lifetime of the modeled application. For instance, consider a marketplace domain where buyers and sellers negotiate products. Sellers advertise their desire to sell products, submitting offers to the marketplace. Buyers access the marketplace in order to buy products. They look for offers that match their needs. They can move to another marketplace in order to look for offers that they did not find in the original one. Alternatively, they can form groups to find offers with a lower price per unit. Fig. 1 shows some instances for the marketplace domain: *Bob's Agent* is an instance of a *ser Agent, lothes Buyer* is an instance of the *Buyer* role, and *Wal-Mart* is an instance of the *Marketplace* organization.

2.2 The Abstractions and Their Categories

TAO classifies the set of abstractions it defines into three distinct categories: (i) *fundamental abstractions* – include the object and agent abstractions, which are the basis for building MASs (Section 3); (ii) *en ironment abstractions* – include definition of environments and events that are used to represent the environmental constraints and characteristics that influence instances of fundamental and grouping abstractions (Section 3.4); (iii) *grouping abstractions* – encompass abstractions for dealing with more complex situations in large-scale systems; it includes organizations and roles to model complex collaborations (Section 4). Fig. 2 presents the TAO abstractions and their relationships: our proposed conceptual framework (metamodel layer).

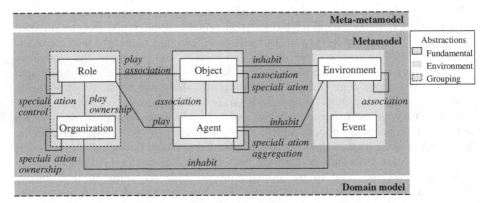

Fig. 2. The abstractions and relationships of the conceptual framework

As shown in Fig. 2, the entity instances defined in the conceptual framework TAO are object, agent, organization, role (agent role and object role), environment and event. Because of similarities among some entities, we have defined a new abstraction called element that is the basis for the definition of most entities.

Element definition
   An element is an entity instance that has properties and relationships with others elements

Objects, agents, environments, organizations, object roles and agent roles are entities whose definitions are based on the element abstraction. Their definitions extend an element by identifying specific properties and relationships. Event is the only entity in TAO that is not based on the definition of element. It is because events do not have state, behavior or relationships.

The *properties* of an element describe its state and behavior characteristics. The *state* of an element defines information about other elements of the system and the *beha ior* of an element defines the actions or operations that the element can perform. An element can change its state and interact with other elements. An element must be related to another element, i.e., a *relationship* must exist between two elements, so that they can interact. The *relationships* link two elements and describe how these elements are related to each other. As illustrated in Fig. 2, different elements are related in different ways, i.e. there are different types of relationships (Section 5). An element *class* defines properties and relationships that are common to all its *instances*. An element instance is a concrete manifestation of an abstraction to which a set of properties and relationships are applied 6 . An element instance of a class fulfills the description of its class.

Besides defining the abstractions, we introduce templates associated with each abstraction in the text. The templates are used to define each abstraction in a schematic way. They list the set of properties and relationships of each element. The templates correspond to the metamodel layer and their instances are related to the domain model layer. In order to exemplify the use of our templates, we have applied them to the marketplace example (Section 2.1) throughout this paper.

2.3   TAO: An Overview

A multi-agent system (MAS) comprises classes and instances of *agents, ob ects* and *organi ations*. Organizations group together the agents of a MAS 45, 64 . Agents, organizations, and objects, inhabit (or are immersed in) *en ironments* 33, 42 that provide *resources* and make available *ser ices*. Resources are non-autonomous entities such as databases or external programs used by agents or organizations. We use objects as an abstraction for modeling resources 45 . While objects represent passive elements, such as resources, agents represent autonomous entities that manipulate objects. Services are the public facilities, or public functions, provided and used by the entities of the system 39 . Entities such as agents, objects, organizations and the environment can make public some of its functions (services) to be used by others entities.

An organization describes a set of *roles* 4 that limits the behavior of its agents, objects and sub-organizations 70 . Agents and objects can be members of different organizations and play different roles in each of them 58 . Every agent of the MAS plays at least one role in an organization. Agents may interact with each other and cooperate either to achieve a common goal, or to achieve their own goals 74 . The agent interactions are based on *relationships* defined between organization roles. An agent may interact with agents from the same organization or from a different one. Two distinct organizations are also related when there are interactions and relationships among their agents.

3 Fundamental Abstractions

This Section describes the fundamental abstractions, object and agent, and the environment abstractions. Each abstraction is described in terms of the following issues: basic definition, state properties, behavior properties, its interplay with other abstractions, its associated template, its application to model the marketplace example. This Section also highlights the most important differences and common features between objects and agents. The types of relationships between abstractions are presented and discussed in Section 5.

3.1 Object

An ob ect is a passi e or reacti e element that has state and beha ior and can be related to other elements

An object is an element that has a state and a number of operations (behavior) to either examine or change its state 29 . An object extends the definition of an element since it defines state and behavior properties, and relationships with other objects or other elements. The *state* of an object does not have any predefined structure. It stores information about itself, about the environment and about other objects. The *beha ior* of an object defines the operations that it is capable of performing. The object *relationships* describe how objects are linked to system's elements, such as other objects, agents, and roles.

An object has control of its state. It performs operations that can modify its state during its lifetime. On the other hand, an object cannot modify its behavior[1] and has no control of it, i.e., an object is not autonomous in the sense it does everything that another one asks it to do. In this way, objects are passive elements that do whatever anyone asks them to do and only when they are asked.

Objects could play roles defined by the organization that uses the object. Because of the importance of the entity role in our conceptual framework, the object role is described in a specific template that is explained in Section 4.2. An object *class* defines the structure and behavior of similar objects 5 . The following template defines the state, behavior and relationships that an object class must have. The object template also lists the events that objects, instance of the object class, can generate and perceive and the roles that objects could play.

```
                           Object

      Object_Class Object_Class_Name
             State   setOf{Information}
             Behavior setOf{Operation}
             Relationships setOf{Relationship_Name}
             Events generated: setOf{Event_Name},
                    perceived: setOf{Event_Name}
             Roles setOf{Role_Class_Name}
      end Object_Class
```

The application of the object template to our case study defines the object class *Offer* that characterizes the seller announcements. This class presents the product, the announcer identifier, the basic operations to change the offer price, and the relationships with objects, environment, roles, and the marketplace organization. The object inhabits the *MarketPlaceEnv* environment, has a *Product* object associated, can be accessed by *Buyers* and *Sellers*, and is defined in the context of the *MarketPlaceOrg* organization.

---

[1] Computational reflection has been introduced in the object paradigm 43 to support the dynamic adaptation of the behavior of object-oriented systems at run-time. However, it is not a property of the objects themselves; it is an extension of the object paradigm.

```
                          Offer

     Object_Class Offer
           State {price, Product, announcerId, count}
           Behavior {get_price, set_price}
           Relationships {Association_Offer_Product,
                 Inhabit_Env_Offer, Association_Offer_Buyer,
                 Association_Offer_Seller,
                 Association_Offer_MarketPlaceOrg}
           Events generated: Announcement_Published
           Roles Announcement
     End Object_Class
```

3.2 Agent

An agent is an autonomous adapti e and interacti e element that has a mental state

Software agents are complex objects with an attitude 7 ; that is, they are elements that extend objects with structured state and agency behavioral properties. According to 25, 34, 52 , agents are interactive, autonomous and adaptive elements, and those are the three fundamental characteristics that define the agent property. Characteristics such as rationality, learning ability and mobility are additional characteristics that are neither necessary nor sufficient for the characterization of a software agent.

The *state* of an agent is expressed through mental components such as beliefs, goals, plans and actions 34, 52, 64 . The set of beliefs, goals, plans and actions is called the mental state of the agent. During the lifetime of an agent, its mental state can change, i.e., the agent can change its beliefs, goals, plans and actions.

An agent has beliefs or knowledge about the world, about itself and about other agents. The beliefs include what the agent knows, what the agent views, its memories and its perceptions about everything that happens in the MAS. The agent's goals consist of future states, or desires, which agents would like to reach, or satisfy. As agents are goal-oriented an agent within a MAS must have at least one goal to be achieved. An agent achieves a goal by executing a plan, which can be selected from a list of plans.

Plans define a sequence of actions that is executed by an agent to achieve goals. An agent updates its mental state, changes its roles, perceives and generates *e ents* and sends and receives messages while executing actions. Actions have a set of pre and post-conditions. An action is executed if its pre-conditions are satisfied according to the beliefs of the agent. After the execution of the action, the agent checks the post-conditions according to its beliefs. If the post-conditions are satisfied the correctness of the action is guaranteed.

The *beha ior* of an agent is expressed through its plans and actions that are based on its agency characteristics, e.g., interaction, autonomy and adaptation. Agents are interactive because they have the ability to interact with other elements when playing roles in an organization. Agents interact with others since they have relationships with other system elements. The *relationships* describe how an agent is linked to another *element*. For example, a relationship describes the roles that an agent plays and the environment that it inhabits. The types of relationships that an agent may have are defined in Section 5.

The autonomy characteristic refers to the proactive capacity of an agent — the agent does not need external stimulus (e.g., user events) in order to carry out a given task. Agents are adaptive elements since they can adapt their state and their behavior by responding to messages sent by the environment or other agents. By assuming a given situation the agent may simply react, or it may reflect upon what should be done.

The agent template defines an agent *class*. An agent *class* describes beliefs, goals, actions, plans and relationships that are the same for all its agent instances. The agent template also lists the events that agents, instances of the agent class, can generate and perceive, and the roles that agents could play. A specific template for agent roles was created and is explained in Section 4.2.

Agent

```
Agent_Class Agent_Class_Name
        Beliefs setOf{Belief_Name}
        Goals setOf{Goal_Name}
        Actions setOf{Action_Name}
        Plans setOf{Plan_Name}
        Events generated: setOf{Event_Name},
                perceived: setOf{Event_Name}
        Roles setOf{Role_Class_Name}
        Relationships setOf{Relationship_Name}
    end Agent_Class
```

We used the agent template in our case study to define an agent called *User_Agent* that represents the users in the system. The agent *User_Agent* knows what is a simple offer, a group offer and the environment it inhabits. Its goal is to deal with products and it can perform actions to deal with sellers and buyers and to request authorization to enter another marketplace. Besides that, it also has strategies for buying and selling products. It plays the roles of *Buyer* and *Seller*. It also plays the role of *Mediator* if it is coordinating a group in order to buy products.

User_Agent

```
Agent_Class User_Agent
    Beliefs {Offer, Offer_for_Group, MarketPlaceEnv}
    Goals {Dealing_products}
    Actions {ask_for_Entering_Authorization,
            deal_with_Seller, deal_with_Buyer}
    Plans {buying_Strategy1, buying_Strategy2,
            selling_Strategy}
    Events generated: Group_Forming
            perceived: Announcement_Published
    Roles Buyer, Seller, Mediator
    Relationships {Inhabit_Env_User_Agent, Play_Buyer,
    Play_Seller, Play_Mediator}
 end Agent_Class
```

3.3   Agent versus Object

We define an agent as an extension of an object, i.e. an agent is an object with additional features, because it extends the definition of state and behavior associated with objects. The state of an agent has a "mentalistic" structure 68 , as we have already seen. The agent's mental state extends the definition of state defined for objects because it adds to its state the definition of its behavior. So the state of an agent, its mental state, consists of also its state and its behavior. The mental state consists of: beliefs, that are equivalent to the object's state, and also goals, plans and actions, that define the agent's behavior. Moreover, the behavior of an agent extends the behavior of objects because: (i) an agent has full control of its behavior, i.e., agents can say no to the requests of other agents, (ii) agents can change their behavior, adding new actions to be executed 64 , and (iii) agents do not require external stimuli to carry out their jobs. These three extensions make an agent an active element and an object a passive element.

Another difference between agents and objects is related to the agency characteristics. As we have already seen, an agent is an autonomous and interactive element that sends and receives messages. The autonomy and interactivity of an agent can vary from a completely reactive agent that interacts frequently with other agents to a completely proactive agent that may not need to interact with anyone to achieve its goals. In the case where the agent is a completely reactive element it may be considered an object. The more autonomous an agent is the less interactive it needs to be. A proactive agent does not need to cooperate with anyone to achieve its goal. On the other hand, the less autonomous an agent is the more interactive it needs to be to achieve its goals.

An object is an interactive element but it is not an autonomous one. Objects are reactive and passive elements since they need the assistance of another element to do their job and since they respond to any request for assistance. Classically, an object interacts a lot with other objects in order to complete their jobs. From the point of view of the autonomy and interaction characteristic, there is no difference between a reactive agent and an object. They both need a request from another element to do their jobs and they both need to interact with other elements in order to do their jobs.

4   Environment Abstractions

An en ironment is an element that is the habitat for agents ob ects and organi ations
An en ironment can be heterogeneous dynamic open distributed and unpredictable

An environment extends the definition of an element since it defines its properties, i.e., its state and its behavior, and its relationships. The *state* of an environment stores the lists of resources and services and associated access permissions. Resources are non-autonomous entities such as databases or external programs used by agents or organizations. We use objects as an abstraction for modeling resources 45 . The resources can be used by objects, by agents or by organizations when playing roles. The permissions associated with resources restrict the access of objects and agents to them. Agents, objects and organizations make services available to other agents and organizations. The permissions associated with the services restrict the access of the agents and organizations.

The *beha ior* of an environment is defined based on its characteristics. An environment can be heterogeneous, dynamic, open, distributed and unpredictable 57 . An environment can be a passive element such as an object or can be an active element such as an agent having agency characteristics such as autonomy, adaptation and interaction. An environment can also have other agency characteristics such as mobility. A palmtop may be considered a mobile environment. Thus, an environment may be seen as an agent when appropriate.

An environment is the habitat of MAS organizations, agents and objects. An organization may inhabit multiple environments but an agent and an object must inhabit only one environment at a given moment. An agent or an object must not be in two or more environments at any given moment. Different environments can be the habitat of different elements and can have different characteristics, resources and services. The *relationships* of an environment describe which elements inhabit it and which other environments are associated with it. These relationships are extensively described in Section 5.

The environment template presents an environment *class*. An environment class defines its state as a set of resources and a set of services, the behavior of its instances as a set of its properties and a set of relationships that are common to all environment instances.

Environment

```
Environment_Class Environment_Class_Name
    Resources setOf{<Resource, Permision, Element_Class_Name>}
    Services setOf{<Service, Permission, Element_Class_Name>}
    Behavior setOf{Properties}
    Relationships setOf{Relationship_Name}
    Events generated: setOf{Event_Name},
           perceived: setOf{Event_Name}
end Environment_Class
```

The environment template was used to define our case study environment. The *MarketPlaceEnv* is the habitat of agents, objects, and organizations. It provides services and resources to deal with products and it is open and heterogeneous.

MarketPlaceEnv

```
Environment_Class MarketPlaceEnv
    Resources {<Offer, read, Seller>, <Offer, read, Buyer>,
              <Offer, write, Seller>, <Offer, write, Buyer>}
    Services {buy_Service, sell_Service, submit_Service}
    Behavior {Open, Heterogeneous}
    Relationships {Inhabit_Env_User_Agent, Inhabit_Env_Offer
              Inhabit_Env_MarketPlaceOrg, ...}
    Events perceived: Group_Forming
end Environment_Class
```

Events are generated in different ways. They can be generated by objects through the execution of their operations, by agents through the execution of their actions and by environment when the environment is an active element 68 . An event generated by the environment, by an agent or by an object can trigger the execution of actions associated with agents or operations associated with objects that perceive the event. As a consequence, events are related to actions and operations that generate them and to actions and operations that perceive them.

5 Grouping Abstractions

MAS comprises a set of grouped agents immersed in one or more environments whose global behavior is derived from the interaction among the constituent agents 74 . The group of agents comprising the MAS defines organizations whose goals are the same as the MAS. A MAS has at least one organization that represents the system and that groups all agents. The organization's agents exist to achieve the goals of the MAS. The agents have individual goals that, when they are grouped together, characterize the goals of the MAS.

5.1   Organization

An organi ation is an element that groups agents which play roles and ha e common goals An organi ation hides intra-characteristics   properties and beha iors represented by agents inside it

Besides the organizations defined by the MAS, the MAS can have other organizations that are sub-organizations. Recursively, each sub-organization can have others sub-organizations defined within it.

From the perspective of elements outside of an organization, the organization can be viewed as an agent. An organization hides intra-characteristics, properties and behavior represented by agents inside it. However, an organization extends the properties and relationships defined by agents. An organization defines a set of rules and laws that agents and sub-organizations must obey. The rules and laws characterize the global constraints of the organization. An organization also defines roles that must be played by the agents and sub-organizations within it. Since all organizations define roles, rules and laws, any agent and any sub-organization is always playing at least one role and respecting the rules and the laws defined by the MAS organizations.

The *state* of an organization is represented by the state of the agents that play roles in it and by the rules and laws defined in the organization. An organization's *beha ior* is based on the behavior of the agents that play roles in this organization. The behavior of an organization typically is more complex than the sum of the behaviors of the agents playing roles. The *relationships* describe how an organization is linked to another *element*. For example, the roles defined by an organization are linked to the organization through the relationship owner, describing that the organization is the owner of the roles. Another example is the association between two organizations characterizing that they will exchange messages. One may observe that interactions between an organization and another element in fact occur between an agent inside the organization and the element.

The organization template presents an organization class that describes the rules and laws as well as the relationships associated with all instances. In relationships we can find the roles that an organization owns, the environment that organization inhabits, and the resources and services that it provides.

```
Organization

Organization_Class Organization_Class_Name
           Rules setOf{Rule}
           Laws setOf{Law}
           Relationships setOf{Relationship_Name}
     end Organization_Class
```

We have defined the organization for our case study by using the organization template. The organization *MarketPlaceOrg* has rules and laws guiding the behavior of agents playing roles and agents within it, like *Mediator_creates_Buying_Groups_and_just_Him* and *Counter_Proposal _has_NMAX*, and it has relationships like *Inhabit_Env_MarketPlaceOrg*, which fix that it inhabits some environment, others like *Owner_Mktp_Role_Buyer* and *Owner_Mktp_Buying_Group_Org*, which fix that it owns some role and some sub-organization.

```
MarketPlaceOrg

Organization_Class MarketPlaceOrg
    Rules {Counter_Proposal_has_NMAX,
           Buiyng_Group_has_MAX_Buyers,
           Verifier_authorizes_only_Buyers_to_Enter}
    Laws {Mediator_creates_Buying_Groups_and_just_Him,
           Everybody_uses_FIPA_ACL_Protocol_to_comunicate}
    Relationships {Owner_Mktp_Buying_Group_Org,
           Owner_Mktp_Role_Buyer, Owner_Mktp_Role_Seller,
           Owner_Mktp_Role_Mediator, Owner_Mktp_Role_Verifier,
           Inhabit_Env_MarketPlaceOrg,
           Association_Offer_MarketPlaceOrg, ...}
    end Organization_Class
```

5.2 Roles

efined in the conte t of an organi ation a role is an element that guides and restricts the beha ior of an agent or an ob ect in the organi ation The social beha ior of an agent is represented by its role in an organi ation

The two most important properties of roles are (i) a role is always defined in the context of an organization and (ii) a role must be played by an agent, by an object or by a sub-organization. A role is an element since it defines a set of properties and relationships.

The *state* and *beha ior* of an object role, similar to what is defined for objects, keep information and operations, respectively. An object role may add information to the state of the object and may restrict access to the object state. An object role also guides and restricts the behavior of an object. On one hand, the object role can add behavior and relationships to the object that plays the role and, on the other hand, can restrict the access to the object 41 .

The *relationships* of an object role describe additional relationships and types of relationships that were not previously available to objects. For example, an object role may add an association to another element that was not defined in the object.

From the point of view of the element that is related to the object that is playing a role, the role identifies the properties that the element can see and identifies the available relationships. The object role template defines the states, behaviors and relationships available to the object that plays the roles and to other elements related to it. The object role template presents the role class, and all role instances of the role *class* have the same states, behaviors and relationships.

Object_Role

```
Object_Role_Class Object_Role_Class_Name
        State  setOf{Information}
        Behavior setOf{Operation}
        Relationships setOf{Relationship_Name}
    end Object_Role_Class
```

An agent role guides and restricts the behavior of an agent because associated with the role are goals, beliefs, duties, rights, protocols and commitments that an agent has while playing the role. An agent role is an element since it has state, behavior and relationships with other elements. The *state* of an agent role is defined by its beliefs and goals. The beliefs of the roles are related to the organization's facts, e.g., information about the other roles and information about the objects available in the organization. The goals of the roles characterize the goals that the agent must achieve while playing the role. The goals of the roles grouped together form the organization's goals.

The duties, rights, protocols and commitments define the *beha ior* of an agent role. The duties of the roles describe the responsibilities 70 of the organization's agents. The duties define actions assigned to the agent playing the role. We will generalize and describe a duty as a set of actions. Besides the rules and laws described in the organization, the rights associated with each role describe the permissions on the resources and services available in the environment and about the behavior of the agents. The portion of the environment that an agent can sense and effect is determined by the agent's specific role. Normally, each agent has a partial notion of the whole system 35, 57 and none of the agents have sufficient competence, resources or information to solve the whole problem 30 .

The protocols and commitments define the interactions between roles and other elements. Protocols define a set of interactions and rules that the elements playing the role and following the protocol must obey. A commitment defines a set of actions that an element playing a role must carry out in relation to other roles.

The definition of the *relationships* of an agent role is based on the protocols and commitments associated with the role. In this way, the agent role adds a set of relations to the agent that plays the role.

The agent role template presents the agent role *class* and the goals, beliefs, duties, rights, protocols and commitments that define the interactions. It also identifies the relationships of the agent roles, i.e., its owner, the agents and organizations that may play the role, the objects associated with the role, and the associations between the roles. All role instances of the role class have the same properties and relationships.

Agent_Role

```
Agent_Role_Class Agent_Role_Class_Name
     Goals setOf{Goal_Name}
     Beliefs setOf{Belief_Name}
     Duties setOf{Action_Name}
     Rights setOf{Permission_Name}U setOf{Action_Name}
     Protocols setOf{Interaction_Class_Name}U setOf{Rule_Name}
     Commitments setOf{Action_Name}
     Relationships setOf{Relationship_Name}
end Agent_Role_Class
```

The agent role template was used to define the role buyer. The role *Buyer* is defined by the organization *MarketPlaceOrg*. Agents playing this role can deal with agents that play roles of *Seller*, *Mediator* and *Verifier*, when they are buying products from *Seller*, or asking to participate in a *Buying_Group*, or asking permission to enter another marketplace, respectively. They also have some duties, such as *buy_Product*, that can generate a commitment, like *pay_for_Product*, and some rights, like *accepting_Offer*. Moreover, their interactions must follow some protocols, such as the *FIPA_Protocol* 14 .

Buyer

```
Agent_Role_Class Buyer
   Goals {buy_products}
   Beliefs {Offer, Product}
   Duties {submit_Offer, analyse_Offer, buy_Product,
           pay_for_Product}
   Rights {making_Counter_Proposal, rejecting_Offer,
           accepting_Offer, receiving_Product}
   Protocols {FIPA_Protocol}
   Commitments {pay_for_Product}
   Relationships {Association_Buyer_Seller,
           Association_Buyer_Mediator,Association_Buyer_Verifier,
           Association_Offer_Buyer, Owner_Mktp_Role_Buyer}
end Agent_Role_Class
```

6 Relationships

This Section presents the relationships between all elements of the conceptual framework. There are eight different relationships classified in two different ways that associate objects, agents, environments, organizations and roles where some are basic and domain-independent relationships and other are domain-dependent relationships. The basic relationships are *play*, *owner* and *inhabit*. These relationships will always appear in any conceptual model since they do not depend on the problem domain.

6.1   Relationship Types

Let A be a set of agents, $a \in A$, E be a set of environments, $e \in E$ and O be a set of objects, $o \in O$. Let Org be a set of organizations, org, subOrg $\in$ Org and subOrg always represents a sub-organization. Let R be a set of roles, $R = RObj \cup RAg$ where RObj is a set of object roles and RAg is a set of agent roles, $r \in R$, $ro \in Robj$ and $ra \in RAg$. For each one relationship presented below, we present its definition, its classification and the elements it links.

- Inhabit (I) : I(habitat, citizen) : I(e,a), I(e,o), I(e,org)
Some elements must inhabit environments and can dynamically change from a habitat, i.e. an environment, to another. The inhabit relationship specifies that the element that inhabits - the citizen - may leave and enter habitats, respecting the habitat permissions. Normally, the habitat does not guide the actions of its citizens and does not impose constraints on when to enter or leave the habitat or what specific actions they must carry out. On the other hand, the habitat restricts which elements can enter, which resources and services they can access and which services they can provide. When a citizen changes its habitat it is no longer subordinated to its old habitat.

When inhabiting environments, agents, objects and MAS organizations must respect the permissions that have been defined by them. Agents and objects inhabit only one environment at a given time, as opposed to organizations, which can inhabit more than one environment at the same time.

- Ownership (Ow) : Ow(owner, member) : Ow(org, r), Ow(org, subOrg)
Some elements must be members of another element. The ownership specifies that an element - the member - is defined in the scope of another element - the owner - and that a member must obey a set of global constraints defined by its owner. Members may be dynamically created or destroyed by their owner.

Organizations are owners of roles and sub-organizations. Each role and sub-organization has one owner organization. Agents or sub-organizations in an organization play roles as defined by their enclosing organization.

- Play (P): P(element, role) : P(a,ra), P(subOrg,ra), P(o,ro)
Objects, agents and sub-organizations must play roles. The play relationship defines that the object, agent or sub-organization that plays the role assumes properties and relationships defined by the role. The behavior of the object, agent or sub-organization is guided by and restricted to the scope of the role.
- Specialization/Inheritance (S) : S(super-element, sub-element) : S(o,o), S(a,a), S(org,org), S(ro,ro), S(ra,ra)

The specialization relationship defines that the sub-element that specializes the super-element may add and redefine the properties and behavior associated with the super-element.

- Control (C)[2] : C(controller, controlled) : C(ro,ro), C(ra,ra), C(ra,ro)

The control relationship defines that the controlled element that plays the role must do anything that the controller element asks it to do. An agent role may control another agent role or an object role. Object roles only can control another object role. An agent playing a role that controls another role played by another agent is related to the other agent by an undirected relationship of control.

- Dependency (D) : D(client, supplier) : D(ro,ro), D(ra,ra), D(ra,ro)

An element - the client - may be defined to be dependent on another one - the supplier - to do its job. The dependency relationship specifies that the client cannot completely do its job unless it asks the supplier. The client changes its behavior according to the supplier but the opposite is not true. The client does not influence its supplier. An agent role may depend on another agent role or on an object role. Object roles can only depend on another object role.

- Association (As) : As(associate1, associate2) : As(r,r), As(e,e), As(o,o), As(a,o), As(o,org)

If an element is associated with another element, it knows that the other element exists. The association relationship must define how an element interacts with another one. Roles may be directly associated with other roles as well as environments.

- Aggregation/Composition (Agg) : Agg(aggregator, part) : Agg(ro,ro), Agg(ra,ra), Agg(o,o), Agg(a,a)

If an element is aggregated with other element, we say that it is part of an aggregator. The aggregator may use the functionalities available in its parts. The parts do not need to know that they are being aggregated to an aggregator, but the aggregator knows each of its parts. Depending on the strength of the aggregation, the part may not exist without the aggregator.

The relationship template is used to define the links between the elements. For each relationship type, the template identifies the elements and its roles in the relationship.

Relationship

```
Relationship Relationship_Name
      INHABIT: habitat, citizen
    | OWNERSHIP: owner, member
    | SPECIALIZATION : super-element, sub-element,
    | PLAY: element, role
    | CONTROL: controller, controlled
    | DEPENDENCY: client, supplier
    | ASSOCIATION: associate1, associate2
    | AGGREGATION: aggregator, part
end Relationship
```

---

[2] We are extending the relationships *control* and *dependency* described in 74 .

As an example, we describe in this paper two kinds of relationships. Below we have an instance of the relationship template ownership that links the organization *MarketPlaceOrg* and the agent *User_Agent* and, net, an instance of the relationship template play linking the *User_agent* and the role *Buyer*.

```
                    Owner_Mktp_Role_Buyer

     Relationship Owner_Mktp_Role_Buyer
            OWNERSHIP: MarketPlaceOrg, Buyer
     end Relationship
```

```
                         Play_Buyer

     Relationship Play_Buyer
            PLAY: User_Agent, Buyer
     end Relationship
```

7 Semantics of the Template-Based Representations

As we have stated previously, the main goal of this paper is to characterize a key set of abstractions that can be used to define a conceptual framework using agents and objects, and clarify the interplay between the agent and object abstractions. For this reason, we have focused on the choice and presentation of these concepts in an informal way rather than on formally defining the semantics of each of the templates. In addition, presenting these concepts using a formal notation would certainly lead us to representations that would be less legible because of their mathematical nature than the light template-based representation that we have adopted.

However, the formal semantics of the schemas and its parts is certainly a necessary result that will be provided as soon as we finish the process of refining our templates to our satisfaction. Even though we do not aim at giving a completely formal semantics for our templates in this paper, in this section we will provide an overview on how they should be formalized to indicate possible formalization choices.

Objects can be formalized in (temporal) logic following the theory we have presented in 1 . Each element class (e.g., an object or agent class) has a specific name and can be defined as a set of possible instances. For example, the names of object and agent element classes in the templates are Object Class Name and Agent Class Name, respectively. If the instances are objects, the class is called object class; if the instances are agents, the class is called an agent class, and so on. Given an element class C, $c_i \in C$ (i 1,...,n) denotes an element of this class. Every instance of an element class has an associated single object identity (or identifier). @C represents the set of possible (element) identifiers of class C.

The formal specification of the object class template can be given as a tuple <DT,AT,AC> in the abstract data type style and a set AX of axioms (or properties), where DT is a data signature (i.e., it defines sorts such as Boolean and function symbols f(x1,...,xn) related to these sorts), AT is a set of attribute symbols a(x1,...,xn) that we call the state of an object, and AC is a set of action symbols g(x1,...,xn). The behavior is defined in our template as a set of properties AX that we call operations in our template. The relationships can be defined as a set of relations Rel: C1 X C2 X ... X Cn, where C1, C2, ..., Cn are element classes.

In order to formalize the agent class template, we need to formalize beliefs, goals, actions, plans, events, roles, and relationships. Relationships are also relations as in the case of objects. Beliefs are facts and rules that may be expressed in first-order logic (FOL) or Prolog. The goals and actions may be expressed in temporal logic with processes (e.g., mu-calculus) used, for example, in 12 . Events can be seen as atomic processes. Roles can be seen as a special relationship. A plan may be described as a sequence <ac1, ac2, ..., can> of actions that should be executed to achieve a certain goal.

Environments were defined in terms of the set of resources (including the permission and the name related to each resource), a set of services (including the permission and name related to each service), a set of properties that describe its behavior, a set of events, and a set of relationships of this environment with other entities. Each resource and service has an identity. Permissions can be characterized as Prolog or temporal logic constraints. Each event can be seen as an atomic process. Services can also be defined using a process style following 12 .

Organizations are defined in terms of a set of rules to which they conform, a set of laws they obey, and a set of relationships with other organizations. The rules can be defined in first-order logic or Prolog. The laws can be defined as constraints in FOL or temporal logic, and the relationships can be defined as mathematical relations. Agent and object roles were also defined. Roles for objects can be formally defined by a specific relation in a way similar to the way views were defined in 1 . In order to define roles for agents, we have to introduce extra attributes in the agent descriptions. However, the formalization may also be based on logic and process.

8 Related Work

A lot of work has been done in the area of developing models, methodologies, methods and languages 8, 27, 39, 42, 54, 57, 71 to help and guide software engineers to create conceptual models of MASs. However, not much has yet been done in the area of conceptual frameworks for MASs.

TAO as well as the work discussed later in this section 10, 28, 68, 73 is focused on the development of a new conceptual framework to explain the interplay among MAS abstractions. As indicated in Fig. 3, TAO and its related research work discussed next addresses the metamodel layer illustrated in the 4 layer metadata architecture proposed by MOF. We did not compare our work to well known methods and methodologies since they belong to the domain model layer of MOF as shown in Fig. 3. In other words conceptual frameworks and methodologies belong to different levels of abstraction.

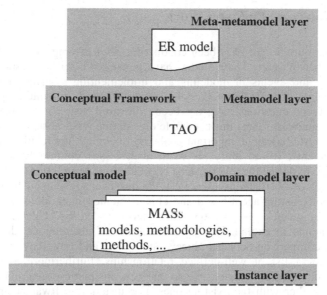

Fig. 3. Locating TAO in the MOF Metadata architecture.

Wagner 68 presents a conceptual framework of agent-oriented modeling restricted to model organizational information systems. Thus, it is not generally applicable to MAS and, consequently, it must be carefully used in the case of other types of systems. Although the proposed framework integrates agents and objects, it does not include important concepts such as actions, goals, organizations and, thus, roles as first class elements. Organizations are defined as institutional agents that are composed of rights and rules. The relationships between the institutional agent and simple agents are not defined. Moreover, the framework does not deal with pro-active agents.

KAOS is a conceptual framework that defines abstractions, such as entity, relationship and agent, as extensions of object 10 . An entity is an autonomous object that is independent of other objects; a relationship is a subordinate object; and an agent is an object that has choice and behavior. In this way, KAOS does not satisfactorily explain the distinction between an entity and an agent and why a relationship should be an object. It does not describe the characteristics of an object or explain how other abstractions extend it. Two other weaknesses of KAOS are: (i) it does not consider organizations and roles as important abstractions, and (ii) it does not describe the relationships between the defined abstractions.

d'Inverno and Luck 28 define a conceptual framework with four important limitations: (i) it does not define all possible relationships between its elements; (ii) it does not define organization and role; (iii) it defines new concepts like server agents, autonomous agents and neutral objects increasing the complexity of understanding the relationship between agents and objects; and (iv) their approach is so generic that it may be very difficult to be used by software engineers and methodology developers.

Finally, Yu and Schmid 73 define a conceptual framework for agent-oriented and role-based modeling. However, it does not define abstractions such as objects, object roles and organizations and, therefore, it does not connect these abstractions with the definitions of agent and role.

9 Discussions and Ongoing Work

Our research group 17, 65 has been conducting a set of empirical studies 15, 49, 62 for a number of years. These studies have generated a set of questions about the use of objects and agents in modeling and implementing systems 16, 18 . After exhaustive review of theories, methodologies and methods for multi-agent systems, we found that our questions have not been addressed yet. We felt the need for a conceptual framework that must completely define the abstractions and their relationships. TAO has three important goals: (i) to explain the relationships between objects and agents; (ii) to unify six main abstractions commonly used to model MASs; and (iii) to define the relationships between those abstractions.

The core set of abstractions used in TAO has been developed based upon our investigation of existing agent-based and object-oriented methodologies 13, 42, 45, 68, 71, 73 , languages 40, 48, 63 , and theories 59, 64, 68 . Our conceptual framework intends to explain how to use this set of abstractions, defining it and introducing a comparison between objects and agents and how they are related. For that we present a list of well-defined relationships. Furthermore, our conceptual framework is intended to be extensible so that new abstractions and relationships can be grouped together with the existing ones. For instance, software components are natural candidates to be included in the framework.

The benefit of having a conceptual framework for a family of problems is to provide support for developing new methodologies, methods and languages based on the essential concepts defined and related in the framework.   Although some methodologies are agent-centered methodologies and do not consider objects as an abstraction, these methodologies also can be based on our conceptual framework. Our framework defines an object as an abstraction but it does not insist that this definition must be used.

Nonetheless, it should be noted that although our agents' template defines the internal architecture of an agent in terms of plans, goals, beliefs and actions, the users of our framework can map these concepts to other internal architecture styles, such as the BDI architecture 38 . Different architectures can utilize our framework, changing the templates and internal definitions of our set of abstractions. Another example occurs with the roles template, which may be completely different than the one presented here.

The conceptual framework was defined to be used to generate conceptual models. Abstractions defined in the conceptual framework are instantiated in the conceptual models. And thus, conceptual models are used to generate computational models. In this way, abstractions used in conceptual models may be mapped to other abstractions used in computational models. We are working on the creation of transformations for the set of abstractions defined in our conceptual framework to computational models. We are also concerned with possible adequate representations of both models.

Another work under way is related to the non-functional requirements. We believe that some non-functional requirements (such as reliability, security, ...) will be common to several abstractions within an application. In this sense, we are investigating how to allow abstractions to support an explicit separation of such crosscutting behavior. The notion of aspect 22, 37, 66 is well understood in the object-oriented context, but only a few preliminary works have been published that discuss it in terms of agent-based software engineering (such as 16, 20).

Related to the MAS dynamic, we intend to study the dynamic of organizations. We will seek to improve reporting about the definition of commitments, protocols, rights, laws and actions. Some questions remain to be answered: How do agents enter and exit organizations Why do they enter and why do they exit How do organizations or agents define an organization's set of rules and laws How do agents that enter an organization learn about and start to obey its conditions Little work in this direction has been carried out 23 .

10 Conclusion

Object-oriented software engineering and its associated theories have already proven to be effective for the development of software systems. Object-oriented theories and respective languages and methodologies have shown how suitably powerful abstractions, like the notions of object and class, can be fully exploited not only to define modeling languages, but also to support methodologies that drive all the phases of the engineering of software systems 56 . However, the advances in networking technologies and the coming of the Internet era are leading towards issues that traditional object-oriented software engineering is not ready to address. Large-scale software systems are now entrusted with typically complex tasks, which can involve massive amounts of passive components as well as autonomous components. These components affect numerous kinds of connected environments, and are subject to the uncertainties of open environments such as the Internet 56 . The inadequacy of object-oriented approaches does not derive from the methodologies, but rather from limitations of the object theories and their abstractions themselves, which are not powerful enough to examine these new issues. To cope with this situation, companies and researchers are investigating how agents can contribute to the mastering of the complexity of modern large-scale systems.

This paper presented a conceptual framework that provides a conceptual setting for engineering large-scale MASs based on agent and object abstractions. The identified set of abstractions is organized in terms of a unifying framework, providing software engineers with a deeper understanding of the fundamental concepts underpinning agent and object notions and their relationships. Objects are viewed as abstractions to represent passive elements, while agents provide a means of representing active elements in the software system. In addition, a set of additional abstractions is provided to model situations where organizations of cooperating agents and objects perform and coordinate their actions in dynamic environments to accomplish the organizations' goals. The core set of abstractions was developed based on our extensive work in investigating existing agent-based and object-oriented methodologies, languages and theories, and our extended experimental work on developing many large scale MASs. As a result, it can be tailored to different domains. Since its basic ontology can be extended to accommodate new abstractions for these domains, it enables different research teams to compare and discuss their formulations based on the unified terminology enabled by the proposed foundations.

Acknowledgments. This work has been partially supported by CNPq under grant No. 140646/2000-0 for Viviane Silva, grant No. 140179/95-0 for Anarosa Brandão, grant No. for Christina Chavez, grant No. 141457/2000-7 for Alessandro Garcia, and by

FAPERJ under grant No. E-26/150.699/2002 for Alessandro Garcia. Viviane Silva, Alessandro Garcia, Anarosa Brandão, Christina Chavez and Carlos Lucena also are supported by the PRONEX Project under grant 7697102900. Paulo Alencar research was supported by the Natural Sciences and Engineering Research Council of Canada (NSERC), Human Resources Development Canada (HRDC) and IBM Canada. The authors would also like to acknowledge the contributions of Don Cowan, Toacy Oliveira and Gustavo Robichez.

References

1. Alencar, P., Cowan, D., Lucena, C.: A Logical Theory of Interfaces and Objects. IEEE Transactions on Software Engineering, Vol. 28, n. 6, June, (2002): 548–575.
2. Basili, V. et al.: Experimentation in Software Engineering. IEEE Transactions on Software Engineering, SE-12(7), July (1986).
3. Bäumer, D. et al.: Role Object. In: Proceedings of the Conference on Pattern Languages of Programs, (1997).
4. Biddle, J., Thomas, E.: Role Theory: Concepts and Research. John Wiley and Sons, New York, (1966).
5. Booch, G.: Object-oriented Analysis and Design with Applications". The Benjamin/Cummings Publishing Company, Inc., 2nd edition, USA, (1994).
6. Booch, G., Rumbaugh, J., Jaconbson, I.: The Unified Modeling Language User Guide. Addison Wesley, (1999).
7. Bradshaw, J.: An Introduction to Software Agents. In: J. Bradshaw (Ed.), Software Agents, American Association for Artificial Intelligence/MIT, Cambridge, (1997): 3–46.
8. Bresciani, P., Perini, A., Giorgini, P., Giunchiglia, F., Mylopoulos, J.: Modeling Early Requirements in Tropos: a Transformation Based Approach. In: Proceedings of the 2nd Workshop on Agent-Oriented Software Engineering, Montreal, Canada, May, (2001).
9. Chen, P.: The Entity Relationship Model – Towards a Unified View of Data. ACM Transactions on Database Systems, vol. 1, no1. March 1976, 9–36.
10. Dardenne, A., Lamsweerde, A., Fickas, S.: Goal-directed Requirements Acquisition. Science of Computer Programming, (1993) 20:3–50.
11. Dieste, O., Juristo, N., Moreno, A., Pazos, J.: Conceptual Modeling in Software Engineering and Knowledge Engineering: Concepts, Techniques and Trends. In: Chang, S.K. (eds.): Handbook of Software Engineering and Knowledge Engineering Fundamentals. World Scientific Publishing Co., Vol.1 (2001)
12. Dong, J., Alencar, P., Cowan, D.: A Behavioral Analysis Approach to Pattern-Based Composition. Journal of Systems and Software, (2003). (To Appear)
13. Elammari, M., Lalonde, W.: An Agent-Oriented Methodology: High-level and Intermediate Models. In: Wagner, G., Yu, E. (eds.): Proceedings of the 1st International Workshop on Agent-Oriented Information Systems (1999).
14. Foundation of Intelligent Physical Agent: FIPA Interaction Protocols Specification, (2002). Available at URL http://www.fipa.org/repository/ips.html
15. Garcia, A., Cortés, M., Lucena, C.: A Web Environment for the Development and Maintenance of E-Commerce Portals based on a Groupware Approach. In: Proceedings of the Information Resources Management Association International Conference (IRMA'01), (2001): 722–724.
16. Garcia, A., Silva, V., Lucena, C., Milidiú, R.: An Aspect-Based Approach for Developing Multi-Agent Object-Oriented Systems. In: Proceedings of the 21st Brazilian Symposium on Software Engineering, Rio de Janeiro, Brazil, October, (2001): 177–192.

17. Garcia, A., Chavez, C., Silva, O., Silva, V., Lucena, C.: Promoting Advanced Separation of Concerns in Intra-Agent and Inter-Agent Software Engineering. In: Proceedings of the Workshop on Advanced Separation of Concerns in Object-Oriented Systems (ASoC) at OOPSLA'2001, Tampa Bay, USA, October, (2001).
18. Garcia, A., Silva, V., Chavez, C., Lucena, C.: Engineering Multi-Agent Systems with Aspects and Patterns. Journal of the Brazilian Computer Society, November, (2002).
19. Garcia, A., Lucena, C. Software Engineering for Large-Scale Multi-Agent Systems – SELMAS 2002. Post-Workshop Report, ACM Software Engineering Notes, August, (2002).
20. Garcia, A., Lucena, C., Cowan, D.: Agents in Object-Oriented Software Engineering. Software: Practice and Experience, Elsevier, (2003). (Accepted to Appear)
21. Genesereth, N., Ketchpel, S.: Software Agents. Communications of the ACM, v. 37, n. 7, July, (1994).
22. Glaser, N., Morignot, P.: The Reorganization of Societies of Autonomous Agents. In: Boman, M., Velde, W. (Eds.): Proceedings of the 8th European Ws. on Modeling Autonomous Agents in a Multi-Agent World, Springer, Berlin, Germany (1997).
23. Harrison, W., Ossher, J.: Subject-Oriented Programming: A Critique of Pure Objects. In: Proceedings of OOPSLA'93, (1993): 411–428.
24. Helfin, J., Hendler, J.: Semantic Interoperability on the Web. In: Proceedings of the 17th National Conference on Artificial Intelligence, (2000): 443–449.
25. Huhns, M., Singh, M.: Agents and Multiagent Systems: Themes, Approaches and Challenges. In: Huhns, M. Singh, M. (Eds.): Readings in Agents. Morgan Kaufmann (1998): 1–23.
26. Iglesias, C., Garrijo, M., Gonzalez, J, Velasco, J.: Analysis and Design of Multiagent Systems using MAS-CommonKADS. In: Singh, M. et al (Eds.), Intelligent Agents IV: Agent Theories, Architectures and Languages, LNCS 1365, (1997).
27. Iglesias, C., Garrijo, M., Gonzalez, J.: A Survey of Agent-Oriented Methodologies. In: Proceedings of the 5th International Workshop on Intelligent Agents: Agent Theories, Architectures, and Languages (ATAL-98), Paris, France, July (1998): 317–330.
28. d'Inverno, M., Luck, M.: Understanding Agent Systems. Springer Series on Agent Technology, Springer (2001).
29. Jacobson, I.: Object-Oriented Software Engineering. Addison-Wesley, (1992).
30. Jennings, N.: Commitments and Conventions: The Foundation of Coordination in Multiagent Systems. Knowledge Engineering Review, Vol.8, n. 3, (1993): 223–250.
31. Jennings, N., Wooldridge, M. Applications of Intelligent Agents. In: Agent Technology: Foundations, Applications, and Markets, Springer, Heidelberg, Germany, (1998): 3–28.
32. Jennings, N., Sycara, K., Wooldridge, M.: A Roadmap of Agent Research and Development. Journal of Autonomous Agents and Multi-Agent Systems, v. 1, n. 1, (1998): 7–38.
33. Jennings, N.: Agent-Oriented Software Engineering. In: Proceedings of the Twelfth International Conference on Industrial and Engineering Applications of Artificial Intelligence, (1999):4–10.
34. Jennings, N.: On Agent-based Software Engineering. Artificial Intelligence, Vol. 117, n. 2, (2000): 277–296.
35. Jennings, N., Wooldridge, M.: Agent-Oriented Software Engineering. In: Bradshaw, J. (ed.): Handbook of Agent Technology, AAAI/MIT Press, (2000).
36. Jennings, N.: An Agent-based Approach for Building Complex Software Systems. Communications of the ACM, v. 44, n. 4, (2001): 35–41.
37. Kiczales, G. et al.: Aspect-Oriented Programming. In: Proceedings of European Conference on Object-Oriented Programming (ECOOP) LNCS, (1241), Springer-Verlag, Finland, June (1997).

38. Kinny, D., Georgeff, M., and Rao, A.: A methodology and modeling technique for systems of BDI agents. In: Van de Velde, W., Perram, J. (eds.): Agents Breaking Away: Proceedings of the Seventh European Workshop on Modeling Autonomous Agents in a Multi-Agent World, Springer-Verlag, Vol.1038 (1996) 56–71.
39. Kinny, D., Georgeff, M.: Modelling and design of multi-agent systems. In: Müller, J., Wooldridge, M., Jennings, N. (eds.), Intelligent Agents III, Springer-Verlag, Vol.1193 (1997) 1–20.
40. Kinny, D.: The   Calculus: An Algebraic Agent Language. In: Intelligent Agents VIII, Springer-Verlag, Vol. 2333, (2002): 32–50.
41. Kristensen, B., Østerbye, K.: Roles: Conceptual Abstraction Theory and Practical Language Issues. Theory and Practice of Object Sytems Vol. 2, n. 3, (1996): 143–160.
42. Lind, J.: MASSIVE: Software Engineering for Multiagent Systems. PhD thesis, University of the Saarland (2000).
43. Maes, P.: Concepts and Experiments in Computational Reflection. In: Proceedings of OOPSLA'87, ACM SIGPLAN Notices, October (1987): 147–155.
44. Mamei, M. et al. Engineering Mobility in Large Multi Agent Systems: a Case Study in Urban Traffic Management. In: A. Garcia et al. (eds), Software Engineering for Large-Scale Multi-Agent Systems, Springer, LNCS, 2003.
45. MESSAGE website, Available at URL http://www.eurescom.de/Public/Projects/p900-series/P907/P907.htm.
46. B. Meyer. Object-Oriented Software Construction. Prentice-Hall, 2nd edition, (1997).
47. Minsky, N., Ungureanu, V.: Law-Governed Interaction: A Coordination and Control Mechanism for Heterogeneous Distributed Systems. ACM Transactions on Software Engineering and Methodology, Vol. 9, n. 3, July, (2000): 273–305.
48. Moss, S., Gaylard, H., Wallis, S., Edmonds, B.: SDML: A Multi-Agent Language for Organizational Modelling. Computational Mathematical Organization Theory, Vol. 4, n. 1, (1998): 43–69.
49. Neto, A., Lucena, C.: CommercePipe: Consumer to Business Commerce Channels on the Internet. SEA (Software Engineering Applications) IASTED, Las Vegas, October (2000)
50. Newcomer, E., Hurley, O.: Web Services Definition. In: Proceedings of the World Wide Web Consortium Workshop on Web Services, April, (2001).
51. Nwana, H.: Software Agents: An Overview. Knowledge Engineering   e iew, 11(3):1–40, 1996.
52. Object Management Group – Agent Platform Special Interest Group: Agent Technology – Green Paper. Version 1.0, September (2000).
53. Object Management Group: OMG MOF – Meta Object Facility (MOF) Specification. Version 1.4, April, (2002). Available at URL http://www.pmg.org/cwm.
54. Odell, J., Parunak, H., Bauer., B.: Extending UML for Agents. In: Odell, J., Parunak, H. and Bauer, B. (Eds.), Proceedings of the Agent-Oriented Information Systems Workshop at the 17th National Conference on Artificial Intelligence, 2000.
55. Omicini, A., Petta, P., Tolksdorf, R.: Engineering Societies in the Agents World II. Proceedings of the 2nd International Workshop on Engineering Societies in the Agents World, Praga, (2001).
56. Omicini, A.: From Objects to Agent Societies: Abstractions and Methodologies for the Engineering of Open Distributed Systems. In: Corradi, A., Omicini, A., Poggi, A. (eds.): WOA (2000): 29–34.
57. Omicini, A.: SODA: Societies and Infrastructure in the Analysis and Design of Agent-based Systems. In: Ciancarini, P., Wooldridge, M. (eds.), Agent-Oriented Software Engineering, Springer-Verlag, (2001): 185–194.
58. Parunak, H., Odell, J.: Representing Social Structures in UML. In: Proceedings of Agent-oriented Software Engineering, (2001): 1–16.

59. Petrie, C.: Agent-Based Software Engineering. In: Ciancarini, P., Wooldridge, M. (eds.), Agent-Oriented Software Engineering, Springer-Verlag, (2001).
60. Rumbaugh et al. Object-Oriented Modeling and Design. Prentice Hall, Englewood Cliffs, New Jersey (1991).
61. Rasmus, D.: Rethinking Smart Objects – Building Artificial Intelligence with Objects. Cambridge University Press (1999).
62. Ripper, P., Fontoura, M, Neto, A., Lucena, C.: V-Market: A Framework for e-Commerce Agent Systems. World Wide Web, Baltzer Science Publishers Vol. 3, n. 1, (2000).
63. Shoham, Y.: Agent0: A Simple Agent Language and its Interpreter. In: Proceedings of the Ninth National Conference on Artificial Intelligence, (1991): 704–709.
64. Shoham Y.: Agent-Oriented Programming. Artificial Intelligence, n. 60, (1993): 24–29.
65. SoC+Agents Group. Separation of Concern and Multi-Agents Systems Group. Available at UR: http://www.teccomm.les.inf.puc-rio.br/SoCagents/.
66. Tarr, P. et al.: N Degrees of Separation: Multi-Dimensional Separation of Concerns. In: Proceedings of the 21st International Conference on Software Engineering, May, (1999).
67. The Semantic Web Portal. Available at URL: http://www.semanticweb.org.
68. Wagner, G.: Agent-Object-Relationship Modeling. In: Proceedings of the 2nd International Symposium: From Agent Theory to Agent Implementation, April (2000).
69. Willmott, S., Dale, J., Burg, B., Charlton, C., O'Brien, P. Agentcities: A Worldwide Open Agent Network. Agentlink News, November, (2001): 13–15.
70. Wooldridge M., Jennings N., Kinny, D.: A Methodology for Agent-Oriented Analysis and Design. In: Proceedings of the Third International Conference on Autonomous Agents (Agents'99), ACM Press (1999): 69–76
71. Wooldridge, M., Jennings, N., Kinny, D.: The Gaia methodology for agent-oriented analysis and design. In: Journal of Autonomous Agents and Multi-Agent Systems, Vol. 3, (2000): 285–312.
72. Wooldridge, M., Ciancarini, P.: Agent-Oriented Software Engineering: The State of the Art. In: P. Ciancarini And M. Wooldridge (Eds.), Agent-Oriented Software Engineering, Springer-Verlag, LNAI, 2001.
73. Yu, L., Schmid, B.: A Conceptual Framework for Agent-Oriented and Role-Based Work on Modeling. In: Wagner, G., Yu, E. (eds.): Proceedings of the 1st Int. Workshop. on Agent-Oriented Information Systems (1999).
74. Zambonelli, F., Jennings, N., Wooldridge, M.: Organizational Abstractions for the Analysis and Design of Multi-agent Systems. In: Ciancarini, P., Wooldridge, M. (eds.): Agent-Oriented Software Engineering, Springer-Verlag (2001).
75. Zambonelli, F. et al.: Agent-Oriented Software Engineering for Internet Applications. In: Omicini, A., Zambonelli, F., Klusch, M. (Eds.), Coordination of Internet Agents: Models, Technologies, and Applications, Springer-Verlag, New York, (2001).
76. Zambonelli, F., Jennings, N., Wooldridge, M.: Organizational Rules as an Abstraction for the Analysis and Design of Multi-agent Systems. Journal of Knowledge and Software Engineering, v.11, n.3, (2001).
77. Zambonelli, F., Parunak, H.: Signs of a Revolution in Computer Science and Software Engineering. In: Proceedings of the Third International Workshop Engineering Societies in the Agents World, Madrid, Spain, (2002).

The Role of Roles in Designing Effective Agent Organizations

James J. Odell[1], H. Van Dyke Parunak[2], and Mitchell Fleischer[2]

[1] James Odell Associates, 3646 West Huron River Drive, Ann Arbor
MI 48103-9489 USA
email@jamesodell.com
http://www.jamesodell.com

[2] Altarum, 3520 Green Court, Suite 300, Ann Arbor,
MI 48105 USA
{van.parunak,mitch.fleischer}@altarum.org
http://www.erim.org/{~vparunak,~mfleischer}

Abstract. Agent-based systems are no longer contained within the boundaries of a single, small agent organization. To meet the demands of large-scale system implementations, agent organizations must deal with environmental forces, interact with other agent organizations, and know how they affect individual agents. In this paper, we look to social and organizational systems theory as a source of inspiration. Many of these techniques have been successful for a hundreds and thousands of years. We believe that the designers of agent-based systems can learn a great deal from organization designers. In the first of a series, this paper examines the notion of *role* and its implications on how agents might behave in group settings.

1 Introduction

We simply have hardly any real experience building truly heterogeneous, realistically coordinated multiagent systems that work together, and ... almost no basis for systematic reflection and analysis of that experience 1 .

Societies need to employ patterned behavior to exist. The behavior of each individual is determined to a great extent by the requirements of these patterns 2 . However, the current practice of MAS design tends to be limited to individual agents and small face-to-face groups of agents that operate as closed systems. We have little principled understanding for:

– organizing sophisticated, interactive, heterogeneous agent-based systems.
– grouping the agents in such systems into very large-scale aggregates that exhibit predictable, stable, and reliable behavior.
– achieving economies of scale and scope within large MAS.
– building and operating such systems *in situ*.

From a scientific standpoint, the foundations for constructing large multiagent systems have a long history. Although researchers have been explicitly thinking about MAS/DAI organizations and attempting to link organization theory with MAS/DAI models for decades, the idea of organization, *per se*, has been only a

A. Garcia et al. (Eds.): SELMAS 2002, LNCS 2603, pp. 27–38, 2003.
© Springer-Verlag Berlin Heidelberg 2003

peripheral theme. MAS/DAI researchers have focused on specific coordination techniques, rather than the central issues involved in MAS organization.

In previous papers, we introduced the notion of groups and roles 9 , initially explored the effect of the environment on agents 10 , and discussed frequently characterized forms of agent interaction 11 . We are now beginning a series of papers that explore ways of designing effective MAS organizations. This paper addresses *roles*. The usefulness of the concept is apparent by the degree to which it is referenced (often intuitively) in newer agent development methodologies, such as Gaia 24 and MESSAGE 25 . Our concern here is to examine in more detail what the notion means and how roles might be employed in agent-based systems. Forthcoming papers will address related issues, such as:

- groups – defining sets of related agent roles that support certain kinds of organizations
- group structures – specifying hierarchic and network configurations among groups
- policies and contracts – expressing rights, norms, rules, agreements, and enforcement mechanisms for agent organizations
- communication and interaction protocols – discussing patterns of communications among roles and their uses
- activity structures – expressing work plans and business processes for agent-based systems
- ontology - building and expressing sets of concepts and their terms adopted by agents and their groups
- goals – defining the state a group is trying to attain (e.g., explicit missions, objectives, critical success factors)
- beliefs, desires, intention – imputing cognition to an organization as a way for external entities to reason about the organization and its members.
- emotions and morale – formalizing the notion and application of "feelings" for agent-based organizations as an approach for its human users to reason and understand agent social behavior.

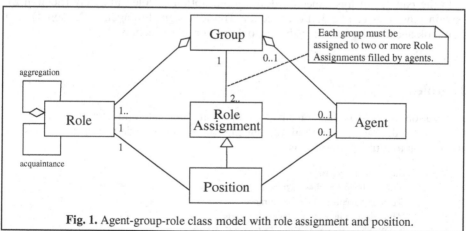

Fig. 1. Agent-group-role class model with role assignment and position.

Using a UML class diagram, Fig. 1 illustrates the primary concepts involved in expressing roles. Below are definitions for some of the key concepts we are using in this paper. In particular, we will be discussing the first four notions more fully (the last three are for background, only).

A *role* is a class that defines a normative behavioral repertoire of an agent. While roles are defined independently from groups, they must be played within groups. Roles can be composed of other roles. Furthermore, roles can have acquaintance associations with other roles, denoting that interaction may occur among the instances of the related roles.

A *position* is a formally recognized role assignment that may occur within a group structure. A position may or may not have an agent assigned to it. Only one agent may be associated with it at any point in time. However, many different agents may be associated with the position over time.

A *role assignment* is the association of a group with a role that may be occupied by an agent. Each mapping of an agent to a role assignment can be a result of an exogenous or an endogenous process.

A *group* is a set of two or more agents that are related via their role assignments, where these relationships must form a connected graph within the group. Agents and Roles are associated with Groups to provide context.

A *social system* consists of a set of interdependent role behaviors, providing a collective pattern in which agents play their parts, or roles.

An *organi ation* is a group whose roles and interactions are typically expected to be relatively stable and change slowly over time.

An *en ironment* provides the conditions under which an entity (agent or object) exists. It includes the groups to which an agent may belong.

In the balance of this paper we develop the notion of role intuitively (Section 2), explain how roles can be defined (Section 3) and assigned to agents (Section 4), and then look ahead to how roles enable us to define groups (Section 5).

2 Roles

The notion of *role* is fundamentally a thespian concept, and attention to how it functions in the theater can reinforce our intuitions and provide useful metaphors for application to multiagent systems.

> All the world's a stage,
> And all the men and women merely players:
> They all have their exits and entrances;
> And one man in his time plays many parts.
>   –W. Shakespeare, *As You Like It*, Act II, Scene 7.

Can it be possible that Shakespeare's lines have anything to do with the field of behavioral science known as *role theory* 12 The similarities between the

Shakespeare's characterization and our present-day usage of *role* are noteworthy. Both express a perspective on human behavior. For Shakespeare, social life was similar to stage acting with its scenes, masks, and airs; in role theory, life *is* the stage. Both also employ a special language. Shakespeare wrote of players and parts that are played; role theory discusses individuals and the roles they play.

As humans, we find the perspective and language of the theater a useful analogy for describing and understanding many of the same complex aspects of individual behavior. The *role* perspective consists of those factors presumed to be influential in governing human behavior. Since we commonly employ this device in real life for conceptualizing human behavior, it may also serve as a useful device for other kinds of individuals in a MAS—be they life forms, active software constructs, or hardware devices. The notion of role permeates other aspects of the theater analogy, such as:

- *Actor* - The individual assigned to play a part, or role. In a MAS, an actor is an agent.
- *Part* - In ancient Greece and Rome, the parts of theatrical characters were literally read from rolls of parchment. When translated into French, the term "roll" becomes "role" 13 . Since the sixteenth century, *role* has been an English synonym for a part that one plays or assumes in society or life 14 . Employing the notion of role for multiagent systems is in keeping with centuries of accepted usage.
- *Script* – In a multiagent system, the social script may be as constraining as that of a traditional play, or it may permit the agent actor some degree of improvisation that is consistent with the role. In other words, role behavior can be strictly or loosely defined. However, even in rote-based scripts a degree of latitude always exists. Here, actors can at least employ their own style and interpretation as well as exercise some degree of variance in terms of appearance, movement, and so on.
- *Performance* – The player acts the part. Actors can at least employ their own style and interpretation of a script (even in a verbatim performance). They can also exercise some degree of variance in terms of appearance, movement, and so on. In society, role performance is determined by social norms; in agent-based systems, performance can be determined by sets of constraints that govern both the behavior of each role and the behavior of all agents in a society, independent of the role.
- *Play* – In the theater, a play is a literary composition in the form of dialogue assigned to specific roles adapted for staged performance. In society, this is present in certain situations or contexts where scripts and role performances are required or expected. For example, a marriage ceremony has well defined roles and a verbatim-style script. In contrast, driving a car involves roles that have no predefined verbal dialogue. Instead, the dialogue of the Driver role involves signals and hand gestures along with driving behavior that is expected to conform to certain social and legal norms. In agent-based systems, the analog of a *play* would be a *system*, *application*, or *scenario*. For example, a scenario for a British auction has a well defined interaction protocol involving agents playing the roles of bidder, seller, and auctioneer.
- *irector* – In a play, the director supervises and controls its production; he or she determines how the roles are to be filled and how the parts should be interpreted. Supervisors, assembly line coordinators, parents, coaches, and police are examples of those who govern individuals and roles in human societies. Agent societies, too, can require supervision and control by agents that have been given authority

known as *distinguished agents*. Distinguished agents can come in either human form (e.g., an agent designer, system architect, or operator) or automated form (a central controller or another agent with the appropriate power). Directors are not always a required element. The directors could be free to determine for themselves how the script is played out. The end result may or may not be as good as having a knowledgeable director to refine the movement of the actors. Yet, improvisational plays are probably best performed without central control.

– *Audience* – The viewers of a play both observe the performance and react to the actors' role playing. An agent system could be similarly observed for several reasons. The primary mechanism would be by monitoring the system and recording its progress and status.

In essence, the role perspective in theater, life, human-resource departments, and agent-based societies assumes that performance results from social proscriptions and individual behavior and that the individual variations in performance are expressed within the framework created by these factors. Here, an individual's behavior is shaped by the demands and rules of others, the individual's own understanding of appropriate behavior, and the individual's competence in the performance. In human-based organizations, defining normative forms of behavior is quite common. For example, human resource departments define and specify roles to ensure some degree of standardization within an organization. Such roles can be defined generally as Staff Member and Manager or, more specialized, as Intermediate Programmer III and Principal Analyst. This perspective does not deny individual differences. Instead, it highlights the social determinants that may be involved in creating such differences. Furthermore, it can help *role designers* focus on those conditions where social determinants will be more influential.

3 Designing Agent Roles

Roles define normative behavioral repertoires for agents. They provide both the building blocks for agent social systems and the requirements by which agents interact. Each agent is linked to other agents by the roles it plays by virtue of the system's functional requirements—which are based on the expectations that the system has of the agent. This section first describes how roles are formed, and second, how roles can be configured both in terms of the number and complexity of actions supported by a given role and the degree of control the agent has over various actions.

3.1 Role Formation

Roles can be assigned to agents in a multiagent system in at least two ways: endogenously (by emergent self-organization as the system runs), and exogenously (by the system designer when the system is constructed or modified).

Endogenous self-organization is a widespread phenomenon in natural systems [3] [4] [5]. As agents interact with each other, system-level structures and patterns emerge that can adapt robustly to changes in the system's environment. Role differentiation in social insects is a prominent example of such self-organization [7]. For instance, individual *Polistes* wasps in a nest spontaneously take on different roles (nurse vs. forager vs. "chief") in response to changing food resources and brood sizes 8 . Synthetic systems can exploit similar dynamics. Experiments with information brokers in a web-based information system 6 show that the brokers can emergently specialize into complementary niches, thus adopting distinct information roles.

Self-organizing role assignment is robust to system change and replaces expensive and time-consuming human design effort with autonomous configuration. Thus it is a particularly attractive way to design systems for domains that are subject to unexpected change. Even the human social structures with which we are intuitively familiar are ultimately generated and maintained by emergent self-organization. Many social psychologists suggest that roles are formed when a recurring set of behaviors is found useful in a group context 15, 16, 17, 18 . Initially, the behavior could have been the actions of a single individual. Over time, however, the individual's actions might be identified as a useful set of behaviors that can be employed by other individuals to produce similar results.   This reusable set of actions becomes standardized in the form of a role. These roles can be extracted analytically by techniques such as social network analysis 23 24 or Dooley graphs 21 .

However, there are several reasons that one might want to begin with existing human structural patterns and impose them exogenously on a multiagent system at design time. These reasons fall into two main categories: cognitive fit and dynamic properties.

Imposed roles may be preferable to emergent roles in a system that must interface closely with human agents. There arc usually several different ways that roles can be assigned to a set of agents with a given function. Those roles that emerge in a self-organizing digital system may not align naturally with those that a human organization would adopt to address the same function. This difference can make it difficult for people to understand the behavior of the digital system. If human stakeholders cannot understand a system, they will not trust it, severely compromising its usefulness.

Dynamically imposed roles may be useful in initiating a system to which one wishes to apply emergent self-organization. One initializes the multiagent system with a set of roles known to provide the desired functionality in human organizations, which greatly reduces the burden of subsequent self-organization. Instead of searching the entire space of possible role assignments, self-organization can be used to fine-tune the initial assignment, reducing the operating time necessary to achieve a desired level of function. By starting with known human roles, one also encourages self-organization to find assignments that are "close" to those roles and thus more tractable to human cognition.

Readers will recognize our interest in and research on self-organizing mechanisms in other publications 3 10 20 . In this paper, we focus our attention on defining patterns of human-like roles that can be imposed at design time. The synthesis of these two approaches is a major area of current research for us.

3.2   Role Configuration

Configuring a role can be thought of along two dimensions: breadth and depth. Role breadth, or *hori ontal speciali ation*, addresses the number and complexity of actions supported by a given role.   Depth, or *ertical speciali ation*, separates the performance of actions from the administration of them. That is, it relates to the degree of control an agent can have over its actions and the actions of other agents 19 .

Horizontal Specialization of Roles

At one extreme, a role could require an agent to be a jack-of-all-trades, handling any kind of request. In this scenario, there is no horizontal specialization—only "fat" homogeneous agents. In small, simple organizations, such versatility can be useful. However, in large, diversified organizations (whether human or MAS systems), agents cannot be expected to do everything. Instead, diversity and limited capability are the guidelines for role design.

In the other extreme, a role could simply require the repertoire of a single, highly specialized action. Such an approach is common in the traditional assembly line where each worker has a single, specific task to perform. Simple roles have two primary characteristics. First, each incumbent of a role assignment can perform its action separately and independently from other role assignments. Second, the incumbent can perform its task without knowing how other assembly–line actions fit together to produce the end product. Simple roles are commonly used because they provide building blocks that are both easier to understand and simpler to develop than more broadly defined roles. However, the resulting population of narrowly defined roles will be larger than more elaborate ones for two reasons. The simpler the individual role, the more roles will be required by a complex activity to accomplish the same goal. Because of their narrow design, simple roles can sometimes require coordinator roles to organize them. Coordination is not always required for simple roles, particularly when it can occur among the roles through mechanisms such as mutual adjustment, standards, and stigmergy. Coordinator roles are just one of many mechanisms for obtaining coordination.

A high level of horizontal specialization is particularly useful when two situations exist: independent action is useful and an understanding exists of how the other actions fit together to deliver the end product. Some degree of horizontal specialization can increase productivity for several reasons:

- Specialized roles can be identified and specified that use repetitive actions which are expected to produce successful results.
- Incremental improvement is encouraged due to its modular nature. As actions become more specialized and standardized they tend to become smaller and simpler units of behavior. Incrementally modifying behavior at a fine-grain level tends to be easier than at a coarse-grain level.
- Role assignment could be based on particular criteria, enabling the system to match and assign an individual agent to a role.

Specialization is a matter of degree, so that a role can include more than one specialized action and actions can be broad rather than narrow. The richer and more complex a role is, the greater the requirements for the agent filling the role assignment. Coarse-grained roles carry with them the problems and benefits of coarse-grained components. For example, driving a hook-and-ladder fire engine requires a front driver, rear driver, and a navigator/radioman. Each performs a separate specialized action that depends on close coordination with the others. Here, actions are predominantly concurrent and interdependent; whereas the assembly-line specialization (described above) involves actions that are predominantly serially dependent in nature. In other words, these roles are less specialized than the traditional assembly line where each worker role is not concerned about close coordination with other roles.

Vertical Specialization of Roles

While horizontal specialization addresses the performance of work, vertical specialization addresses the management of work. More precisely, vertical specialization addresses the degree of control that a role has over its actions as well as the actions of other roles. Management roles implement those tasks associated with planning, coordination, and monitoring of the agents within a group. The primary purpose of specializing roles vertically is to insure that horizontally specialized behavior results in the identified goals. In essence, then, these roles define management functions that administer the linkage among agents playing planned horizontal roles. Manager roles differ both in terms of how, why, where, and who they control, as well as the breadth and management level of their control. In all cases, they manage behavior that leads to specific goals.

At one extreme, the role of an agent that simply carries out its activities only when directed by another agent is very narrow vertically. In contrast, the role of an agent that assumes control of much of the decision making for other agents is vertically broad. The shift from passive responder to active manager is another way of saying that a role's vertical dimension shifts from narrow (or specialized) to broader (or more general). At the far extreme of vertical generalization, a fat jack-of-all-managers role would control the actions of every agent including itself.

In between these extremes exists a range of possibilities. For example, a manager role could still require management in a system where every agent requires checks and balances. And a very simple agent could follow simple rules involving agent-based pheromones. For instance, if it detects a pheromone, it will follow the "scent" gradient towards the "food." No manager role is necessary. In fact, many effective solutions for agent-based organizational designs employ swarm intelligence techniques that require little or no vertical specialization. Some forms of human organizations do not require management roles, either. Without vertical specialization, however, many human-based organizations, such as most armed forces and legal systems, would fail utterly.

4 Role Assignments and Positions

Roles are established so that actors may play them. When an agent is actually assigned to play a role, this is known as *role assignment*. Assignments to roles can be made by a distinguished agent or established upon request by the agent itself. In either case, a set of prerequisite conditions must be met for the assignment to be made.

> A *role assignment* is the association of a group with a role that may be occupied by an agent. Each mapping of an agent to a role assignment can be a result of an exogenous or an endogenous process.

Formally, a role assignment is a relation between an agent and a role. However, having a role-filling mechanism that does not always have a particular agent assigned is also useful. These are called *positions*.

A *position* is an officially recognized potential for role assignment within a group structure. A position may or may not have an agent assigned to it. Only one agent may be associated with it at any point in time. However, many different agents may be associated with the position over time.

The notion of "position" is useful to organization designers, because it encourages the designer to identify and specify those jobs that need to be performed. This is accomplished before any agents physically exist to fill the positions. A position can be established to last for long periods of time or merely created for a brief, ad hoc, usage. For example, long-term positions could include positions such as facilitators and librarians. Short-term positions could be established for each instance of a workflow activity. For instance, the workflow for Order 12345 would include activities such as Accept Order, Fill Order, and Ship Order. Here, a temporary position could be requisitioned for each activity defined for Order 12345 and filled by a qualified agent. The manager agent in charge of the Order 12345 workflow would be responsible for creating and filling each position. When each activity completes its job, the position is "vacated" and terminated. In fact, even the manager job could be requisitioned as a short-term position in an Order workflow, to be filled as needed by an agent designed as a general order-processing manager.

In other words, defining positions enables system designers and agent managers:

- to anticipate organizational needs by specifying positions first and populating them later.
- to create positions on-the-fly and fill them with agents they deem qualified.
- to remove an agent from its position when it cannot function effectively (e.g., its platform is down, or the agent is overloaded with other activities at a particular moment) and be replaced with another agent.
- to fill the same position serially with different agents over time, allowing agents to be purchased from different vendors, constructed for specific platforms using particular languages, or adapted over time to fill a given position.

In short, a position is a specification for an agent to fulfill *potentially*. It specifies the role to be assigned, criteria for occupying the position, and the supervisory relationship that it might have with other positions.

By their nature, positions partition the organization into discrete processing units, thereby placing barriers across the organization. Organizations that were thought of as seamless entities instead become aggregations of positions that must communicate and coordinate. The more positions there are, the more complexity there is within the organization—whether the positions are vertical or horizontal. The fewer positions, the more complexity there is inside of the *agent*. Also, the more complex the environment, the more positions there can be.

Position specialization also creates a balancing problem. When positions are partitioned into more specialized positions, how many of each kind should be created For example, if all the Sales positions are specialized as either Merchandise Sales or

Service Sales positions, how many of each should be created If there were ten Sales positions before, should there now be five of each new specialization What is the optimal number What happens when the number required at any time swings widely from needing many Service Sales positions to needing many Merchandise Sales positions Having a single type of Sales position handles all situations. Yet, if merchandise and service sales situations are vastly different, a single type of Sales position could require too many duties, skills, responsibilities, and supervisory relationships for any one agent to adequately satisfy.

5 Groups – The Next Frontier

The only class in Fig. 1 that we have not discussed is the Group. As defined earlier:

> A *group* is a set of agents that are related via their roles, where these relationships must form a connected graph within the group.

This definition implies not only that a group is a function of the roles contained within it, but also that roles have no meaning without their group referent. Hence, our ability to understand roles is limited by our ability to understand the groups of which they are a part. As with roles, groups may be deliberately established (i.e., by a system designer) or they may be emergent. In human organization terms, a deliberately established group could be a department or other workgroup that has been defined by some organizational authority. In contrast, an emergent group might be a social group that forms when several individuals decide to go out for a beer after work. Over time, they define themselves as a group ("My Friday Afternoon Drinking Buddies").

In a subsequent paper we will consider the properties of agent groups and how they can either be deliberately established or system parameters set in order to foster the emergence of more effective groups. Some questions that we expect to address in that subsequent paper include:

• What system parameters affect emergent group formation and group effectiveness
• What (if anything) differentiates deliberate groups from emergent groups
• How should positions be grouped To form groups that support individual, assemblage, team, or workflow activities—or some other organization unit
• How should groups be aggregated into larger groups
• To what extent should group structure and content be standardized
• What is the purpose and function of the manager roles in each group
• How much administrative power should be delegated to the manager agents and how much to the other agents in each group

6 Conclusion

Societies need to employ patterned behaviors to exist. The behavior of each individual is determined to a great extent by the requirements of these patterns. In this paper, we have begun examining human-based organizational techniques as a source of inspiration for designing effective agent-based organizations. In particular, this paper has addressed the notion of *roles*: what the notion means and how roles might be employed in agent-based systems. Forthcoming work will address groups, group structures, policies and contracts, communication and interaction protocols, activity structures, ontology, goals, BDI's, and emotions and morale for agent organizations.

References

1. Gasser, Les, Perspectives on Organizations in Multi-Agent Systems, *Multi-Agent Systems and Applications*, Michael Luck *et al* eds., Springer-Verlag, Berlin, 2001, pp. 1–16.
2. Katz, Daniel, and Robert L. Kahn, *The Social Psychology of rgani ations*, (2nd ed.), John Wiley and Sons, New York, 1978.
3. Parunak, H. V. D., 'Go to the Ant': Engineering Principles from Natural Agent Systems, *Annals of perations esearch* 75: 69–101, 1997.
4. Bonabeau, E., M. Dorigo, et al., *Swarm Intelligence rom Natural to Artificial Systems*, New York, Oxford University Press, 1999.
5. Camazine, S., J.-L. Deneubourg, *et al* , *Self- rgani ation in Biological Systems* Princeton, NJ, Princeton University Press, 2001.
6. Kephart, J. O., J. E. Hanson, *et al* , "Dynamics of an Information-Filtering Economy," *ooperati e Information Agents II* M. Klusch and G. Weiss, eds. Berlin, Springer-Verlag. 1435: 160–170, 1998.
7. Beshers, S. N. and J. H. Fewell, Models of Division of Labor in Social Insects, *Annual e iew of Entomology*, 46: 413–440, 2001.
8. Theraulaz, G., S. Goss, *et al* "Task Differentiation in *Polistes* Wasp Colonies: A Model for Self-Organizing Groups of Robots," *irst International onference on Simulation of Adapti e Beha ior*, MIT Press, 1991.
9. Parunak, H. Van Dyke, and James Odell, Representing Social Structures in UML, *Agent- riented Software Engineering A SE II*, Michael Wooldridge *et al* eds., Springer-Verlag, Berlin, 2002, pp. 1–16.
10. Odell, James, H. Van Dyke Parunak, Mitch Fleischer, and Sven Brueckner, Modeling Agents and their Environment, *Agent- riented Software Engineering A SE III*, Fausto Giunchiglia *et al* eds., Springer-Verlag, Berlin, 2003 (forthcoming).
11. Parunak, H. Van Dyke, S. Brueckner, M. Fleischer, and J. Odell, "Co-X: Defining what Agents Do Together," In *Proceedings of Workshop on Teamwork and oalition ormation*, AAMAS 2002, 2002.
12. Biddle, Bruce J., and Edwin J. Thomas, *ole Theory oncepts and esearch*, John Wiley and Sons, New York, 1966.
13. Moreno, J.L. ed., *The Sociometry eader*, The Free Press, Glencoe, IL, 1960.
14. Oxford English Dictionary, (2nd ed.), Oxford University Press, Oxford, 1992.
15. Bormann, E.G., and N.C. Bormann, *Effecti e Small roup ommunication* Burgess Publications, Minneapolis, MN, 1988.
16. Burke, Peter J., The Development of Task and Social-emotional Role Differentiation, *Sociometry*, 30 (December), 1967, pp. 379–92.
17. Burke, Peter J., Role Differentiation and the Legitimation of Task Activity, *Sociometry*, 32 (June), 1968, pp. 159–68. Reprinted by Warner Modular Publications, Inc. (R466), 1973.
18. Diamond, M.A. and Seth Allcorn, Role Formation As Defensive Activity In Bureaucratic Organizations, *Political Psychology*, Vol. 7, No. 4, December, 1986.

19. Mintzberg, Henry, *Structure in i es esigning Effecti e rgani ations*, Prentice Hall, Englewood Cliffs, NJ, 1993.
20. Zambonelli, F. and H. V. D. Parunak, "From Design to Intention: Signs of a Revolution," First International Conference on Autonomous Agents and Multi-Agent Systems (AAMAS 2002), Bologna, Italy, 2002.
21. Parunak, H. V. D., "Visualizing Agent Conversations: Using Enhanced Dooley Graphs for Agent Design and Analysis," Second International Conference on Multi-Agent Systems (ICMAS'96), 1996.
22. Krackhardt, D. and J. Hanson, "Informal Networks: the Company behind the Chart," *Har ard Business e iew*, 71(4), July/Aug., 1993, pp. 104–111.
23. Rogers, E.M. and D.L. Kincaid, *ommunication Networks toward a new paradigm for research*, New York: Free Press, 1981.
24. Wooldridge, M., N.R. Jennings, and D. Kinny, The Gaia Methodology for Agent-Oriented Analysis and Design. *International ournal of Autonomous Agents and Multi-Agent Systems*, 3(3), September 2000, pp. 285–312.
25. Evans, R., et al., *Methodology for Agent- riented Software Engineering*, EURESCOM, Project P907 Deliverable 3, final report, 20 September, 2001.

Requirements Engineering for Large-Scale Multi-agent Systems

Luiz Marcio Cysneiros[1] and Eric Yu[2]

[1] Department of Mathematics and Statistics
York University
cysneiro@mathstat.yorku.ca
[2]Faculty of Information Studies
University of Toronto
yu@fis.utoronto.ca

Abstract. Large-scale software systems typically involve a large number of actors playing different roles, interacting with each other to achieve personal and common goals. As agent-based software technologies advance, systematic methods are needed to support the development of large-scale multi-agent systems. As with other kinds of software systems, successful system development relies on in-depth understanding of stakeholder needs and wants, and their effective translation into system requirements, and eventually into executable software. This paper presents a requirements engineering methodology based on agent concepts at the requirements modeling level. The strategic actor is used as the central organizing construct during requirements elicitation and analysis. In considering alternative arrangements of work processes and system interactions, strategic actors seek to exploit opportunities and avoid vulnerabilities. The methodology starts by building a lexicon as a preliminary step. The relevant actors are then identified. A breadth coverage step produces a first-cut model of the domain and the social relationships within it. The models are then developed depth-wise to capture organizational and individual goals and to explore alternatives. The methodology complements and extends the *i** modelling framework. By taking into account agent characteristics such as autonomy, intentionality, and sociality starting from the requirements level, the methodology leads naturally into the development of large-scale systems that employ multi-agent software technologies. An example from the healthcare domain is used to illustrate the methodology.

1 Introduction

Imagine the widespread use of software agents to support healthcare on a large scale. Healthcare professionals, patients, and even family members would be supported in their interactions and decision making by various kinds of software agents personalized to meet their information and communication needs. Information technology is widely recognized as a key ingredient for improving healthcare quality and cost-effectiveness. Compared to conventional information systems, agent-based systems have the potential to offer greater flexibility, enhanced functionalities, and better robustness, reliability, and security.

While many elements of agent technologies are advancing beyond experimental stages, methods for building large-scale real-world applications are only beginning to be developed 19 20 . Such systems are characterized by large numbers of players, with complex relationships, and often conflicting goals. Humans, hardware, and

A. Garcia et al. (Eds.): SELMAS 2002, LNCS 2603, pp. 39–56, 2003.
© Springer-Verlag Berlin Heidelberg 2003

software interact in much more intricate ways then in conventional systems which automate routine work processes. A critical factor in the successful development of such systems is therefore the understanding of stakeholder needs and wants, how technologies might alter their relationships, facilitation of their negotiations, and communication of those needs to system developers.

Requirements engineering is an area of growing importance as it focuses on identifying and characterizing "what" the system should do, while subsequent software engineering stages elaborate on the technology-oriented "how". Various approaches, including models, languages, methodologies, and tools have been developed to assist and support requirements activities such as elicitation, analysis, negotiation, verification and validation 10 .

This paper presents a methodology that uses the strategic actor concept as the central organizing construct. Unlike traditional requirements modeling techniques (e.g., 5 13) that assume well-defined activity steps, input-output flows, or object interactions, strategic actors may act autonomously within the constraints of their social relationships with other actors. As new technologies and work arrangements are being proposed, various players explore alternatives and seek to advance or protect their strategic interests as they face uncertainty and turbulence in their environments.

The methodology builds on the *i** framework for agent-oriented requirements engineering 15 16 . This paper extends earlier work by introducing the use of a lexicon control as a front-end to guide model construction, as well as systematic steps on how to use the i* framework to elicit requirements. A broader methodology based on *i** covering the full range of software engineering activities is outlined in 2 . This present paper elaborates on the very early stages of software development.

By incorporating agent characteristics such as autonomy, intentionality, and sociality into the earliest stages of requirements analysis, the methodology facilitates the development process for large-scale multi-agent software systems. For detailed analysis, strategic actors are refined into agents that play roles or occupy positions. Each of these may be used to represent composite actors such as organizational units consisting of multiple positions, roles, and agents. Composite actors may have goals that complement or conflict with those of individual actors.

The methodology is illustrated with an example from the healthcare domain. The scenario is the provision of automated support to assess patients with chronic diseases through the use of a set of "guardian angel" software agents integrating all health-related concerns, including medically-relevant legal and financial information, about an individual. This personal system will help track, manage, and interpret the subject's health history, and offer advice to both patient and healthcare provider. The example setting has been proposed as an exemplar for advancing research in agent-oriented software development methodologies 17 , and is based on the Guardian Angel project proposal 14 . Although the methodology could be presented more concisely with a simpler pedagogical example, we have chosen to use a realistic example to illustrate the complexity of issues that can arise in a large-scale application.

2   Agent-Oriented Modeling for Requirements Engineering

Most requirements modelling techniques have focused on the specification of processes in terms of activity steps, input and output flows, or interactions and message exchanges among mechanistically-behaving objects (e.g., 5 , 13). Agent-based systems function in environments where humans, as well as hardware and software, have considerable autonomy. Thus their behaviours are not so well defined or predictable. Instead, they are better characterized by intentional concepts – goals, beliefs, abilities, and social relationships such as interdependencies and commitments.

The *i** modelling framework 15 was developed to introduce an intentional and social ontology for requirements engineering. Systems and their environments are described in terms of intentional relationships among strategic actors. Actors are taken to be intentional in that they have goals, beliefs, etc., and strategic in that they seek to exploit opportunities and to mitigate vulnerabilities. *Actors* may be abstract (*roles* defining responsibilities), concrete (*agents* – human and non-human individuals or classes with specific capabilities), or other organizational constructs (e.g., *positions* which package a number of *roles* together to be assigned to a single concrete *agent*). Composite actors may be composed of constituent actors.

External relationships among actors are expressed in the *Strategic   ependency* (SD) model. Actors depend on each other for goals to be achieved, tasks to be performed, resources to be furnished, and softgoals to be satisficed[1]. Internal relationships among the intentional elements within an actor's reasoning are expressed in the *Strategic   ationale* (SR) model. Rationales are modelled through means-ends relationships, task decompositions, and softgoal contributions. SD models are used to represent different configurations of relationships, for example, representing different ways in which multi-agent systems can be used within a healthcare context, whereas SR models are used to make the reasoning about such alternate configurations explicit.

The *i** concept of strategic actor is an abstraction used to hide the detailed actions within the actor's discretion. Strategically significant elements of work processes are described in terms of dependency relationships among actors. The agent-oriented modelling approach offers a higher-level description that is a more faithful representation of reality as real-world agents frequently depart from standardized routines and procedural process specifications.

Note that during the requirements stages, agent concepts are used to encompass both human and non-human agents. The agent-based ontology is used to bring out complex social relationships, so as to expose strengths and vulnerabilities in the existing process. This allows the stakeholders and analysts to conceive of alternatives to the existing process, guided by goals and evaluation criteria. Such alternatives might, and often does, introduce software agents into the process.

3   The Methodology

An initial step aims to develop an informal understanding of the domain by systematically collecting and analyzing the vocabulary used by stakeholders. A Lexicon is constructed using supporting tools.   The lexicon is then used to help construct an agent-oriented model of the social structure of the domain. A first -cut

---

[1] We use here the same notion used in 3 that an NFR can rarely be said to be satisfied. Goal satisficing suggest that the solution used is expected to satisfy within acceptable limits. The term satisfice was coined by Hebert Simon to express "good enough" alternatives

Strategic Dependency (SD) model is then constructed to provide an overview of the existing processes and related systems. As the elicitation proceeds, the first-cut model provides a scaffolding for stakeholders to voice their concerns and aspirations, critique the current processes and organizational arrangements, and to articulate possible new arrangements. These elaborations will be used to construct more detailed models where the achievement of *goals* are evaluated, leading stakeholders to explore alternate systems and organizational arrangements which will allow them to achieve their *goals* more effectively. Figure 1 illustrates the process as an SADT (Structured Analysis and Design Technique) model 12

The methodological steps presented in this paper address primarily the early stage in requirements elicitation and analysis. During this stage, one develops an understanding of the problem by analyzing organizational structures, processes, and social relationships. Alternatives to the existing process are explored, including the possible introduction of software agents, and how these different alternatives might contribute to overcome problems and improve the process.

A subsequent stage in the methodology, not illustrated in this paper, addresses the late requirements where the system-to-be is introduced and therefore its requirements

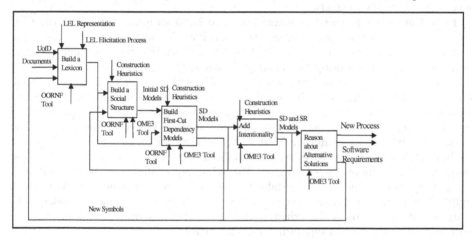

Fig. 1. An SADT Model of the Overall Methodology

are to be detailed, modeled and analyzed in the presence of quality requirements (also known as Non-Functional Requirements 1). Tradeoffs will have to be made, some of them requiring one more time social and organizational concerns to be brought to light.

3.1 Understanding the Vocabulary

Dealing with complex domains demands to first understand the vocabulary used in the domain. Clarifying the vocabulary can help avoid many problems typically caused by the naive assumption that it is easy to understand what the stakeholder is talking about 4 6 . The methodology starts by constructing a controlled vocabulary to act as front-end support for the *i** modelling process, as an ongoing resource for the project, as well as for future reuse. It serves to facilitate and focus communication with stakeholders and among development team members.   LEL, Language Extended Lexicon proposed by Leite 9 , is used to capture the vocabulary used in practice in the domain. Its objective is to register the vocabulary of a given UofD[2]. It is based upon the following simple idea: understand the problem's language without worrying about deeply understanding the problem. LEL is mainly used to register terms (words or phrases) relevant to a specific field of application.

LEL is based on a controlled vocabulary system composed of symbols where each symbol is an entry expressed in terms of notions and behavioural responses. The notions record the meaning of the symbol and its fundamental relations with other entries. The behavioural responses specify the connotation of the symbol in the UofD. Each symbol may also be represented by one or more aliases and will be classified as a subject, a verb or an object.

The construction of the lexicon is guided by the principles of minimal vocabulary and circularity. The circularity principle prescribes the maximization of the usage of lexicon symbols when describing lexicon entries, while the minimal vocabulary principle prescribes the minimization of the usage of symbols exterior to the lexicon when describing lexicon entries.

First Contact: Open-Ended Interview – To build an initial version of the LEL we start by conducting an open-ended interview 7 with some or all of the stakeholders (depending on their availability, and taking into account possible political sensitivities). During this meeting we will try to get a first idea of the domain and to capture some initial lexicon symbols. We will also try to identify possible documents that we can use to further elicit other symbols. Although we are not yet worried about capturing intentions, if there are already some preconceived notion of a target system, one question must be asked now: Why do you need this system The answer will be used to delimit the context in which we will focus our work. Try also to find out the main stakeholders involved in the domain. All actors discovered should be included as symbols of the lexicon. The relatively neutral activity of eliciting a vocabulary allows the RE to establish rapport with and among stakeholders, cultivating a collaborative atmosphere for potentially more contentious issues later. This activity also affirms the primacy of the stakeholders in determining eventual outcomes, with the RE in a supporting, facilitating role.

LEL is useful not only for understanding the domain but also as a starting point for creating different models throughout the process. In addition, capturing the vocabulary in an organized form benefits the reuse of the domain knowledge.

Domain Knowledge Construction – Start to register all the relevant words or phrases peculiar to the domain using the lexicon. This process leads to a spiral growth of our knowledge about the domain and continues until no new symbols are found.

Validating the Lexicon with Stakeholders – Because the lexicon uses a natural language structure, it can be validated by stakeholders without much difficulty. At every stage, validating the Lexicon with the stakeholders is very helpful in gaining additional knowledge about the domain.

---

[2] *" ni erse of iscourse is the general conte t where the software should be de eloped and operated The   of includes all the sources of information and all known people related to the software These people are also known as the actors in this of "*

3.2 Outlining the Social Structure

To appreciate the complexity in a large-scale application, it is helpful to begin by identifying the main actors and roles and outlining how they relate. That gives the RE a better context for understanding the processes and the political landscapes. To build an outline of the social structure, we will use the lexicon and semi-structured interviews. The social structure is depicted in a model consisting of *actors* and the structural relationships among them (an agent *play*ing some role, *occupy*ing some position; a position *co er*ing some roles; an actor being *part-of* another actor; an actor *is-a* specialization of another actor). *Actors* may be differentiated into *agents*, *roles*, and *positions* but may also be generic, if the distinctions are not clear at this point. For example, Figure 2 depicts the idea that an agent physician person occupies the physician position which in turn may cover either the role of a physician in a hospital or the role of a physician in a practice. Notice that these two roles will certainly encompass different goals, meaning that each one might have different requirements for the software to be built.

Identifying the Main Actors - We start by picking up all the symbols classified as subjects in the lexicon. They are strong candidates to be actors. For each symbol represented as an actor in the model, check if other symbols categorized as subjects appear in the Notions of that symbol in the lexicon. The presence of other subject symbols may suggest the possibility of a structural relationship between these two actors. Once we do it to all the symbols in the lexicon we should get an initial idea of the domain's social structural relationships.

Validating the Social Structure with Stakeholders - This can be done by using semi-structured interviews where the model will be explained and presented to the stakeholders so they can confirm it or help correct it.

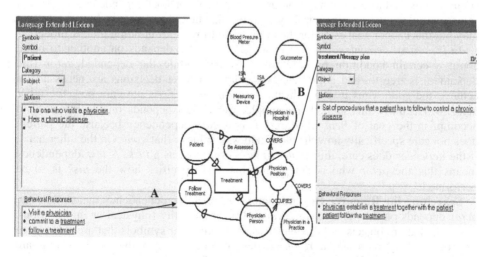

Fig. 2. Finding Goals and Resources Dependencies

3.3 Building a First-Cut Dependency Model

At this stage we are trying to understand and model the "as-is" processes and systems. Initially, we will be mostly aiming to construct a Strategic Dependency (SD) model 15 . The SD model depicts a process through the use of a network of dependency relationships among *actors*. In *i**, a *dependency* is a relationship in which one *actor* (the *depender*) depends on another *actor* (the *dependee*) for something (the **dependum**) to be achieved. A *dependum* can be a *goal task resource or softgoal*, reflecting the types of freedom allowed by the relationship, as detailed below.

    Identifying the Main Dependencies - To start building an SD model, we revisit the symbols in the lexicon. Other elicitation techniques (open-ended interviews, document reading, observation and protocol analysis 7) can also be used to enhance the initial model derived from the lexicon.

    For each symbol that has been identified as an actor in the social structure model, check if the behavioural responses have any other symbol that is a subject (another probable *actor*), or have sentences with two symbols that are subjects. These suggest the presence of a *dependency*. Since not all dependencies can be discovered through the lexicon, a complementary approach is to using the social structure model (Section 3.2) to ask each actor in the model: 1) On Whom do you depend to do your job 2) What other people/devices do you interact with 3) Who depend on you to do their job In addition, dependency types may not be directly apparent from the lexicon. Hence, the RE may need to elicit from actors the nature of the dependency relationships. The lexicon can provide further help in the following ways:

    Searching for Goal or Task Dependencies - Symbols that are verbs and are present in the behavioural responses of other subject symbols suggest a task or goal dependency. Arrow A in Figure 2 illustrates this heuristic Also, checking every symbol classified as a verb may lead us to many task or goal dependencies, although sometimes we may be seeing a task or goal that is internal to an actor. In that case, we may put this task or goal aside for the moment until we start building the SR models.

    In *i**, a *goal dependency* is one in which one *actor* depends on another to bring about a certain condition or state in the world, while the depended *actor* (the dependee) is free to, and is expected to, make whatever decisions are necessary to achieve the *goal*. Thus it also indicates that one *actor* does not care how the other *actor* will achieve this *goal*. For example, the Patient depends on the Physician to accomplish the goal of *Being Assessed*. It is a *goal* dependency because the patient does not care specifically how the physician will achieve that *goal*. On the other hand, if the *depender* does care, this *goal* will be represented as a *task*. A *task* dependency means that the *actor* who is delegating this *task* specifies how the *task* is to be performed.

    Searching for Resource Dependencies - A *resource* dependency means that one *actor* depends on the other for the availability of an entity (physical or information). Symbols that are objects and that have one or more other symbols that are subjects in its notions may represent a *resource* dependency between the symbols that are subjects. Arrow B in Figure 2 shows an example of this heuristic.

    Figure 3 depicts the First-Cut model.

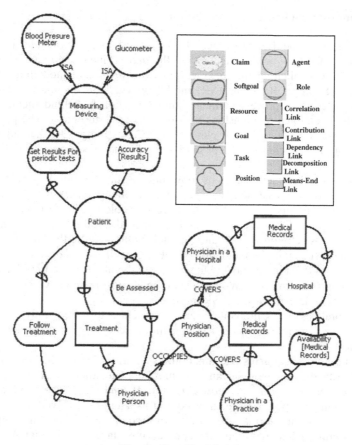

Fig. 3. First-Cut Model

The first-cut dependency model aims to provide a broad-brushed picture of the major relationships and associated processes.   oals are recorded as they are recognized, but no attempt is made to further pursue their "hows" and "whys". Understanding the "whys" requires that one have at least a basic understanding of the "whats" (actual process). The same applies for *softgoals* A *Softgoal* is similar to a goal in that it is a condition in the world that an actor would like to achieve. However, the criteria for the condition being achieved are not sharply defined. Therefore, *softgoals* are satisficed (sufficiently achieved) rather than satisfied 3 . In Figure 5 we can see the *softgoal* Availability regarding Medical Records. This *softgoal* appears in the first-cut model because the Physician Working in a Practice may have major problems for obtaining Patient's Medical Records from Hospitals where the Patient had been visiting before consulting with this Physician. Hence, being a major concern for a Physician Working in a Practice, this *softgoal* can be elicited even if we are not concerned about *softgoals*.

3.4 Elaborating on Processes and Rationales

At this stage we would have a general idea of the main *actors* and their external *dependencies*. We now need to understand the *actors'* internal implementation of the processes through eliciting the *tasks* within each *actor* and modelling them in SR models. The Strategic Rationale (SR) model provides an intentional description of processes in terms of process elements and the rationale behind them. SR models describe the intentional relationships that are "internal" to *actors*. The primary focus at this stage is on eliciting *task* elements, without going into the rationales. The elicitation of the *task* elements helps clarify the boundaries of responsibilities among *actors*.

Building the SR model enables us to go into details that not only help understand certain needs but also disclose new *dependencies* among *agents*. To do that, we focus on finding the main *tasks* that each *actor* is responsible for. *Tasks* tend to be easier to identify than *goals*. They are more tangible since the stakeholders or the end-users carry them out as activities. *oals* and rationales that underlie the business will be the focus of our next step in the methodology. However, if some *goals* are evident at this stage, we record them in the model but will not elaborate on them until later.

Examining the Lexicon - We will, once again, use lexicon symbols classified as verbs to be candidates for *tasks* in SR models.

Behavioural responses in symbols that represent actors frequently hide a *goal* or *task*, while behavioural responses that have an object symbol may disclose a resource dependency.

Drawing Some Scenarios – at this point, scenarios 18 can be helpful in refining *tasks* and expanding on an *actor* (an actor may be understood as any possible instance of an actor, i.e. *agent role and position*). To expand on an *actor*, we may ask the stakeholders in what possible scenarios could this agent be involved.

The scenario is an informal way of eliciting requirements and is non-intentional. It is more useful in late requirements engineering stage and is playing more of a supporting role at this early stage of requirements elicitation. Be careful to only describe scenarios that are pertinent to the problem and therefore not to expand the UofD more than it needs to be. If one has created the scenario by reading documents, validate each scenario with the stakeholders.

Asking Questions - Also, for each *role* or *position* in the models we may frequently ask: Who are the actors involved with this *role position*. Furthermore, for each or *actor* we must ask two questions: 1) What is this person responsible for 2) What are the processes in which this person is involved Answers to these questions may be directly modeled in a SR model or be the trigger for drawing a scenario.

This process continues until no more *tasks* are found. We confirm with the stakeholders that the process is now correctly understood and modeled. Any new symbol found during the process has to be added to the lexicon and the process repeats looking for new *actors*, new *dependencies* and new *tasks*.

Managing Viewpoints - Stakeholders typically have different viewpoints about one subject matter. Different stakeholders may view the same process in different ways or have different ways of achieving the same *goal*. Different viewpoints can be represented as different models and later consolidated, or expressed as alternative ways of achieving a *goal softgoal*.

Finally, it is also very important to maintain consistency between SD and SR models as new findings in SR models may arise in this step of the methodology.

Figure 4 shows some of the *tasks* that were found through the use of the above heuristics. We can see for example that in order to Follow a Treatment, a Patient have to Control the Evolution of the Disease, Follow a Prescribed Load of Exercises, Take Medication and Follow a Specific Diet   On the other hand we can see that a Physician to Assess a Patient has to Manage Medical Records, Make Medical Decisions and Establish a Treatment. The *goal* Get Professional Recognition appears in this model because we arrived to this *goal* because it was not clear why a Physician depends on a Patient to Follow the Treatment. As happened with the Availability *softgoal* in the First-Cut model, although at this stage we are not yet concerned about intentions, since we got to know a *goal* we have to model it. Later we can further reason about this *goal*, for now it is enough to represent it in the model.

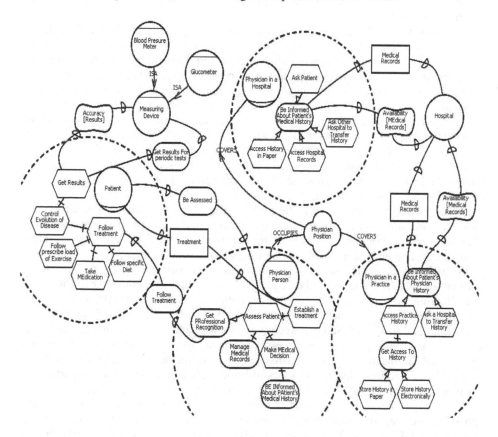

Fig. 4. Elaborating on Processes and Rationales

3.5   Elaborating on the Intentional Dimension

Once we have a model representing the process as-it-is today, we elicit the *goals* that underlie the process, why the process is the way it is, what are the *goals* that have to be achieved so the business can be successful. Here we will be seeking higher-level *goals* that will represent among other things the business objectives. We will also be looking for individual *goals*, i.e., *goals* that are particular to an *actor*. In this step we will mostly use semi-structured and open-ended interviews and eventually document analysis 7 . When using these techniques, one may keep asking the following questions: Why does this *actor* need to perform this *task* Why does it have to be performed this way To discover *goals* that are currently not satisfied, one could ask: What is wrong with the process   What are the things you (the *actor*) dislike most What should be changed What are the major weaknesses Aside that,   discovering the major strengths in the current process/system would suggest *goals* that are currently satisfied.

It is important to have in mind that this is not a top-down process and neither a bottom-up one. Since we depart from already elicited *tasks*, it is more likely that we start using a bottom-up approach rather than a top-down approach. However, we recognize that in some situations the opposite approach might be more suitable.

At this point in the methodology, it is important to be careful about privacy and political aspects. A stakeholder may be reluctant to disclose negative aspects of a process because he or she may have fears about sanctions or reprisals. Thus, interviews with more than one stakeholder at a time should be carefully handled and better avoided. Also, if one stakeholder says there is no problem with the actual process, while others say the opposite, one could suspect that important personal interests might be at stake. These should be probed further as they may suggest or preclude possible future alternatives.

Aside from *goals*, we will also be looking for *softgoals*. Some *softgoals* can be identified and modeled during the previous phases, but we defer the comprehensive elicitation and elaboration of softgoals until this stage since *softgoals* are typically used as selection criteria in evaluating and suggesting process alternatives. The notion of the *softgoal* elaborated here is related to that of non-functional requirements 3 , but our *softgoals* relate to *actors* that can be a human agent or a computer agent.

Following a taxonomy of common *softgoals* during elicitation from the stakeholders can be very helpful. For example, for each *task* and *goal* we may ask: Does this *task goal* need Safety Accuracy Performance Whenever the answer is yes, we may represent it as a *softgoal* and refine it until we have the operationalizations that will satisfice this *softgoal*. Refinement can be either top-down or bottom-up, and more likely it is a mix of both. Refinements may also be part of the taxonomy and must be used as guidance instead of a mandatory approach.

After we refine all the *softgoals*, we may check for possible interdependencies, (positive and negative contributions, among *softgoals*). To do that, we use the approach used in 4 . This approach proposes three heuristics to search for interdependencies: 1) Evaluate different graphs for the same type of softgoal, e.g., all the graphs related to performance. 2) Evaluate graphs for softgoals that are frequently conflicting, e.g. Usability and Security. 3) If the number of graphs is not too large, pair wising different graphs (of course excluding graphs that have already been compared within the two previous heuristics). Where negative contributions are found, tradeoffs will have to be made among possible alternative solutions.

To check for model completeness at this stage, we check if all *goals* are evaluated. *oals* are related to tasks through *means-ends links*. The *tasks* are the different ways in which the *goal* can be accomplished. Each *task* may consist of *subgoals subtasks resources and softgoals* (via the *task decomposition link*). All elements of a *task* must be satisfied in order for a *task* to be satisfied. A *goal* is satisfied if any of its alternative tasks is satisfied (via the means-ends links). Note that (hard) goals can be satisfied, while softgoals can only be *satisficed*.

Softgoals have also to be evaluated through a qualitative reasoning that can be carried out using contribution links among *softgoals*. The semantics of the links are based on the concept of satisficing 3 . The most common contribution types are *Help Hurt* (positive/negative but not sufficient to meet the parental goal), *Some   Some-* (positive/negative of unknown degree), whereas *Make Break* indicates positive/negative of sufficient degree, i.e., strong enough to say that the softgoal is met or not met. Although these distinctions are coarse grained, they are enough to decide whether we need further refinement and search for more specific *softgoals* and operationalizations or not.   *ontribution links* allow one to decompose *softgoals* to the point that one can say that the operationalizations to this *softgoal* have been reached (i.e., the goals are no longer "soft").

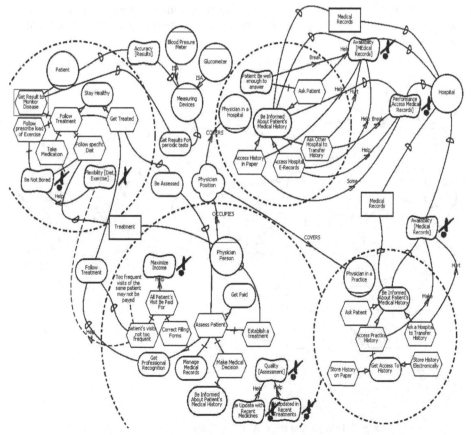

Fig. 5. Addressing the Intentional Level

Figure 5 shows part of the model after we addressed the intentional level. We can see for example that a Patient has a *goal* of Staying Healthy, which can be achieved by Getting Treated and Following a Treatment. We can also see that further refinements addressing the intentional level lead to find out that in order to Follow a Prescribed Load of Exercise and to Follow a Specific Diet, a Patient does not want to Be Bored. This is because an inflexible load of exercise can pushes the Patient to the level of not doing any exercise at all (expressed by the *softgoal* Flexibility with a *help contribution link* to the *softgoal* Be not Bored). The same way, a fixed diet that does not allow one to make changes can lead to frequent occurrences of improper meals, which in turn might lead to the need of changing medications. This may, in turn, lead to frequently visits to the physician. Since Physicians depends on the Patient to Follow a Treatment in order to Maximize Income (Frequent visits may not be paid), having the *softgoal* Be not Bored evaluated as weakly denied clear indicates a point for further reasoning to take place in the next step of the methodology.

We can also see in Figure 5 that in order to satisfice the *softgoal* Quality regarding the Assessment, the Physician may be Updated with Recent Medicines as well as to be Updated in Recent Treatments (both *softgoals* have a *help contribution link* to Quality). Once these two *softgoals* were considered partly denied because treatments and drugs evolve too fast, the Quality *softgoal* is automatically evaluated as partially denied since none of the *softgoals* that might contribute to its satisficing are satisfied or at least weakly satisfied.

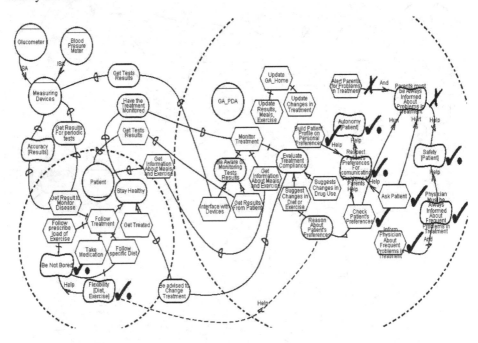

Fig. 6. Introducing the GA PDA Software Agent as an Alternative

3.6 Exploring Further Alternatives

By this time in the process, a space of alternatives would likely have already emerged for achieving some of the *goals*. We may pay special attention to the problems raised and therefore to *goals* (hard or soft) that are not currently being achieved. We may look for possible ways of achieving these goals. For example, diminishing the dependency one *agent* has on another may diminish the vulnerability of this *agent* against the other and lead to a more satisfactory process. This is particularly true when one agent is frequently not achieving a *goal* that is delegated by another *agent*. It is also worth considering whether adding new *actors* (either human or software) to the process may help. Software agents can absorb some responsibilities previously performed by a human agent, or can introduce new capabilities.

It is also important to compare different viewpoints. Focus on how each viewpoint contributes positively and negatively to achieve the *goals*. For example a Physician in a Practice has a different viewpoint for the *goal* Be informed about Patient's Medical History than the Physician in a Hospital does. Eventually, a compilation of two or more different viewpoints can bring the best solution. If possible, conduct a group meeting with the

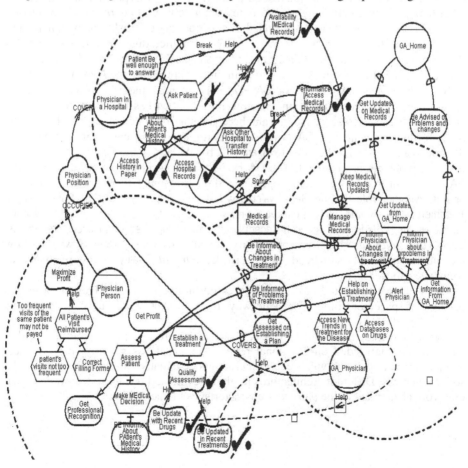

Fig. 7. Introducing the GA Physician Software Agent as an Alternative

involved stakeholders to elaborate on new alternatives. One has yet to be aware about political and personal constraints since different alternatives may lead to different redistribution of power as typically indicated in the stakeholders' personal *softgoals*.

Figure 6 shows the introduction of a new software agent GA_PDA as one possible alternative to the actual process. The GA_PDA is understood as a software agent running in a PDA a Patient will carry constantly. The Patient will depend now on the GA_PDA to Have the Treatment Monitored. This *dependency* will be enforced by a *task* Monitor Treatment that refines this goal within the GA_PDA. Among other refinements, this *task* is decomposed by the *goal* Evaluate Treatment Compliance. Suggesting Changes in Drug use or Suggesting Changes in Diet or Exercise can satisfy this *goal*. By Reasoning About Personal Preferences to suggest changes in diet or exercise we would contribute positively (*help correlation link*) to the Patient's Flexibility *softgoal* Furthermore, we need to respect the Autonomy that a Patient may have and in extension the Autonomy his GA_PDA may have. To Satisfice this Autonomy it is necessary to Respect Patient's Preferences for Communicating Problems to Parents. Further Refinement indicates that in order to comply with this *softgoal* the GA_PDA must check Patient's Preferences or Ask the Patient either the GA_PDA must send a notification to the parents or not. On the other hand, this alternative might contributes negatively (*hurt contribution link*) to the *softgoal* Parents Must be Always Informed About Problems in Treatment, which in turn refines the Safety *Softgoal*. An alternative way to satisfice this *softgoal* is to Keep the Physician Always informed About Frequent Problems in the Treatment. This way, the Safety *Softgoal* can be at least weakly satisfied without compromising the Autonomy *softgoal*.

Since the Patient now can tell the GA_PDA not to contact the parents about frequent occurrences of problems in treatment, now the Physician has to be Alerted Regarding Frequent Problems in Treatment so he can check whether or not changes may have to be made to the treatment. The GA_Physician software agent will carry this out and it is illustrated in Figure 7. The GA_Physician will be alerted by the GA_Home about any frequent problems in treatment. The GA_Home will in turn receive an alert from the GA_PDA about frequent problems together with instructions either to alert the parents or not. Another role for the GA_Physician will be to Help Physicians on Establishing a Treatment. This would have positive contributions (*help contribution links*) to the Physician *softgoals* Be Updated with Recent Drugs and Be updated with Recent Treatments. Those two *softgoals* that were previously considered weakly denied will be now reevaluated to weakly satisficed. In its turn the *softgoal* Quality is now evaluated as weakly satisficed.

Other alternatives could have been addressed but we limit ourselves to those two because of space constraint. The same way, the GA_Home would have to be refined and evaluated.

During the late requirements phase, these new software agents will be further detailed and analyzed. Non-functional requirements such as security, performance, availability and privacy will be considered and evaluated to their impact in the software design. Different architectures might be evaluated trying to determine which one would better suit to the particular characteristics of each agent.

4   Conclusions and Future Work

Recently, many different approaches have proposed solutions for analyzing and designing multi-agent systems 19 20 . This work extends the agent-oriented approach to requirements engineering, particularly at the early stages. The methodology aims to address some of the special challenges arising from the intentional and social dimensions of complex organizational environments. Agent characteristics such as autonomy, sociality, and intentionality are used to address the needs arising from large-scale software systems which may involve large number of stakeholders, playing different roles, with different goals and viewpoints.

The methodology presented in this paper is part of the Tropos Project 2 . The Tropos Project recognizes that existing methodologies such as object orientation and structured analysis have been motivated from programming languages rather than from characteristics of the world, and hence do not cope well with today's ever-changing world.

In our case studies, the methodology has been instrumental in guiding the elicitation and modelling activities. The agent-oriented focus helped surface many conflicting views, divergent goals, different ways of accomplishing goals, as well as issues of politics and power. Conventional techniques would not offer any support for dealing with these issues, even if the requirements engineer can recognize some of these complexities based on personal experience or intuition.

Studies of systems in use have long recognized how social factors can lead to system success or failure (e.g., 8). An agent-oriented methodology offers a more explicit and systematic treatment of the intentional and social dimensions as an integral part of the system development process. An agent-oriented requirements methodology could also lead naturally into systems that employ agent-based software technology 2 16 . Agent-centred modelling abstractions originating from the requirements phase can be used to preserve notions of autonomy and intentionality as the development process progresses to architecture to design to implementation, resulting in systems that are more flexible and robust, with an awareness of their social surroundings.

Large-scale software frequently suffers in later phases from not being able to model and justify many decisions that were made during the elicitation process. Since the methodology captures intentions it is possible to keep a rationale showing why one alternative was chosen over another.

We have been conducting case studies at three major hospitals in the Toronto area. We worked with stakeholders to explore how software could help overcome the many problems in the discharge process in these hospitals. We were able to propose a different discharge planning process supported by a new software agent with encouraging results. We are now investigating whether the same solution can be extended to the other two hospitals. Since the three hospitals deal with different types of patients and assessments and have different balance of powers among physicians, nurses and social workers, the answers are not immediately apparent.

Although results were positive, the case studies also revealed a number of limitations and ideas for future work. Complementary use of other techniques (such as scenarios and viewpoint management) in a more systematic way should be explored. Scenarios can be used to help identify missing actors or relationships. Viewpoint techniques can be used to uncover how different actors perceive processes and relationships, and also how they would achieve goals. In our case studies, we found more than four different ways in which a patient is discharged. They achieve their higher-level goals in different ways some better than the others. Exploring the different roles involved in the domain enhances the chances of finding inconsistencies in the model as well as different ways of achieving a goal.

Better coupling between the lexicon tool and the *i** modelling tool can provide support for consistency checks and traceability. Semi-automated heuristic support for recognizing intentional concepts from natural language descriptions would be very desirable.

The methodology should also provide more guidance in the use of modelling constructs, e.g., typical uses of the agents, roles, and positions. Lighter weight versions of the methodology would also be useful for less demanding types of organizational environments.

We intend to expand the methodology to deal with the late phase of requirements engineering proposing a systematic approach to further refine requirements for software agents including the reasoning about possible software architectures. Links to other methodologies should also be the subject of future work. Some initial work on linking *i** to UML, particularly to Use Cases and Class diagrams, have recently been done 11 2 .

References

1   Boehm, Barry e In, Hoh. *"Identifying   uality- e uirement   onflicts"*. IEEE Software, March 1996, pp. 25–35
2   Castro, J., M. Kolp, J. Mylopoulos. "A Requirements-Driven Development Methodology", 13th International Conference on Advanced Information Systems Engineering CAiSE 01, Interlaken, Switzerland, June 4–8, 2001.
3   Chung, L., B.A. Nixon, E. Yu, J. Mylopoulos. *Non- unctional e uirements in Software Engineering*. Kluwer Academic Publishers, 2000.
4   Cysneiros, L.M. and Leite, J.C.S.P. "Using UML to Reflect Non-Functional Requirements", Proc. of the CASCON 2001, Toronto, Nov 2001.
5   DeMarco, T. *Structured Analysis and System Specification* New York, Yourdon 1978.
6   D'Souza, D.F and A.C. Will. *b ects   omponents and   rameworks With   ML The atalysis Approach*. Addison-Wesley 1999.
7   Goguen, J. and C. Linde. *"Techniques for Requirements Elicitation" irst International Symposium on e uirements Engineering*, IEEE Computer Society Press, pp152–164, 1993.
8   Kling, Rob (ed.). *omputeri ation and   ontro ersy   alue onflicts and Social hoices* 2nd. Edition. San Diego: Academic Press. 1996.
9   Leite J.C.S.P. and A.P.M. Franco "A Strategy for Conceptual Model Acquisition " in Proceedings of the *irst IEEE International Symposium on e uirements Engineering San iego a IEEE omputer Society Press* pp 243–246, 1993.
10 Nuseibeh,B.A. and Easterbrook,S.M. Requirements Engineering: A Roadmap , In A. C. W. Finkelstein (ed) *The uture of Software Engineering* . (Companion volume to the Proc. of the 22nd Int. Conf. on Software Engineering, ICSE00) IEEE Computer Society Press.

11 Santander, V. and Castro, J. "Deriving Use Cases from Organizational Modelling" IEEE Joint International Requirements Engineering Conf. pp:32–39 Essen, Germany, Sept 2002.

12 Ross, D. "Structured Analysis: A language for Communicating Ideas" *IEEE Trans on Software Eng   1 pp 1 –*   Jan. 1977.

13 Rumbaugh, J., Jacobson, I. and Booch,G. *The   nified Modeling Language   eference Manual* Addison-Wesley, 1999.

14 Szolovits, P., Doyle, J., Long, W.J. "Guardian Angel:Patient-Centered Health Information Systems" Technical Report MIT/LCS/TR-604,
http://www.ga.org/ga/manifesto/GAtr.html

15 Yu, E. "Towards Modelling and Reasoning Support for Early-Phase Requirements Engineering" *in Proc   f the   rd IEEE Int Symp on   e uirements Engineering*, pp:226–235, 1997.

16 Yu, E. "Agent-Oriented Modelling: Software Versus the World". Agent-Oriented Software Engineering AOSE-2001 Workshop Proceedings. LNCS 2222.

17 Yu, E. and Cysneiros, L.M. "Agent-Oriented Methodologies-Towards a Challenge Exemplar" in Proc of   the 4th Intl. Bi-Conference Workshop on Agent-Oriented Information Systems (AOIS 2002) Toronto May 2002.

18 Wirfs-Brock R., B. Wilkerson and L. Wiener. *esigning   b ect- riented Software*, Prentice Hall 1990.

19 The International Workshop series on Agent-Oriented Information Systems, http://www.aois.org/

20 The International Workshop Series on Agent-Oriented Software Engineering, http://www.csc.liv.ac.uk/ mjw/aose/

Requirements Traceability in Agent Oriented Development

Jaelson Castro[1], Rosa Pinto[1], Andréa Castor [1], and John Mylopoulos [2]

[1] Centro de Informática, Universidade Federal de Pernambuco, Av. Prof. Luiz Freire S/N, Recife PE, Brazil 50732-970, +1 55 81 3271 8430
{jbc,rccp, aop}@cin.ufpe.br
[2] Dept. of Computer Science University of Toronto, 10 King's College Road Toronto M5S3G4, Canada, +1 416 978 5180
jm@cs.toronto.edu

Abstract. Agent-oriented development is emerging as the software development paradigm of this new century. Indeed, software developers are using agents as a new metaphor for understanding, modeling, and implementing software that operates in dynamic, open, and often unpredictable environments. The growth of interest in software agents has led to the development of new methodologies based on agent concepts. However, requirements traceability has been recognized as an important prerequisite for developing and maintaining high quality software. It is intended to ensure continued alignment between stakeholder requirements and various outputs of the system development process. In this paper we present a general traceability framework, which can be used during agent-oriented development. We also sketch an approach to enhance the Tropos methodology to support traceability. An e-commerce case study is used to demonstrate the applicability of the approach.

Keywords: requirements traceability, agent-oriented software development.

1 The Introduction

Progress in software engineering over the past two decades has been made through the development of increasingly powerful and natural high-level abstractions. Procedural abstraction, abstract data type, and, most recently, objects and components are all examples of such abstractions. We claim that agents represent a similar advance in abstraction: they have been used by software developers as a way to understand, model, and develop software that operates in dynamic, open, and often unpredictable environments. 27 .

The growth of interest in software agents has recently led to the development of new methodologies based on agent concepts. Methodologies -- such as, Gaia 28 , MaSE 26 , AUML 20 , and Tropos 3 , among others -- have become the focal point of research in the emerging area of agent-oriented software engineering. These methodologies propose different approaches in using agent concepts and techniques at various stages during the software development lifecycle (2 ; 11 ; 12).

A. Garcia et al. (Eds.): SELMAS 2002, LNCS 2603, pp. 57–72, 2003.

It is well established that a lack of attention on system requirements leads to systems that do not meet stakeholder expectations. Capturing information necessary to understand requirements evolution, validation and verification can facilitate requirements management. However, few agent-oriented methodologies are requirements-driven 18 .

The main goal of the requirements engineering process is to understand stakeholder goals, refine these goals into requirements, deal with conflicts between requirements, and specify these in a concise and clear description that meets stakeholder desires and serves as basis for system design and implementation. Therefore, an important task of this process is keeping track of bi-directional relationships between requirements and the development process artifacts in order to facilitate the maintenance and verification of the system 21 .

Requirements are supposed to be selected by stakeholders on the basis of system scope, complexity, constraints, cost and the like. A requirement is *traceable* if one can discover its origin, why does it exist, what other requirements are related to it, and how that requirement relates to systems designs, implementations and user documentation. Hence, requirements traceability refers to the ability to describe and follow the lifecycle of a requirement in both a forward and backward direction -- i.e., from its origins, through its specification and development, to its subsequent deployment and use, and through periods of on–going refinement and iteration 9 .

During *design*, traceability allows designers and maintainers to keep track of what happens when a change request is implemented before a system is redesigned. Traceability is helpful if it can link designs to justifications, important decisions and assumptions behind them, as well as the contexts in which design solutions are arrived. Thanks to traceability, accurate costs and schedules of changes can be defined, even if the original development team is no longer available. Last, but not least, *test procedures*, if traceable to requirements or design, can be modified when errors are discovered.

As a consequence of these different uses and perspectives on traceability, there are wide variations on the format and content of traceability information across different system development efforts. In fact, a reference model is needed to facilitate the construction of requirements traceability models 25 .

In this paper we argue that requirements traceability must be considered in agent-oriented methodologies. In particular we show how a general-purpose traceability approach 25 can be used in the context of agent-oriented development. To illustrate this point, we sketch how the Tropos framework could be enhanced to support requirements traceability.

The structure of the paper has as follows. Section 2 presents the models that support requirements traceability and Section 3 describes the Tropos methodology for agent-oriented development. In Section 4 we discuss traceability in the context of Tropos, while Section 5 concludes the paper.

2 Support for Requirements Traceability

In   24 and   25 a general framework to support requirements traceability is presented. It includes a meta-model defining the language in which traceability models can be defined and a set of reference models that can be customized within the scope defined by the meta-model.

The meta-model can be used to represent the following dimensions of traceability information:

- *What* information is represented – including salient attributes or characteristics of the information
- *Who* are the stakeholders that play different roles in the creation, maintenance and use of the various artifacts and traceability links across them
- *Where* is it represented in terms of sources that "document" traceability information.
- *How* is this information represented – both by formal and informal means and how it relates to other components of traceability
- *Why* was a certain conceptual artifact created, modified, or evolved
- *When* was this information captured, modified, and evolved

Requirements traceability is defined as the ability to describe and follow the lifecycle of a requirement, in both forward and backward direction, within the context of four composite, interrelated and parallel layers: environment, organisation, management and development:

- *En ironment* represents constraints on the universe where an organisation is embedded.
- *rganisation* represents an element (with goals and decisions) of the universe.
- *Management* is related to activities such as management of people, budget and contracts that can be performed by an organisation.
- *e elopment* is related to artifacts produced by some development process.

In the sequel the reference model is divided into three sub-models for clarity: Requirements Management, Design Allocation and Rationale Management.

- *e uirements Management sub-model* deals with issues of requirements understanding, capture, tracking, validation and verification.
- *ationale sub-model* is used to capture the rationale or assumptions on which requirements or designs are based.
- *esign sub-model* is used to refer to any activity that creates artefacts, including implementation.

Elements are related to each other through links with associated semantics. The notation used to represent the proposed links is based on UML stereotypes.

Before we proceed to present the sub-models we briefly discuss some of the links/relationships used in the sub-models:

- *Satisfy* specifies that an activity must be realized in the target element in order to attend the needs of the source element. The activity to be realized depends on the target element type.
- *esource* represents information needed to understand a specific element.
- *enerali ation* provides a mechanism for structuring classes.
- *Aggregation captures* the decomposition of composite requirements into one or more simpler requirements.
- *Allocate* means that the source element pertains to the target element.
- *esponsibility* associates stakeholders with software elements.
- *epresents* captures the requirements representation in other languages like modelling or programming ones

2.1 The Requirements Management Sub-model

The INFORMATION element is the sub-model root. The recursive *resource* link is inherited by its sub elements and the *satisfy* link between it and CONSTRAINT element represents that all sub elements linked with INFORMATION should obey the imposed constraints so that the system could be implemented. The *responsibility* link between the INFORMATION and STAKEHOLDER elements express the stakeholders that contribute or are responsible for the development of diagrams, programs, requirements, etc.

The ENVIRONMENT INFORMATION and ORGANIZATIONAL INFORMATION elements represent, respectively the environmental and organizational view of the Requirements Management sub-model (see Figure 1). These abstract concepts are extremely important if we want systems that comply with the real expected user's needs. The ENVIRONMENT INFORMATION element is used to represent all the concepts external to the organization that affect the system in some way. The ORGANIZATIONAL INFORMATION element represents goals, rules or procedures of the organizational world in which the system will be inserted. We need to capture organizational requirements to define how the software system fulfils the organizational objectives, why it is necessary, what are the possible alternatives, what are the implications to the involved parts.

The *resource* link between ORGANIZATIONAL INFORMATION and ENVIRONMENT INFORMATION indicates that there are elements outside of the organization that can affect some of its goals and consequently its systems. The model also expresses that ORGANIZATIONAL INFORMATIONs can be derived and/or aggregated with other ones. They are also resource for TASKs and should satisfy some CHANGE PURPOSEs.

The SYSTEM GOALs represent clear objectives to be achieved by the software system.

TASK CONSTRAINT and RE UIREMENTs elements are part of the management layer.

CONSTRAINTs are imposed by the environment of the system. The TASK element represents the management tasks to be performed by the project manager. Its links to

ORGANIZATIONAL INFORMATION, SYSTEM GOALS and RE UIREMENTS elements means that each one of them are resources for the tasks to be carried out.

The *resource* link between the TASK and SYSTEM GOAL elements indicates that the system goals only can be met if the resources are available.

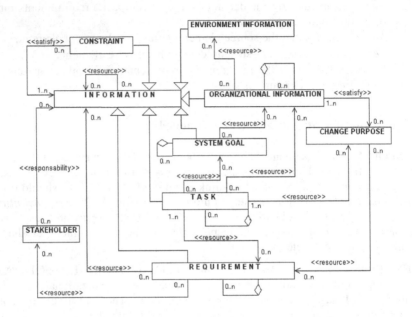

Fig. 1. Requirements Management Sub-model

To control the changes in a system the model includes the CHANGE PURPOSE element linked to TASK, RE UIREMENTS and ORGANIZATIONAL INFORMATION. The *resource* links means that the CHANGE PURPOSE will be satisfied by requirements and the TASK element is the resource required to accomplish the requested change while the *satisfy* link means that CHANGE PURPOSEs must be in according with at least one ORGANIZATIONAL INFORMATION.

To be effective, requirements have to be linked to the stakeholders that proposed them. This is illustrated in the model by the STAKEHOLDER element and its links to the RE UIREMENT element. The link *resource* expresses that a stakeholder is a source of information.

2.2 The Rational Sub-model

The specification, elaboration, decomposition, derivation and modifications of requirements, diagrams, etc. generate issues or conflicts, often due to the differing interpretations, assumptions, interests, viewpoints, experience, and objectives of the stakeholders. Information about how decisions are made to resolve these issues must be maintained throughout the system lifecycle to ensure that customer requirements are understood and satisfied 21 . Figure 2 presents our rationale sub-model.

There are *resource* links between SUBJECT element and ORGANIZATIONAL INFORMATION and SYSTEM GOAL expressing that a SUBJECT is information needed to understand some of them. The SUBJECT can be any problem that requires a discussion or resolution. The problem does not need to be related to a requirement. Various POSITIONS or alternatives that address the resolution should be considered and for each one of them there will be one or more ARGUMENTS that will support or contradict it. The relationships *support* and *contradict* indicates that a position can have as resource none or many arguments that support or constradict it.

The *resource* links between CONSTRAINT/ASSUMPTION and SUBJECT expresses that the formers can be resources of information to understand the SUBJECT. The same happens with the link between CONSTRAINT and DECISION, CONSTRAINTs also can be resources of information to understand a DECISION. Note that we are using can be because of the cardinality between these elements. Obviously a stakeholder gives an argument so we have two links between the elements ARGUMENTS and STAKEHOLDER. The link *resource* indicates the stakeholder who provides the argument and the link *responsibility* indicates the stakeholder who is responsible for the argument that generates the decision.

Although the proposed model is rich enough to capture the full rationale behind the decision taken, in practice, only a subset of it is used. This is due to the overhead generated as well as the lack of current appropriate tool support. However, simple descriptions of rationale on which requirements are based may be recorded along with the ASSUMPTIONS behind them.

2.3 The Design Sub-model

The sub-model in Figure 3 indicates that the DESIGN ELEMENT is the root of DIAGRAM, PROGRAM and SUBSYSTEM elements. The RE UIREMENTs are *resources* for PROGRAMs that are *resources* for TESTs. Due to various reasons changes may be required and should be recorded by the CHANGE PURPOSE element and its link to DESIGN ELEMENT indicates that it has a *resource* dependency with some design elements.

TASK is always related to project management, i.e., tasks to be performed by the manager to support some organizational need, implement a requirement or a diagram. The *satisfy* link betweeen the elements TASK and DESIGN ELEMENTexpresses that the satisfaction of the tasks depends on some design elements. The *allocate* link between RE UIREMENTs and SUBSYSTEMs express that requirements are assigned to one or more subsystems.
In the next section we review an agent-oriented framework, Tropos, which can be extended to support traceability.

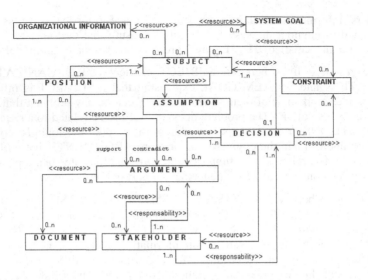

Fig. 2. The Rational Sub-model.

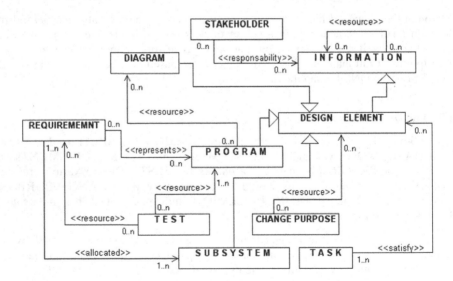

Fig. 3. Design Sub-model

3 Tropos

Tropos is founded on concepts used during early requirements analysis. To this end, we adopt the concepts offered by *i** 29 a modeling framework offering concepts such as *actor*, *agent position* and *role*, as well as social dependencies among actors, including *goal softgoal task* and *resource* ones.

It is worth pointing out that the lack of documentation of links between artifacts may cause increased overtime in situations of system maintenance, validation and verification. The Tropos framework, which is centered on requirements, is the natural framework candidate to be extended to support traceability.

The proposed framework spans four phases of software development:
- Early requirements *concerned with the understanding of a problem by studying an e isting organi ational setting the output of this phase is an organi ational model which includes rele ant actors and their respecti e goals*
- Late requirements *where the system-to-be is described within its operational en ironment along with rele ant functions and ualities*
- Architectural design *where the system's global architecture is defined in terms of subsystems interconnected through data and control flows*
- Detailed design *where each architectural component is defined in further detail in terms of inputs outputs control and other rele ant information*

In the sequel we review the phases and make some remarks of how traceability issues could be addressed.

3.1 Early Requirements

During early requirements analysis, the requirements engineer is supposed to capture and analyze the intentions of stakeholders. These are modeled as goals, which, through some form of a goal-oriented analysis, eventually lead to the functional and non-functional requirements of the system-to-be 16 . Tropos uses i to describe early requirements, which are assumed to involve social actors who depend on each other for goals to be achieved, tasks to be performed, and resources to be furnished. The *i** framework includes the S*trategic ependency S model* for describing the network of relationships among actors, as well as the S*trategic ationale S model* for describing and supporting the reasoning that each actor goes through. The framework has been presented in detail in 29 and has been applied to different application areas, including requirements engineering, business process reengineering, and software processes.

A Strategic Dependency model is a graph, where each node represents an *actor*, and each link between two actors indicates that one actor depends on the other for something in order that the former may attain some goal.

We call the depending actor the *depender* and the actor who is depended upon the *dependee*. The object around which the dependency centers is called the *dependum*. By depending on another actor for a dependum, an actor is able to achieve goals that it is otherwise unable to achieve on its own, or not as easily. At the same time, the depender becomes vulnerable. If the dependee fails to deliver the dependum, the depender would be adversely affected in its ability to achieve its goals. Once the relevant stakeholders and their goals have been identified, a means-ends analysis determines how these goals (including softgoals) can actually be fulfilled through the contributions of other actors.

Figure 4 presents the SD i model for a Media Shop. Media Shop is a store selling and shipping different kinds of media items such as books, newspapers, magazines, audio CDs, and the like. The basic objective for its new system is to allow an on-line customer to examine the items in the Medi@ Internet catalogue and place orders. The Medi@ system is used in our case study.

As shown in Figure 4, actors are represented as circles; dependums – goals, softgoals, tasks and resources – are respectively represented as ovals, clouds, hexagons and rectangles; and dependencies have the form *depender→ dependum → dependee*.

The main actors are Customer, Media Shop, Media Supplier and Media Producer. Customer depends on Media Shop to fulfill its goal: Buy Media *Items*. Conversely, *Media Shop* depends on *ustomer* to *increase market share* and make *"customers happy"*. Since the dependum *Happy ustomers* cannot be defined precisely, it is represented as a softgoal. The *ustomer* also depends on *Media Shop* to *consult the catalogue* (task dependency). Furthermore, *Media Shop* depends on *Media Supplier* to supply media items in a continuous way and get a *Media Item* (resource dependency). The items are expected to be of good quality because, otherwise, the *ontinuing Business* dependency would not be fulfilled. Finally, *Media Producer* is expected to provide *Media Supplier* with *uality Packages*

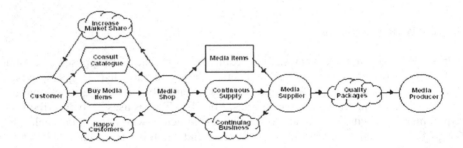

Fig. 4. i Model for a Media Shop

The actors in the SD model should be stored in the STAKEHOLDER element of the Requirements Management sub model to be linked to the INFORMATIONs that they are responsible for, as also the RE UIREMENTs of which they are information resources. These links are extremely important to maintain because they store information about the stakeholders and their contributions for the system to be. When a change is required for some reason the stakeholders involved have to be questioned about how to implement it so that their needs continue to be satisfied and the conflicts could be resolved.

3.2 Late Requirements Analysis

Late requirements analysis results in a requirements specification document which describes all functional and non-functional requirements for the system-to-be. In Tropos, the software system is represented as one or more actors, which participate in a strategic dependency model, along with other actors from the system's operational environment. In other words, the system comes in to the picture as one or more actors, which contribute, to the fulfillment of stakeholder goals.

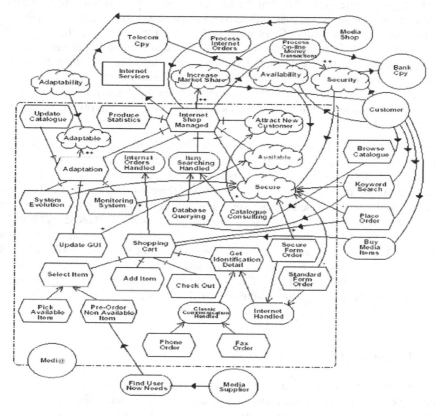

Fig. 5. Strategic Rational Model for Medi@

Although a Strategic Dependency model provides hints about why processes are structured in a certain way, it does not sufficiently support the process of suggesting, exploring, and evaluating alternative solutions. That is the role of the Strategic Rationale model, which is a graph with four main types of nodes—goal, task, resource, and softgoal—and two main types of links—means-ends links and process decomposition links. A Strategic Rationale graph describes the criteria in terms of which each actor selects among alternative dependency configurations.

In Figure 5 we provide a description of our Media Shop example. Observe that the actor representing the software to be, i.e., Medi@ is expanded to provide some more insights. A root task *Internet Shop Managed* to the softgoal *Increase Market Share*. That task is firstly refined into goals *Internet rder Handled* and *Item Searching Handled*, softgoals *Attract New ustomer*, *Secure* and *A ailable*, and tasks *Produce Statistic s*and *Adaptation*. To manage Internet an order, Internet Order Handled is achieved through the task *Shopping art* that is decomposed into subtasks *Select*

Item, *Add Item*, *heck ut* and *et Identification etail*. The latter (task) is achieved either through sub-goal *lassic ommunication Handled* dealing with phone and fax orders or *Internet Handled* managing secure or standard form orderings. To allow for the ordering of new items not listed in the catalogue, *Select Item* is also further refined into two alternative subtasks, one dedicated to select catalogued items, the other to preorder unavailable products. To provide sufficient support (++) to the *Adaptable* softgoal, *Adaptation* is refined into four subtasks dealing with catalogue updates, system evolution, interface updates and system monitoring. The goal *Item Searching Handled* might alternatively be fulfilled through tasks *atabase uerying* or *atalogue onsulting* with respect to customers' navigating desiderata, i.e., searching with particular items in mind by using search functions or simply browsing the catalogued products.

All the relationships and nodes presented in the Strategic Rational Model in figure 5 can be stored in the Requirements Management sub model presented in section 2. For example, in the ENVIRONMENT INFORMATIONs element we have to store the information about the communication company (*Telecom py*) and the financial company (*Bank py*) because both pertain to the outside world of the system but have a great impact in it. The goal *Increase of Market Share* is the ORGANIZATIONAL INFORMATION of the sub model. Tasks such as *atabase uerying atalogue onsulting Select Item and Pick A ailable Item* are example of RE UIREMENTS, which could be derived, aggregated, composed as well as have their versions controlled. The CONSTRAINTs are for example the limited number of credit cards processed by the *Bank py* or the availability of the services provided by the *Telecom py's* services.

3.3 Architectural Design

System architecture constitutes a relatively small, intellectually manageable model of system structure, which describes how system components work together. By now, in addition to classical architectural styles (e.g., 23), software architects have developed catalogues of style 10 such as *Thin Web lient*, *Thick Web lient*, *Web eli ery* for e-business applications. Unfortunately, these architectural styles focus only on web concepts, protocols and underlying technologies but fail to consider neither business processes nor non-functional requirements of the application. As a result, the organizational architecture styles are not described nor the conceptual high-level perspective of the e-business application. In *Tropos*, we have defined organizational architectural styles (7 ; 14) for cooperative, dynamic and distributed applications like mutli-agent systems to guide the design of the system architecture.

Organizational theory 22 and strategic alliances 8 study alternatives for (business) organizations. These alternatives are used to model the coordination of business stakeholders—individuals, physical or social systems—to achieve common goals. Using them, we view a software system as a social organization of coordinated autonomous components (or agents) that interact in order to achieve specific, possibly common goals. We adopt (some of) the styles defined in organizational theory and strategic alliances to design the architecture of the system, model them with i^*, and specify them in Telos 17 . Kolp in 13 briefly discuss ten common organizational styles: *flat structure   structure-in-   pyramid   oint   enture   bidding   takeo er   arm's-length   hierarchical   contracting   ertical integration and co-optation*

The evaluation of the styles can be done with respect to software quality attributes identified as relevant for distributed and open architectures such as multiagent ones. The   quality   attributes   are: **1**:*Predictability*;   **2**:*Security*;   **3**:*Adaptability*; **4**: *ooperati ity*;   **5**: *ompetiti ity*;   **6**:*A ailability*;   **7**:*Integrity*;   **8**:Modularity   and **9**:*Aggregability*.

Due to lack of space, we do not detail them here; an interested reader may refer to 13 where a full description of such attributes is presented.

In our example, we have left three (soft) goals (*A ailability Security Adaptability*) in the late requirements model. The first goal is *A ailability* because we propose to allow system agents to automatically decide at run-time which catalogue browser, shopping cart and order processor architecture fit best customer needs or navigator/platform specifications. Moreover, we would like to include different search engines, reflecting different search techniques, and let the system dynamically choose the most appropriate. The second key softgoal in the late requirements specification is *Security*. To fulfil it, we propose to support in the system's architecture a number of security strategies and let the system decide at run-time which one is the most appropriate, taking into account environment configurations, web browser specifications and network protocols used. The third goal is *Adaptability,* meaning that catalogue content, database schema, and architectural model can be dynamically extended or modified to integrate new and future web-related technologies. These software quality attributes (*A ailability Security Adaptability*) will guide the selection process of the appropriate architectural style.

The Joint Venture architectural style is the better solution in this case. The system was decomposed into three principal partners (*Store   ront, Billing Processor* and *Back Store*) controlling themselves on a local dimension and exchanging, providing and receiving services, data and resources with each other.

The usefulness of the Rationale sub-model may be demonstrated if we discuss the Tropos' architectural design phase. Recall (see Figure 4) that the availability, adaptability and security goals were chosen to drive the selection of the architecture. For example the goal availabitlity was proposed to allow system agents to automatically decide at run-time which catalogue browser, shopping cart and order processor architecture would fit best customer needs or navigator/platform specifications (further details in 3).

Each one of the three sub-goals identified should be represented in the SUBJECT element of the Rational sub-model, because they are motivations for the decisions taken (i.e. the choice of Joint Venture architectural style). The GOAL of all the SUBJECTs is to choose the architectural style of the system. The architectural styles should be represented as the POSITIONs to each of the SUBJECTs. Thus for each SUBJECTs there is a POSITIONs related to them. The notation used in NFR diagrams (++, +, --, -) to demonstrate the suitability or not of certain architecture style should be recorded as ARGUMENTs. In this case the choice is given not by the stakeholder but in accordance with the Correlation Catalogue described in 3 .

3.4 Detailed Design

The Detailed Design phase is intended to introduce additional detail for each architectural component of a system. In our case, this includes actor communication and actor behaviour. To support this phase, Tropos proposes to adopt existing agent communication languages like FIPA-ACL 15 or K ML 5 , message transportation mechanisms and other concepts and tools. One possibility is to adopt extensions to UML, like AUML, the Agent Unified Modeling Language (1 ; 20) proposed by the FIPA (Foundation for Physical Intelligent Agents) 6 and the OMG Agent Work group.

The Design sub model presented in section 2.3 should be used to store information about the Detailed Design phase. In this way the DESIGN ELEMENTs will be each one of the architectural components of the system.

4 Forward and Backward Traceability

In this section we discuss two examples of traceability. We begin with backward traceability and then present a case of forward traceability. Please recall that in our original example the metaphor of a SHOPPING CART was chosen. This preference should be stored in the rationale sub-model because it central to system development.

As an example of backward traceability we will use the Plan Diagram for Checkout presented in 3 . In this plan one of detailed activities is the performance of a task that updates the customer profile after the sale has finished. Suppose that the developer wishes to know why this task is necessary. She will be able to trace it to the class *ustomerProfiler* identified in the detailed design phase. Moreover, if the decisions about actors *Store   ront Back Store* and *Billing Processor* (described in the architecture phase) were stored by the original developer a link to the   goal *Profile ustomer* might be detected. The developer will also learn that this goal was not generated in the late requirements analysis or in the early requirements analysis so it was either a design decision   or its origin was not properly documented.

Suppose that the Media Shop decided instead of selling media items to AUCTION them. How can we identify and measure the impact of this change in the system as a whole If the proper traceability information is recorded this could be an easy task. This change would first require the developer to store the new POSITION and ARGUMENTS behind the new concept of sale, namely auctioning. Then the proper impact analysis could be performed. Recall from figure 4 that originally the goal *Internet   rder Handled* was achieved through the task *Shopping   art which* was decomposed into subtasks *Select Item, Add Item,   heck ut* and   *et Identification etail.* Under the auction scenario the goal and some of its sub-tasks will be affected. The goal will be changed to *Internet Auction Handled* Although tasks *Add Item* and *Select Item* are still required, their meaning and implementation may be altered. Of course task *Shopping   art* will no longer be necessary, being substituted for the task *Auction* The system architecture in general will not be dramatically affected but the actor *Store   ront* responsible for customer interaction through an usable front-end web application, will be significantly affected by the auctioning concept. There would also be a knock-on effect on the detailed design phase. For example, class *Auction* will substitute class *Shopping art* New attributes such *bid current bid* and *time left* are also introduced. A new plan, *place a bid* is also required.

It is work mentioning that in a complex system development; traceability support can be the difference between project success or failure.

5 Related Work

Some agent-oriented methodologies are extensions of object-oriented methodologies (for example, Gaia 28 and MaSE 26), while others are extensions of knowledge engineering methodologies (for example, KGR 12).

Gaia makes an important distinction between an analysis phase (which deals with *abstract* concepts) and a design phase (which deals with *concrete* concepts), and provides several models to be used during each phase In essence, the Gaia methodology supports the construction of a society of agents, defining the role and capabilities of each individual agent, as well as the structure of the society.

MaSE takes an initial system specification, and produces a set of formal design documents in a graphical style. The primary focus of this methodology is to guide a designer through the software lifecycle from a prose specification to an implemented agent system. KGR consists of two viewpoints. The external viewpoint describes the social system structure and dynamics. It includes an Agent Model and an Interaction Model. The internal viewpoint is composed of three models: the Belief Model, the Goal Model, and the Plan Model. These models specify how an agent perceives the environment and how it chooses its actions based on this perception.

The comparison of these methodologies is outside the scope of this work, but we agree that none of them support requirements traceabilty explicitly. However, some of them are more easily adaptable because they do capture some of the information required by a traceability mechanism.

6 Conclusions

If we are to be successful in making agent-oriented software development widely used practice, we must deal with the critical issue of requirements traceability. Failure to do so will result in higher costs and longer corrective and adaptative maintenance. Unfortunately most agent-oriented methodologies are not addressing this issue.

In this work we proposed an extension to the Tropos framework to address requirements traceability concerns. By doing so, we have demonstrated that it is possible to provide a sound methodology that also supports traceability.

Further work is required to make a comparison between issues of requirements traceability for object–oriented systems versus agent-oriented ones. Proper tool support for traceability in the context of an agent-oriented software development environment is another topic that needs to be addressed.

References

1   Bauer, B., Muller, J. , and Odell, J. "Agent UML: A Formalism for Specifying Multiagent Interaction", in *Proceedings of the irst International Workshop on Agentriented Software Engineering A SE'* , pages 91–104, Limerick, Ireland, 2001.

2   Castro, J., Kolp, M. and Mylopoulos, J. "Tropos: A Requirements-Driven Software Development Methodology", in *1 th International onference on Ad anced Information Systems Engineering aiSE' 1* Interlaken, Switzerland, June 2001. LNCS 2068, pp. 108–123.

3   Castro, J. Kolp, M. and Mylopoulos, J. *Towards e uirements- ri en Information Systems Engineering The Tropos Pro ect.* Information Systems Journal , Elsevier, 2002. Vol 27, pp. 365–89

4   Chung, L. K., Nixon, B. A., Yu, E., and Mylopoulos, J. *Non- unctional e uirements in Software Engineering*, Kluwer Publishing, 2000.

5   Finin, T., Labrou, Y. and Mayfield, J.. *K ML as an Agent ommunication Language.* In J. Bradshaw, editor, *Software Agents.* MIT Press, 1997.

6   FIPA. The Foundation for Intelligent Physical Agents. At http://www.fipa.org, 2001.

7   Fuxman, A., Giorgini, P., Kolp, M., and Mylopoulos, J. "Information Systems as Social Structures", in *Proceedings of the Second International onference n ormal ntologies for Information Systems IS' 1*, Ogunquit, USA, Oct. 2001.

8   Gomes-Casseres, B. *The Alliance e olution The New Shape of Business i alry*, Cambridge, Harvard University Press, 1996.

9   Gotel, O. *ontribution Structures for e uirements Engineering.* Ph.D Thesis. Department of Computing, Imperial College of Science, Technology, and Medicine, London, U.K., 1996.

10   IBM. Patterns for E-business. At http://www.ibm.com/developerworks/patterns, 2001.

11   Iglesias, C. A., Garijo, M. and Gonzáles, J. C "A Survey of Agent-Oriented Methodologies", in J. P. Muller, M. P, Singh, and A. S. Rao (Ed), *Proceedings of the ifth International Workshop on Agent Theories Architectures and Languages ATAL-* , July 2-8, 1998, LNAI, Springer – Verlag, 1999

12   Kinny, D., Georgeff, M. and Rao, A. "A Methodology and Modelling Technique for Systems of BDI Agents", in W. Van Der Velde and J. Perram, editors., Agents Breaking Away: *Proceedings of the Se enth European Workshop on Modelling Autonomous Agents in a Multi-Agent World MAAMAW'* (LNAI Volume 1038). Springer-Verlag, 1996.

13   Kolp, M., Castro, J., and Mylopoulos J. "A Social Organization Perspective on Software Architectures", in *Proceedings of the irst International Workshop on rom Software e uirements to Architectures ST AW' 1*, pages 5–12, Toronto, Canada, May 2001.

14   Kolp, M., Giorgini, P., and Mylopoulos, J. "A Goal-Based Organizational Perspective on Multi-Agents Architectures", in *Proceedings of the Eightth International Workshop on Intelligent Agents Agent Theories Architectures and Languages ATAL' 1*, Seattle, USA, Aug.2001.

15   Labrou, Y., Finin, T. and Peng, Y. "The Current Landscape of Agent Communication Languages," *Intelligent Systems*, 14(2):45–52, 1999.

16   Letier, E. and van Lamsweerde, A. "Agent-Based Tactics for Goal-Oriented Requirements Elaboration", in *Proceedings of the Twenty- ourth International onference on Software Engineering I SE* , Orlando, Florida, May 19-25, 2002.

17   Mylopoulos, J., Borgida, A., Jarke, M., Koubarakis, M. Telos: "Representing Knowledge About Information Systems," *A M Transactions on Information Systems*, 8 (4), Oct. 1990, pp. 325 – 362.

18   Mylopoulos, J and Castro, J. Tropos: "A Framework for Requirements-Driven Software DDevelopment", J. Brinkkemper, A. Solvberg (eds.), *Information Systems Engineering   State of the Art and   esearch Themes*, Springer-Verlag, pp. 261–273, June 2000.

19   Mylopoulos, J., Kolp, M.   and Castro, J. " UML for Agent-Oriented Software Development: The Tropos Proposal", in *Proceedings of the   ourth International   onference   n the   nified Modeling Language   ML' 1*, Toronto, Canada, Oct. 2001.

20   Odell, J., Parunak, H. V. D. and Bauer, B. "Extending UML for Agents", in *Proceedings of the Second International Bi- onference Workshop on Agent- riented Information Systems A   IS' *, pages 3–17, Austin, USA, July 2000.

21   Ramesh, B. and Jarke, M. "Towards Reference Models For Requirements Traceability." *IEEE Transactions on Software Engineering*, vol. 27, pp. 58–93, Jan. 2001.

22   Scott, W. R.   rgani ations   ational Natural and   pen Systems, Upper Saddle River, N.J., Prentice Hall, 1998.

23   Shaw, M., and Garlan, D. *Software Architecture   Perspecti es on   Emerging   iscipline*. Prentice Hall, 1996.

24   Toranzo, M and Castro, J A "Comprehensive Traceability Model to Support the Design of Interactive Systems", in *WIS   M´   - International Workshop on Interacti e System   e elopment and   b ect Models*, 1999, Lisboa. 1999.   Also included in   Nunes, N., et al, Interactive System Design and Object Models In: International Workshop on Interactive System Development and Object Models, 1999, Lisboa. **ECOOP'99 - Workshop Reader**. London: Springer Verlag - Lecture Notes in Computer Science, 1999. v.1743. p.267 – 287.

25   Toranzo, M. *A   ramework to Impro e   e uirements Traceability* (in Portuguese: Um Framework para   Melhorar o   Rastreamento de Requisitos). Ph.D thesis, Centro de Informática daUniversidade Federal de Pernambuco - UFPE, Brazil, 2002.

26   Wood, M. and DeLoach, S. A. "An Overview of the Multiagent System Engineering Methodology", in the   irst International Workshop on Agent- rientes Software Engineering A   SE-   , June, 10, 2000 – Limerick. Ireland

27   Wooldridge, M. *"Intelligent Agents "* in G. Weiss, editor. *Multiagent Systems*, the MIT Press, April 1999.

28   Wooldridge, M., Jennings, N. and Kinny D. "The Gaia Methodology for Agent-Oriented Analyis and Design,"   ournal of Autonomous Agents and Multi-Agent Systems, 2000.

29   Yu, E. and Mylopoulos, J., "Understanding 'Why' in Software Process Modeling, Analysis and Design," in *Proceedings Si teenth International   onference on Software Engineering - I   SE*, Sorrento, Italy, May 1994.

The Reflective Blackboard Pattern: Architecting Large Multi-agent Systems

Otavio Silva, Alessandro Garcia, and Carlos Lucena

Grupo TecComm – SoC + Agents
Departamento de Informática – PUC-Rio
Rua Marquês de São Vicente, 225 – Ed. Pe. Leonel Franca, 10º Andar Rio de Janeiro – Brazil
{otavio, afgarcia, lucena}@inf.puc-rio.br
http://www.teccomm.les.inf.puc-rio.br

Abstract. Software architectures of large multi-agent systems (MASs) are inherently complex and have to cope with an increasing number of system-wide properties and their corresponding control policies. With the openness and increasing size and complexity of these systems a more sophisticated software architectural approach becomes necessary. In this context, we propose the *eflecti e Blackboard* architectural pattern, which is the result of the composition of two other well-known architectural patterns: the *Blackboard* pattern and the *eflection* pattern. The proposed pattern provides, early in the architectural design stage, the context in which more detailed decisions related to systemic properties and associated policies can be made in late stages of MAS development. The pattern allows for a better separation of concerns, supporting the separate handling of control strategies by means of the computational reflection technique. Moreover these control activities are handled independently from the application data and agents, providing a better architecture for real-life multi-agent systems. An electronic marketplace architecture, with the goal of interconnecting providers and consumers of goods and services to find one another and transact business electronically, is assumed as a case study through the paper to clarify all the expressed concepts and to show the applicability of our proposal.

1 Introduction

Software technology is undergoing a transition from monolithic architectures, constructed according a single overall design, into open architectures composed of conglomerates of collaborative, heterogeneous, and independently designed agents and multi-agent systems (MAS). These architectures are driven by additional system-wide properties, such as coordination 28, 33 , adaptability 21 , mobility 22 , security 23, 38 and manageability 28 . Each of these system properties encompasses policies (or strategies) that control the application agents and data. Among the problems inherent in such architectural transition, none is more serious than the difficulty to incorporate and compose multiple control strategies, requiring a more sophisticated software architectural approach. The basic functionalities of agents already are quite complicated in large-scale multi-agent architectures, and so control strategies should be designed separately from the agents' basic behaviors. The degrees to which quality requirements (e.g. reusability and maintainability) are met on

A. Garcia et al. (Eds.): SELMAS 2002, LNCS 2603, pp. 73–93, 2003.

an MAS are largely dependent on its software architecture 34 . Hence, if an MAS architecture that includes suitable support for handling multiple control strategies is chosen from the outset, it is more likely that distinct quality attributes will be achieved throughout the development of multi-agent software.

Software architecture 34 has emerged as a central discipline for software engineers of complex systems in the last decade. This discipline is concerned with defining high-level styles and patterns for fundamental structure and organization of software systems. An architectural pattern 5 provides a solution to a recurring problem, defining a set of components as well as rules that organize the relationships between them. Architectural patterns are the building blocks of large-scale software architectures, which are likely to include instances of more than one of these patterns, composed in arbitrary ways 3 . A specific composition of architectural patterns, which occurs often in a given domain, is defined as another pattern. In the context of MAS, the blackboard architectural pattern has been widely used as a useful metaphor for communication and coordination of heterogeneous and separately designed agent organizations, providing low temporal and spatial coupling 6, 20 .

The idea of blackboard architectures is not new, and they were first introduced in the Hearsay II project 7 . Nowadays they are experiencing a renaissance with various industry-strength tuplespace architectures, such as IBM TSpaces 25 and JavaSpaces 9 . The *Blackboard* pattern 5 encompasses the definition of components and rules of blackboard architectures: multiple *knowledge sources* or independent *agents* are the components that implement specific parts of the application logic, and interact with each other by using the *blackboard* component; the blackboard is a data structure that is used as the general communication and coordination mechanism for the multiple agents, and is managed and arbitrated by a *controller* component. However, the pattern does not specify explicitly how the controller component deals with distinct control strategies to manage the blackboard, and how to separate such strategies from the application agents and data, which leads to multi-agent software architectures that are difficult to maintain, understand and reuse.

In this paper we propose the definition of the *eflecti e Blackboard* architectural pattern that is built from the composition of two well-known architectural patterns 5 : the *Blackboard* pattern and the *eflection* pattern. As a result of the proposed composition, the components of the Reflection pattern are used to refine the overall structure of the Blackboard pattern and promote better separation of concerns. Separation of concerns is a fundamental principle of software engineering, and it is achieved in reflective architectures by separating the system in two levels: the *base le el* and the *meta-le el*. The Reflective Blackboard architectural pattern follows this organization: the controller is situated at the meta-level of multi-agent systems, while the application agents and data are encapsulated at the base level. Our primary claim is that systemic properties of an MAS are handled at the meta-level, completely separated from its basic functionality, and achieved by applying reflection mechanisms upon the blackboard operations and by invoking appropriate control strategies. The combination of the Reflection pattern with other patterns has already been successfully used to define new patterns for other complex domains 8, 14, 15 .

The Reflective Blackboard architectural pattern is independent of programming languages and specific implementation frameworks, and its use can minimize the complexity caused by the presence of numerous system-level properties in MASs. The proposed pattern is targeted first of all to engineers of complex multi-agent applications who must define and implement the different control strategies that drive their systems. The proposed pattern can also be interesting for developers of different types of blackboard infrastructures and frameworks since they can decide to incorporate reflective capabilities directly into their products. The remainder of this paper is organized as follows. Section 2 presents the Reflective Blackboard architectural pattern. Section 3 discusses the proposed pattern and a collection of other related patterns, together with guidelines for their implementation, combination, and practical use in MAS development. Section 4 points out some concluding remarks and directions for future work.

2 The Reflective Blackboard Architectural Pattern

2.1 Motivation Example: Electronic Marketplace

Consider a marketplace application where buyers and sellers negotiate products and services. Sellers advertise their desire to sell products or services, submitting offers to the marketplace. Buyers access the marketplace to submit bids in order to buy products and services, and simultaneously to find prospective sellers. Once the buyers have found an appropriate seller, they continue to communicate indirectly through the marketplace in order to negotiate and make proposals and counterproposals. Some buyers eventually join up with each other to buy products together and minimize costs. The marketplace is open, i.e. agents can join or leave it at any time, and agents are not initially aware of their counterparts. Buyers and sellers visit different marketplaces in the network in order to achieve their individual goals.

The blackboard architectural pattern is a natural solution for the marketplace problem and is widely used in practice to develop sophisticated marketplaces [1, 2, 17, 37]. Blackboards are the commonplace where commerce transactions are conducted and products or services are traded. Different blackboards represent distinct marketplaces (Fig 1) and work as a message exchange infrastructure, used by the agents to communicate and coordinate their activities. Buyer and seller agents are the knowledge sources that cooperate and compete to process sales transactions for their owners. Agents write and read messages on the blackboards, with each message encapsulating a bid, an offer, a proposal or a counterproposal. Each host holds one or more marketplaces (i.e., blackboards). The controller component manages the marketplace by ensuring its control policies.

In marketplace applications, one of the strategies must deal with the communication control in the presence of mobility. Distinct marketplaces are spread over the network and, as a consequence, buyer and seller agents move to different hosts to find products and services required by their owners. In the beginning of their conversation the negotiating agents know each other's locations and can send messages to the destination host and the target marketplace so that the receiver can read and process them. However, since buyer and seller agents must visit different marketplaces, the hosts where they exist are likely to change. After moving from a marketplace to another the agent needs to continue receiving all the messages that were addressed to it. On the other hand, the agent that will be sending messages does not necessarily know that the receiver has moved to another marketplace and thus can continue sending messages to the previous marketplace. Since every message must reach its eligible receiver, they must be forwarded to the receiver's new marketplace. This strategy for controlling the communication by forwarding messages across multiple hosts should be seamless to both agents, so that they do not need to be aware of it.

This example is illustrated in Fig 1. In (i) Ag1 and Ag2 are agents that know each other's locations. Ag2 can thus send messages to Ag1 directly to the blackboard which represents Ag1's marketplace. In (ii), Ag1 has moved to a different marketplace, and in (iii) Ag2 has sent another message to the environment where Ag1 used to live. In this way, a control strategy that redirects the message to Ag1's new marketplace should exist. This control strategy is represented in (iv), and is termed *mobile communication strategy*. In addition to this communication strategy, robust marketplaces must contain control strategies for *coordinating* agent activities, *managing* the marketplace transactions, insuring *secure* commerce, providing *reliable* communication between agents and so forth. We use the mobile communication strategy to illustrate the use of the proposed pattern in the next section. Section 3 shows how our pattern provides a suitable structure for incorporating and integrating multiple control policies into a MAS based on a reflective blackboard architecture.

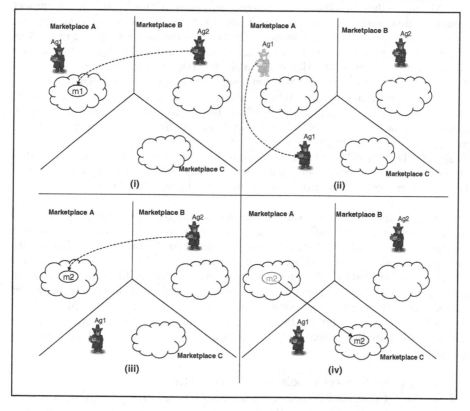

Fig. 1. Motivation example illustrated

2.2 Problem

The blackboard architectural style already has been widely used to tackle problems that have non-deterministic solutions 5 . When MASs 29 are concerned, this architectural pattern is widely accepted to implement the agents' communication 20 and coordination 6 . Recent research also has achieved positive results in using blackboards to implement agents' mobility and persistence 36 . As described previously, the Blackboard pattern structure is divided into three components: the blackboard itself, a group of knowledge sources (or agents), and a controller component. The left upper side of Fig 2 shows the components of the blackboard pattern. The blackboard is the central data store of the MAS. Data elements of the blackboard are application data (like messages, information, and so on) and control data (or meta-data). The blackboard provides an interface that enables all agents to read from, remove (take) from and write data to it. Agents use these operations to communicate indirectly with each other, and coordinate their activities. Agents use effectors to issue operations on the blackboard, and use sensors to perceive changes in the blackboard (for simplicity, we overlooked sensors and effectors in Fig 2).

Although the blackboard structure has proven itself to be a proper communication interface between software agents, it lacks a more precise specification of its controller component. The control component proposed in 5,34 is simply defined as a loop that monitors the changes on the blackboard and decides what action to take next. However, real-life MASs encompass a number of application-dependent and -independent control policies used to manage various system-wide properties, like mobility, communication, coordination, and security. The problem is that the main liability of the blackboard pattern is the difficulty of dealing with multiple control strategies in large MASs 5 ; the pattern does not provide architectural support for handling several control strategies separately. Finally, the blackboard pattern does not provide separation between application data and control data; the controller component is responsible for storing both kinds of data. However, access to control information should be prohibited to some agents.

As far as the motivation example (Section 2.1) is concerned, the problem stated above is related to the difficulty associated with the definition of the mobile communication strategy in a way that is transparent to the buyer and seller agents. During negotiation processes, agents are moving across distinct marketplaces and should not keep control of their negotiation partners' location. In addition, the use of the blackboard pattern amalgamates control data – e.g. data informing about the agents' actual location - and application data – e.g. representing bids, offers, proposals and counterproposals. In addition, the pattern does not support the separate handling of mobility, reliability, management and security policies for the marketplace application.

There are some *forces* associated with this problem:
- Control policies for some system properties are usually different in distinct execution environments. So the software architecture must be sufficiently flexible to enable adaptation to changes in the underlying environments, as well as to changes in application requirements related to control policies.

- MAS architectures must have a high degree of modifiability, i.e. facilitate the incorporation of changes once the nature of the desired change has been determined. In addition, the software architecture must support exchange, addition or removal of control strategies at run-time.
- The MAS architecture should guide the designer and the programmer on reusability of strategies across different projects when numerous control strategies are used.

2.3 Solution

We propose the composition of the blackboard architectural pattern with the reflection architectural pattern 5 to solve the problem stated in the previous section. The reflection architectural pattern provides a mechanism for changing the structure and behavior of a system dynamically 5 . The right upper side of Fig 2 illustrates the reflection pattern, which divides software systems into two different levels: base level and meta-level. The *base le el* contains the application logic, which is implemented by *agents*; the *meta-le el* is composed of *meta-ob ects*, which encapsulates data and behavior. Meta-objects' data is called metadata (or control data) that represent information about application data stored in the base level, while its associated behavior may be understood as the reaction to changes performed at the base-level 26 . The interface between the base-level and the meta-level is provided by a

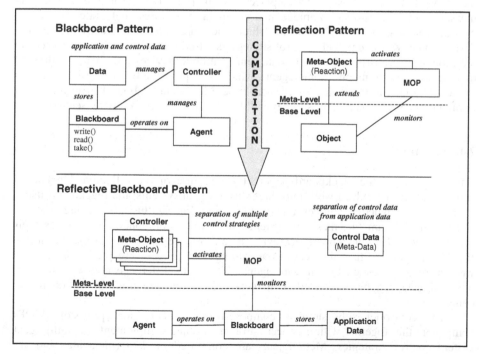

Fig. 2. The Composition of the Blackboard Pattern and the Reflection Pattern

separate component called *Meta- b ect Protocol* (MOP). The MOP is responsible for redirecting the control flow at the base-level to the meta-level in the execution points of certain systems.

The proposed composition results in three major changes to the blackboard solution: (i) the controller component and control data (metadata) are moved to the meta-level, (ii) the MOP intercepts the blackboard operations transparently, (iii) the controller semantics is distributed into separate meta-objects (i.e, reactions and metadata). According to these changes, data written in the blackboard may be associated with meta-objects located in the system's meta-level. The meta-objects behave like rules, which state how the system should behave when specific operations are performed in the blackboard. For example, a meta-object may specify that whenever a specific piece of data is taken out of the blackboard, the agent that wrote it will be notified of this data removal. In this way, the control of the agent communication, which is performed in the blackboard, allows us to inject system-wide properties transparently at the meta-level.

The application of this solution to the marketplace example allows the mobile communication strategy be implemented at the meta-level controller, separated from the buyer and seller agents that are located at the base level. This is done by creating, meta-objects on the meta-level that specify that message forwarding strategies are created whenever an agent moves from one environment to another. These message-forwarding strategies are responsible for forwarding messages addressed to agents that have left their "home" marketplaces, to their destination marketplaces. The message pointers also are implemented as meta-level rules that state that every message addressed to the agent to which they are related is redirected to the destination environment. This control strategy is based on the same idea proposed by the mobile IP protocol 32 , where data sent to mobile devices are always addressed to their home environment (home agent), which is responsible for forwarding the data to the environment where the device actually is. More details about the dynamics and implementation of this control strategy will be provided in the following sections.

2.4 Structure

As it happens in the blackboard pattern the structure of the reflective blackboard pattern can be divided, as well, into three different subsystems: the blackboard itself, a group of knowledge sources and a controller. Fig 3 illustrates, using a UML component diagram 4 , these subsystems, their main components as well as their dependencies. The blackboard behavior is almost the same as proposed in the Blackboard pattern. It is the central data storage structure where pieces of data are written, read or deleted by software agents. The main difference now is that every piece of data can be associated with meta-objects that are used in the controller component.

The controller subsystem is composed of a meta-object protocol (MOP) component that together with a collection of meta-objects implement the multi-agent system control strategies. Meta-objects are composed of data (metadata) and are responsible for associating specific behavior (reactions) to operations performed over specific pieces of data. These meta-objects can transparently modify the normal behavior of the blackboard, thus implementing the multi-agent system control strategies. Different agents can act over the blackboard by means of their sensors and effectors, which can respectively sense and perform changes in the blackboard that can be considered their environment. The agents do not communicate directly; they only write and read data from the blackboard.

Whenever an agent performs any operation over a specific piece of data stored at blackboard, the MOP component verifies if there is any meta-object associated with it. If positive it executes the reaction associated with the meta-object, i.e. its behavior. The meta-object execution can access the blackboard writing and deleting data. In this way, in a reflective blackboard architecture the semantics of a blackboard operation, in fact, is the result of the execution of the meta-objects associated with it. Meta-objects also may exist in the control subsystem without correspondent data in the blackboard. In this way the multi-agent system can associate reactions to data that is part of the multi-agent system vocabulary and probably will be written in the blackboard at runtime.

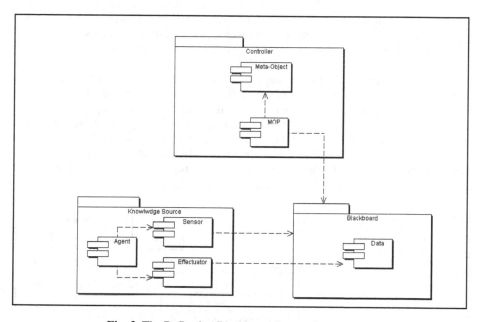

Fig. 3. The Reflective Blackboard Pattern Structure

2.5 Dynamics

Reflection is used to intercept and modify the effects of operations of the blackboard. From the point of view of application agents, computational reflection is transparent: an agent writes a piece of data on the blackboard, and has no knowledge this write operation has been intercepted and redirected to the meta-level. The following scenario illustrates the general behavior of the Reflective Blackboard architecture:

1. A knowledge source (or agent) performs an operation on the blackboard (write for example), supplying a piece of data and expecting some other piece of retrieved data;
2. This operation is intercepted by the meta-level's MOP, which will perform, if specified, control activities over the performed operation;
3. The MOP checks for the existence of meta-objects associated with the blackboard data and related to the performed operation. If the knowledge source has performed a write operation on the blackboard, the searched meta-objects will be those related to the written piece of data. On the other hand, if the knowledge source has performed read or delete operations, the searched meta-object will be related to the piece of data read from the blackboard;
4. If the searched meta-object exists, its behavior (i.e., its reaction) is executed. The possible effects of the Reaction must be specified by the implementation of the Reflective Blackboard pattern (section 3.3). Depending on the implementation, the reaction can modify blackboard data, activating other agents or other reactions, among other types of control activities.

Fig 4 uses a UML 4 sequence diagram to visually illustrate this scenario.

Concerning the motivation example presented in Section 2.1, this scenario can be specialized into two different ones. The first refers to the update of the message forwarding strategy while the second refers to the message forwarding strategy itself. The message forwarding strategy update scenario starts when Agent1 decides to move to another host and notifies its home environment, represented by *BlackboardA*, that it is going to leave. This notification is represented by the *MobileAgent ata* that is written in the blackboard. The write operation is intercepted by the MOP, which

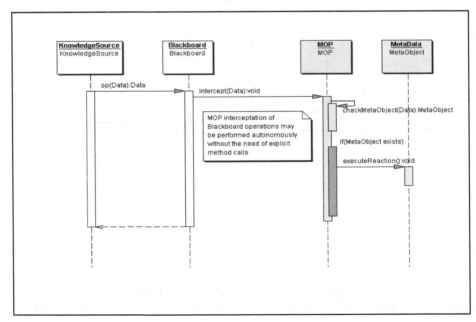

Fig. 4. Reflective Blackboard dynamics

checks the existence of any meta-object associated with the *MobileAgent ata*. If such meta-object exists, in fact it will be responsible for updating the message forwarding strategy as specified in Section 2.3. In this way, the reaction (i.e. behavior) associated with this meta-object is responsible for creating a new message forwarding strategy and consequently notifying the MOP that a new meta-object exists. At this point, the meta-level operation ends and Agent1 can actually move to its destination environment. This scenario is represented in Fig 5 using an UML sequence diagram.

After the message pointer is updated, every message addressed to Agent1 will be forwarded to its new environment. In the motivation example scenario Agent2 sends a message, addressed to Agent1, to *BlackboardA*. This process is represented by the operation write performed by Agent2 over *BlackboardA*. This operation is intercepted by the MOP, which will check the existence of any meta-object associated with the written message. Such meta-object is in fact the message forwarding strategy that was created in the scenario presented above. This meta-data is responsible to associate a reaction, responsible to the message forwarding process, to messages addressed to Agent1. If the searched meta-object exists on the meta-level its reaction will be executed. The reaction execution will remove (take) the message from *BlackboardA* and write it on *BlackboardB*. After the reaction execution, the meta-level operation ends and Agent1 can read the message from *BlackboardB*. This scenario is represented in Fig 6 using an UML sequence diagram.

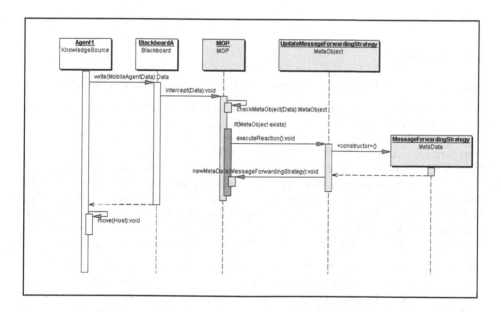

Fig. 5. Updating the message forwarding strategy

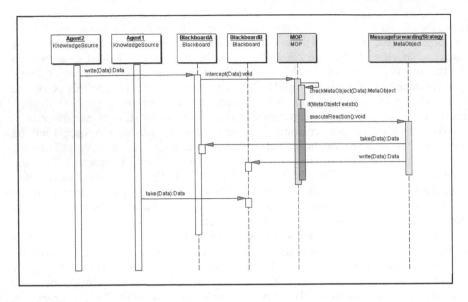

Fig. 6. Dynamics for the message forwarding strategy

2.6 Consequences

The Reflective Blackboard architectural pattern promotes the following **benefits**:

Separate handling of control concerns The use of reflective blackboard architectures to develop MASs promotes the separation of their control policies from their basic functionality. In addition, it separates application data from control data. These kinds of separation enable the smooth handling of different control aspects of the system. Moreover, the different control strategies are composed independently from the application at the meta-level. The application developers focus their attention on the intra-agent concerns at the base level. This is particularly important when a large MAS is involved since it is often composed of organized societies of agents, with each particular society having different, very complex control policies. These policies are difficult to handle if they are tangled with system basic data and functionality.

Impro ed reusability and maintainability Agents' code is not intermingled with explicit invocations of control strategies. The MOP does these invocations in a way that is transparent to the application functionality. As a consequence, it improves readability, which in turn promotes reusability and maintainability. Reuse and maintenance also are improved due to the separate incorporation of control strategies. Different applications demand different implementations of control strategies. So reuse of the application logic (i.e. the agents) can be gathered, since such control strategies are implemented at the meta-level. In this way, the separation of concerns achieves reuse at different levels: the agent level, the control-strategy level and the systemic-property level.

Increased e pressi eness Architectures of large MASs often comprise isolated agents and organizations of independently designed agents. The presence of the MOP and meta-objects allows writing and associating code of control strategies with various levels of an MAS, e.g. the agent-level, the organization-level and the system-level. In this way, the complexity of MAS can be controlled in a flexible and systematic manner, and control strategies can be added at the levels where they are needed. However, care should be taken while improving the power of the meta-level and meta-information. Unnecessary expressive power may complicate both using the proposed architecture and understanding of the MAS code, increasing the probability of error introductions and making the testing phase more difficult.

Acceleration of the MAS de elopment process In complex systems, the process is likely to involve several software engineers, and a good separation of concerns contributes decisively to acceleration of the development process by paralleling the development of different architectural components and the handling of different system aspects. The proposed pattern enables engineers of multi-agent software to work separately on the abstraction levels of different systems . *Meta-le el software engineers* decide how to refine the meta-level components to incorporate and compose the system's control policies, and *base-le el software engineers* are concerned only with the internal architecture of agents and its basic functionality.

ynamic econfiguration. Distributed multi-agent applications typically have dynamic systemic requirements that need more complex algorithms. The pattern defines an approach that supplements standard blackboard architectures with a general reflective mechanism for injecting control activities dynamically into the communications between software agents. So dynamic reconfigurability is achieved through the extensive use of reflection since the meta-level comprises reflective facilities to expose the structure and behavior of MAS components to the meta-level engineers, enabling dynamic inspection and adaptation. Algorithms that support systemic requirements are separated from functional components but may be invoked whenever agents communicate using the blackboard. Since the MOP component provides an interface to change the application behavior dynamically, meta-level engineers can reconfigure the meta-level to inject new control policies, remove existing ones, and decide which policy should be enforced in a given system's execution point at run-time.

On the other hand, using a Reflective Blackboard architecture has some **liabilities**:

Performance o erhead A possible disadvantage of this pattern is that reflective architectures are usually slower than non-reflective architectures. This problem occurs because of the additional computation that is needed to change dynamically control flow from the base level to the meta-level and to activate meta-objects responsible for implementing control activities.

Increased number of architecture components. The resultant architecture of a Reflective Blackboard system is naturally more complex than a Blackboard architecture. This complexity is associated to the architecture implementation. However, once the architecture has been built, it can be reused in different multi-agent applications.

2.7 Known Uses

Tuplespace architectures are a classic implementation of blackboard architectures. **TSpaces** 25 is a well-known tuplespace architecture that implements the Reflective Blackboard pattern. TSpaces is a Linda-like blackboard architecture for network communication with database capabilities. It provides group communication services, database services, and event notification services. The TSpaces Event notification engine plays the role of the MOP component of the Reflective Blackboard pattern. TSpaces reactions are called callback objects and TSpaces meta-data contains information about the operation and the data monitored by the event engine. When implementing an MAS, the TSpaces event monitoring services are used to establish control strategies. MASs implement this by registering events that notify agents that relevant data has been written in the blackboard. Since agents are notified of a specific event, the associated control strategy is performed.

MARS 6 is another implementation of the proposed pattern. It defines Linda-like blackboards, which can be programmed to react with specific actions to the accesses made by agents. MARS is implemented using the JavaSpaces 5 technology. MARS was created to help in the task of defining coordination strategies in mobile agents applications. MARS meta-data are called meta-tuples and contain information about the agent that performs a specific operation over specific pieces of data. The MOP protocol is implemented using template-matching searches on a meta-level blackboard where meta-data is stored.

TuCSoN 31 is a coordination model that can be thought of as an implementation of the Reflective Blackboard pattern. This model is based on the notion of tuple centers, which are in fact programmable blackboards. Tuple centers are programmed by associating reactions to specific data and operations. Reactions are created using a proprietary specification language and are handled separately from application basic logic and data.

T-Rex 36 is also an implementation of the Reflective Blackboard Pattern. T-Rex implements a reflective model (MOP and meta-data) that is similar to MARS. On the other hand, while MARS uses the reflective blackboard architecture only to implement agents' coordination, T-Rex also uses it to implement mobility, communication, persistence and also the systems' dependability.

3 Reflective Blackboards and the Development of Large MASs

The Reflective Blackboard pattern provides, during the architectural design stage, the context in which more detailed design decisions related to system-level properties are made in later MAS development stages. Thus, this section builds up the overall picture; it discusses how meta-level and base-level engineers proceed from the architectural phase to the design and implementation phases of MAS construction. Since the proposed architecture has been chosen, MAS engineers must describe how multiple control policies are introduced into the system (Section 3.1), how the reflective blackboard pattern is connected with other related patterns that cover additional aspects of MAS development (Section 3.2) and how the components of the pattern can be implemented (Section 3.3).

3.1 Achieving Multiple Control Strategies

Large-scale MASs are driven by multiple, complex control strategies that encompass system-level properties and are not part of an application's basic functionality. This section illustrates how introducing some particular system-wide properties into MASs based on the reflective blackboard solution, which is the structural foundation upon which more detailed pattern languages for systemic properties can be developed. We illustrate the benefits of the proposed pattern to inject typical systemic properties in the marketplace application (Section 2.1), such as coordination activities, security policies and management strategies.

oordination Coordination, which is defined as the management of dependencies between agents in order to foster harmonious interaction between them 27 , is indispensable for effective cooperation between autonomous agents, as well as for safe competition between them 28 . With regard to the marketplace example, coordination strategies are needed in several contexts, e.g. in the case that multiple buyers eventually join up with each other to buy products together and minimize costs. Coordination activities include accessing the bids of a marketplace and communicating and synchronizing with cooperating mobile agents that are visiting

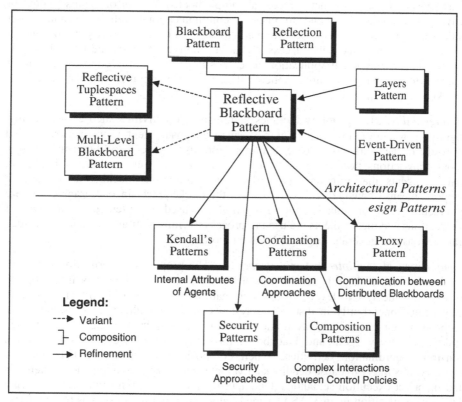

Fig. 7. The Reflective Blackboard Pattern and its Related Patterns

other distributed marketplaces in order to find the best price proposal. In a complex open system, coordination activities encompass application-dependent strategies – related to the specific roles of the application agents – and application-independent ones – related to the interaction of the agents with the other agents of the same application and with the visited execution environments – which should be separated 40,39 . The Reflective Blackboard pattern clearly supports separating the application-dependent coordination activities (base level) and the application-independent ones (meta-level). Hayden et al propose a system of patterns for multi-agent coordination 18 .

Security Security involves confidentiality and integrity factors and is primarily a combination of policies for access control, intrusion detection, authentication and encryption 3, 21 . Each of these policies traditionally are implemented by controlling the communication process that involves the application components. The use of a reflective blackboard architecture allows us to incorporate easily such security policies since the agent communication is centralized on the blackboard. Meta-level engineers use meta-objects to implement each security policy and the MOP to intercept operations issued on the blackboard in order to activate these meta-objects. In the marketplace example, security is a fundamental requirement since the marketplace is open. So meta-objects are implemented to control agents joining or leaving the marketplace and to encrypt communications, reliably sending user authentication from marketplace to marketplace (and pass if along to dependent requests), and to check the access rights of mobile agent requests. All this is independent of the actual application code. Yoshioka et al. 38 propose a system of patterns to implement security policies that can be combined with the Reflective Blackboard pattern.

Manageability. Manageability includes administrative activities such as accounting, logging, configuration management, performance measurement, report generation and so forth. In the marketplace case, administrators usually need to obtain information about transactions performed in their marketplaces, as well as information about visiting agents that join and leave them. The reflective blackboard architecture supports means of analyzing the activities of the marketplace since all transactions are conducted upon the blackboard. The MOP is used to intercept operations of transactions and meta-objects are used to process the information associated with such transactions and generate logging files and reports.

omposition of Multiple Systemic Properties The proposed pattern allows system-level properties and strategies be entirely implemented separately as meta-objects. However, some system-level properties are naturally interactive. In practice, because they occur concurrently in distributed systems, multiple policies can interfere with each other. For example, many replication strategies require logging and distributed updates on every agent and blackboard modification and security policies often constrain coordination activities. When composition conflicts are not managed properly, it is likely to cause deadlocks, livelocks, dangling resources, inconsistencies, and incorrect execution semantics. One approach to dealing with interference during strategy composition in an MAS is using composition patterns. Composition patterns, such as the Mediator pattern 10 and the Chain of Responsibility pattern 10 provide a means of allowing safe integration of interactive properties at the meta-level. The

Mediator pattern, for instance, defines an object that encapsulates how a set of objects interact; this solution promotes loose coupling by keeping objects from referring to each other explicitly, and it lets you vary their interaction independently.

3.2 Architectural Refinements and Design Decisions

Our pattern is the basis for the composition of multiple known patterns during the refinement of complex multi-agent software architectures. The previous section discussed how meta-level engineers incorporate specific properties using the proposed pattern. This section discusses related architectural and design patterns, methods and guidelines that help with taking design decisions and refining the basic architecture of reflective blackboards. Most important, this section shows how the Reflective Blackboard pattern is connected with other patterns, with which other patterns it can be refined and combined, which variants it exposes and which other patterns solve the same problem in a different way. Fig 7 illustrates the interconnections of the Reflective Blackboard pattern with other architectural and design patterns.

Internal Architecture of Agents Base Le el . The architecture of a single agent is very complex since it encapsulates a mental state and a number of behavioral features, such as autonomy, adaptation, collaboration and learning. Kendall et al. 24 examine design patterns for agents with a layered architecture. They illustrate patterns applicable to each layer constructing the agents. Garcia et al. propose an aspect-oriented method to structure the internal design of software agents 13 and compare it with a pattern-oriented method 16 .

eflecti e Tuplespaces Base Le el In this variant, the blackboard component of the proposed pattern is structured as tuplespaces, which are shared, associatively addressed memory spaces that are composed of a bag of tuples. Tuplespace architectures originate from the Linda project at Yale University 11 . Being a global memory, tuplespace architectures are often characterized as special kinds of blackboard architectures. The meta-level components are structured as tuples, stored in meta-level tuplespaces. TSpaces, MARS, TuCSoN, and T-Rex, the known uses presented in Section 2.7, implement this variant of the proposed pattern. The next section shows how to implement this variant of the proposed pattern.

E ent- ri en Blackboard Base Le el The Reflective Blackboard pattern can be combined with the Event-Driven architectural pattern 34 . An event model is used to signal when changes are made to the blackboard and to notify the agents that something changed. An event could trigger the activation of a set of agents or the controller could dynamically determine which agent to start. In addition, the meta-level could activate a control strategy based on a specific event.

Meta-Le el rgani ation Meta-Le el . The general structure of a reflective architecture is very much like the Layers architectural pattern 5, 34 . The metal-level and base level are two layers, each of which provides its own components. However, in contrast to a layered architecture, there are mutual dependencies between both layers. The base level builds on the meta-level, and vice-versa. An example of the latter occurs when meta-objects implement behavior that is executed in case of an exception. The kind of exception handler that must be executed often depends on the current state of computation. In a pure layered architecture, these bi-directional dependencies between layers are not allowed. Every layer only builds upon the layers below. Another issue is that the meta-level of the proposed pattern can use the structure of the Layers pattern to refine its meta-level in multiple meta-levels, leading to a variant termed *Multi-le el Blackboards* (Fig 7) This variant is composed of a tower of meta-levels, where each level incorporates different control levels.

istributed Blackboards Meta-Le el The meta-levels of different blackboards may have to communicate with each other in order to implement a given systemic property. The Proxy design pattern 10 is a solution for remote communication. The proxy pattern provides a surrogate or placeholder for another object to control access to it. Proxy is applicable whenever there is a need for a more versatile or sophisticated reference to an object than a simple pointer. A remote proxy provides a local representative for an object in a different address space, and hides the fact that an object resides in a different address space. A protection proxy controls access to the original object, which is useful when objects should have different access rights.

3.3 Implementation Issues

The software architecture proposed in this paper has been identified and developed based on our extensive work implementing the T-Rex framework 35,36 and other reflective architectures 35,14,15 , and on our study of a number of related implementation architectures 6,25,31 . Since the proposed pattern is independent of programming languages or implementation architectures, a wide range of MAS developers can employ it. This Section points out issues that software engineers should consider to implement the proposed architectural pattern, and the procedure by which such issues are realized in the T-Rex framework:

Step 1: How will meta-objects be structured? A fundamental issue is deciding which meta-information will be available in the meta-objects components. In fact this decision depends on the specificity of the control implemented by the multi-agent system. Common meta-objects contain references to the base level data, agent identification and blackboard operation 6,36 . However it can also contain more application-specific information such as the hypothesis level of abstraction and degree of certainty. In the T-Rex framework's implementation meta-objects are implemented through meta-tuples 35,36 , which associate a specific **reaction** to a given **operation** performed by an **agent** over a piece of **data** stored on the blackboard. In this way, the meta-objects' meta-information are 4-tuples that have the following strucuture: (reaction, operation, agent, data).

Step 2: How will the MOP be implemented? Another important issue is deciding how the meta-object protocol will act over meta-objects. A possible implementation is to use another blackboard to store meta-objects, and thus the MOP will use standard blackboard operations to write and search for meta-objects. Using Linda-like tuple spaces 11 in this "meta-level blackboard" implementation can help this task since it is useful to use template match searches while looking for meta-data. By using another approach, one could also use native reflective architectures such as Guaraná 30 to implement meta-level activities. The MOP in T-Rex is implemented through reflective tuple spaces where any operation executed over the base-level blackboard is intercepted. After this interception the control is deviated to the meta-level and meta-objects associated with the performed operations are searched. If there exists any associated meta-object, its associated reaction is executed.

Step 3: Which components will be able to access the meta-level? It is important to establish the access policies to the multi-agent system's meta-level, where its control strategy will be implemented. It can be defined that the meta-data is written only in the implementation phase and remains unchanged at runtime. On the other hand, the system administrator and even agents can insert meta-data at runtime. The adoption of this access policy may require special attention to the meta-level control and implementing a meta-meta-level could be useful to deny harmful changes to the control component. The T-Rex framework does not provide access restrictions to the meta-level. In this way meta-objects can be created or deleted at runtime, by the MAS administrator or even by the agents that belong to the system. Specific implementations of the framework are able to use meta-meta-level tuple spaces to enable access control policies on the meta-level, following the same idea proposed by the Reflective Blackboard pattern.

Step 4: Which components will the reactions be able to modify? Reactions are components that specify changes in the normal system's behavior. It is an important decision establishing which components they can access. In general, by accessing the multi-agent systems' blackboard it is possible to change the systems' overall behavior, since it will change the agents' environment and thus be acting directly upon the agents' sensors. On the other hand, to implement some control strategies it might be necessary to allow reactions to access the other system specific components, such as the operational system functions file system or the network. In the T-Rex framework there are no access restrictions to reactions. These restrictions should be implemented on the applications that are developed using the reflective infrastructure provided by T-Rex.

4 Conclusion and Ongoing Work

Agent technology has been revisited as a complementary approach to the object paradigm, and has been applied in a wide range of realistic application domains. The inclusion and composition of system-level properties and their control strategies into MASs is one of the major sources of software complexity. For complex MASs, most code is not devoted to implementing the desired functional behavior, in terms of its agents, but rather to providing system-wide properties (and their control strategies) like coordination, security, reliability and manageability. Hence, many ongoing investigations are concerned with mastering this software complexity by means of effective software engineering techniques in order to enhance system reusability, maintainability and stability. Patterns are a useful technique for MAS engineers since they capture existing, well-proven experience in software development and help to promote good design practice.

This article describes an architectural pattern that enables a more complete separation of systemic properties implementation from agent functionality, allowing these properties to be developed, maintained, and modified with minimal impact on agent implementations. The Reflective Blackboard pattern is quite useful when developing multi-agent systems with huge numbers of agents and whose control strategies are very complex. Its use can minimize development efforts since it promotes a better separation of concerns. The base level specifies the interface for exploiting application functionality. The meta-level layer defines the MOP to modify the control strategies, implemented by meta-objects. The basic idea of this pattern is that since communication and coordination, the basic properties in MAS, are centralized on the blackboard, we may easily control it and insert new systemic properties in the desired points to the agents' functionality in a largely transparent way. This pattern provides a loosely coupled meta-level controller. This component is handled separately, keeping control aspects independent from the functional aspects of an MAS and, consequently, improves its maintainability and reusability. Our pattern is the basis for the composition of multiple known patterns during the construction of complex MASs. In this sense, this paper also discussed how the proposed pattern is integrated with other known patterns, enabling the effective use of reflective blackboard in MAS development.

As future work, we are planing to create domain specific patterns for each internal feature of an agent and for specific system-wide properties, investigate their scalability and accumulate more practical know-how to construct a pattern language. Section 3 described some guidelines to deal with different systemic properties based on a reflective blackboard. However, we need to conduct some case studies and experiments to understand better how traditional software concerns (like privacy and dependability) and MAS-specific concerns (like coordination and emergent behavior) manifest and interact with each other during different MAS development stages. Up to now, we developed a first empirical study 16 to understand how the internal concerns of agents interact with each other and can be explicitly separated during software lifecycle phases, using a pattern-oriented method 16 and an aspect-oriented method 12 .

Acknowledgements. This work has been partially supported by CAPES for Otavio and CNPq under grant No. 141457/2000-7 for Alessandro, and by FAPERJ under grant No. E-26/150.699/2002 for Alessandro. Otavio, Alessandro and Carlos are also supported by the PRONEX Project under grant 7697102900. We would also like to thank the anonymous referees for the good suggestions during this work.

References

1. J. Bailey, Y. Bakos. "An Exploratory Study of the Emerging Role of Electronic Intermediaries". International Journal of Electronic Commerce 1(3), Spring 1997.
2. Y. Bakos. "The Emerging Role of Electronic Marketplaces on the Internet". CACM, August 1998.
3. M. Barbacci. " uality Attributes". Technical Report, CMU/SEI-95-TR-021, December, 1995.
4. G. Booch, J. Rumbaugh. "Unified Modeling Language – User Guide". Addison-Wesley, 1999.
5. F. Buschmann, R. Meunier, H. Rohnert, P. Sommerlad, M. Stal. "Pattern-Oriented Software Architecture: A System of Patterns", John Wiley & Sons, 1996.

6. G. Cabri, L. Leonardi, F. Zambornelli, "MARS: A Programmable Coordination Architecture for Mobile Agents", IEEE Internet Computing, Vol. 4, No. 4, pp. 26–35, July-August 2000.
7. L. Erman, F. Hayes-Roth, V. Lesser, D. Reddy. "The HEARSAY-II speech-understanding system: Integrating knowledge to resolve uncertainty". Computing Surveys 12(2): 213–253.
8. L. Ferreira, C. Rubira, "The Reflective State Pattern". Proceedings of the 5th Patterns Languages of Programs Conference (PLoP'98), August 98, Monticello, EUA.
9. E. Freeman, S. Hupfer, K. Arnold, "JavaSpaces(TM) Principles, Patterns and Practice", Addison-Wesley Pub Co, 1999
10. E. Gamma et al. "Design Patterns: Elements of Reusable Object-Oriented Software". Addison-Wesley, Reading, 1995.
11. D. Gelernter, "Generative Communication in Linda" ACM Transactions on Programming Languages and Systems, vol. 7 - No.1, pp 80–112, 1985
12. A. Garcia, V. Silva, C. Lucena, R. Milidiú. "An Aspect-Based Approach for Developing Multi-Agent Object-Oriented Systems". XXI Brazilian Symp. on Software Engineering, Rio de Janeiro, Brazil, October 2001, pp. 177–192.
13. A. Garcia, C. Chavez, O. Silva, V. Silva, C. Lucena. "Promoting Advanced Separation of Concerns in Intra-Agent and Inter-Agent Software Engineering". Workshop on Advanced Separation of Concerns in Object-oriented Systems (ASoC) at OOPSLA'2001, Tampa Bay, USA, October 2001
14. A. Garcia, C. Rubira. "A Architectural-based Reflective Approach to Incorporating Exception Handling into Dependable Software". In: A. Romanovsky et al (Eds). Advances in Exception Handling Techniques . Springer-Verlag, LNCS-2022, April 2001, pp. 189–206.
15. A. Garcia, C. Rubira. "A Unified Meta-Level Software Architecture for Sequential and Concurrent Exception Handling". The Computer Journal, Special Issue on High Assurance Systems Engineering, January 2002.
16. A. Garcia, V. Silva, C. Chavez, C. Lucena. "Engineering Multi-Agent Systems with Aspects and Patterns". Journal of the Brazilian Computer Society, Special Issue on Software Engineering and Databases, August 2002.
17. R. Guttman, A. Moukas, P. Maes. "Agent Mediated Electronic Commerce: A Survey". Knowledge Engineering Review, June, 1998.
18. S. Hayden, C. Carrick, . Yang. "Architectural Design Patterns for Multiagent Coordination". In Proceedings of the International Conference on Agent Systems '99 (Agents'99), Seattle, WA, May 1999.
19. M. Huget, F. Dignum, J. Koning (Eds.). Proc. of the Workshop on Agent Communication Languages and Conversation Policies. AAMAS 2002, Bologna, Italy, July 2002
20. M. Huhns, L. Stephens. "Multiagent Systems and Societies of Agents", in *Multiagent Systems – A Modern Approach to istributed Artificial Intelligence*, ed. G. Weiss, MIT Press, 2000
21. Institute of Electrical and Electronics Engineers. "IEEE Standard Computer Dictionary: A Compilation of IEEE Standard Computer Glossaries". New York, 1990.
22. N. Karnik, A. Tripathi. Design Issues in Mobile-Agent Programming Systems . IEEE Concurrency, vol. 6, n. 3, 1998, pp.52–61.
23. N. Karnik, A. Triphathi, "Security in the Ajanta Mobile Agent System", Software – Practice and Experience, January 2001.

24. E. Kendall, P. Krishna, C. Pathak, C. Suresh, "A Framework for Agent Systems", in *Implementing Applications rameworks b ect riented rameworks at Work*, ed. M. Fayad, D. Schmidt, R. Johnson, John Wiley & Sons, 1999.

25. T. Lehman, S. McLaughry, P. Wyckoff. "TSpaces: The Next Wave". Hawaii International Conference on System Sciences (HICSS-32), January, 1999.

26. P. Maes. "Concepts and Experiments in Computational Reflection". ACM SIGPLAN Notices, 22(12), pp 147–155, 1987

27. T. Malone, K. Crowston. "The Interdisciplinary Study of Coordination". *A M omputing Sur eys* , 1 (March), 87–119.

28. N. Minsky, V. Ungureanu. "Law-Governed Interaction: A Coordination and Control Mechanism for Heterogeneous Distributed Systems". ACM Transactions on Software Engineering and Methodology, Vol. 9, No. 3, July 2000, pp. 273–305.

29. Object Management Group – Agent Platform Special Interest Group. "Agent Technology – Green Paper – Version 1.0", OMG, September 2000.

30. A. Oliva, I.Garcia, L.Buzato, "The reflexive architecture of Guaraná". Technical Report IC-98-14, Institute of Computing, State University of Campinas, April 1998

31. A. Omicini, F. Zambonelli, "TuCSoN: a Coordination Model for Mobile Information Agents". 1st International Workshop on Innovative Internet Information Systems (IIIS'98), Pisa (I), June 1998

32. C. E. Perkins, Mobile IP, IEEE Communications Magazine, vol. 35, no. 5, pp. 84–99, May 1997

33. A. Porto, G. Roman (Eds.). Coordination Languages and Models. Proc. of the 4th International Conference COORDINATION 2000, Limassol, September 2000. LNCS 1906, Springer.

34. M. Shaw, D. Garlan. "Software Architecture: Perspectives on an Emerging Discipline", Prentice Hall, 1996.

35. O. Silva, A. Garcia, C. Lucena, "A Unified Software Architecture for System-Level and Agent-Level Dependability in Multi-Agent Object-Oriented Systems", 7th ECOOP Workshop on Mobile Objects Systems, Budapest, Hungary, June 2001

36. O. Silva, A. Garcia, C. Lucena, "T-Rex: A Reflective Tuple Space Environment for Dependable Mobile Agent Systems". III WCSF at IEEE MWCN 2001, Recife, Brasil, August 2001

37. M. Tsvetovatyy, M. Gini, B. Mobasher, Z. Wieckowski. MAGMA: An Agent Based Virtual Market for Electronic Commerce. International Journal of Applied Artificial Intelligence, September 1997.

38. H. Yoshioka, Y. Tahara, A. Ohsuga, S. Honiden. "Security for Mobile Agents". In Proc. of the 1st International Workshop on Agent-Oriented Software Engineering at ICSE 2000, Limerick (IR), June 2000.

39. F. Zambonelli, N. Jennings, M. Wooldridge. "Organizational Abstractions for the Analysis and Design of Multi-Agent Systems". In Proc. of the 1st International Workshop on Agent-Oriented Software Engineering at ICSE 2000, Limerick (IR), June 2000.

40. F. Zambonelli, G. Cabri, L. Leonardi. "Developing Mobile Agent Organizations: A Case Study in Digital Tourism". Proceedings of the 3rd International Symposium on Distributed Objects & Applications (DOA) 2001, Rome (I), September 2001.

A Declarative Approach to Agent-Centered Context-Aware Computing in Ad Hoc Wireless Environments

Gruia-Catalin Roman[1], Christine Julien[1], and Amy L. Murphy[2]

[1] Department of Computer Science and Engineering
Washington University
Saint Louis, MO 63130
{roman, julien}@cse.wustl.edu
[2] Department of Computer Science
University of Rochester
Rochester, NY 14627
murphy@cs.rochester.edu

Abstract. Much of the current work on context-aware computing relies on information directly available to an application via context sensors on its local host, e.g., user profile, host location, time of day, resource availability, and quality of service measurements. We propose a new notion of context which includes in principle any information available in the ad hoc network infrastructure but is restricted in practice to specific views of the overall context. The context of each view is defined in terms of data, objects, or events exhibiting certain properties, associated with particular application agents, residing on particular hosts, and part of some restricted subnet. Location, distance, movement profiles, access rights, and much more can be used in view specifications. The underlying system infrastructure interprets the view specifications and continuously updates the contents of user-defined views despite dynamic changes in the specifications, state transitions at the application level, mobility of hosts in the physical space, and migration of code among hosts. In systems that are large-scale in terms of both space and numbers of agents, this local restriction will prove necessary for providing timely context information to application agents.

1 Introduction

The foundation of this work is the notion that context-aware computing holds the key to achieving rapid development of dependable mobile applications in ad hoc networks. *Context-aware computing* refers to the explicit ability of a software system to detect and respond to changes in its environment, e.g., a drop in the quality of service on a video transmission, a low battery level, or the sudden availability of much needed access to the Internet. Initial context-aware systems like Olivetti's Active Badge [1] and Xerox PARC's PARCTab [2] focused on user location to provide context-aware information in an office environment, while more

A. Garcia et al. (Eds.): SELMAS 2002, LNCS 2603, pp. 94–109, 2003.

recent systems use location information for context-aware tour guides [3,4]. Gradually, other aspects of context have been fed into applications, including time, weather, and user information, allowing, for example, researchers in the field to attach varied contextual information to their notes with FieldNotes [5]. With the increase in the variety and complexity of context information, much needed frameworks and systems for generalizing its treatment are being developed. The Context Toolkit [6] generalizes interaction among components through context widgets, while the Context Fabric [7] provides a service infrastructure. By and large, these systems limit the context to what a component can immediately sense, ignoring what other networked components can sense. While this need has been hinted at in discussions of context-aware software [8], no wide-spread system allows such access. When the needs of the application must reach beyond the basics (e.g., the application requires access to services available at a remote location), the programmer needs to contend with more complex processes that include discovery and communication. While these extra costs may be acceptable in wired networks where connections persist over extended periods of time, in ad hoc networks the complexity of managing frequent disconnections can significantly increase the programming effort. Yet, mobile systems do need access to a broad range of resources, maybe even more so than traditional distributed applications. Of interest to us is the ease with which resources can be acquired and retained in the presence of mobility. Our specific environment consists of logically mobile agents that operate over a network of physically mobile hosts. These mobile agents coordinate with each other to accomplish their individual application needs. In many scenarios this network may include many agents and span a large physical space. Our work extends the notion of declarative specifications to a broad set of resources and provides the mechanisms needed to maintain access to the specified resources despite rapid changes in the environment caused by the mobility of hosts, migration of software components, and changes in connectivity. For instance, an application on a palmtop should be able to declare its need for printer access and, as the owner travels along, a printer should always appear on the desktop, as long as some printer exists within wireless communication range. Of course, building such an application with today's technology is feasible, but coding it cannot be reduced to the simple act of providing a declaration in the program. We contend that we can accomplish the latter (and more) by extending the notion of context-aware computing and by developing a software infrastructure that continuously secures the resources declared by the application program. In building these specialized contexts, we also recognize that different applications interact with available information in different ways. For these reasons, we introduce four distinct context-aware models that provide unique styles of interaction.

The remainder of this paper is organized as follows. Section 2 discusses the nature of declarative specifications. Section 3 provides details about four different models of context-awareness. Finally, conclusions appear in section 4.

2   Declarative Specification of Views

In our computing model, hosts can move in physical space, and the applications they support are structured as a community of software components called agents that can migrate from one host to another. Thus, an agent is the unit of modularity, execution, and mobility, while a host is a container characterized, among other things, by its location in physical space. Communication among agents and agent migration can take place whenever the hosts involved can physically communicate with each other, i.e., they are connected. Since the notion of context is always a relative one, we will use the term *reference agent* to denote the agent whose context we are about to consider, and we will refer to the host on which this agent is located as the *reference host*. An agent's location is always a host, while a host's location is always a point in some physical or logical space.

2.1   Informal View Definition

A mobile ad hoc network is an opportunistically formed structure that changes rapidly in response to the movement of the mobile hosts involved. Initially, communication in such networks was point to point over a physical broadcast medium, the air waves. However, growth in performance and capabilities has allowed some mobile units to serve as mobile routers for others in the area. Through transitivity, routing in ad hoc networks has expanded the connectivity pattern beyond the limits of an immediately accessible region. In principle, the context associated with a given agent consists of all the information available in the ad hoc network. This includes all information stored by all hosts in the network as well as the context information (e.g., location, temperature, time) sensed by agents on those hosts. We refer to this as the *maximal context* of the reference agent. Of course, such broad access to information is generally costly to implement. In addition, various parts of the same application may need different resources at different times during the execution of the program. For this reason, we believe that it is important to structure the context in terms of fine-grained units which we call views. A *view* is a projection of the maximal context together with an interpretation that defines the rules of engagement between the agent and the particular view.

The concept of view is agent centric in the sense that every view is defined relative to a reference agent with respect to its needs for resources from and knowledge about its environment. An agent sees the world through a set of these individualized views. The set may be altered at will by defining, redefining, and deleting views as processing requirements demand. The software engineering gains derive, to a great extent, from the flexibility and simplicity we can offer the application programmer. Our strategy focuses on declarative specifications and employs a rich set of criteria. For instance, one ought to be able to describe the view contents in terms of phrases such as:

All specials (reference to objects) posted by family restaurants (reference to agents) within one mile (implicit reference to hosts) of my current location (property of the reference host).

In general, constraints on the attributes of the desired resources (data or objects) and the agents that own them are an effective way to restrict a view's contents. They must be combined, however, with constraints on the attributes of the hosts on which the agents reside and with properties of the ad hoc network in the immediate vicinity. Security and network considerations emerge as important research issues in any effort to design a language for view specification. At the network level, for instance, an application may want to limit context to a connected subnet of the ad hoc network forming a region around the reference host. The network topology, geometry, physical distribution in space, and security enforcement procedures play a role in determining the shape of the region of interest. These considerations are new to context-aware computing and are injected by our focus on ad hoc mobility.

The next section provides a more formal treatment of this declarative view specification. The notation is only illustrative and assumes the underlying data representation to be that of a tuple space. Tuple space representations based on the Linda tuple space model [9] enjoy a great deal of popularity due to the content-based manner in which data is accessed. In mobile computing specifically, several systems have found success using shared tuple spaces. MARS [10] focuses on logical mobility, or the movement of agents over physically stationary hosts, using a tuple space to allow coordination among co-located mobile agents. LIME [11] combines support for logical mobility with support for physical mobility and relies on transient sharing of tuple spaces among agents and hosts within communication range. Each agent carries its own tuple spaces, and tuple spaces of connected agents logically merge to form a global tuple space as long as the agents are connected. This work reuses this notion of transient sharing of tuple spaces, combines it with a more flexible tuple representation, and allows more general access to the tuple space.

2.2   Formal View Definition

We assume a tuple to be an unordered set of fields, each with a unique name. An individual agent owns tuples which it keeps in a local tuple space. Fundamentally, tuple access occurs by matching a provided pattern against the contents of the tuple. While adhering to the content-based nature of Linda pattern matching, we extend the traditional semantics to allow the provision of more flexible constraint functions over fields. The matching function, $\mathcal{M}$, described in detail in [12] requires that, for every constraint provided in a pattern, a field that satisfies the constraint exists in the tuple. While the matching function does require that each constraint be satisfied, it does not require that there be a constraint to match every field in the tuple.

In our model, the data, the agents owning the data, the hosts where the agents are located, and the paths to those hosts must all satisfy application-provided constraints. An agent can provide the view's data constraints through a pattern. The matching function, $\mathcal{M}$ is then used to filter the data tuples using this pattern. Hosts and agents in the system provide *profiles* containing personal information. Host profiles handle logical properties of the host, and may relate to the user of the computer. Examples of such properties may include the host's id, the identity of the owner of the computer, or services provided by the computer. Agent profiles, on the other hand, are likely to contain properties related to the application on whose behalf the agent is running. The view's host and agent constraints then reduce to a pattern of constraints over a profile, and these constraints can also be evaluated using the matching function, $\mathcal{M}$. An agent provides network constraints by forming an abstraction of the network topology and its properties. This abstraction, detailed in [13], generates a subnet of the network around the specifying host. For example, the application can restrict its context with respect to the physical distance to other hosts. The subnet constructed includes hosts only within the application-specified distance; all other hosts are excluded.

In any shared data space, access control becomes a real problem. Our model addresses this issue by adding the notion of an access control function. Each agent specifies an individualized function that limits the ability of other agents to access its local data. From the opposite direction, an agent specifying a view attaches to the view a set of credentials that verify it to the other agents. Additionally, the specifying agent declares the operations it intends to perform over the view. These operations can include simple reading or removal of data or more complex operations such as reacting to the appearance of a particular piece of data. The provision of the operations can be viewed as a contract between the specifying agent and the system. Any attempt by the specifying agent to perform an operation that it didn't declare will result in an exception. When determining the contents of a view, the system evaluates each contributing agent's access control function over the view's credentials and potential operations. The fact that the access control function is evaluated on an individual basis for each tuple adhering to the view constraints provides a very fine level of granularity.

Figure 1 shows our computational model. A host, the outer rectangle in the figure has a physical location and a profile describing its properties. Each host contains mobile agents, the smaller rectangles in the figure. Each agent also stores its properties in a profile and has a logical location, the host on which it is located. Additionally, agents can define

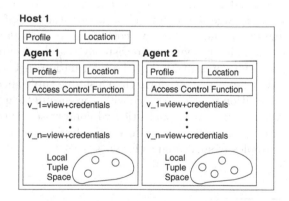

Fig. 1. The computational model.

views which consist of the view specification, described in detail below, and the credentials provided for that view. For evaluating the view specifications of other agents, each agent also defines an access control function. Finally, every agent owns a local tuple space that contains its data items.

Given a reference host r, we first define η, the subnet of the ad hoc network that satisfies the provided network constraints (n), to be a subset of the closure of r's network. η must be a tree, r must belong to η, and η must satisfy n. Given the host constraints (h), the agent constraints (a), the data constraints (d), the agent's credentials (κ), and the operations that will be performed on the view (ops), a view specified by a reference agent, r contains the tuples defined by:

$$\text{view}_r(n, h, a, d, \kappa, ops) \triangleq$$
$$\langle \text{set } \eta, \gamma, \alpha, \theta : \eta \subseteq Closure(r) \wedge tree(\eta) \wedge r \in \eta \wedge \eta \text{ sat } n$$
$$\wedge \gamma \in \eta \wedge \mathcal{M}(\gamma.\text{profile}, h) \wedge \alpha.\text{loc} = \gamma \wedge \mathcal{M}(\alpha.\text{profile}, a)$$
$$\wedge \theta \in \alpha.T \wedge \mathcal{M}(\theta, d) \wedge \alpha.acf(\kappa, ops, \theta)$$
$$:: \theta \rangle. {}^{1}$$

where γ is a host, α is an agent, and θ is a tuple. $\alpha.\text{loc}$ refers to the host on which agent α is currently running, $\alpha.T$ refers to α's local tuple space, and $\alpha.acf$ to α's access control function. A tuple belongs to a view only if it satisfies the view constraints and the reference agent meets the requirements of the access control function of the agent owning the tuple.

As hosts and agents move and the available data changes, the view is updated to reflect the changing set of available tuples. From the application's perspective, all of these changes are transparent and manifest only in changes to the set of available data items. Therefore, the application agent can operate over a view without regard to the changes occurring in that view. The application also has the freedom to change the constraints associated with its view dynamically, and, when it does, the model adjusts the view to reflect the application's new needs.

The adoption of a declarative context specification is motivated by our belief that transparent context management will shift to the underlying middleware many of the burdens programmers face in the development of applications for use in ad hoc networks. Moreover, the programmer controls the scope of the view (a large or small neighborhood), the size of the view (the range of entities included), and the relative cost of executing a particular operation on that view (by defining the level of consistency, e.g., best effort versus transactional semantics). The presentation of the information in this view to the programmer can take a more abstract form than a simple tuple space. A variety of data structures in addition to a tuple space will prove useful to applications in different domains. Additionally, more sophisticated context-sensitive interactions can be provided through veneers that build on the basic model. The next section details some examples of such models in our system.

---

[1] The three-part notation $\langle \text{op } quantified\_variable : range :: expression \rangle$ used here is defined as follows: variables from $quantified\_variables$ take on all possible values permitted by $range$. Each such instantiation of the variables is substituted in $expression$, producing a multiset of values to which **op** is applied, yielding the value of the expression. If no instantiation of the variables satisfies $range$, the value of the expression is the identity element for **op**, e.g., $true$ when **op** is $\forall$; zero if **op** is "+".

3   Models of Context-Awareness

Because we see ad hoc mobility as a fundamental challenge to developing the next generation of consumer, industrial, and military applications, we seek to develop new models of context-awareness able to accommodate the complexities of mobile computing, to build middleware that embodies these models, and to evaluate both on interesting application test beds. This section offers a broad-brush discussion of the four types of context-awareness models we are currently developing. Our models reflect those popular in distributed computing, but we expect new technological advances to result from our special focus on their applicability to ad hoc networks, the introduction of declarative specifications of context, and automatic context maintenance. To show how an agent's interaction with the view differs among the four models, we introduce an example that we will revisit throughout this section. Consider a team of robots exploring an uninhabited planet. The robots need to perform experiments that require precise relative locations and instrumentation that no single robot can carry. For example, some robots may be able to precisely sense their locations, some may be able to sense the ambient temperature, others may sense atmospheric pressure, and still others may collect data about the soil composition. All of these pieces of information have the potential to contribute to the operating context of any agent in the system. Now consider a specific reference agent that requires two pieces of location information from other robots (for determining relative locations) and a single piece of temperature information (for performing its particular experiment). To satisfy its needs, the agent defines two views. The first is defined to contain the location data items that are between some minimum and maximum distance from the agent's robot. The second view contains temperature data items within a specified number of network hops. The agent can dynamically adjust its view specifications as its needs change. The agent's style of interaction with these views depends upon the features of the context-awareness model in use by the system. As we describe our context-awareness models, we will revisit this example to elucidate how the agent interacts with its temperature view in each model.

3.1   Context-Sensitive Data Structures

In many distributed systems, data access serves as the primary form of interaction among components. In mobile computing, several systems have used shared tuple spaces as a coordination medium. As discussed previously, MARS [10] employs a single tuple space per host to facilitate coordination among co-located mobile agents while LIME [11] relies on transient sharing of tuple spaces among agents on the same host and among hosts within communication range. Other systems have explored different data structures. PEERWARE [14], for example, stores documents in trees and adjusts the contents of the tree to account for mobility. All these systems assume a symmetric and transitive model of sharing. When a group of components is formed, they all share the same data, and they perceive it in the same manner. By contrast, our proposed model allows each

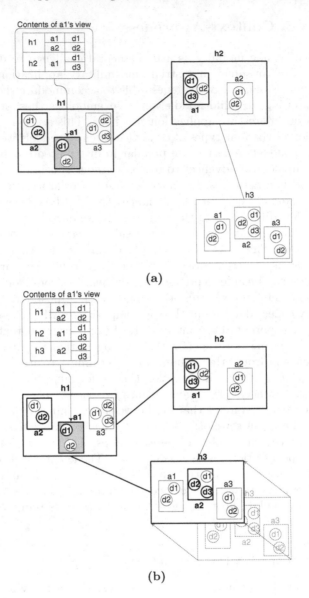

Fig. 2. View dynamics. Data items visible to reference agent a1 located on host h1 before and after h3 moves into h1's range. Hosts, agents, and data items with darkened borders contribute to the view, while ones with lighter borders do not satisfy the specification.

individual agent to define its own perspective of the data available in the world in terms of one or more views. This asymmetry, a distinguishing feature of our model, allows each agent to assume responsibility for and control over the size and scope of the data it accesses. For example, an agent associated with a managing robot that monitors the activities of other robots in its vicinity might define a view that includes the locations and activities of all other robots within a certain distance, which may be continuously adjusted as the exploration progresses. One of the worker robots, however, may define a view containing only information it needs to accomplish its individual task; this view may have nothing to do with the monitoring agent.

In general, the agent's view contains a *representation* of a subset of the data available in the ad hoc network. The choice of representation is a defining feature of each specific instantiation of the general model. In the context-sensitive data structures model, the view's representation is a simple data structure (e.g., a tuple space). The three remaining models build on this foundation. The choice of data included in the view, i.e., its *contents*, is determined by the view specification. The latter is given in a declarative manner by stating constraints on the network, hosts, agents, and data that contribute to defining the view. One can impose restrictions on network properties (e.g., number of hops, distances, bandwidth, etc.) so as to define a connected subnet immediately surrounding the reference host. This kind of locality will help control the context maintenance costs while meeting the needs of most mobile applications. Within this contextual setting, an application can impose further restrictions on the properties of the physically mobile hosts (e.g., power availability, devices supported, etc.) in the subnet and of the mobile agents supported by the admissible hosts. Finally, data associated with the remaining eligible agents can be filtered to produce the actual contents for that view. As hosts and agents move and properties of the network components change over time, the contents of the view must be transparently updated for the reference agent.

The dynamic nature of the view definition is illustrated in Figure 2, where the depicted view of agent a1 changes as the distance between hosts h1 and h3 decreases. Agent a1 is grayed to indicate that it is the agent specifying the view. Hosts, agents, and data items that contribute to the view are shown with darkened borders. In part (a) of the figure, due to a1's specification, only hosts h1 and h2 qualify to contribute agents to the view. Because of the restrictions on agent and data properties, only certain data items on certain agents on these hosts appear in the view. The balloon pointing to a1 shows a table of the hosts, agents, and data items contributing to a1's view. As part (b) shows, when host h3 moves closer to h1, it satisfies the view's constraints. Again, only certain data items on certain agents appear in the view. Exactly which hosts, agents, and data items contribute is determined by the application-provided view specification.

In the context-sensitive data structures model, the view representation takes the form of a standard data structure. For the purposes of discussing our example, we assume this data structure is a tuple space with which the robot agent interacts by performing standard tuple space operations. Figure 3 shows this general pattern of interaction. This figure and all subsequent ones show a virtual picture of an agent's view where both remote and local tuples are included in a single "soup." The actual distribution of information in logical and physical space (as shown in Figure 2) is omitted. Tuple space operations, or requests, can include reading and removing data from the view. Additionally, the tuple space can provide reactive behaviors whereby a robot agent can react to the appearance of new data items in the view. As discussed previously, tuples match operations or reactions through content-based pattern matching, i.e., an agent selects data by specifying constraints over the values of the tuples' fields. In the robot example, tuples from temperature sensors might contain fields including a unique id identifying the probe, the string temp indicating that the probe is a temperature probe, the value of the temperature at that probe, and other fields. The agent can provide constraints over all of the data item's fields or over a subset of them. A robot agent might gain an initial temperature reading by performing a read operation for a tuple corresponding to any probe (p), labeled as temperature data (by the string temp), with any temperature value (v):

$$\text{read}(\langle probeId : \text{p}, probeType = \text{temp}, probeValue : \text{v}\rangle)$$

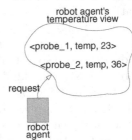

This request constrains only the fields explicitly mentioned; it places no restrictions on other fields in the tuple. When the request completes, the probe id and value are stored in the local variables, p and v, respectively. (The reader is reminded that this notation and all similar notation is for illustration purposes only.) If the robot wants to receive later readings from the same temperature probe (p) that differ from the initial reading by more than 5 degrees, it might register a reaction:

Fig. 3. Agent/view interaction in the context-sensitive data structures model.

$$\text{react to}(\langle probeId = \text{p}, probeType = \text{temp}, probeValue : \text{v}' :: (\text{v} - 5) < \text{v}' < (\text{v} + 5)\rangle, \text{A})$$

The action A will be performed whenever the temperature probe p outputs a new temperature reading that satisfies both the view specification and the value constraints provided in the react to operation.

3.2   Context-Sensitive References

Traditional distributed systems, like CORBA-compliant systems [15] and Jini [16] hide many of the details of object distribution from the programmer. The general pattern of interaction requires a client to find an object using a lookup service and then bind to it, allowing the programmer to invoke methods on the remote object as if it were local. If the remote object fails, the client must revisit the lookup service to retrieve a new reference. This style of interaction, while common in traditional distributed systems has received only limited attention in ad hoc networks [17]. Our next model extends the context-sensitive data structures model so the view contains objects and object references instead of data items. An agent obtains an object reference and description from the view through a request similar to those used in the previous model. Because the object description contains information about the interface of the object, the application agent can use this information to interact with the remote object directly by invoking methods on the reference. The agent can continue to use the reference but receives no guarantees regarding the stability of the remote object because the interaction occurs outside the view.

In using the context-sensitive references model in the robot environment, the temperature data is encapsulated in objects. Instead of reading data items directly from the view, the robot agent reads an object reference based on requirements it provides. The agent provides these requirements as a pattern that is matched (again, in a content-based fashion) against the object description stored in the tuple space. The reference returned indicates the remote object's location and information about how to interact with it (i.e., the object's interface). Figure 4 shows this style of interaction. A robot agent might request from the view a reference to a temperature object at a location (loc) within 2 meters of the agent's current location ($here$):

$$read(\langle objectReference : r, probeType - temp, location : loc :: |loc - here| < 2m\rangle)$$

For a more complicated request, the agent could require that the object reference returned provide a particular method. Because the object reference is bound to r when the read operation returns, the robot agent can interact directly with the remote object by invoking methods on r. For example, a temperature object might have methods getCelsius() and getFahrenheit(), and the robot agent could call either method depending on its needs:

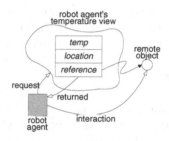

Fig. 4. Agent/view interaction in the context-sensitive references model.

$$r.getCelsius()$$

The agent can hold the reference as long as it desires, however, if the reference object disappears, an exception will be generated the next time the robot agent attempts to use the stale reference. In such a case, the agent must obtain a new reference from the view. Additionally, because both the robot agent and the agent holding the temperature object are mobile, the distance between them could grow to more than two meters without the robot agent's knowledge. The next model of context-awareness, while incurring additional overhead, helps the application programmer transparently cope with these deficiencies.

3.3   Context-Sensitive Bindings

The need for load-balancing [18] and fault-tolerance [19] have been addressed in extensions to the CORBA specification. These additions accomplish their respective tasks by selecting from among a set of object replicas for each remote object call. In the case of load-balancing, consecutive remote method calls are not necessarily forwarded to the same object; instead calls are spread to multiple replicas. For fault-tolerance, consecutive calls can be forwarded to the same object instance until that object fails. In these cases, a different replica services later remote object calls. The DENO (Decentralized Network Objects) [20] system also attempts to address these problems in the context of mobile and unreliable networks, adding object replication to increase efficiency, availability, and fault-tolerance. Our context-sensitive bindings model attempts to solve similar problems in the ad hoc environment. Instead of addressing the replication problem, however, our model concentrates on the binding aspect. The view abstraction allows our model to provide a more general and transparent solution.

In the mobile ad hoc environment, objects move, and bindings are even more likely to break. The middleware supporting the view concept transparently manages bindings, hiding both the lookup service and object mobility from the programmer. In general, the view contains a set of objects (and associated object descriptions) owned by connected agents. The set of available objects depends on the reference agent's view specification. However, the programmer does not access this set of objects directly. Instead he requests bindings to objects in the view, subject to certain policies. For example, if multiple objects available in the view match the binding request, the application might desire the nearest match. As agents and the objects associated with them move, the bindings are maintained and transparently updated to select new objects as needed. If an object matching the binding request in the view better satisfies the binding policy, the application's bound object is updated to reference the better match. Additionally, when bound objects move outside the view, a new object satisfying the binding request and located in the view replaces it. The change from one satisfying object to another is under the indirect control of the programmer through the binding policies he provides. Any effects of this rebinding are therefore the responsibility of the application itself.

As an example of a view, consider a reference agent responsible for printing documents. Its view might contain all printers available on the current floor in the current building. The agent might then request a binding to the highest quality printer. As the agent moves, the set of available printers changes, and therefore the binding automatically changes. This model may be added as a thin veneer over the context-sensitive references model. This veneer hides the view contents and services a binding request by locating an object in the view that matches the binding specification and policy and by creating the connection to it for the agent. The layer also responds to changes in the available set of objects in order to maintain, update, and break bindings when necessary.

Because the robot agent requires a single temperature reading, when using the context-sensitive bindings model, the agent requests a single binding to a temperature object. Because this model allows the agent to specify a binding policy which helps select the "best match" for the binding from among the objects in the view, the agent might request to bind to the temperature probe with the highest precision. Even though the object description might contain a wealth of information, the requesting agent can choose which fields of the description to provide constraints for. A binding request might look like:

$$\mathsf{bind}(\langle \mathit{objectReference} : \mathbf{r}, \mathit{probeType} = \mathsf{temp}\rangle) \; \mathsf{highest\_precision\_policy}$$

The agent interacts with the object by invoking methods on the binding:

```
r.getCelsius()
```

Figure 5 shows these interactions. If the bound object disappears from the view, or a new object appears that better satisfies the binding policy, the middleware automatically updates the binding. The system generates an exception only when no object in the view satisfies the binding request. An agent can also request

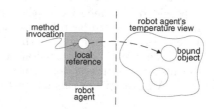

Fig. 5. Agent/view interaction in the context-sensitive bindings model.

to receive a special notification that the bound object has changed to a new object.

3.4   Context-Sensitive Events

The final model allows agents to interact through a language of events. In this case, the view contains events generated by components in the system. For example, an agent monitoring robot activity might define a view containing events generated when new robots (hosts) connect and are within a certain physical distance. Event-based interactions have become common in distributed systems. The JEDI system [21], for example, defines a distributed event dispatcher through which active entities communicate by generating events and registering to receive events. The SIENA event distribution service [22] addresses scalability issues by aggregating similar event subscriptions. Recent work [23] has targeted publish/subscribe systems for the ad hoc environment, specifically addressing reconfiguration algorithms much needed in the highly dynamic ad hoc environment. These systems address specific implementation concerns, while our goal is to apply the view's scope limiting concept to publish-subscribe models. Our generalized view concept provides allowances for ad hoc mobility and the capability to restrict the scope of visible events based on the network, hosts, agents, objects, and the events themselves.

In this case, objects themselves are not directly visible to agents, only the events they generate are visible. These events are filtered by an event specification. Agents operate on this resulting view of events by binding callback functions to events or prescribed sequences of events which pass through the filter. Any application-defined object can generate events, allowing agents to respond to both application specific events as well as generic events such as a change in an object data field. An agent must subscribe to receive particular event notifications, and an agent receives a notification only if it is subscribed for the event at the time it is generated. To ensure a unified treatment of all events and uniformity of the view contents, we introduce (for specification purposes) virtual objects so named as to refer to application agents, hosts, and network resources abstractly. These special objects pass on system generated events to the context, but their implementation is hard-coded in the middleware. The existence of these virtual objects allows an application agent to react to, for example, the appearance in the view of a new contributing agent. The context-sensitive events model is provided as a veneer over the context-sensitive data structures model.

In this model, the example robot agent registers to receive temperature events from its view. As shown in Figure 6, this registration attaches a callback function provided by the agent to the generation of the relevant events. As the figure indicates, this style of interaction completely hides the view's contents from the robot agent. An example of this interaction using our illustrative notation is:

$$\mathsf{subscribe}(\langle \mathit{probeType} = \mathsf{temp}\rangle, \mathsf{C})$$

In this example, the callback function is called anytime a temperature probe generates a temperature event. Whether events are generated at a certain frequency or upon a temperature change is determined at the application level by the temperature probe's implementation. The callback function receives an instance of the event, which contains information about the event itself and about the tem-

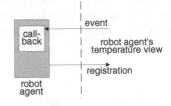

Fig. 6. Agent/view interaction in the context-sensitive events model.

perature probe object generating the event. The agent will, however, receive all events generated by all temperature probes in the view. To handle this, the agent has several choices. One is simply to filter these events locally, at the application level. A second option would detect a single "first" event and remember the source, probe p. The callback for this event would deregister the initial registration and register the agent for only events originating at p. This second registration might look like:

$$\mathsf{subscribe}(\langle \mathit{probeId} = \mathsf{p}, \mathit{probeType} = \mathsf{temp}\rangle, \mathsf{C}')$$

Of course, this option requires the agent to explicitly handle the failure or disappearance of probe p by subscribing to events generated by the temperature probe's virtual object. As previously described, this virtual object and the events it generates are defined by the middleware, and an API for accessing this information is provided to the application programmer.

Even for this simple example, each model has advantages and disadvantages. The model chosen for use depends on factors as varied as the guarantees required by the system and the application developer's preferred programming paradigm.

4   Conclusions

Our experiences in the ongoing development of the LIME middleware provide us with a foundation for beginning this model's implementation. A prototype implementation of the basic context-sensitive data structures model builds directly on top of LIME and provides most of the capabilities outlined in this paper. This initial prototype allows us to begin the development of the applications that spurred this investigation. Further work on the middleware's development will provide the true asymmetric behavior and will allow for performance evaluation studies to be carried out. We approach this development effort from a bottom-up perspective. The lowest level requires algorithms and protocols for gathering information from sensors and disseminating that information in a timely fashion. We have already developed an algorithm for consistent group membership [24] that uses location information to provide the appearance of announced disconnection in spite of host mobility. Other work on providing an abstraction of the network based on properties of network paths [13] establishes a foundation for implementing the view abstraction required in this model. Each layer of the implementation must address key issues related to the highly dynamic ad hoc environment. As mentioned in the introduction, one such issue concerns the application's ability to specify the level of consistency guarantees it requires for particular operations over particular views. As always, another key element of the final implementation involves tradeoffs between system expressiveness and the efficiency of its implementation. In particular, the view specification language should be as flexible as possible without losing the efficiency gains associated with the provision of the asymmetric model. The prototype will be useful in evaluating possible specification mechanics, but conclusive evaluation results will only be available once the implementation of the asymmetric model is fully operational. As software must function in settings that are increasingly open and highly dynamic, software development is becoming more complex. While we cannot eliminate intrinsic complexities of software artifacts operating under such demanding circumstances, we can reduce the complexity of application development by shifting much of the burden onto the system support infrastructure. Programming power can be amplified by allowing the developer to think at a new and high level of abstraction. Effective use of the limited resources often associated with mobile systems can be achieved by having the system infrastructure explicitly know what the application needs are at any given point in time.

Acknowledgments. This research was supported in part by the National Science Foundation under Grant No. CCR-9970939 and by the Office of Naval Research MURI Research Contract No. N00014-02-1-0715. Any opinions, findings, and conclusions or recommendations expressed in this paper are those of the authors and do not necessarily reflect the views of the National Science Foundation or the Office of Naval Research.

References

1. Harter, A., Hopper, A.: A distributed location system for the active office. IEEE Networks **8** (1994) 62–70
2. Want, R., et al.: An overview of the PARCTab ubiquitous computing experiment. IEEE Personal Communications **2** (1995) 28–43
3. Abowd, G., Atkeson, C., Hong, J., Long, S., Kooper, R., Pinkerton, M.: Cyberguide: A mobile context-aware tour guide. ACM Wireless Networks **3** (1997) 421–433

4. Cheverst, K., Davies, N., Mitchell, K., Friday, A., Efstratiou, C.: Experiences of developing and deploying a context-aware tourist guide: The GUIDE project. In: Proceedings of MobiCom, ACM Press (2000) 20–31
5. Ryan, N., Pascoe, J., Morse, D.: Fieldnote: A handheld information system for the field. In: First International Workshop on TeloGeoProcessing. (1999) 156–163
6. Salber, D., Dey, A., Abowd, G.: The Context Toolkit: Aiding the development of context-enabled applications. In: Proceedings of CHI'99. (1999) 434–441
7. Hong, J., Landay, J.: An infrastructure approach to context-aware computing. Human Computer Interaction **16** (2001)
8. Schilit, B., Adams, N., Want, R.: Context-aware computing applications. In: IEEE Workshop on Mobile Computing Systems and Applications. (1994) 85–90
9. Gelernter, D.: Generative communication in Linda. ACM Transactions on Programming Languages and Systems **7** (1985) 80–112
10. Cabri, G., Leonardi, L., Zambonelli, F.: MARS: A programmable coordination architecture for mobile agents. Internet Computing **4** (2000) 26–35
11. Murphy, A., Picco, G., Roman, G.: LIME: A middleware for physical and logical mobility. In: Proceedings of the 21st International Conference on Distributed Computing Systems. (2001) 524–533
12. Julien, C., Roman, G.C.: Egocentric context-aware programming in ad hoc mobile networks. In: Proceedings of the $10^{t}h$ International Symposium on the Foundations of Software Engineering (FSE-10). (2002) 23–30
13. Roman, G., Julien, C., Huang, Q.: Network abstractions for context-aware mobile computing. In: Proceedings of the 24th International Conference on Software Engineering. (2002) 363–373
14. Cugola, G., Picco, G.: PEERWARE: Core middleware support for Peer to Peer and mobile systems. Technical report, Politecnico di Milano (2001)
15. Emmerich, W.: Engineering Distributed Objects. John Wiley and Sons, Ltd. (2000)
16. Edwards, K.: Core JINI. Prentice Hall (1999)
17. Handorean, R., Roman, G.: Service provision in ad hoc networks. In: Proceedings of the 5th International Conference on Coordination Models and Languages. (2002) 207–219
18. Othman, O., O'Ryan, C., Schmidt, D.: Strategies for CORBA middleware-based load balancing. IEEE Distributed Systems Online **2** (2001)
19. Object Management Group: Fault tolerant CORBA specification. OMG Document ptc/2000-04-04 (2000)
20. Keleher, P., Cetintemel, U.: Consistency management in Deno. Mobile Networks and Applications **5** (2000) 299–309
21. Cugola, G., Nitto, E.D., Fuggetta, A.: The JEDI event-based infrastructure and its application to the development of the OPSS WFMS. IEEE Transactions on Software Engineering **27** (2001) 827–850
22. Carzaniga, A., Rosenblum, D., Wolf, A.: Design and evaluation of a wide-area event notification service. ACM Transactions on Computer Systems **19** (2001) 332–383
23. Cugola, G., Picco, G., Murphy, A.: Towards dynamic reconfiguration of distributed publish-subscribe middleware. In: Third International Workshop on Software Engineering and Middleware. (2002)
24. Roman, G., Huang, Q., Hazemi, A.: Consistent group membership in ad hoc networks. In: Proceedings of the 23rd International Conference on Software Engineering. (2001) 381–388

Engineering Mobility in Large Multi Agent Systems: A Case Study in Urban Traffic Management

Marco Mamei[1] and Michael Mahan[2]

[1]Dipartimento di Scienze dell'Ingegneria – Università di Modena e Reggio Emilia
Via Vignolese 905 – 41100 Modena – ITALY
mamei.marco@unimo.it

[2]Nokia Research Center
Agent Technology Group
5, Wayside Road, Burlington, Massachusetts, USA
michael.mahan@nokia.com

Abstract. The complexity raised in modern software systems seems to be no longer affordable in terms of the abstractions and methodologies promoted by traditional approaches to computer science and software engineering and radically new approaches are required. This paper focuses on the problem of engineering the motion coordination of a large-scale multi-agent system, and proposes an approach that takes inspiration from the laws of physics. Our idea is to have the movements of agents driven by force fields, generated by the agents themselves and propagated via some infrastructure or by the agents in an ad-hoc way. A globally coordinated and self-organized behavior in the agent's movements can then emerge due to the interrelated effects of agents following the shape of the fields and dynamic fields re-shaping. The approach is presented and its effectiveness described with regard to a concrete case study in the area of urban traffic management.

1   Introduction

Computer science is in deep trouble, structured design is a failure and systems, as currently engineered, are brittle and fragile. They cannot be easily adapted to new situations and small changes in requirements entail large changes in the structure and configuration. These problems are going to be exacerbated by the new information technology scenario that is rapidly forming under the eyes of everybody: computing systems are going to be everywhere and will be always connected and active. On the one hand, computer systems are going to be embedded in every object, e.g., in our everyday clothes, in our home furniture, in our homes themselves, not to mention the computing capabilities of handheld computing devices and cellular phones, which are already a reality. On the other hand also due the advances in wireless technologies, network connectivity will be pervasive, and every computing device will be somehow connected in a network, whether the "traditional" Internet or some ad-hoc networks. Modeling this scenario as a large-scale multi agent system seems the most natural choice, but a new set of engineering principles that can be applied to effectively build flexible, robust, evolvable and efficient multi agent system is required 18, 22 .

We think that one of the main topics, in the research of these new engineering principles, will be to conceive new ways to let the agents of a system to communicate

A. Garcia et al. (Eds.): SELMAS 2002, LNCS 2603, pp. 110–122, 2003.

and coordinate each other in a powerful and flexible way and to support these new paradigms with innovative middleware and programming models. The contribution of this paper is to present a new methodology to coordinate the respective movements of large number of agents. The goals of their coordination can be various: letting members meet somewhere 5 , distribute themselves accordingly to specific spatial patterns 1, 23 , or simply move in the environment without interfering with each other and avoiding the emergence of traffic jams 8 . The core idea of the proposed approach is to provide agents with simple yet contextual information supporting and facilitating the required coordination activities. Context aware agents, by exploiting the available contextual information, can coordinate each other via very simple algorithms in a robust and flexible way. On the contrary, context-unaware agents blind with regard to what is around them, and moving in an environment unable to provide them suitable contextual information, may require very complex built-in algorithms to coordinate with each other, limiting their capability of dealing with dynamics and resource constraints. In our model, context-related information is expressed in the form of "computational fields" (o- $ields$). We can imagine that each agent of the system can generate specific fields conveying some application-specific information about the local environment and/or about itself. Agents can perceive these fields and can react accordingly, i.e., following the gradient downhill, uphill, or by following its equipotential lines. Therefore, agents' activities and movements are simply driven by these "force" fields, without any central controller. Engineering a coordination policy is mainly a bottom-up approach and consists in specify local interactions: how agents generate fields, how these fields are propagated in the environment and how agents subscribe and react to the fields. A case study for assisting users to avoid traffic jams while driving their cars is adopted through the paper to exemplify the main concepts and use of the Co-Fields approach and its suitability in effectively providing support for several coordination problems.

The following of the paper is organized as follows. Section 2 introduces the case study. Section 3 outlines the limitation of current middleware models and overviews the Co-Fields model. Section 4 details the use of Co-Fields model in the case study and presents the results obtained. Section 5 discusses related works. Section 6 concludes the paper and discusses future works.

2   The Case Study

To fix the ideas on an application scenario and to clarify our model, we introduce a simple case study application consisting in a system to enable the coordination of the respective movements of a group of users driving their cars in a city. In this scenario, we can suppose that the city is provided with an adequate computer network embedded in its streets/corners, and that cars are equipped with a computer executing a navigator agent. In particular: on the one hand, there will be a network of computer hosts, each capable of communicating with each other and with the mobile devices located in its proximity. The number of the embedded hosts and the topology of the network depend on the city, but basically the requirement is that each host represents and manages a meaningful zone of the city, and that the embedded network topology mimics the topology of the city plan. Also, we require some sort of localization mechanism (e.g. GPS) to be enforced by the infrastructure. On the other hand, a car is provided with a computer running a digital assistant capable to offer different services to its user based on the location-dependent information it is able to retrieve by connecting to the city infrastructure (see figure 1). Given the above scenario, in particular we focus on how users can be supported in coordinating with each other. More in detail the coordination problem taken in consideration is helping a user to avoid traffic or queues while driving across the city (thus realizing a sort of load balancing between cars and city's streets/corners).

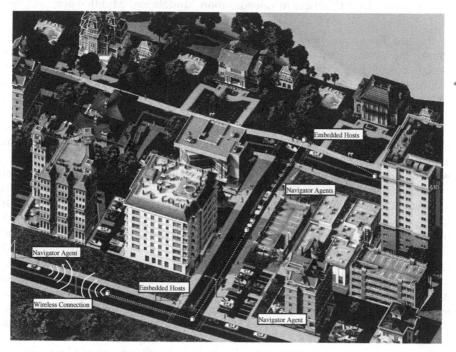

Fig. 1. Multi agent system for traffic management.

3   Towards the Co-fields Model

In this section we are going to briefly survey the current best practices in managing the interactions and the coordination activities of a multi agent system, showing why we think that they are inadequate to treat a case study like the one presented in section 2. Then we are going to describe our proposal: the Co-Fields model, stressing on what are its contributions respect to the current approaches.

Central to the following discussion will be the concept of context awareness. In our opinion by its own nature coordination implies the need for context awareness. An agent can coordinate with other entities only if it is somehow aware of "what is around" (i.e. its context). In the traffic management application, for example, agents' need some information about where the traffic is, where is their destination and how to get there. Agents cannot have enough information for their coordination tasks from scratch, because they are embedded in a possibly unknown, open and dynamic environment –the city-. So the core of their coordination activities will be to gather somehow this contextual information and then exploit it properly. As we will show in the next paragraphs, in our opinion, the problem of the current models is that they do not provide enough contextual information or they provide it in the wrong way.

3.1   Current Best Practices in Coordination Models and Middleware

In the last few years, several middleware and coordination models, addressing – among the others – the problem of coordination and interaction in a multi-agent system (more generally, in a distributed multi-component system), have been proposed. We briefly discuss them by grouping into three categories: *i* models based on direct communication *ii* models based on shared data-spaces *iii* and models based on event publish/subscribe.

In *direct communication models*, a distributed application is designed by means of a group of components that are in charge to communicate with each other in a direct and explicit way. Systems like Jini 9 , UPnP 20 , FIPA-based agent systems 3 , as well as P2P systems like JXTA 11 are examples of middleware infrastructures rooted on a direct communication model. The problem of this approach is that agents are placed in a "void" space: the model, per se, does not provide any contextual information, they can only perceive and interact with other components/agent, and the middleware support is mostly reduced to helping in finding communication partners. Thus, each agent has to "manually" become context aware by discovering the other entities in the environment. For instance, in the case study, a user agent has to explicitly retrieve via some service the city map, it has to discover which other cars are currently driving in its same area, and explicitly negotiate with them to agree on a specific traffic management policy. Therefore, the approach does not generally suits the coordination needs of pervasive scenarios, in that it requires agents' notable efforts (both computational and communication) to acquire context-awareness and end up with ad-hoc solutions for a contingent coordination problem (decisions which are, consequently, brittle, not flexible, and not adaptable).

Shared data-space models exploit shared localized data structures in order to let agents interoperate and coordinate with each other. These data structures can be hosted in some data-space (e.g., tuple space), as in JavaSpaces 7 , or they can be carried on by agents themselves, as in Lime 16 and XMiddle 13 . In these cases, agents are no longer placed in a void space but they live in an environment that can be modeled and described in terms of the information stored in the data spaces that, being accessible only from a locality, can provide some sort of contextual information to agents without forcing agents to directly communicate with each other. For instance in our example, one can assume the each street and corner provides a data-space, which stores messages left by the other agents about their presence and eventually their intended next location. An agent accessing several data-spaces would have to build an internal representation of the actual traffic condition and then decide either by negotiating with other agents or accordingly to a predefined set of rules its next movement. Still, the problem of the approach is that contextual information usually expresses raw local data that can be difficult for agents to "understand" and exploit to achieve their coordination tasks. In other words, coordination decisions have still to be taken directly by agents on the basis of the available data (thus requiring computational efforts), accordingly to some global policy that is either previously established (and thus is not flexible and adaptive) or it has to be acquired (thus requiring further communication efforts among agents). Programmable tuple space models, such as MARS 5 and TuCSoN 14 may alleviate agents' computational efforts by hosting coordination policies in the tuple space. Still, these policies tend to be strictly local to a tuple space and cannot easily support the coordination of physically distributed agents.

In *e ent-based publish subscribe models*, a distributed application is modeled by a set of components interacting with each other by generating events and by reacting to events of interest. Typical infrastructures rooted on this model are: Jedi 6 , Jini Distributed Events 9 and UPnP General Event Notification Architecture (GENA) 20 . Without doubt, event-based model promotes stronger context-awareness, in that components can be considered as embedded in an active environment able of notifying them about what's happening around. This frees agents from the need of explicitly querying the environment or the other agents (as in direct and data-space models), and thus leads to software systems that can be both computationally and communication efficient.   Current software engineering practices are based on designing each agent's program by specifying how the events update agents' internal state (which encode agent's context awareness) and how they trigger actions to let the agent behave accordingly to its perceived context. For instance, in the case study, a possible use of this approach would be to let each agent to notify its movements across the city, to update (accordingly to other agents' notified movements) its internal representation of the traffic condition (i.e. context-awareness) and then move properly. The problem of this approach is that it is still too complicated: even if they are provided with all the information they need, agents have to apply a complex decisional algorithm to infer the right decision, about where to go, from their internal knowledge.

In the next sub-section we are going to describe our proposal, stressing on how it improves current best practices, trying to solve the described problems.

3.2   The Co-fields Model

The core idea in the Co-Fields model is to delegate to the infrastructure all the activities needed to set-up the proper conditions required to let the agents' coordinate in an almost automatic way. In particular we would like the infrastructure to build a global view of the environment tailored ad-hoc to specific agents' coordination tasks. Agents perceiving this coordination-specific view would be able to achieve their goal effortlessly, because the view represents the agents' context in the exact way needed for the agents' coordination task. Although the models surveyed in the previous section are interaction models, prescribing only data exchange mechanisms, they typically induce coordination models on the application level. In fact, the standard practice to exploit the above interaction models is to have contextual information represented by some kind of general purpose data, and to let agents acquire and process this data to take decisions relevant for their coordination task. This tends to keep the context representation and its usage by the agents strongly separated, typically forcing agents to execute complex algorithms to exploit the contextual information. On the contrary, designing context-representation together with the mechanism agents will use to exploit this information makes the process automatic because the context has been represented knowing in advance what will be the agent's reaction to that information. While the infrastructure is in charge of tailoring this artificial, coordination-specific view, the agents simply have to blindly follow the prepared coordination policy. Such characteristics also imply that agents' activities are automatically adapted to the environmental dynamic, which is reflected in a changing view of the environment, without forcing agents to re-adapt themselves. All of this means that the approach we propose is based on a design-as-a-whole perspective 15 , in which agents are not designed in isolation, but as part of a global organization. Following this approach, agents achieve their goal not because of their capabilities as single individuals, but because they are part of an (auto)organized system that leads them to the goal achievement. The fact that the goals are accomplished is not a merit of the single agents, but of the system as a whole.

The Co-Fields model can be schematized in the following four points:

1. The environment is represented and abstracted by "computational fields", spread by agents and by the infrastructure. These fields convey some useful information for the agents' coordination tasks and provide agents with strong coordination-task-tailored context awareness.
2. The coordination policy is realized by letting the agents to move following the "waveform" of these fields.
3. Environment dynamics (through the infrastructure) and agents' movements induce changes in the fields' surface, composing a feedback cycle that influences agents' movement (point 2).
4. This feedback cycle lets the system (agents, environment and infrastructure) to auto-organize, so that the coordination task is finally achieved.

In the following paragraphs, we are going to detail how the Co-Fields model can be realized, by specifying what is a field and how agents interact with the sensed fields.

A field can be defined as a distributed data structure composed by a unique identifier, a value (representing the field magnitude in that particular point), and a propagation rule. Fields can be generated by the agents or by the environment, and are propagated through the *space* as specified by their propagation rule. To support fields' propagation a proper infrastructure or middleware is required. This middleware can be based on an external server in charge of storing fields' values, but it can also be embedded in agents themselves and rely on an ad-hoc (epidemic) communication schema. The final shape of the field surface will be determine both by the field's propagation rule and by the infrastructure topology 1 . Fields can be static or dynamic, basically a field is static if once propagated its magnitude does not change over time; it is dynamic if its magnitude does. A field can be dynamic because for example its source moves and the field, with some propagation delay, changes accordingly its magnitude, or because for example its propagation rule its designed to remain active and to change field value after some time. In a given environment, several different types of fields can exist and be propagated, accordingly to field-specific laws. Application-specific fields can also be defined and spread in an environment by application agents, to support application-specific problems. The achievement of an application-specific coordination task relies on the evaluation of an application-specific *coordination field*, as a combination (e.g., linear) of some of the perceived fields. The coordination field is a new field in itself, and it is built with the goal of encoding in its shape the agent's coordination task. Once a proper coordination field is available, agents can achieve their coordination task by simply following (deterministically or with some probability) the shape of their *coordination field*, as if they were walking upon the *coordination field* associated surface. Basically their actions will be based on following downhill the decrease of the *coordination field*, on following its increase uphill, or on following one of its equipotential lines (see Figure 2). Our view is to consider a Co-Fields based system as a simple dynamical system. Agents are simply seen as balls rolling upon a surface whose shape is described by the coordination field. Complex movements are achieved not because of the agent will, but because dynamic re-shaping of this surface.

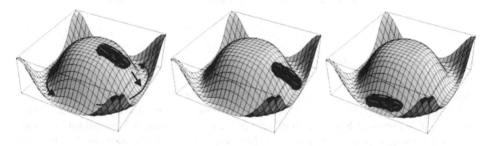

Fig. 2. A car agent following the surface of its coordination field; (left) the agent follows the decrease of its coordination field; (center) the agent follows the increase of its coordination field; (right) the agent follows an equipotential line of its coordination field.

4   Coordinating Mobility in the City with Co-fields

Implementing the Co-Fields' model to the application scenario described in section 2 is straightforward: we assume the presence of a host in each of the city's street and corners, connected with each others accordingly to the city plan, and providing the ability to determine which car is in which place. The networked infrastructure of the city is used to store and propagate different types of fields, representing different aspects of the environment. Agents access the infrastructure by connecting to their closest host. Once connected, an agent can access only to the host's stored fields and to the fields stored in the host's closest neighbors (we will consider one-hop-radius neighbors). In this way a strong locality scope for agent perception and interaction is enforced. Accessing at least a small hosts' neighborhood is required, because agents' movements are based on the locally perceived gradient of a field (see Figure 2) and that gradient can only be determined by evaluating the difference between fields' magnitude in different hosts. To model the coordination problems of the case study the two simple fields described in the next sub-sections are required, to be composed in an application-specific way to achieve the coordination task.

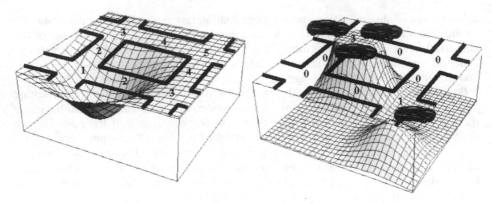

Fig. 3. Street/Corner Fields (**left**). Traffic Field (**right**)

4.1   Street/Corner Field

This is a field generated by every city street/corner. It simply has value 1 in the street/corner that generates it and its value increases as the distance from the source (measured in terms of hops number) increases. In particular, we can simply imagine the field value is increased by 1 at every hop. Figure 3 – left shows a simple city map, with some fields values reported. Because the propagation rule follows a breadth first algorithm, problems related to multiple paths are avoided. The above fields are static and they do not change over time. As it will be clear in the following, the shape of this kind of fields has been chose so that an agent following downhill a room field will inevitably reach the source street or corner.

4.2   Traffic Field

The *traffic-field* measures the amount of traffic in a street/corner, and it is evaluated by considering the cars present in that place (i.e. connected to a certain server). The infrastructure evaluates the traffic field by simply considering the number of cars connected to the infrastructure and normalizing that number to the dimensions of the street/corner (see Figure 3 - right). The traffic field is dynamic and adjusts its values over time, depending on agents' movements. The shape of this field has been chosen so that an agent, following downhill the traffic field, tends to stay away from crowded areas.

4.3   Traffic Management

The aim of this service is to help a user to avoid traffic or queues while visiting the city. We assume that each street/corner in the city propagates the corresponding *street corner field* and that the infrastructure computes the *traffic field* as described above. The model implementation is then quite straightforward: basically each agent evaluates its *coordination field*   as the sum between a minimum combination of the *street corner fields* S in its visit schedule (fields are combined by taking the in each point the minimum one) and the traffic field T .

$$= \min (S_1, S_2, ..., S_n) + \lambda \cdot T$$

The first term of the coordination field, expresses a field surface having its minimum points in correspondence of the street/corners the agent has to visit. So, because each agent follows downhill the coordination field, this term guides the agent to visit the street/corners in its schedule. In order not to get stuck in a minimum, when the user completed the visit of a place, the corresponding field is removed from the combination. The place is thus removed and so it does not represent a minimum anymore. The second term of the coordination field takes into consideration the traffic management. In fact the term $\lambda \cdot T$ with $\lambda \geq 0$ is a field that has its maximum points where the traffic is particularly intense. When this term is added to the minimum combination it changes the steepness of the coordination field in the crowded zones. In particular a crowded zone tends to be a peak in the coordination field and thus it tends to repulse the income of other agents. It is easy in fact to understand that the agent will follow the "greed path" - the one indicated by $\min (S_1, S_2, ..., S_n)$ - only if   decreases towards the same direction indicated by $\min (S_1, S_2, ..., S_n)$. For this reason λ can be regarded as a term specifying the relevance of the traffic field. If λ is too high the agent will suggest the user to follow alternative (possibly longer) uncrowned paths towards the destination whenever the "greed" one will be a bit crowded. If λ is too low the agent will accept always to remain in the "greed" path disregarding the traffic conditions.

To evaluate the performance of the Co-Fields model and its soundness in the traffic management problem, we developed a simulation of the city using the Swarm Simulation Toolkit 19 , a powerful tool for this kind of multi agent system simulation. In particular, we tried a set of simulations in which a group of agents roam the city independently visiting the street/corners in the city according to their schedule. We compared the case in which the agents are interested to the traffic field, and thus the traffic management applies, to the case in which agents are not interested in the traffic field and no traffic management applies (figures 4, 5). The results confirm the effectiveness of the approach and its suitability in managing large multi agent system consisting of more than one hundred agents.

5   Related Works

Several proposals in the last years are challenging the traditional ideas and methodologies of software engineering and inspired to physical, biological models are entering in the distributed application and multi agent system research frameworks. Our Co-Fields model is rooted in this emerging trend.

Fig. 4. Without traffic management (left) large traffic jams appears. These traffic jams are avoided when the traffic management is active (right).

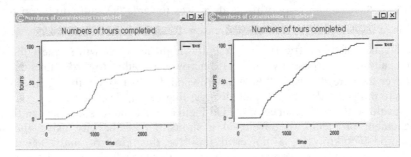

Fig. 5. Performance comparison between the case without traffic management (left) and the case with traffic management (right). The throughput notably increases due to Co-Fields traffic management.

In the next paragraphs we are going to briefly overview some systems that share along with the Co-Fields this physical or biological inspiration, stressing on differences and commonalities. In particular, we think that field based approaches to robotics 10, 12 , the MMASS 2 multi agent systems model and way in which Non Player Characters are controlled in the videogame "The Sims" 17 are those that best match the Co-Fields approach.

In robotics, the idea of potential fields driving robots movement is not new 12 ; one of the most recent re-issue of this idea, the Electric Field Approach (EFA) 10 , has been exploited in the control of a team of Sony Aibo legged robots in the RoboCup domain. Following this approach, each Aibo robot builds a field-based representation of the environment from the images captured by its head mounted camera, and decides its movement by examining the fields' gradients of this representation. Although very close in spirit, EFA and Co-Fields are very different form the implementation point of view: in Co-Fields, fields are distributed data structure actually spread in the environment; in EFA, fields are just an agent internal representation of the environment and they do not actually exists. Co-Fields requires a supporting infrastructure to host fields' data structures, but it completely avoids the complex algorithms involved in field representation and construction

The MMASS formal model for multi-agent coordination, described in 2 , represent the environment as a multi-layered graph in which agents can spread abstract fields representing, different kinds of stimuli, through the nodes of this graph. The agents' behavior is then influenced by the stimuli they perceive in their location. In fact agents can associate reactions to these stimuli, like in an event-based model, but because of the explicit representation of the environment these events and reactions are location dependent. The main difference between this and our approach is that in our approach agents combine perceived fields and are constantly guided by the field produced. In their approach fields tend to be considered separately and they trigger one-shot reactions instead of guiding agents behaviors. Moreover also the application domain is quite different, while we are using this approach for the coordination of a multi agent system in an embedded computing scenario, they are mainly focused on an agent approach to simulation (using a MAS to simulate artificial societies and social phenomena).

Another closely related approach is the one exploited to control the Non Player Character in the videogame "The Sims" 17 . The Sims are characters, living in a virtual world, whose behavior is directed by a happiness landscape : the Sims traverse a spatial landscape of happiness values trying to increase their happiness. Characters behave by climbing gradients of happiness, if they are hungry, their perceive a happiness landscape where things providing food will have higher peaks. So if they happen to be on the slope of a fridge, they will start climbing that slope until getting to the fridge. After eating, all of a sudden the peak will collapse and a new landscape will appear to represent character happiness new requirements 21 . We think that the main difference between this and our approach is that "Sims' happiness fields" tend to be static and generated only by the environment. On the contrary in our approach fields are dynamic and can change over time and agents themselves are able to generate fields and thus a stronger (auto)organizational perspective is enforced.

6   Conclusions and Future Works

In this paper we presented Co-Fields, a new model to coordinate the respective movements of a large number of agents in an environment. The model is based on the concept of computational force fields: distributed data structures providing to the agents an abstraction of the environment in terms of force fields driving agents towards the achievement of specific coordination tasks. A concrete case study has been presented to show the feasibility and the effectiveness of the approach.

Co-Fields main advantages can be summarized as follows:

- In Co-Fields, agents are provided with simple yet effective contextual information, enabling them to coordinate their movements in an implicit and natural way. This makes it possible to automatically adapt the global behavior of a system to the characteristics of a changing or unknown environment;

- Implicit coordination minimizes the agents' efforts in achieving a coordination task, which suits a power limited mobile computing scenario.

Co-Fields main disadvantage is that:

- A general engineered methodology to map a coordination policy into the fields' shape is still missing. Unfortunately, this heavily constrains the kind of coordination problems that can be managed with the Co-Fields approach. This is not a specific problem of our approach and all the described related works suffer from the same problem

Our future work will proceed towards two main directions. On the one hand we are currently completing the definition of a light, micro-kernel, event-based infrastructure 4 , suitable as a supporting middleware for pervasive applications and resource limited devices. Such infrastructure will be used for testing the Co-Fields model in practice. On the other hand, we are trying to extend the field mode. Our perception is that the model can be applied well beyond the case study application described in this paper. For example, it can be applied to guide users visiting a building while carrying personal digital assistants, or in a manufacturing control scenario, to route pieces towards processing machines and optimize the overall throughput. Moreover, the approach could be exploited addressing more general coordination problems that do not deal with some physical movements: in these cases, a coordination field can be thought as spread in an abstract coordination space and agents would follow their coordination fields not by moving, but by doing other kind of actions.

Acknowledgements. Work supported by the Italian MURST in the project "MUSI UE – Infrastructure for oS in Web Multimedia Services with Heterogeneous Access" and by the Nokia Research Center, Boston, USA.

References

1   H. Abelson, D. Allen, D. Coore, C. Hanson, G. Homsy, T. Knight, R. Nagpal, E. Rauch, G. Sussman and R. Weiss, "Amorphous Computing", Communications of the ACM, 43(5), May 2000.

2   S. Bandini, S. Manzoni, C. Simone, "Heterogeneous Agents Situated in Heterogeneous Spaces", 3rd International Symposium From Agent Theories to Agent Implementations, Wien (A), April 2002.

3   F. Bellifemine, A. Poggi, G. Rimassa, "JADE – A FIPA2000 Compliant Agent Development Environment", 5th International Conference on Autonomous Agents (Agents 2001), pp. 216–217, Montreal, Canada, May 2001.

4   G. Cabri, L. Leonardi, M. Mamei, F. Zambonelli, "Engineering Infrastructures for Mobile Organizations", 2nd International Workshop on Engineering Societies in the Agents' World, LNAI No. 2203, Dec. 2001.

5   G. Cabri, L. Leonardi, F. Zambonelli, "Engineering Mobile Agent Applications via Context-Dependent Coordination", IEEE Transactions on Software Engineering, 2002, 28(11):1040:1058, Nov. 2002.

6   G. Cugola, A. Fuggetta, E. De Nitto, "The JEDI Event-based Infrastructure and its Application to the Development of the OPSS WFMS", IEEE Transactions on Software Engineering, 27(9): 827–850, Sept. 2001.

7   E. Freeman, S. Hupfer, K. Arnold, "JavaSpaces Principles, Patterns, and Practice", Addison-Wesley, 1999.
8   A. Howard, M. Mataric, G. Sukhatme, "An Incremental Self-Deployment Algorithm for Mobile Sensor Networks", Autonomous Robots, 13(2):113–126, Sept. 2002.
9   Jini, http://www.jini.org, Sun Microsystems
10   S. Johansson, A. Saffiotti, "Using the Electric Field Approach in the RoboCup Domain", RoboCup 2001: 399–404, Seattle, WA, USA, 2001.
11   JXTA, http://www.jxta.org, Sun Microsystems
12   O. Khatib, "Real-time obstacle avoidance for manipulators and mobile robots", The International Journal of Robotics Research, 5(1):90–98, 1986.
13   C. Mascolo, L. Capra, W. Emmerich, "An XML based Middleware for Peer-to-Peer Computing", In Proc. of the IEEE International Conference of Peer-to-Peer Computing (P2P2001), Linkoping, Sweden, Aug. 2001.
14   A. Omicini, F. Zambonelli, "Coordination for Internet Application Development", Autonomous Agents and Multi-Agent Systems 2(3). Kluwer Academic Publishers, September 1999.
15   H. V. Parunak, S. Brueckner, J Sauter, "ERIM's Approach to Fine-Grained Agents", NASA Workshop on Radical Agent Concepts, Greenbelt, MD, USA, Jan. 2002.
16   G. P. Picco, A. L. Murphy, G. C. Roman, "LIME: Linda Meets Mobility", In Proceedings of the 21st International Conference of Software Engineering (ICSE'99), Los Angeles, USA, May 1999.
17   The Sims, http://thesims.ea.com
18   G. Sussman, "Robust Design through Diversity", DARPA/MIT Amorphous Computing Workshop, September 1999.
19   Swarm Simulation Toolkit, http://www.swrm.org
20   Universal Plug and Play, http://www.upnp.org
21   S. Johnson, "Wild Things", Wired, pp. 78–83, March 2002.
22   F. Zambonelli, V. Parunak, "From Design to Intentions: Sign of a Revolution", 1st International Joint Conference on Autonomous Agents and Multi-agent Systems, Bologna (I), July 2002.
23   F. Zambonelli, M. Mamei, A. Roli, " What Can Cellular Automata Tell Us About the Behavior of Large Multi-Agent Systems ", in this volume.

Sustainable Information Ecosystems

Rune Gustavsson and Martin Fredriksson

Department of Software Engineering and Computer Science,
Blekinge Institute of Technology,
Box 520, S-372 25 Ronneby, Sweden
{rune.gustavsson,martin.fredriksson}@bth.se

Abstract. Fundamental challenges in engineering of large-scale multi-agent systems involve qualitative requirements from, e.g., ambient intelligence and network-centric operations. We claim that we can meet these challenges if we model our multi-agent systems using models of evolutionary aspects of living systems. In current methodologies of multi-agent systems the notion of system evolution is only implicitly addressed, i.e., only closed patterns of interaction are considered as origin of dynamic system behaviour. In this paper we argue that service discovery and conjunction, by means of open patterns of interaction, are the basic tools for sustainable system behaviour. In effect, we introduce a framework for sustainable information ecosystems. Consequently, we describe basic principles of our methodology as well as a couple of applications illustrating our basic ideas. The applications coexist on our supporting agent society platform SOLACE and their respective behaviour is visualized using our system analysis tool DISCERN. The paper is concluded with a summary and a number of open research issues in the area.

1 Introduction

Current approaches for networked information systems with a societal focus can be characterized as emphasizing the notion of coordinated behaviour and openness. Systemic properties, such as trustworthiness, adaptation, and robustness, of these systems are key aspects to address. To that end, we argue that methodological approaches of such systems would benefit from a holistic and context-sensitive framework, i.e., a framework for information ecosystems [5].

Our framework for information ecosystems will allow us to explicitly address important systemic properties of future large-scale multi-agent systems (web of agentfied services), as well as highlighting important mechanisms and models to support dynamics in such systems. We argue that frameworks for complex multi-agent systems should focus on the dynamically changing interdependencies among certain key concepts, and in what way such concepts help us in maintaining what could be described as sustainable system behaviour.

The paper is organized as follows. In Section 2 – *Setting the scene* – we outline three key concepts of computational ecosystems and in what way they are interrelated. That is, the interplay between environment, structures, patterns, and processes. In Section 3 – *Methodological issues* – we introduce the main

A. Garcia et al. (Eds.): SELMAS 2002, LNCS 2603, pp. 123–138, 2003.

concepts of our methodology; an adaptive software development process and components of a methodological approach (focused on a worldview of computational ecosystems). We also identify the importance of the worldview in the concepts of environment and information ecosystems. The section also includes descriptions on developed systems and related research activities.

In Section 4 – *Methodological practice* – we present our current focus on developing tools and platforms to support the relevant concepts of computational ecosystems. In Section 5 – *Sustainable ecosystems* – we address some fundamental issues of information ecosystems, e.g., co-evolution and feedback loops, and discuss the relevance of those concepts in computational ecosystems. In Section 6 – *Information societies* – we introduce some new concepts that allow us to address semantic issues in a proper way.

Then, in Section 7 – *Sustainable information societies* – we follow up on methodological issues raised in earlier sections. Specifically we address issues related to intelligent service conjunction and system dynamics. In Section 8 – *Assessment of methodologies* – we introduce a short comparison of our methodological approach with respect to contemporary agent methodology approaches. Finally, the paper is concluded with Section 9 – *Conclusions and future work* – where the paper is summarized with remarks regarding our current work and a number of suggestions for future work.

2   Setting the Scene

Mainstream system development of today is largely possible to characterize by means of networking. During the last decades we have witnessed a shift of focus from mainframe computing, i.e., via client-server and Internet connectivity models, grid computing, peer-to-peer computing, and web services, towards so called network-centric computing. Prominent examples of the latter system types include ambient intelligence and pervasive computing as well as military applications such as network-centric operations. We can regard this model of system development as guided by a bottom-up system abstraction approach.

We network (smart) equipment and we form networks of networks. As the complexities of the systems increase, we also have to deal with different kinds of vulnerabilities that degrade the systems as well as offers opportunities of adversaries to exploit those vulnerabilities in harmful and even disastrous ways. Moreover, issues of scalability, emergent behavior, and maintenance become more and more pressing to harness in a satisfactory way. From a user point of view, issues of trustworthy systems are becoming a key acceptance factor. A challenging question is how we perceive, design, implement, and maintain these new kinds of network-centric systems. Current approaches of software system engineering are, as we know, not sufficient for many reasons [1][2][11][14][17].

In parallel with the mainstream computing development addressed above, we have also had an almost separate trend guided by a top-down cognitive approach. Here we have a trend from stand alone knowledge-based systems via distributed intelligence problem solving to multi-agent systems. Viewing distributed applications as multi-agent societies allows us to introduce new high-level concepts such as coordination, negotiations, team formations, and contracts in our system modeling. However, most of current agent applications have been closed applications, i.e., agent ensembles that are more or less isolated from the possible influence of other agent's in concurrent network-centric applications. Even here, we have only recently begun to address methodological issues.

We therefore claim that our view of system development and maintenance should undergo a complete reassessment. In order to deal with methodologies for network-centric systems of the kind mentioned above, we suggest the introduction of sustainable computational ecosystems. The concept of information ecosystems refers to coexistence of applications in niches, co-evolution of new applications based on feedback and feed forward loops. Furthermore we will both have cooperation as well as (even hostile) competition. The concept sustainable refers to that we have to introduce and use systemic concepts such as sustainability invariants to guarantee, e.g., trust criteria, or harness emergent behaviour.

3   Methodological Issues

A comprehensive methodology consists of components and processes that aim at delivering a set of products, i.e., systems: *frameworks, theories, models*, and *practices* (see Fig. 1). As a framework for the process model, we use the approach of *Adaptive software development* [6]. We have identified this methodology as particularly suitable since its origins lies in recent ideas of complex adaptive systems, but also since, it has the actual focus of delivering practical results and systems, not just theories and models. As such, the approach supports emergent order in system development, as opposed to the traditional style of an imposed order. Emergent order in system development reflects the type of ecosystem applications we have in mind. In particular, the approach enables us to replace the traditional plan–build–revise model with one of speculate–collaborate–learn (see Fig. 2).

In essence, the framework of *Adaptive software development* specifically addresses the evolutionary adaptation of domain-specific system dynamics and structures in complex software systems. Consequently, we need to introduce specific theories and models of these key aspects of software development. The worldview of a computational ecosystem consists of the environment, structure (components of the information system itself), patterns, and processes.

The figure also indicate that the interaction between the environment and the information system must be trustworthy, meaning that people using the information system must trust that the interactions between the system and the environment give support for relevant interactions with the environment. Patterns and processes support the dynamics of the computational ecosystem at hand. Crucially important is therefore the development of suitable tools that support methodological issues as identified in terms of relevant frameworks, theories, and models.

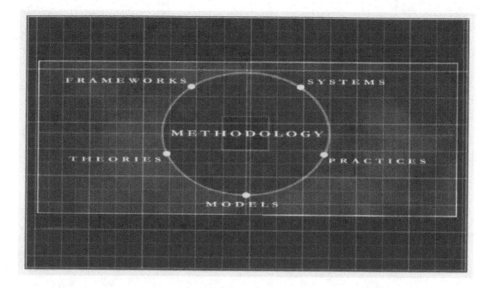

Fig. 1. Methodology - A comprehensive methodology, targeting theoretical as well as practical issues in observation and construction of complex systems, involves the following components: *frameworks, theories, models, practices*, and *systems*.

4   Methodological Practice

The most characteristic requirement of computational ecosystems is a natural support for construction and observation of complex system behavior. We consider construction to be a matter of integration and interaction, i.e., the ability of an agent to enter or leave a particular location in some system and the ability of agents in the system to interact with each other, by means of integration. We must also be able to observe and analyze the fundamental constructs involved in some system, in order to achieve a sustainable behavior by means of instrumentation. In order to address observation and construction of computational ecosystems we have developed two platforms: SOLACE and DISCERN.

4.1   Service-Oriented Layered Architecture for Communicating Entities

We have developed a distributed *Service-oriented layered architecture for communicating entities* (SOLACE), which supports the construction of computational ecosystems. This architecture explicitly supports the abstraction layers of *fabric, system*, and *domain*. We have omitted support of the environment perspective in SOLACE because the architecture as such is only supposed to support the abstract perspectives characterizing constructs that are an integral part of the physical environment. That is, we consider the architecture to be an integral part of the physical environment and not vice versa.

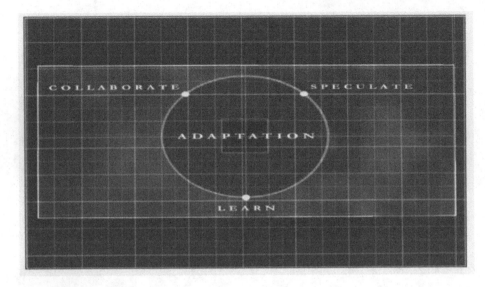

Fig. 2. Adaptation - In the approach of *Adaptive software development*, key components of the evolutionary development process includes the following iterative activities: *collaborate, learn,* and *speculate.*

In terms of current requirements of service-oriented architectures, the fabric layer of computational ecosystems must explicitly account for the notion of scalability and the support for mediation. In doing so, SOLACE provides for the automatic and localized coupling and decoupling of fabric nodes.

We do this by means of multiple classes of broadcast protocols that, at regular intervals, advertise a particular node's existence in the surrounding environment. Nodes that already exist in the environment receive these broadcasts and acknowledge the presence of the signaling node. The platform thereby provides system entities with support for mediation, interaction, and observation, irrespective of their physical locality.

A number of computational entities exist as an integral part of each node in the fabric of computational ecosystems that, by means of mediated interaction, form complex, and dynamic system behavior. By means of the fabric, SOLACE supports each entity – i.e., agent or service – in the continuous feedback loops of articulation, construction, observation, and instrumentation.

As soon as we launch an entity, which temporarily resides on a particular fabric node, it is automatically coupled with and accessible by its neighboring system entities. In essence, our architecture supports all entities at the system level with the essential mechanisms for discovery, addressing, and routing. These mechanisms provide all agents with the support needed by a sustainable information ecosystem.

4.2   Distributed Interaction System for Complex Entity Relation Networks

In practice, observation of some systemic phenomenon aims at acquiring certain quantifications of some domain's characteristic qualities. We can acquire these measurements by means of certain instruments. In addition, we consider these quantifications to be the basis in an actual instrumentation of some particular system under study. We have therefore implemented a *Distributed interaction system for complex entity relation networks* (DISCERN) that explicitly addresses the dynamic and real time observation and instrumentation of computational ecosystems residing on SOLACE. DISCERN enables the observation of qualities and quantities in multiple domains of computational ecosystems.

We consider a layered perspective of qualities in computational ecosystems, in terms of environment, fabric, system, and domain. DISCERN is therefore applied in the observation of domain specific qualities with respect to these four perspectives. However, even though SOLACE does not address the notion of a physical environment, this is of utmost importance in DISCERN in order to immediately provide a human agent and observer with the current context. In a similar manner, the fabric, system, and domain layers of computational ecosystems are represented in DISCERN by means of a volumetric space that is navigable.

In addition to the possibility of a human agent to observe and instrument the qualities of computational ecosystems, DISCERN also provides support of quantification. That is, by means of the constructs accounted for by SOLACE, any quality available in some accessible open computational system can dynamically be quantified and further analyzed in DISCERN. Since DISCERN supports real time observation and instrumentation of computational ecosystems, the quantities acquired in some particular context can be used in further studies on automated analysis and in the continuous feedback loop of articulation, construction, observation, and instrumentation.

4.3   Challenges

In addressing issues of sustainable information ecosystems, we consider platform efficiency in providing support for service discovery (observation) and service conjunction (construction) to be crucial design issues. Consequently, we envision typical processes of evolution in the system as comprised by the following scenario.

> "A lookup service receives a service request, which initiates a search for matching services. The lookup service matches the resulting set against specific constraints and, if necessary, the identified services are adapted for reuse. After this procedure of adaptation, service conjunction takes place. Finally, due to possible side effects of service conjunction, the lookup service initiates system administration."

Effective processing of service conjunction requires distributed lookup services with agent capabilities and services that are possible to match with each other. An open question is therefore the performance tradeoffs of intelligence between the lookup services and the complexity in service descriptions. Techniques for (partial) pattern matching and dialogue management are crucial for effective support of the processes outlined above.

To address those topics we evaluate techniques developed within semantic web efforts, e.g., XML for content, RDF for meta-information, and OIL for processing and reasoning. Efficient processing of service discovery in a setting of distributed lookup services is also crucial. Here we investigate search algorithms and caching mechanisms developed in peer-to-peer architectures.

4.4   Experimentation

With a strong focus on theory in practice, we argue that the challenges and proposed support for practical aspects of a methodological approach has to be validated in real life application domains. Consequently, we are currently addressing and evaluating the previously outlined challenges by means of support for service discovery and conjunction in two separate application domains executing in the form of two concurrent systems on SOLACE. We have developed two systems: *Conceptual demonstrator for network services* (CONDENS) and *Delegation and interaction in care environments* (DICE).

Research and development of information systems for defence and warfare have changed most dramatically during the last decade; from weapons of mass destruction to sustainable systems of services, i.e. network-centric warfare. Consequently, at the core of CONDENS is the development of a sustainable multiagent system where interacting entities and services temporarily come together in a physical setting; in order to perform a particular assignment under dynamic and hostile conditions. In essence, the system developed is subject to a validation of qualities such as scale, dynamics, and perception.

Treatment of elderly people and citizens in need of professional care is one of the most important aspects of any society to consider, i.e., proactive support for citizens' quality of life. However, since the involved organizations to a great extent are of a centralized nature, patients need to transport themselves to the hospital in order to receive treatment. If the organizations could be decentralized and still reach out to patients in need of treatment, this would be of great benefit for all of the involved parties.

Consequently, we are currently developing a system for *Delegation and interaction in care environments* (DICE), where interacting and coordinated entities and services temporarily come together in a physical setting; in order to perform sustainable and effective behaviour under dynamic and life-dependent conditions. In essence, the system developed is subject to a validation of qualities such as information fusion, coordination, and normative constraints.

By means of DISCERN we can analyze and interact with both systems via a distributed set of observation services. Furthermore, we govern the behavior of both CONDENS and DICE by means of instantiating patterns on the appropriate levels of system structures (see Fig. 3). This arrangement provides us

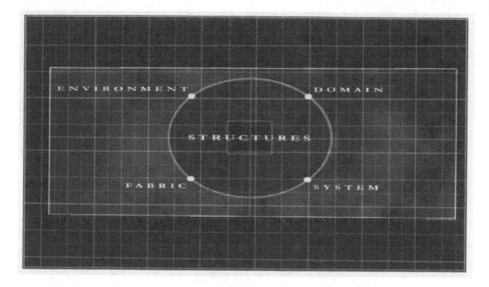

Fig. 3. Structures - The structures undergoing continuous evolution and adaptation in complex software systems can be considered in terms of their *environment, fabric, system,* and *domain.*

with systems that are open with respect to several criteria as well as robust and scalable.

5   Sustainable Ecosystems

The introduction of sustainable information ecosystems is to explicitly support a methodology for what we believe to be the next generation of qualitative requirements in engineering of large-scale multi-agent systems behaviour. In doing so, we emphasize the three components of system dynamics (structures, processes, and patterns), as well as the four components of system structures (environment, fabric, system, and domain). In combination with each other these components of a methodology for information ecosystem reflect ideas from general system theories, especially with respect to theories about living systems, i.e., autopoesis [10].

The structure of a living organism is continuously changing according to regulatory processes, e.g., ageing. Such processes are by nature constrained by systemic invariant criteria that in effect maintain the existence of organisms. In this holistic context we consider patterns to hold the generic descriptions of a particular system. Furthermore, we treat grounding of patterns in terms of physical structures that undergo change by means of certain processes. The notion of controlled feedback loops is an important type of pattern in information societies, as they capture the principles of regulated and coordinated information flows and exchange between organizations, technologies, and users (see Fig. 4).

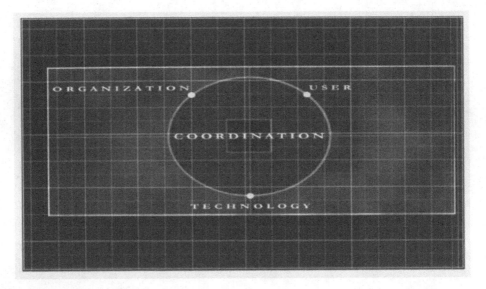

Fig. 4. Coordination - Key concepts and interdependencies in coordinated adaptation and evolution of sustainable information ecosystems typically involves *organizations, technologies*, and *users*.

We claim that the metaphors above, concerning living systems, can be reinterpreted and applied to system characteristics of information ecosystems and information societies. Furthermore, important requirements on systemic properties can be formulated in terms of sustainability criteria that guide us in introduction of information systems in societal contexts.

The introduction of a new information technology in an environment should, e.g., maintain and respect individual users by means of trustworthy computational ecologies. A challenge is, consequently, to develop and respect certain (open) patterns of interaction for a particular type of information society. We argue that multi-agent technologies are key enablers in the design and maintenance of such systems and mechanisms.

A framework for information ecologies as defined in [12] is comprised by the following key concepts: people, practices, values, technologies, and places. This corresponds to the environment component of our view on structures in computational ecosystems (see Fig. 5). In [12], contrary to our view, the information system itself is not in focus. In essence, our computational ecosystems consist of an environment component (the information ecology in [12]) and an information system component.

It should be noted that all of the involved concepts typically reflect a qualitative perspective on system behaviour, but also that the manifestations of these concepts are considered as situated in some particular local and physical environment. Therefore, information ecosystems are characterized as being adaptive and open systems (external flow is the primary qualitative constraint of behaviour).

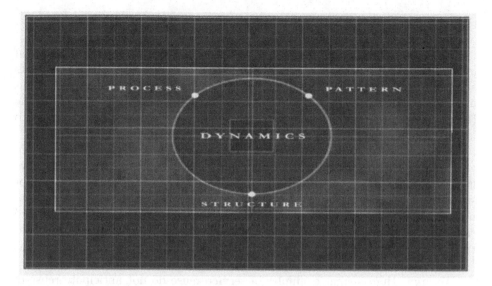

Fig. 5. Dynamics - In sustainable information ecosystems, we consider the dynamics taking place in terms of open *structures*, *processes*, and *patterns*.

Consequently, an aspect of information ecosystems of utmost concern is their evolutionary mechanisms, e.g., feedback and existence (survival of the fittest or, more relevant in our cases, arrival of the fittest). That is, required capabilities of constituents in information ecosystems are continuous assessment of current situations by means of observing patterns of interaction and, consequently, adaptation by means of constructing patterns of interaction.

Due to the complexity of an information ecosystem, i.e., constituents and interdependencies, they can be modelled as universal information ecosystems.[1] From an organizational perspective, multi-agent systems have proven themselves to be a quite successful metaphor in design and implementation of societal and networked information systems [8].

However, it should be noted that current methodologies of multi-agent systems mainly consider applications of a closed nature, i.e., system constituents and interactions are modelled as affected only by closed patterns of interaction, e.g., auction protocols in computational markets. In essence, this situation occur when we model systemic properties to be formed by agent ensembles that are more or less isolated from the possible influence of other agent's in concurrent network-centric applications.

From a holistic perspective this corresponds to a situation where system evolution only occurs as a result from dynamic interaction, according to a predefined pattern of interaction. Still, system evolution is necessarily also comprised by situations where the (interacting) constituents of a particular system undergo a continuous change – triggered by external factors – in order to survive. In cur-

---

[1] http://www.cordis.lu/ist/fetuie.htm

rent methodologies of multi-agent systems the notion of system adaptation is, consequently, only implicitly addressed.

We argue that in dealing with large-scale multi-agent systems and universal information ecosystems of an open nature, i.e., when both system constituents and interactions are evolving by means of open patterns of interaction, current methodologies for multi-agent systems are no longer sufficient in capturing the (holistic) notion of system evolution [3]. This is also the case when it comes to identification and maintenance of systemic invariants (sustainability criteria).

To meet the sustainability criteria of constructing patterns of interaction, as a result from observation and assessment, service-oriented architectures have lately been proposed by several proponents, e.g., Microsoft's .NET. The major strength of such architectures has been advocated in terms of their effectiveness of runtime insertion and exclusion of particular services, e.g., printers and cameras. However, this is a typical example of system constituents that by nature do not evolve. That is, reuse of services is hampered by service descriptions (patterns) that are defined by a particular service designer at design time.

We argue that current examples of service reuse do not anticipate reuse of services from perspectives other than that originally intended by their designer. Adaptation and sustainability of services is at the moment mostly a coincidental result from demonstrating the only possible reuse of physically grounded services (c.f. a printer is a printer and can only be reused as a printer).

A problematic situation of system (service) adaptation occurs when our conception of some particular service changes and we have no apparent way of relating the designers service description to the new context at hand. To meet the challenge of service reuse we advocate a decoupling of design–use into design–affordance–use. That is, we argue that the actual added value of some service must be explicated at design time, but also that this description of the service typically will change during its lifetime and therefore needs to be dynamic in nature. In practice, this decoupling[2] is manifested by a cognitive decomposition of the universal information ecosystem into the abstraction levels of *environment*, *fabric*, *system*, and *domain* [3] (see Fig. 3).

6 Information Societies

In essence, a purposeful and principled reuse of system components, e.g., web of services in complex networked environments, requires what we could characterise as a systemic approach to evolution. That is, harnessing enabling technologies – such as network-centric applications, service-oriented architectures, and new models of connectivity – into opportunities to create new applications. But also to, in the process of engineering such systems, make sure that they fulfil both functional properties as well as non-functional qualities, e.g., engineering trustworthy multi-agent systems.

---

[2] Consider Newell's introduction of the knowledge level for knowledge-based systems, enabling reuse of problem solving methods and application domains [13].

In order to identify and engineer such properties and qualities we have to proceed in a systematic way. In short, we have to address the complexity of information ecosystems embedded in our societal fabric. In this endeavour we consider adaptation and grounding to be of utmost importance to address.

Firstly, application generation in ecologies typically means reuse and adaptation of components and services. Secondly, in order to ground the application in a trustworthy way we start by identifying a suitable model of the environment (typically by means of a three-dimensional ortographic projection in DISCERN) to ground our system components of fabric, system, and domain.

To that end we extend the concept of information ecologies by adding system components of organisations and their coordination mechanisms, e.g., societal constructs such as institutions, communities, norms, and roles. In short, we aim at an information society [4]. Issues regarding how we can utilize and manage the full potential of smart and networked technology embedded in our societal systems, and how we can support a shift of focus from products and applications to adaptable services, can be reformulated in terms of articulation, construction, observation, and instrumentation of sustainability in dependable systems, i.e., information societies.

The introduction of societies and communities allows us also to introduce a semantic closure of our systems. Given this semantic closure we can have more intelligent services and support systems. It will also enable us to formulate semantically sensitive patterns of interaction (see Fig. 5). Using this we can, for instance, increase security and integrity by imposing semantic constraints on availability and access, thus extending for instance the traditional syntactic role-based access control.

7   Sustainable Information Societies

Information societies have to deal with dysfunctional behaviour of users and systems as well as with the positive side of life. A particular threat to trustworthiness in information societies is the notion of evolutionary aspects of security and integrity in network-centric information ecosystems. It is well known that information security is and ongoing process of information warfare, including feedback loops in terms of interaction patterns of protection–detection–response processes.

This is but one reason why we advocate a methodological approach that supports construction and observation activities of the universal information ecosystem, e.g., design and maintenance, to support sustainable information ecosystems. The evolutionary activities of construction and observation concern all abstraction levels of a universal information ecosystem's structures, and are therefore considered as crucial tools in sustainability of invariance criteria.

As such, sustainability is expressed in terms of invariance of system qualities, e.g., trustworthiness, respect of certain values, or profitability. Still, the notion of sustainability requires a basic set of system tools that support observation and construction of the real system. We argue that the foremost of such tools, required for runtime sustainability, is that of service conjunction.

Service conjunction is a basic tool for (evolutionary) creation and adaptation of new services and sustainability in service provisioning. However, it should be noted that the tool is highly context-dependent. An evolutionary approach towards service conjunction requires, as we previously stated a decoupling of the design–use pair. Consequently, we advocate a structural shift from a system–infrastructure view into domain–system–fabric–environment view (see Fig. 5).

As such, this decoupling allows us to introduce a more flexible and informed approach towards service conjunction and reuse. In principle, the basic procedure involved in adaptation and dynamics of information ecosystems encompasses the following key concepts: structures, patterns, and processes. Consequently, we argue that sustainable system adaptation and evolution involves the following considerations:

- *Structure adaptation.* We need to remove context-dependent descriptions of physical components, if we want to identify and reuse them in new contexts, i.e., aiming at sustainable structures
- *Pattern adaptation.* We need to remove closed patterns of interaction if we want to reuse (partial) patterns in new contexts, i.e., aiming at supporting sustainable ecologies.
- *Process adaptation.* We need to remove static processes of service assembly if we want to make particular species of behaviour survive in continuously changing environments, i.e. aiming at sustainable processes.

In summary, the notion of sustainable information ecosystems emphasizes the need for qualitative services and automated reuse of them, by means of informed mechanisms for context assessment and service conjunction as an integrated ability of each and every service / agent.

8   Assessment of Methodologies

In this section we briefly assess other methodological approaches towards multi-agent systems. Recent approaches include GAIA and ROADMAP [16][19][18][9]. Overviews and comparisons of different agent methodologies from different aspects have also appeared [7][15]. A common feature of current agent methodologies is that they are in reality partial theories with respect to the methodology (see Fig. 1).

Typically the process view is only rudimentary addressed if at all. Also there is typically no explicit identification of the underlying models, theories, or systems. Since there never has been or will be an all-encompassing methodology suitable for all kind of systems (we already have specific methodologies for, e.g., real time systems or database systems) such explicit constraints are essential in choosing proper models and tools.

Again referring to Fig. 1, most of the current set of agent methodologies implicitly addresses specific or preferable formal models, in order to validate certain aspects of the implicit agent systems at hand. Moreover, current methodologies aims at developing individual systems (in a top-down approach) that is, at least implicitly, isolated (closed) systems. The ROADMAP approach, however, extends the GAIA model to cover some of its shortcomings with respect to openness and practical support from tools and platforms.

It should be noted that our proposed methodology is rather a framework with the following messages. In system development, or rather service development, in a computational ecology it is important to identify the whole range of proper frameworks, theories, models, and best practice with respect to a specific goal system.

Given these methodological constraints we can then address the adaptation of systemic structures, processes, and patterns. A first step in identifying the proper methodological components is, consequently, to address the goal system's environment. After this, we can start to identify a proper set of sustainability invariants (methodological conflicts can effectively be resolved at this point).

Examples of related theory and model components of our methodology for construction and observation of sustainable information ecosystems can be found in the following areas of research: economic theories, risk management theories, activity theory, software engineering, and social and cognitive science. Given these different theories and models it is important to have a common methodological framework to coordinate and orchestrate the different efforts.

9   Conclusions and Future Work

We argue that contemporary approaches to research and development of large-scale multi-agent and service-oriented systems does not provide the proper methodologies and tools for service conjunction in a scalable manner. To that end, we have introduced an information ecosystems approach towards understanding and maintenance of ensembles of large-scale multi-agent systems. We also propose systemic sustainability invariants as the means for adaptation of information societies.

An information ecosystem approach presupposes tools for observation and construction, specifically for sustainable service conjunction and system evolution. Much work remains in order to validate our approach. However, experiments on our SOLACE platform and the DISCERN visualization tool have been very promising. The next step involves implementation of more advanced scenarios and complex services together with our industrial partners (civilian as well as defense-oriented).

Acknowledgements. The authors would like to acknowledge the substantial development efforts provided by the personnel at *Societies of computation laboratory* (SOCLAB).[3] Furthermore, it should be noted that the development of

---

[3] http://www.soclab.bth.se.

SOLACE, DISCERN, CONDENS, and DICE in part was funded by a national research project called *Service-oriented trustworthy distributed systems* (SOTDS). Industrial partners in the project include KOCKUMS and GATESPACE.

References

1. Blair, G., Coulson, G., Robin, and Papathomas, M. (1998) An Architecture for Next Generation Middleware. In *Proceedings of Middleware '98*. The Lake District, England.
2. Dertouzos, M. (1999). *The future of computing*. Scientific American.
3. Fredriksson, M. and Gustavsson, R. (2002) Theory and practice of behavior in open computational systems. In Müller, J. P. and Petta, P. (eds.) *From agent theory to agent implementation*. AT2AI3.
4. Gustavsson, R. and Fredriksson, M. (2002) Humans and complex systems: Sustainable information societies. In Olsson, M. O. and Sjöstedt, G. (eds.) *Revealing complex structures: Challenges for Swedish systems analysis*. FORMAS.
5. Gustavsson, R. and Fredriksson, M. (2001) Coordination and control of computational ecosystems: A vision of the future. In Omicini, A., Zambonelli, F., Klusch, M., and Tolksdorf, R. (eds.) *Coordination of Internet agents: Models, technologies, and applications*, pp. 443–469. Springer Verlag.
6. Highsmith III, J. A. (2000) Adaptive Software Development. In *A Collaborative Approach to Managing Complex Systems*. Dorset House Publishing Co., Dorset. ISBN 0-932633-40-4.
7. Iglesias, C., Garijo, M, and Gonzales, J. (1999). A Survey of Agent-Oriented Methodologies. In *Intelligent Agents V – Proceedings of the Fifth International Workshop on Agent Theories, Architectures, and Languages (ATAL-98)*. Lecture Notes in Artificial Intelligence, Springer-Verlag, Heidelberg.
8. Jennings, N. R. (1999) Agent-based computing: Promise and perils. In *Proceedings of Sixteenth international joint conference on Artificial intelligence*, pp. 1429–1436.
9. Juan, T., Pearce, A., and Sterling, L. (2002). ROADMAP: Extending the Gaia Methodology for Complex Open Systems. In *Proceedings of the First International Joint Conference on Autonomous Agents and Multi-Agent Systems, AAMAS 2002*, ACM Press, 3–10.
10. Maturana, H. and Varela, F. (1980) Autopoesis and cognition. D. Reidel, Dortrecht, Holland, 1980.
11. Milnar, N., Gray, M., Roup, O., Kirkorian, R., and Maes, P. (1999). Hive: Distributed Agents for Networking Things. In *Proceedings of ASA/MA'99*.
12. Nardi, B. A. and O'Day, V. L. (1999) *Information ecologies: Using technology with heart*. The MIT Press. ISBN 0-262-14066-7.
13. Newell, A. (1982) The Knowledge level. In *Artificial intelligence*, no. 18, pp. 87–127.
14. Waldo, J. (1999). The Jini Architecture for Network-centric Computing. In *Communications of the ACM*, 76–82.
15. Wooldridge, M and Ciancarni, P. (2001). Agent-Oriented Software Engineering: The State of the Art. In Ciancarni, P and Wooldridge, M. (eds.) *Agent-Oriented Software Engineering*, Springer-Verlag Lecture Notes in AI, Volume 1957.
16. Wooldridge, M., Jennings, N., and Kinny; D. (2000) The Gaia Methodology for Agent-Oriented Analysis and Design. In *Journal of Autonomous Agents and Multi-Agent Systems*, 3 (3), 25–312.

17. Yokete, Y. (1992). The Apertos Reflective Operating System: The Concept and its Implementation. In *Proceedings of OOPSALA'92*, ACM, 414–434.
18. Zambonelli, F., Jennings, N., Omnicini, A., and Wooldridge M. (2001) Agent-Oriented Software Engineering for Internet Applications. In A. Omicini, F. Zambonelli, M. Klusch, and R. Tolksdorf (eds.) *Coordination of Internet Agents*, Springer-Verlag, 326–346.
19. Zambonelli, F., Jennings, N., and Wooldridge, M. (2000) Organisational Abstractions for the Analysis and Design of Multi-Agent Systems. In *Proceedings of First International Workshop on Agent-Oriented Software Engineering*, Limerick, Ireland, 127–141.

Achieving the Promise of Reuse with Agent Components

Martin L. Griss[1] and Robert R. Kessler[2]

[1] Computer Science Department 349BE, University of California, Santa Cruz
1156 High Street, Santa Cruz, CA 95064
griss@soe.ucsc.edu
http://www.soe.ucsc.edu/~griss
[2] University of Utah, School of Computing, 50 S. Central Campus Dr. 3190,
Salt Lake City, UT USA 84112
kessler@cs.utah.edu

Abstract. Using software agents as next generation flexible components and applying reuse technologies to rapidly construct agents and agent systems have great promise to improve application and system construction. Whether built on conventional distributed computing and application management platforms, on a specialized agent platform, on web service technology or within a P2P infrastructure, agents are a good match for independent development, for scalable and robust systems and dynamic evolution of features, and for autonomic self-managing systems. In this paper we describe the vision and progress we have made towards developing a robust infrastructure, methods, and tools for this goal.

1 Introduction

For some time now, component-based software engineering (CBSE) has promised, and indeed delivered, significant improvements in software development 1 . Greater reuse, improved agility and quality are accessible benefits. CBSE produces a set of reusable assets (usually components) that can be combined to obtain a high-level of reuse while developing members of a product-line or application family. Typically, one first performs domain analysis to understand and model commonality and variability in the domains underlying the product-line, and then a layered modular architecture is defined, specifying layers and core components, key subsystems and mechanisms. Finally, high-level specifications and interfaces are defined for pluggable or generated components. Implementation begins with the development or selection of a framework that implements one or more layers of the architecture. Delivering the reuse potential as a well-designed domain-specific kit carefully allocates variability to a combination of components, frameworks, problem-oriented languages, generators and custom tools 2 .

Once this is done, components can be (largely) independently developed, or in closely related sets, doing detailed design and careful implementation of components and generator templates. Sometimes, when defects are to be repaired or new features

A. Garcia et al. (Eds.): SELMAS 2002, LNCS 2603, pp. 139–147, 2003.

added, it is a simple matter of enhancing a component or developing a new conforming component. However, at other times, the architecture has to be changed, new interfaces must be defined, and change ripples to many components.

Software agents offer great promise to build loosely-coupled, dynamically adaptive systems on increasingly pervasive message-based middleware, P2P and component technology, Java, XML, SOAP and HTTP 3 . Agents are specialized kinds of distributed components, offering greater flexibility than traditional components. There are many kinds of software agents, with differing characteristics such as mobility, autonomy, collaboration, persistence, and intelligence. Research in our group, previously at Hewlett-Packard Laboratories 4 , 5 , and now at UC Santa Cruz in collaboration with the University of Utah, is directed at the use of multi-agent systems in the engineering of complex, adaptive software systems. An important step is to simplify and improve the engineering and application of industrial-strength multi-agent systems and intelligent web-services to this problem. The research integrates several different areas, combining multi-agent systems, component-based software engineering, model-driven software reuse, web-services, and intelligent software.

In this paper, we will highlight some of the issues and our progress involved in making this step toward more robust, scalable and evolutionary systems using agent components and reuse techniques.

2 Multi-agent Systems

Multi-agent based systems have several characteristics that support the development of flexible, evolving applications, such as those behind E-commerce and web-service applications. Agents can dynamically discover and compose services and mediate interactions. Agents can serve as delegates to handle routine affairs, monitor activities, set up contracts, execute business processes, and find the best services 6 . Agents can manage context- and location-aware notifications and pursue tasks. Agents can use the latest web-based technologies, such as Java, XML and HTTP, UDDI, SOAP and WSDL. These technologies are simple to use, ubiquitous, heterogeneous and platform neutral. XML will become the standard language for agent-oriented interaction, to encode exchanged messages, documents, invoices, orders, service descriptions and other information 7 , 8 . HTTP, the dominant WWW protocol, provides many services, such as robust and scalable web servers, firewall access and levels of security.

An overview of agent capabilities from a large-scale AOSE/CBSE perspective can be found in books (9 , 10 , 11), papers (6 , 12 , 13 , 14 , 15) and web sites (http://agents.umbc.edu/ , http://www.hpl.hp.com/reuse/agents).

While there are many definitions of agents, many people agree that: *an autonomous software agent is a component that interacts with its en ironment and with other agents on a user's behalf*   Some definitions emphasize one or another aspects such as mobility, collaboration, intelligence or flexible user interaction. Organizations such as FIPA (Foundation for Intelligent Physical Agents) are defining reference models mechanisms and agent communication language standards 16 .

There are several different kinds of agent system 17 ; our work at Hewlett-Packard Laboratories 4 focused on two types of agents:

- **Personal agents** interact directly with the user, presenting some personality or social skills, perhaps as an anthropomorphic character, monitoring and adapting to the user's activities, learning the user's style and preferences, and automating or simplifying certain rote tasks.   Examples include meeting scheduling agents, mail agents, software development, etc.

- **Collaborative agents** communicate and interact in groups, representing users, organizations and services. Multiple agents exchange messages to negotiate, share information, etc. Examples include online auctions, planning, negotiation, logistics and supply chain and telecom service provisioning.

In particular, in our prototyping we use personal agents as 24/7 user representatives to find, organize and interact with a set of collaborating team and service agents for meeting arrangers, e-commerce systems and email management 4 , 5 .

Many varieties of agent system and toolkits have been developed and described in the literature or on the web. Recently, even numerous Java-based, FIPA compliant systems are seeing use in the wider community. We have done most of our work using two Java-based toolkits: ZEUS 18 and JADE 19 .

In the rest of the paper, we discuss agents as next-generation components and discuss some features and variants appropriate to the integration of reuse and agent technologies. We then discuss our research program and summarize the progress we have made to date, with an emphasis on our latest results in model-driven agent behavior choreography.

3 Agents as Next Generation Components

Multi-agent systems have a number of features that make them attractive for highly dynamic, evolving applications, in which a multiplicity of external systems, services, users, appliances and developers interact and change. These features are related to those of components, web services, workflow, and rule-based systems, but in combination provide a distinct software engineering capability. Agent systems are described with many different sets of features; the ones we find most compelling, and plan to exploit and extend in our research are discussed in detail in 17 , 20 , 21 where we provide a graphical model and discuss several of the characteristics of a typical agent system. As indicated, the more of each of these attributes, the more agent-like the component system becomes, and the more appropriate the use of an Agent-Oriented Software Engineering (AOSE) approach. These characteristics are supported by mechanisms and interfaces in the underlying infrastructure, as well as by models and policies configured in each agent or group of agents.

The key aspects that make agents suitable as next generation components 3 , 17 , include:

- **Loosely coupled, message-oriented.** The components conform to a message-oriented rather than method-oriented framework. As components, they have a dynamic component lifecycle; as agents, they can introspect on their own state, leading to some degree of self-management, and negotiate with other agent-components for services. The coupling is loose, similar to that obtained with a software bus; typically agents are not built assuming the existence of other specific components. Services are invoked by sending messages, and multiple agents can respond to those messages, or an appropriate agent found by searching for them dynamically, and have alternative strategies and exception handling for coping with the absence of a needed agent service. Dynamic registration and discovery of components by name and features, and the loose coupling are a much greater degree of independent development. A new agent can be loaded and activated while the system is running, and can be found on next lookup.

- **Reactive and proactive autonomy** – Agents pursue their own agendas of activities, and respond to and initiate asynchronous events. Typically they have explicit representations of goals, tasks, priorities, plans, and so can make quite significant adjustments in behaviors when exceptional conditions are discovered, if other agents disappear, or if they refuse to respond. The key is to treat an agent as a collection of reactive behaviors, not just a collection of methods. Agent communication languages and protocols provide a clear framework and expectation of errors, timeouts and service refusals that are to be explicitly handled.
- **Collaboration and coordination** – Techniques and models to choreograph a planned or *ad hoc* society of agents. These include workflow, and state machines, sub-goal delegation and management. Most interesting is emergent behavior as new agents are added, discover each other, and a growing capability.
- **Adaptability and intelligence** – Agents can learn from experience, and adjust themselves to changing situations. We have explored a tasteful integration of machine learning, rule-based and information retrieval techniques, with a blackboard/event-bus style coordination of independent elements.
- **Other salient attributes** – Each agent can be responsible for autonomic self-management, load balancing, etc. We can exploit component and reuse technologies such as frameworks, patterns, generators, and aspects to build individual agents and compatible societies of agents. In particular, the decomposition of behaviors and corresponding protocols across members of a multi-agent society are amenable to a natural aspect-oriented realization.

Agent-oriented software development extends conventional component development, promising more flexible componentized systems, less design and implementation time, and decreased coupling between the agents. In the same way that models, collaborations, interaction diagrams, patterns and aspect-oriented programming help build more robust and flexible component and component systems, the same techniques can be applied to agent components and agent systems 10 , 13 , 14 , 20 , 22 , 23

Agent infrastructures provide services and mechanisms so that agents have fewer yet richer interfaces, increasing opportunities for dynamic composition. Agent-oriented programming (AOP) 15 , and methods such as GAIA 14 decomposes large complex distributed systems into relatively autonomous agents, each driven by a set of beliefs, desires and intentions (BDI). An agent-oriented developer creates a set of agents (with different beliefs and goals) that collaborate among themselves by exchanging carefully structured messages.

4 Progress Towards Reuse Engineering with Agent Components

Our vision is fairly ambitious, and thus we report on a work in progress so far. We do not yet have a complete, coherent solution. Our research agenda towards the systematic integration of reuse and agent technology has two primary goals:

- Treating software agents as loosely-coupled next-generation components. This yields components and frameworks that are more flexible, adaptable, robust and self-managing, combining agents, workflow and services. We build on existing agent systems, standards and infrastructure such as JADE, ZEUS, FIPA, JAS and J2EE.
- Applying software reuse and model-driven development techniques to the rapid and problem-specific construction of multi-agent systems. This exploits combinations of technologies such as customizable components, patterns, micro-frameworks, aspect-oriented composition, domain-specific kits, generators, visual-builders and use of UML to generate multi-agent protocols and behaviors, and complete agent systems.

Work so far has comprised several threads, and produced several results:

- Developing a robust, industrial-strength infrastructure for agent operations; this has been done by delivering our agents as compatible services in a J2EE environment, producing a system called BlueJADE 24 , 25 .
- Developing UML-based tools, and some UML extensions to model groups of agents and the protocols between agents 22 . We will discuss this recent work in more detail in the next section.
- We have analyzed the multi-agent architectures and behavior engines of several agent platforms, notably ZEUS, JADE and FIPA-OS 26 , 27 and are now ready to embark on a refactoring and reengineering of these systems to make the basic parts more reusable and composable. Some guidance is provided by the Java Agent Specification (*http c s sourceforge net cgi-bin iewc s cgi as*
- We are developing a more complete reuse-based model-driven methodology, integrating feature-oriented domain-analysis and use-case driven development to model families of systems, followed by a combination of patterns for collaborations, component-based and aspect-oriented generation of components 20 . This leads to a highly incremental development model, which deals with both agent societies and individual agents.

5 Model-Driven Agent Behavior Choreography

A key mechanism that makes multi-agent systems highly flexible, but initially more complex, is the interaction between agents using structured messages. Instead of the interaction between agent components being described by multiple, distinct interfaces defined using an IDL, a standard *agent communication language* (ACL) is used through a single interface.

A component-interface contains a syntactic description of each method, its parameter names and types, return values, and possible exceptions; typically the semantics is implicit, and must be understood from documentation. Instead of defining many interfaces and methods, the agent approach is to use a simple interface with more complex, structured messages. These messages can be extended dynamically as the system evolves, avoiding a costly re-design and re-implementation.

Of extreme interest in this message-based multi-agent setting is how to coordinate the interactions in the form of message-exchange between multiple agents. While some agents are used individually, groups of agents can collaborate to perform more complex tasks. For example, to purchase books, a group of agents will exchange messages in a conversation to find the best deal, bid in an auction, arrange financing, select a shipper, and track the order. Other B2B interactions include service provisioning, supply chain, negotiation, and fulfillment. The grouping can be static or dynamic. The conversation can be between people and agents, or between agent and agent, or a mix. Groups can be statically or dynamically determined.

We need to coordinate the interactions between the agents to achieve a higher-level task, such as requesting, offering and accepting a contract for some services. We call this choreography or conversation management." An agent group will have a series of stylized message exchanges to accomplish this task, perhaps by advertising and using a brokered service, bidding during an auction, responding to a call for proposals, or negotiating a price.

There are several possible levels of choreography of the expected message sequences, depending on the need for a relatively loose or more tight control of allowed interactions 17 , ranging from built-in handling of certain conditions such as time-outs and exceptions, to rule-based systems, and state-machines and workflow for protocols. While earlier work combined workflow and agents 21 , 28 , 29 , we have most recently focused on combining rules and hierarchical state machines.

- *ules* - A set of rules can be defined for any agent, or community of agents. For example, to determine how long to wait for a response, the number of other agents an agent can talk to at one time, and what sort of responses to make to a specific message from various types of agent. Not all request/response patterns are constrained by the rules; rules can be used where appropriate to select which messages to respond to, and how to respond. A standard rule language can be used, such as the forward chaining rule system provided by ZEUS 18 , or our use of Jess™ with JADE.

- *on ersation protocols* - Often a group of agents must lock-step through a standard protocol of messages; if A says x then B says y . For example, bidding during an auction, or responding to a call for proposals. These protocols can be expressed as FIPA protocol diagrams, UML interaction diagrams, finite state machines, UML state charts or Petri-nets. Each participant can have the same or a compatible model, stepped through explicitly to determine the action and response any incoming message. Our work has used UML state charts 22 .

Our current approach uses hierarchical state machines to define the detailed flow of messages, rules to act as message filters, and a rule-based flexible action language for the semantics. Rather than extending interaction diagrams, as done in AUML, we have directly used hierarchical UML State Machines, embedding an event-driven state machine engine within the JADE behavior mechanisms. We developed a visual tool (using Visio) and a set of Java templates and libraries that allow us to completely generate agent behavior code from a UML model 22 . One of the primary benefits of full hierarchical state machines is that we can neatly factor typical exceptional and common timeout behaviors into surrounding composite states, allowing the nested state to focus on the main part of the protocol. We are now working on a way of generating a set of agents and a set of compatible protocol parts by hierarchically decomposing a single state machine describing the agent society into a set of independent state machines. A reengineered version of this event-driven, state machine behavior engine and generator will be released to the JADE community early in 2003.

6 Related Work

AUML 13 extends UML with enhanced interaction diagrams to make more explicit some of the message and protocol handling. UML models of vocabularies, workflow, role diagrams, patterns, and feature trees will drive aspect-oriented generators to create highly customized agent systems 20 , 23 , The Iconic Modeling Tool 30 uses visual techniques and UML to assemble and control mobile agent programs and itinerary, using a variant of interaction diagrams to show connections.

Agents and workflow can perform a range of simple or complex workflow- like tasks, such as automatic notification via email of the availability of a report, sending a reminder or re-scheduling a meeting 1 , or negotiating on a users behalf 6 . Several authors have explored workflow as an important part of the choreography of multiple agents: a light-weight, dynamic agent infrastructure in Java 29 , supports on demand, dynamic loading of new classes to extend agents with domain-specific XML interpreters, new vocabulary parsers or workflow. Agents can collaborate to perform a workflow, *e g telecom pro isioning BT or ser ice pro isioning HP* Agents can represent the participants and resources, the society of agents collaborate to enact the workflow 32 . Agent systems have been used to implement or augment workflow systems (10 , 33 , 34).

Gschwind's Agent Development Kit (ADK) provides an AgentBean model to allow some agents to be assembled from smaller Java-bean components 31 . ZEUS includes a visual generator of agent systems from role models 18 . Kendall uses agent role models and patterns to feed an aspect-based implementation 23 .

7 Conclusions

Multi-agent technologies will combine with web-service technologies to produce a robust environment for constructing complex, adaptive systems. To help make this adoption and mainstreaming of agent technologies happen soon, we need to produce robust agent platforms, integrated with J2EE and web-service platforms, and create powerful agent construction toolkits, model-driven generators, and visual builders to quickly define and generate (large parts of) of individual agents and agent systems.

We expect UML, AUML, and workflow techniques to play a large role in the definition, generation and execution of choreographed multi-agent interactions.

Further research and experimentation is needed to make it easier to define and implement different agent systems directly in terms of their features and capabilities. An agent, or set of compatible agents, will be constructed by combining aspects and components representing key capabilities.

References

1. Heineman, G., Councill, W.(eds): Component-Based Software Engineering, Addison-Wesley (2001)
2. Griss, M., Wentzel, K.: Hybrid Domain-specific Kits, Journal of Systems and Software, Sep (1995)
3. Griss, M., Pour, G.: Accelerating Development with Agent Components, IEEE Computer, 34(5): 37–43, May (2001)
4. Griss, M., Letsinger, R., Cowan, D., Sayers, C., VanHilst, M., Kessler, R.: CoolAgent: Intelligent Digital Assistants for Mobile Professionals – Phase 1 Retrospective, HP Laboratories report HPL-2002-55(R1) , July (2002)
5. Fonseca, S., Griss, M., Letsinger, R.: An Agent-Mediated E-Commerce Environment for the Mobile Shopper, HPL-2001-157, June (2001)
6. Maes, P., Guttman, R., Moukas, A.: Agents that buy and sell, Communications of the ACM, Vol.42, No.3, March (1999) 81–91
7. Glushko, R., Tenenbaum, J., Meltzer, B.: An XML framework for agent-based E-commerce. Communications of the ACM, Vol.42, March (1999)
8. Meltzer, B., Glushko, R.: XML and Electronic Commerce, ACM SIGMOD. 27.4 December (1998)
9. Huhns, M., Singh, M.: Readings in Agents, Morgan-Kaufman, (1998)
10. Jennings, N., Wooldridge, M.: Agent Technology, Springer (1998)
11. Bradshaw, J.: Software Agents, MIT Press, (1997)
12. Genesereth, M., Ketchpel, S.: Software Agents, Communications of the Association for Computing Machinery, July (1994), 48–53
13. O'Dell, J.: Objects and Agents Compared, Journal of Object Technology, Vol 1, Number 1, May, (2002); also http://www.auml.org/
14. Wooldridge, M., Jennings, N., Kinny, D.: The Gaia Methodology For Agent-Oriented Analysis And Design, AAMAS (2000)
15. Shoham, Y.: Agent-Oriented Programming, Artificial Intelligence, Vol. 60, No. 1, (1993), 139–159.
16. O'Brien, P., Nicol, R.: FIPA: Towards a standard for intelligent agents. BT Technical Journal, 16(3), (1998); also http://www.fipa.org
17. Griss, M.: My Agent Will Call Your Agent, Software Development Magazine, Feb (2000)
18. Nwana, H., Nduma, D., Lee, L., Collis, J.: ZEUS: a toolkit for building distributed multi-agent systems, in Artificial Intelligence Journal, Vol. 13, No. 1, (1999) 129–186; also http://more.btexact.com/projects/agents/ZEUS
19. Bellifemine, F., Poggi, A., Rimassi, G.: JADE: A FIPA-Compliant agent framework, Proc. Practical Applications of Intelligent Agents and Multi-Agents, April (1999), 97–108; also http://sharon.cselt.it/projects/jade
20. Griss, M.: Implementing Product-Line Features By Composing Component Aspects, Proceedings of 1st International Software Product Line Conference, Denver, Colorado, August (2000)

21. Griss, M.: Software Agents as Next Generation Software Components, In Component-Based Software Engineering, George T. Heineman & William Councill (eds), Addison-Wesley, May (2001)
22. Griss, M., Fonseca, S., Cowan, D., Kessler, R.: Using UML State Machines Models for More Precise and Flexible JADE Agent Behaviors, HPL 2002–298(R) and AAMAS AOSE workshop, Bologna, Italy, July (2002)
23. Kendall, E.: Role Model Designs and Implementations with Aspect-oriented Programming, in Proc. of OOPSLA 99, Denver, Co., ACM SIGPLAN, Oct, (1999) 353–369
24. Cowan, D., Griss, M.: Making Software Agent Technology Available to Enterprise Applications, 1st International Workshop on Challenges in Open Agent Systems, AAMAS'02, Bologna, Italy, July (2002)
25. Cowan, D., Griss, M., Kessler, R., Remick, B., Burg, B.: A Robust Environment for Agent Deployment , AAMAS 2002 – Workshop on Challenges in Open Agent Environments, Bologna, Italy, July (2002)
26. Fonseca, S., Griss, M., Letsinger, R.: Agent Behavior Architectures – A MAS Framework Comparison, AAMAS 2002 – 1st International Conference on Multi-Agent Systems and Applications; also, HPL-2001-332, Dec (2001)
27. Fonseca, S., Griss, M., Letsinger, R.: Evaluation of the ZEUS MAS Framework, HPL-2001–154, June (2001)
28. Chen,   ., Chundi. P., Dayal, U., Hsu, M.: Dynamic Agents for Dynamic Service Provisioning, Intl. Conf. on Cooperative Information Systems, August (1998)
29. Chen,   ., Hsu, M., Dayal, U., Griss, M.: Multi-Agent Cooperation, Dynamic Workflow and XML for E-Commerce Automation, Autonomous Agents 2000, June (2000), Barcelona
30. Falchuk, B., Karmouch, A.: Visual Modeling for Agent-Based Applications.   IEEE Computer, Vol. 31, No. 12, December (1998), 31–37
31. Gschwind, T., Feridun, M., Pleisch, S.: ADK – Building Mobile Agents for Network and Systems Management from Reusable Components, in Proc. of ASA/MA 99, Oct, Palm Springs, CA, IEEE-CS, pp 13–21; also http://www.infosys.tuwien.ac.at/ADK/
32. Sutton Jr., S., Osterweil, L.: The design of a next generation process programming language, Proceedings of ESAC-6 and FSE-5, Springer Verlag, (1997) 142–158
33. Kaiser, G., Stone, A., Dossick, S.: A Mobile Agent Approach to Light-Weight Process Workflow, In Proc. International Process Technology Workshop, (1999)
34. Shepherdson, J., Thompson S., Odgers, B.: Cross organizational Workflow Coordinated by Software Agents, WACC '99- Work Activity Coordination and Collaboration Workshop Paper, February (1999); also http://www.labs.bt.com/projects/agents/index.htm

Application-Specific Reuse of Agent Roles

Tom Holvoet and Elke Steegmans

Department of Computer Science, KULeuven
Celestijnenlaan 200A
B-3001 Heverlee, Belgium
+32 16 32.76.38
{Tom.Holvoet,Elke.Steegmans}@cs.kuleuven.ac.be

Abstract. In this paper, we argue that "programming in the large" for reactive multi-agent systems (MAS) should imply a reuse method that allows two things: (1) to describe multi-agent systems in an abstract, application-independent way, and (2) to reuse such abstract multi-agent system through application-specific adoptions. This allows reuse not only of code and design, but also of behavioral aspects, experiments, tests of the abstract multi-agent system. We present our work on MASORG (Multi-Agent System ORGanizations), focusing on the specification and reuse of roles in reactive multi-agent system. We use statecharts to model the abstract roles and we introduce statechart extension mechanisms to add application-specific functionality in the statechart of the abstract role. We work out an example of a role on the abstract level, and reuse and extend this role within an application in the domain of manufacturing control.

1 Motivation

This paper reflects on reuse in multi-agent system development as a key element in software development as an engineering task. In particular, we focus on MAS with relatively simple, mainly reactive agents, as opposed to the purely cognitive agents that use classical (or adopted) AI techniques for reasoning, planning and learning. The overall behavior of a reactive MAS emerges from the individual, simple actions of the constituent agents. However, the use of relatively simple agents does not imply that a simple method suffices to do "programming in the large". MAS are typically very complex, hard to develop and reason upon, debug, and so on.

In the domain of agent-oriented software engineering there has already been done a lot of work in the area of agent-oriented methodologies, well-known examples are Gaia [30], AUML [24], Tropos [15] and MESSAGE [3]. On the other hand in reactive multi-agent system software development, there is almost no reuse except for "the ideas". E.g. several applications (such as active networking, ant colony optimization applications, manufacturing control) make use of "the ideas" known from biological systems, e.g. social insects such as ants, bees, termites [1]. However, there are no methods to assist the development of applications based on these concepts. Almost all current implementations incorporate

A. Garcia et al. (Eds.): SELMAS 2002, LNCS 2603, pp. 148–164, 2003.

the corresponding concepts in an ad hoc, hard-coded fashion. The past few years, several approaches for agent-oriented software engineering are being investigated (for one overview, see [28]). Most approaches, however, focus on reuse of application-specific concepts at the analysis, design and implementation level (roles, protocols [20], agent architectures). Few research is conducted towards generic "organizational abstractions" [31] - such as structures and patterns - for generic (i.e. application-independent) models. That is a real pity, as there is a large potential of reusing generic multi-agent systems in concrete application domains. An overview of possible reuse:

design and code reuse: similar as for "traditional" software systems, reuse of design and implementation abstractions is the prime requirement for any software development method;

reuse of organizations: rather than consisting of separate, individual entities, a MAS is typically an organization consisting of several kinds of agents which exhibit particular roles in a particular environment [18]; a MAS development methodology should therefore support each of these abstractions equally;

extendibility, adaptability, manageability, ... : any software development method should support the well-known "-ities" known from software engineering;

reliability and correctness: correctly reusing software to build a new application entails that the application can rely on the outcome of the analysis of the software by its original developers (this is especially important for highly complex systems):

- correctness tests and experiments for a large range of side conditions can be applied in concrete applications with concrete side conditions;
- if the software is provided with formal specifications, new applications based on this software can rely on formal analysis results, such as behavior of the system, resistance to change, and so on.

In short, we aim to support reuse of generic multi-agent systems in a variety of application-specific contexts. We do not claim to propose one single method for software engineering that is suitable for all kinds of multi-agent systems. It seems obvious that the development of "intelligent, cognitive expert agents" requires concepts, support and analysis techniques that are completely inappropriate for developing "purely reactive multi-agent systems", and vice versa. Our work focuses on mainly reactive, cooperative multi-agent systems. As such, we do not presume a particular agent architecture (in the sense of [25,29]). Instead, we consider agents to be primarily entities with autonomous, pro-active behavior, possibly exhibiting different roles, and which can communicate with other agents through the environment.

This paper is a report on research on an entire method for MAS development, called MASORG. The main point of the paper is that it is important to describe abstract, application-independent MAS separately, and that applications may reuse these abstract MAS in order to reuse the organizations, autonomous behavior, formal results, experiments, and so on. We elaborate on a particular approach to augment generic role specifications through statechart extension mechanisms.

In section 2 of this paper we argue that reusability of multi-agent systems is an important research aspect and we propose our approach MASORG. In section 3 we focus on the reusability of agent roles. Abstract roles are described using statecharts and we propose five statechart extension mechanisms to reuse and extend these abstract roles in different applications. Section 4 gives an example of reusing and extending an abstract role in the "product path planning" example in the domain of manufacturing control. Finally section 5 concludes this paper and gives an overview of the most important future work topics.

2   Reuse of Multi-agent Systems

2.1   Background

Our approach (called MASORG - MAS Organizations) is largely inspired by three pillars of today's software engineering practice and research, namely object-oriented mechanisms, separation of concerns and design patterns and frameworks.

Object-oriented mechanisms. Object-orientation has proven its advantages (and deficiencies) during the last two decades. Encapsulation and reuse through subtyping (inheritance) are two essential mechanisms that are responsible for its success. Although we adopt these mechanisms, and we do work in an object-oriented setting (as a programming paradigm), we refuse, however, to consider MASORG to be an extension of object-orientation towards agent systems. Agent-orientation is a completely different paradigm, and as such has its own specific requirements and concepts that are not present in object-orientation.

Separation of concerns (SOC). Separation of concerns is the generic idea that indicates that by identifying "concerns" as separate software units makes them more suitable for reuse and adaptation. Besides the fact that this is a general characteristic of object-orientation, this term has been exploited (with success) in the latest developments on aspect-oriented programming (AOP) and other advanced SOC ideas and techniques.

Frameworks and design patterns. Reuse of generic - application-independent - software is recognized within the object-oriented community and has lead to the concepts such as design patterns and frameworks. We want to apply similar ideas in MAS development.

2.2   Our Approach – MASORG

The starting point of our position is that the two most interesting and fundamental concerns in MAS are: (1) the generic - application-independent - MAS model/organization on the one hand, and (2) application-specific adaptations of this model on the other hand. There is a large body of work in the area of "separation of concerns" under the name of aspect-oriented programming. Originally, aspects were considered as concerns that are scattered around over different classes or modules of an application design or implementation. Nowadays, the scope of aspects has been broadened, and [10] convincingly discusses two necessary conditions for AOP, namely quantification and obliviousness. Obliviousness refers to the fact that developers of a base class or module should do so obliviously of anything related to the aspect. Quantification is then used to indicate under which conditions, aspect-related behavior is added to the base class or module. In a way, we are aiming to achieve an aspect-oriented approach in that we want developers of generic MAS to be oblivious about any application-specific details. Quantification can then be used by application developers to indicate how the behavior of the generic MAS is to be adopted to cope with application-specific behavior.

In MASORG, there are two phases or levels in the development of a MAS. On an abstract level, an application-independent MAS is modeled. As a multi-agent system is an organization consisting of several kinds of agents which exhibit particular roles in a particular environment, modeling a multi-agent systems consists of (1) defining (or reusing existing) roles - partial behaviors - which are active in a particular environment, and (2) assigning roles to agents, either statically or dynamically. At the level of concrete application building, the developer starts from an abstract MAS and complements it with application-specific functionality and behavior. This means that the developers needs to map the abstract units in the model (the abstract environment, roles and organization) onto very specific application logic. In this paper we only focus on the description and reuse of "roles". A role is a partial specification of agent behavior. Roles represent more than a set of interface operations, but rather incorporate their own autonomous behavior. An agent may exhibit several roles at one time, and several agents may play an identical role in an multi-agent system. The existence of a role depends on the existence of the agent that performs the role. An agent and its roles have one identity. Our definition of roles is close to the concept of roles as defined by Depke e.a. [4,5], they also have investigated this concept of roles and inspected whether or how roles are supported in the UML. This illustrated that the concept of roles is richer than their adoption in generally accepted object-oriented mechanisms.

Moreover, as our concern is mainly in augmenting pre-defined roles with application-specific behavior, standard object-oriented techniques do even worse. We give one small example of a typical way to realize behavior extension of roles. This illustrates the typical problem we occur when reusing generic concepts in an application-specific context. A role and its application-specific implementation could be modeled using the Strategy pattern [13]. An algorithm for the behavior of this role would rely on abstract operations, which could later be implemented in concrete, application-specific classes. Specific patterns for modeling roles are proposed in [12], but for simplicity, we only consider the most simple way to model roles, using the Strategy pattern. This approach however lacks flexibility, and does not separate the concerns completely. The lack of flexibility stems from the fact that the abstract algorithm must foresee all possibly useful application-specific additions. Our experience is that it is hard to write algorithms that cover all possible uses, and that application developers are quite demanding on how to add application-specific items. This also entails that the abstract algorithm is polluted by aspects that are irrelevant at that generic level. Moreover, the only interface between the abstract and the specific classes is a set of operations. This is clearly deficient, as the application developer must understand the entire autonomous behavior of the role before it can be reused successfully, and not just the points - the operations - in which new code can be added. An informal documentation that describes the autonomous behavior is mostly ambiguous and insufficient for non-trivial behavior.

Aspect-oriented programming seems like a better approach to seamlessly add new "slices of behavior" to existing entities. However, employing only a programming level approach (e.g. by applying AspectJ [22]), does not suffice either. First, this does not provide a model of the autonomous behavior of the role. Second, it is actually unclear whether either the roles should be described as aspects and the application-specific parts as plain objects and close, or whether the application-independent MAS should be developed using plain objects and classes, and application-specific parts are modeled as aspects. A justification can be found for both alternatives. However, for both alternatives, specifying a concrete application is a cumbersome, error-prone job, often requiring artificial constructs. Attempts in this direction [14,21] are hence only partially useful as a reuse method. Mind that we are not implying that these problems cannot be overcome using a programming language approach only, but rather a conceptual mismatch exists between pointcuts and advices on the one hand, and roles with their own autonomous behavior on the other. Another approach, XRole [2], is an XML-based system designed to define roles for agent applications. The greatest strength of XRole is the fact that it can be exploited at the different phases of the software production process: the design phase, the implementation phase and at runtime. Within this approach fully abstract versions of roles are offered and need to be filled in by the application which wants to use this role. Within our approach, we want to go a step further by offering abstract roles, where the basic behavior already is offered, tested and implemented. These abstract roles can be reused and extended by the applications for their application-specific needs, so we emphasize on mechanisms by which different applications can reuse and extend them on an easy way.

MASORG. What is required is an abstract, but explicit representation of the behavior of the roles, which is part of the specification of the role - besides the interface operations. This entire abstract representation is the contract between the developers and the re-users of the agent roles. At best, the abstract representation is a formal one, which allows formal reasoning on the behavior of the role as well as on the behavior of the entire multi-agent system. A visual yet simple formalism makes the specifications accessible to application developers. Moreover, the formalism should provide a form of refinement that allows to specify the behavior at different levels of abstraction. Besides the abstract specification, we need to provide mechanisms to add application-specific functionality. These requirements are met by the well-known formalism called statecharts [17], which we extend with reuse mechanisms. For now, we consider only Mealy-like statecharts [23], in which actions are associated with transitions, and not with states.

The behavior of every role is specified by means of a statechart. In object-oriented methodologies, a statechart specification describes the correct sequences of method invocations on the object. The interpretation of a statechart in our approach is completely different. The statechart describes the autonomous behavior of the role. An agent exhibiting a role may decide to perform any of the (autonomous) actions that are "enabled" in its current state. Non-deterministic behavior of the agent (role) is limited to performing any of the enabled actions in the current state. The hierarchical nature of statecharts, also used in [16], allows us to define subtyping of roles through refinement of states in a statechart. As one agent consists of several roles, the entire behavior of an agent can be conceived as the composition of the respective statecharts as "orthogonal states". It also allows to synchronize the behavior of different roles within one agent.

3 Describing Roles in MASORG

Within MASORG, we focus on two aspects, first of all on describing roles in an abstract way and secondly on the reusability and extendibility of roles within different applications. For this purpose we distinguish between the abstract level and the application level of a role in MASORG. On the abstract level a high-level description of the behavior of roles is given. The behavior of the role is described in a statechart, consisting of states, transitions and actions on transitions. The purpose of these high-level descriptions of roles on the abstract level is making them reusable within different applications. On the application level the complementing of the abstract role with application-specific needs is the main focus. This is achieved by extending the statechart of the role with preconditions, pre- and post-actions and pre- and post-state-actions. In this paper we illustrate the abstract level of MASORG through an example based on the behavior of ants in an ant system. On the application level we illustrate how particular application problems that can benefit from ant-like solution algorithms, can reuse and extend this ant behavior.

As we distinguish between the abstract level and the application level, we offer two views on roles within MASORG, the generic view describing the role on an abstract level, and the application view describing the abstract role reused and extended with application-specific functionality. Those two views are explained in more detail in the next two subsections.

3.1   The Generic View of MASORG

Within the generic view of MASORG the generic - application-independent - behavior of an agent is modeled using statecharts. Such a statechart represents the role an agent plays in the organization; it describes the behavior of the agent in an abstract way. For describing this abstract version of the role we use the concepts of a Mealy statechart [23]:

- a state, describing the state of the agent at a certain moment of time;
- a transition, connecting two states with each other;
- an action added to a transition, describing the agent goes from the old state it is into the new state by performing the action.

We illustrate this through an example. In Figure 1 the behavior model of the role "Scouting" is depicted. It describes the behavior of an ant-like role, namely walking through the environment, dropping pheromones in an environment consisting of a graph (a number of nodes which are connected through channels). In this explanation, we assume that the reader is familiar with ant-like multi-agent systems [8,9,27]. However, rather than a life-like ant behavior, this is only an abstract, simple role that is useful to illustrate our point. The main addition to the normal scouting behavior of an ant in this version of the "Scouting" role is that the ant clones new ants with the same behavior when the node it is sitting in has more than one neighbor node. This cloning part is added to cover in a short time a large part of the environment we are exploring.

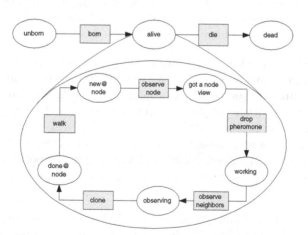

Fig. 1. The "Scouting" Role

Initially, an agent performing this role is in the state "unborn", from which it can perform (autonomously) the action "born" in order to find itself in the state "alive". On a certain moment in the life of the agent, it is satisfied by performing its role, the action "die" is executed and the agent arrives in its final state "dead". Being in the "alive" state the agent finds itself initially in the state "new@node", stating that it has arrived/sitting in a node. Being in this node, the agent performs the action "observe node", observing the environment by inspecting the node on which it resides, leading to the state "got a node view". Performing the "drop pheromone" action leads the agent to the "working" state in which it performs the "observe neighbors" action to know in the "observing" state how many agents it needs to "clone", to finally come into the "done@node" state and to "move" itself to the next node and to repeat its role. The abstract version of this "Scouting" role allows to develop, experiment, test and reason upon the behavior of a multi-agent system consisting of a graph environment and a number of agents, performing this role.

3.2   The Application View of MASORG

Now, we need mechanisms for applications to reuse this behavior: e.g. if we need to build an application based on an ant-like MAS, how can we reuse the abstract MAS version of the previous section? This can be done within the application view of MASORG, where we want application developers to be able to indicate where/when/what application-specific add-ons need to be performed by the agent exhibiting this role, called quantification in [10]. For this purpose we offer five new mechanisms to extend the statechart of an abstract role out of the generic view. The reasons for introducing these mechanisms are: first, we introduce these new mechanisms for their great advantages in expressive comfort. Second, adding application-specific functionality can be considered as another "concern" (cf. separation of concerns), that should not change the abstract behavior. In specific, the mechanisms offered are:

preconditions for actions: applications may influence the non-deterministic behavior of the role by specifying additional action preconditions;

pre-actions and post-actions: an application developer may indicate that particular application-specific code must be performed before (resp. after) a particular action is executed;

pre-state-actions and post-state-actions: an application developer may indicate that particular application-specific code must be performed just before the role arrives in a particular state, or just before it leaves a particular state;

Precondition for actions. Within the Mealy statechart definition, there is no limit on the number of actions which can depart from within one state. This can result in a non-deterministic behavior of the agent in that particular state. To limit this non-determinism while reusing the role within the applications, we offer a new concept to application developers to be able to use: a precondition related to an action. So by specifying additional action preconditions, an application limits the non-deterministic behavior of the role described in the statechart. The application developer can add a precondition in the following way to the statechart:

- a precondition is attached to the transition of the action on which the application developer wants the precondition to be valid. When such a precondition is added it must be satisfied before performing the action following the precondition in the current state.

In Figure 2 (a) an abstract example of adding two preconditions to a statechart is given. The informal semantics of adding preconditions is that the next state is chosen randomly between the all states that are associated with "true" preconditions:

```
chooseRandomlyTruePrecondition(precondition1, precondition2);
if (precondition1 chosen)
  actionA();
else
  if (precondition2 chosen)
    actionB();
```

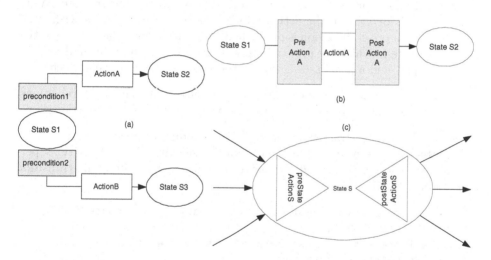

Fig. 2. Using Preconditions (a) Pre- and post-action (b) Pre- and post-state-action (c)

Pre-action and post-action. In the abstract description of a role, an agent goes always from one state to another by performing an action. On the application level, we want to offer a possibility to the application developer to extend this action by adding some application-specific functionality before or after this action. This is achieved by so-called pre-actions and post-actions. The application developer can add a pre- and a post-action in the following way to the statechart:

- a pre-action is attached to an action by placing it just before the action on its transition in the statechart.

– a post-action is attached by placing it just after the action on its transaction in the statechart.

In Figure 2 (b) an abstract example is given of adding a pre-action and a post-action to a statechart. Informally, the semantics of the statechart behavior, i.e. the sequence of actions performed going from one state to another state, are:

```
preActionA();
actionA();
postActionA();
```

Pre-state-action and post-state-action. Within the Mealy statechart it is not possible to perform the same action by all the incoming transitions in the new state or all the transitions leaving the old state. By adding the concepts, pre- and post-state-action, it is possible for the application developer to indicate that particular application-specific code must be performed just before the role arrives in a particular state, or just before it leaves a particular state. While a pre-action is defined on the action which can be performed from within the current state, a pre-state-action is performed from each transition arriving in this particular state to which the pre-state-action belongs. The application developer can add a pre- and a post-state-action in the following way to the statechart:

– a pre-state-action is put into a state on the side of the incoming transitions.
– a post-state-action is put into a state on the side of the outgoing transitions.

In Figure 2 (c) an abstract example is given of adding a pre-state-action and a post-state-action to a statechart. The informal semantics, i.e. the actions performed just before arriving and just before leaving the state from any transition arriving and leaving this state, is:

```
for (all transitions just before arriving in the state S)
    preStateActionS();
for (all transitions just before leaving the state S)
    postStateActionS();
```

4   Applications

Ant-like multi-agent systems are successfully deployed in - amongst others - the application domains of active networking [6,7] and manufacturing control [7, 27]. To evaluate our approach, we developed an application for both domains by reusing the above abstract "Scouting" role and adding application-specific functionality. As it happens, the "Scouting" behavior of the agents fits very well in these two applications for solving their needs and the environment of these applications is a graph too [26]. These two facts were good reasons for choosing these two as test applications domains. Here we only have a closer look at an application worked out within the domain of manufacturing control. A short example of the active networking can be found in [19].

One of the best known applications within the domain of manufacturing control is the "product path planning" application. This application plans the path of the manufacturing of a product through the assembly line of the factory. The assembly line is built of a number of resources which are connected with each other, where each resource can perform a number of operations. A product is manufactured by executing the sequence of operations needed for manufacturing this product. For example for each product there is an agent, which tries to find the best path through the assembly line to manufacture its product.

4.1   "Product Path Planning" Example

The example worked out here is the "product path planning" of the painting process of a car which is a part of the assembly line of the manufacturing of a car in a particular factory [11]. One agent is responsible for searching for paths through the assembly line to paint a car. The purpose of this agent is first of all to find a path in the part of the paint assembly line on which it can finish the sequence of operations needed to paint cars. And secondly, it calculates how much time is needed on each resource to perform its corresponding operation. When the agent is finished with its behavior, another agent uses the information the previous agent has left, the path information and the timing information, and decides which path is the fastest path to paint cars.

The painting of a car starts with carefully cleaning the entire body of the car by dipping it into a huge tank of cleaning solution, e.g. using a phosphate dip. Then it gets an electro-galvanized coating (e-coat), as the first phase of preparing the raw sheetmetal to receive the paint. After this the body goes through a primer bake oven, to prepare the body for the primer spraying phase, followed when the body comes out of the oven. After the body has a primer coat, it is finished by getting sprayed over an enamel coat and baking it in the special enamel baking oven. These are the steps needed to paint a car, for this purpose the agent must find a path through the assembly line which provides the following sequence of operations: cleaning, e-coating, primer baking, primer spraying, enamel coating and enamel baking.

The main focus of this example is to explain how applications can reuse and extend roles and in particular the "Scouting" role. The wanted behavior within this application is the behavior offered by the "Scouting" role, in which the walking around in the environment is restricted and some extra functionality is needed.

Environment. In Figure 3 the start situation of the car painting example is sketched, everything except for the underlined information depicted in the figure belongs to the start situation of the example. The painting part of the assembly line is depicted as a graph consisting of a number of nodes connected with each other through unidirectional channels. Each node represents a resource. Looking at the figure, the paint assembly line consists of the following resources:

- resource A is a "phosphate dip" with "cleaning" operation.
- resource B is a "primer electro-galvanizo" with "e-coating" operation.

- resources C&D are "primer baking oven"s with "primer baking" operation.
- resources E&F are "primer spray booth"s with "primer spraying" operation.
- resource G is an "enamel spray booth" with "enamel spraying" operation.
- resource H is an "enamel baking oven" with "enamel baking" operation.

Each unidirectional channel represents the connection of two resources with each other, indicating that the product can pass through the assembly line from the one resource to the other resource in the direction the arrow of the channel indicates.

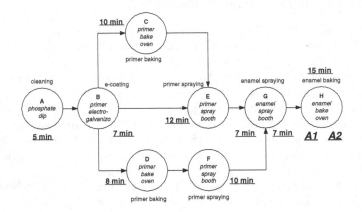

Fig. 3. The paint assembly line

Agent. The agent can perfectly reuse and extend the behavior of the abstract "Scouting" role to find a path through the assembly line to fulfill the painting of cars and to calculate the operation times in each resource through the path. The application view of the "Scouting" role is depicted in Figure 4, where the application-specific functionalities added are:

- when the agent arrives at a resource, it needs to be able to perform a calculation of the time needed to perform the particular operation by that resource. This is added in the abstract version of the "Scouting" role by the post-action "count the operation time" after the "observe node" action.
- the agent needs to be able to leave some extra information behind in the particular resource. This information consists of the operation time of the operation which can be performed by this resource. In the abstract version of the "Scouting" role this is achieved by adding a pre-action, "drop operation time", before the "drop pheromone" action.
- the agent already has the functionality to observe the neighbor nodes of the node it is sitting in, but in this application the agent does not need to know all the neighbor nodes, but only those where the agent can perform the next operation of the painting process. For this purpose, a filter is needed for

reducing the possible neighbor nodes. A logical consequence of this is that the agent also only needs to clone the number of agents which is equal to the number of calculated neighbors. This extra functionality is achieved by adding a post-action "filter neighbors on next operation" after the "observe neighbors" action and by the pre-action "calculate the number of clones" just before the "clone" action.
– the agent needs to stop observing when it has run through all the operations in the process of painting a car, or in other words, when the agent arrives in the ending resource. This is achieved by adding a precondition to the "observing" state, "process finished" in which case the agent has run through the sequence of operations and it can die. When this precondition is false, the agent performs the "calculate the number of neighbors" pre-action.

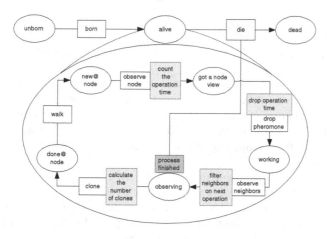

Fig. 4. The application view of the "Scouting" Role

Result. In Figure 3 the end situation of the above example is sketched. The end situation is represented by the entire figure, so including the underlined information depicted in the figure, which leaves in each node the time needed to perform the corresponding operation available as extra information and where in the ending resource H two agents have arrived. The final result is the fact that there are two agents with A1 and A2 as its identities, where agent A2 is a clone created by agent A1. The agent A1 has followed the path A-B-C-E-G-H through the assembly line, while the agent A2 has followed the A-B-D-F-G-H path.

Looking at Figure 4, we explain some parts of the behavior of the agents. Starting in resource A, the agent with identity A1 counts the operation time of the "cleaning" operation and leaves this information behind in the resource, 5 min. In the next step of its behavior it checks which are the neighbor nodes, the next resources to which he can move the product, in this case there is just one neighbor resource to which the product can move and in which the next operation "e-coating" can be performed. The agent does not create any clones and moves itself to resource B where it repeats its behavior. Arrived in resource B, it again counts the time the "e-coating" operation requires and leaves this information available in the "primer electro-galvanizo" resource, 7 min. The agent observes three neighbors, but the filter only leaves two of the three resources available because in resource E the agent can not perform the next operation "primer baking", this can only be done in the resources C and D. For this reason the agent creates just one clone of itself, agent A2 and moves itself to resource C, while agent A2 moves to resource D and they both repeat their behavior. The agents A1 and A2 stay executing their behavior and finally both stop when they arrive in the ending node in this case. As mentioned earlier, another agent can now walk through the assembly line and can observe the information left by the agents A1 and A2 to find the shortest path through the assembly line to paint the body of the car.

5   Conclusion

In this paper we presented ongoing research about a reuse methodology for reactive multi-agent systems. In particular, our aim is to support reuse of generically described multi-agent systems. Building a concrete application based on a generic MAS is reduced to augmenting the generic agent roles with application-specific aspects and provide a mapping of other generic concepts onto an application-specific counterpart.

We focussed on application-specific reuse of roles. A role is generically described by a Mealy-like statechart that specifies its autonomous behavior. Concrete application agents are built as a set of roles that are augmented with application-specific functionality. Therefore, we provided five mechanisms to add functionality to statecharts: preconditions, pre- and post-actions, and pre- and post-state-actions. This approach allows to separate completely the generic agent behavior from application behavior. We performed a first validation of the approach by building two applications that reuse a simple ant-like multi-agent system. Both application domains, active networking and manufacturing control, have been able to reuse the abstract version of the "Scouting" role and to extend it with application-specific functionality.

Reusing an abstract MAS allows to reuse not only software design and implementation, but also behavior, formal analysis, experiments and tests. Actually, in the application worked out in the previous section we could reuse: (1) the (simple) design of the MAS (a graph environment that can host one kind of agents - the scouting behavior) (2) the implementation of the abstract, autonomous behavior (which schedules the different actions the agent may take) (3) experiments (and ideally also formal results) with the MAS which ensures the "good" emergent behavior of the system. In contrary to other approaches referred to earlier in this paper, we do not need to forsee all possibly useful application-specific additions and places in the role at the abstract level within MASORG. The applications can add their application-specific functionality on a user-friendly and easy way, by making use of the extension mechanisms we added to statecharts, preconditions, pre- and postactions, and pre- and post-state-actions. The main contribution of our work is the fact that the designing, implementing and testing of the same behavior for agents does not need to be done over and over again by the different applications. These applications can simply use the techniques offered in MASORG.

MASORG is still ongoing research and in the future we will focus on the following topics: first we will have a look at the possibility to let the applications refine the roles much further then described already in this paper, by letting the applications refine the states of the abstract version of the role. This can result in a possible new abstract variant of the initial abstract role. Secondly, one of the results we aim to accomplish is to build a library of useful roles. For this purpose, we will focus on defining new useful roles. Finally, in this paper we only considered agents having one role. The intention is certainly to extend this to agents having multiple roles. For this purpose we want to investigate in techniques of composing roles making use of statechart techniques.

Acknowledgement. This paper presents results from research sponsored by the research council of the K.U.Leuven. The results have been obtained in the Concerted Research Action on Agents for Coordination and Control - AgCo2 project.

References

1. Bonabeau, E., Dorigo, M., Theraulaz, G.: Swarm Intelligence: From Natural to Artificial Systems. Santa Fe Institute Studies in the Sciences of Complexity, Oxford University Press (1999) ISBN 0-19-513159-2
2. Cabri, G., Leonardi, L., Zambonelli, F.: Separation of Concerns in Agent Applications by Roles. Proc. 2nd International Workshop on Aspect Oriented Programming for Distributed Computing Systems at ICDCS, Vienna, Austria, July (2002)
3. Caire, G., Garijo, F., Gomez, J., Pavon, J., Leal, F., Chainho, P., Kearney, P., Stark, J., Evans, R., Massonet, Ph.: Agent Oriented Analysis using MESSAGE/UML. Second International Workshop on Agent-Oriented Software Engineering 2001 (AOSE-2001)
4. Depke, R., Heckel, R., Küster, J.M.: Improving the agent-oriented modeling process with roles. Proc. Fifth Int. Conf. on Autonomous Agents (AGENTS-2001), Montreal, Canada (2001)
5. Depke, R., Engels, G., Küster, J.M.: On the integration of Roles in UML. Technical Report 214, Univ. PAderborn, August (2000)
6. Di Caro, G., Dorigo, M.: AntNet: Distributed Stigmergic Control for Communication Networks. Journal of Artificial Intelligence Research, 9, (1998)
7. Dorigo, M., Di Caro, G., Gambardella, L.M.: Ant Algorithms for Discrete Optimization. Artificial Life, 5, 2 (1999) 137–172
8. Dorigo, M., Maniezzo, V., Colorni, A.: The Ant System: Optimization by a Colony of Cooperating Agents. IEEE Transactions on Systems, Man, and Cybernetics, Part B, 26(1) 29–41
9. Ferber, J.: Multi-Agent Systems: An Introduction to Distributed Artificial Intelligence. Addison-Wesley (1999) ISBN 0-201-36048-9

10. Filman, R.E., Friedman, D.P.: Aspect-Oriented Programming is Quantification and Obliviousness. ECOOP Workshop on Aspects and Dimensions of Concerns (2000)
11. Flammang, J.: How a Taurus/Sable is Built. http://www.suntimes.com/mediakit/specialads/ford/story3.html
12. Fowler, M.: Dealing with Roles. Proc. 4th Annual Conf. on Patterns Languages of Programs, Monticello, Illinois, USA (September 1997) 2–5
13. Gamma, E., Helm, R., Johnson, R., Vlissides, J.: Design Patterns: Elements of Reusable Object-Oriented Software. Addison Wesley, Reading, MA, USA (1994) 315–323
14. Garcia, A., Lucena, C.J.: An Aspect-Based Object-Oriented Model for Multi-Agent Systems. Advanced Separation of Concerns Workshop at ICSE'2001 (May 2001)
15. Giunchiglia, F., Mylopoulos, J., Perini, A.: The Tropos Software Development Methodology: Processes, Models and Diagrams. Third International Workshop on Agent-Oriented Software Engineering 2002 (AOSE-2002)
16. Griss, M.L., Fonseca, S., Cowan, D., Kessler, R.: Using UML State Machine Models for More Precise and Flexible JADE Agent Behaviors. Third International Workshop on Agent-Oriented Software Engineering 2002 (AOSE-2002)
17. Harel, D.: Statecharts: a Visual Formalism for Complex Systems. Science of Computer Programming 8, 3 (June 1987) 231–274
18. Holvoet, T., Berbers, Y., Steegmans, E.: Organisation = Roles + Environment. Technical Report, KULeuven, Belgium, 11 pages (2001)
19. Holvoet, T., Steegmans, E.: Application-specific reuse in multi-agent system development. Proceedings of the International Workshop on Software Engineering for Large-Scale Multi-Agent Systems (A. Garcia and C. de Lucena, eds.) (2002) 51–55
20. Huget, M.-Ph.: Extending Agent UML Protocol Diagrams. Third International Workshop on Agent-Oriented Software Engineering 2002 (AOSE-2002)
21. Kendall, E.A.: Role Modeling for Agent System Analysis, Design, and Implementation. IEEE Concurrency, Agents and Multi-Agent Systems, Vol. 8–2 (2000) 34–41
22. Kiczales, G., Hilsdale, J., Hugunin, J., Kersten, M., Palm, J., Griswold, W.G.: An overview of AspectJ. J. Lindskov Knudsen (Ed.): ECOOP 2001, LNCS 2072 327–353
23. Mealy, G.H.: A method for synthesizing sequential circuits. Bell System Technical Journal, 34(5) (1955) 1045–1079
24. Odell, J., Van Dyke Parunack, H., Bauer, B.: Extending UML for Agents. AOIS Workshop at AAAI 2000.
25. Rao, A.S., Georgeff, M.: BDI Agents: from theory to practice. Proc. First Int. Conf. on Multi-Agent Systems, ICMAS-95, San Francisco, CA (1995) 312–319
26. Steegmans, E., Holvoet, T., Janssens, N., Michiels, S., Berbers, Y., Verbaeten, P., Valckenaers, P., Van Brussel, H.: Ant Algorithms in a Graph Environment: a Meta-scheme for Coordination and Control. Proceedings of Artificial Intelligence and Applications 2002 (M. Hanza, ed.), ACTA Press (2002) 435–440
27. Valckenaers, P., Van Brussel, H., Kollingbaum, M., Bochmann, O.: Multi-agent coordination and control using stigmergy applied to manufacturing control. Lecture Notes in Artificial Intelligence, 2086, Springer-Verslag 317–334
28. Wooldridge, M., Ciancarini, P.: Agent-Oriented Software Engineering: the State of the Art. Proc. First International Workshop on Agent-Oriented Software Engineering, Limerick, Ireland, LNCS 1957 (June 2000) 1–28
29. Wooldridge, M., Jennings, N.R.: Intelligent agents: Theory and practice. The Knowledge Engineering Review, 10(2) (1995) 115–152

30. Wooldridge, M., Jennings, N.R., Kinny, D.: The Gaia Methodology for Agent-Oriented Analysis and Design. Autonomous Agents and Multi-Agent Systems, 3, Kluwer Academic Publishers (2000) 285–312
31. Zambonelli, F., Jennings, N.R., Wooldridge, M.: Organisational Abstractions for the Analysis and Design of Multi-Agent Systems. Proc. First International Workshop on Agent-Oriented Software Engineering, Limerick, Ireland, LNCS 1957 (June 2000) 127–141

Assisting the Development of Aspect-Based Multi-agent Systems Using the Smartweaver Approach

J. Andrés Díaz Pace , Federico U. Trilnik , and Marcelo R. Campo

ISISTAN Research Institute, Facultad de Ciencias Exactas, UNICEN University
Campus Universitario, (B7001BB0) Tandil, Buenos Aires, Argentina
Also CONICET-Argentina
{adiaz,ftrilnik,mcampo}@exa.unicen.edu.ar

Abstract. Current software engineering trends are increasingly reasoning about large-scale applications in terms of multi-agent systems (MAS). Along this line, frameworks have been regarded as useful instruments to express a variety of agent models. However, despite the advantages of this approach, the MAS paradigm also introduces additional complexity into the development process. The central problem is that developers usually have to understand, select and organize a broad set of agency features in order to build final applications. Moreover, these features tend to be not orthogonal with respect to object structures. Thus, aspects appear as a promising alternative to achieve a better separation of concerns in MAS. In this context, the article presents an approach called *Smartwea er*, which basically gives assistance for the development of MAS applications, using a combination of multi-agent and aspect frameworks. A novel aspect of this work is the use of planning techniques to generate sequences of programming tasks to guide the implementation of applications on top of these frameworks. By doing so, the approach allows developers to better take advantage of MAS patterns, components and frameworks.

1 Introduction

The spreading of multi-agent systems (MAS) in software development 4, 13 has been steadily fostering new ways of designing applications that emphasize qualities such as modularity, autonomy, distribution and adaptability. However, despite the perceived advantages of MAS 13 , they have also introduced more complexity into the design process, because developers usually have to understand, select and organize a broad set of features in order to build MAS applications. For example, different types of agents can be developed by taking a set of basic capabilities such as perception, action, representation and manipulation of mental states, communication or mobility, and integrating them in multiple ways. For these reasons, many researchers have take advantage of object-oriented models to express agent concepts, based on the argument that a combination of agent-oriented with object-oriented techniques can help to alleviate the problem, by providing computational models with better modularity and adaptability. In particular, it is argued that object-oriented frameworks 10 can play a key role in this context, as they can be useful instruments to describe reusable designs and capture the essence of (agent-oriented) patterns, components, algorithms and architectures. Along this line, many MAS frameworks

A. Garcia et al. (Eds.): SELMAS 2002, LNCS 2603, pp. 165–181, 2003.

with different kinds of support for agent models have been reported in the last years 1, 14, 19 .

Nonetheless, the introduction of agents in object models poses also a number of additional problems 11 , because many agency features are sometimes intrusive or not orthogonal with respect to object structures. Examples of such features are autonomy, adaptation, interactions, learning, mobility and collaboration, among others. Most of the current MAS frameworks typically encapsulate core agent behavior and state as a single object, but they provide little support for handling agency features separately. For instance, consider the provision of communication capabilities in order to permit the agents to interchange information with other agents and collaborate to accomplish specific goals. This capability generally involves the implementation of certain communication protocols. However, it is not necessary to equip every agent in a MAS with communication capabilities. Furthermore, some groups of agents may implement different communication variants. Therefore, the way communication capabilities should be designed to interact with the core agent functionality is not always straightforward. Things get even more complicated, because communication may affect other features such autonomy, adaptation and collaboration.

In this context, AOP (Aspect-Oriented Programming) technologies 9 appear as an alternative approach to express agency features more cleanly. Essentially, these technologies make available novel means to achieve the principle of separation of concerns 17 , by providing mechanisms for modularizing certain design decisions in units called aspects, and also for specifying the interaction of these aspects with functional components. Among the advantages of AOP, we can mention better comprehension, easy of change, customizability, and simplified component integration. Although several aspect-oriented approaches have been proposed in the literature, each of them designed to address different requirements, they are mostly concerned with support for the abstraction, reuse and composition of functional components and aspects to produce the overall system. As regards MAS, the use of aspects can permit developers to keep core object functionality from its crosscutting agency aspects, thus lending to MAS the expected benefits of AOP.

Given the complexity of MAS frameworks, this work presents an environment called *Smartwea er* that gives assistance for the development of aspect-based applications 8 . In particular, the approach has been targeted to the development of MAS, using a combination of multi-agent and aspect-oriented frameworks. More specifically, *Smartwea er* is an extension of the *Smartbooks* method, a special documentation technique that, by means of a planning engine, provides semi-automated support for framework instantiation activities. The *Smartwea er* approach builds on the former ideas, but it also incorporates support for aspect-oriented models. Basically, a special engine allows the user to specify the set of functional requirements for an aspect-based application. Then, the tool can respond with a list of programming activities that should be carried out to implement such application on top of a given framework support. For instance, these activities can refer to advice on which classes should be specialized, what methods should be overridden, or what parameters should be set with specific values, etc. In order to elaborate this plan, the engine relies on structured *Smartbooks* knowledge provided beforehand by framework developers, which documents the way different functionality items can be delivered by a target framework. From this perspective, we can naturally think of tailoring the *Smartwea er* approach to work in a MAS context, in order to facilitate the management of agency aspects in MAS applications. By doing so, we aim at reducing the important grasp of experience and design skills often required to implement MAS applications. The rest of the paper is organized into 4 sections. In section 2, we discuss the suitability of frameworks to support MAS and aspects, and also describe two specific object-oriented frameworks. Section 3 introduces the *Smartwea er* approach itself. Section 4 presents a workflow case-study based on a real-life system, and illustrates how the approach proceeds. Finally, section 5 rounds up the conclusions of the work.

2 Framework Support for Agents and Aspects

From an object-oriented perspective, frameworks 10 can be seen as open languages to capture both agent models and aspects, offering a general and reusable skeleton of classes and behavior patterns for a given domain. In the case of multi-agent systems, a MAS framework 1, 14, 19 usually permits the construction of different types of agents with several properties/capabilities, and it allows programmers to extend or adapt certain components/patterns according to the application requirements. This is accomplished by means of the traditional mechanisms for reuse available at the framework level (e.g., abstract methods, inheritance, template and hook methods). Nonetheless, to ameliorate the flaws of traditional MAS frameworks regarding crosscutting agency features, it is interesting to explore their integration with a AOP frameworks. Indeed, this perspective is taken by the *Smartwea er* approach. In the case of aspects, an AOP framework 3 typically supports the definition of both aspects and joinpoints, allowing programmers to customize aspects and relationships among them. In addition, the framework may enable the implementation of general and flexible policies for aspect handling.

Within *Smartwea er*, a central part of the approach is the provision of a framework infrastructure as underlying support. In other words, developers need to select both a predetermined MAS framework and an AOP framework, and then document the frameworks following the *Smartbooks* prescriptions, before the guidance process can take place. With this purpose, we briefly describe two specific framework examples (see Figure 1), which will serve later in the paper to illustrate how to apply the proposed approach.

- *Bubble:* This framework was developed using a multi-agent approach based on reactive agents 4, 7 . The basic elements of the system are agents described by an internal state and a set of executable tasks. The interaction among these agents is performed through events that the agents produce and receive. The agents are also equipped with associated sensors (like filters) that are registered to hear certain kinds of events with a defined criterion of relevance (local, by group, by event strength, regional, etc.). The behavior of a reactive agent is defined through tasks using a condition-action style, i.e. a task is a module composed by a series of actions to be executed by the agent (action part) when certain conditions are fulfilled (condition part). Conditions can be related either to the internal state of the agent or incoming events. The framework also admits agents containing groups of other agents, and tasks composed by groups of predefined tasks. The framework *Bubble* has been used to support the development of a software application called

In uality¹ which provides a set of workflow management tools oriented to structured document-based applications and quality control processes (see section 4 for more details).

- **Aspect-Moderator:** In this aspect-oriented framework 3 (AMF), a specially designated component called moderator performs the weaving, coordinating the interaction between functional components and aspects. This interaction refers both to semantics and activation order of aspects. The approach introduces the concept of aspect bank, from where the moderator may initially need to collect all the required aspects, and then decide about the aspect integration policies. Aspects are first-class abstractions and upon creation they should be registered within the aspect moderator. A proxy object controls the access to the class functionality. This proxy object uses the factory pattern to create aspect objects for each method of the functional component that has to be associated with some aspects. Within the proxy, each participating method is guarded by a pre-activation and post-activation phases. These phases are implemented in the aspect moderator. During the former phase, the proxy intercepts requests for access to the functional components and calls the moderator to evaluate all the required aspects. If the pre-activation phase returns successfully, then the proxy will call the actual participating method. Once this execution is complete, the proxy will initiate the post-activation phase and call again the moderator to evaluate the associated aspects.

2.1 Related Work

Some empirical results on the contribution of MAS and AOP techniques regarding separation of concerns have been reported in 6, 15 . In a way, aspect models can be modeled in terms of events and event patterns, as advocated by 5 . If we assume that interesting points of a program can be defined as events emitted during execution, a crosscutting relationship would relate different program points or execution points. Here, aspects can be suitably expressed as set of rules *e ent pattern   action*. Notably, this fact is observed in *Bubble* where the inclusion of certain architectural features (e.g., events and implicit invocation, uniform decomposition and competing tasks) naturally favors aspects such as autonomy and communication. This confers a high degree of flexibility to the overall architecture, so that different agent capabilities can be easily combined without the need of explicit AOP support. Nonetheless, other aspects such as scheduling and synchronization are not managed at the framework-user level, rather they are provided as built-in features of *Bubble*. As design decision, this gives a better usability of the framework, but at the same time it may limit, for example, the possibility of defining alternative concurrency policies.

On the other hand, in 11, 12 the authors propose a design model to separate the different agency properties and capabilities in object models using AOP, so that it supports the construction of reusable multi-agent designs. The model deals with features such as agent's core state and behavior, agent types, agency properties, particular agency aspects, collaborative aspects, and agent evolution. These features refer mostly to non-functional requirements. The approach additionally prescribes how to compose agent aspects in a disciplined and non-intrusive manner. The model

---

¹ *In uality®* is a commercial software developed by Analyte, Lab Technology Solutions, Buenos Aires, Argentina.

can be seen as an AOP-MAS framework, and the composition process seems to rely mainly in built-in capabilities of this framework. Although the model is useful at essence, as demonstrated by the reported applications, little structured guidance is given on how to use it in terms of framework infrastructure.

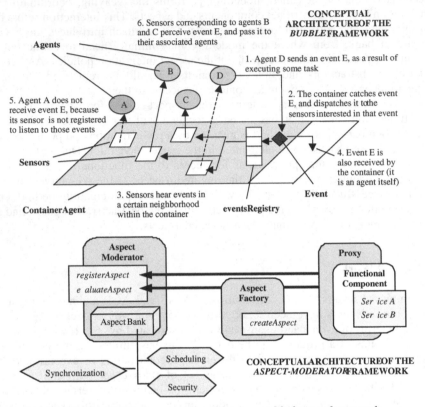

Fig. 1. The *Bubble* framework and the *Aspect-Moderator* framework

3 Knowledge-Driven Weaving: The Smartweaver Approach

Supporting aspects at the design phase can greatly improve aspect-oriented development 2 , because aspects can be identified and incorporated earlier in the development process. An ideal tool supporting AOP should allow designers to describe the required functionality for a specific application along with its associated aspects, and then the tool should automatically generate an application implementing it.

Unfortunately, existent technologies are far to provide the aforementioned assistance. At the current stage of research, an intermediate approach is to think about a knowledge-based engine able to prescribe the developer what activities should be done to implement a given application. From the combination of frameworks and agents in the context of aspects, we can narrow our original statement to the one of providing smart guidance for the instantiation of MAS frameworks. This leads us to the *smart-wea ing* concept 8 .   Essentially, we want developers to specify their requirements by means of general functionality items and aspect models, and then a special engine will translate these requirements to particular aspects programs. The difficulty resides on determining which activities have to be executed for creating a given application, and also how these activities need to be combined to obtain the desired functionality. Assuming an engine provided with adequate knowledge about the different functions that can be implemented using the framework resources, this engine could guide developers with the programming steps required to implement a given set of requirements. In particular, frameworks can naturally fit in this context. If we focus on the process of framework instantiation, it can be seen as a composition of relatively simple programming activities, which must be carried out in some meaningful order. For instance, these activities can include advice on which classes should be specialized, what methods should be overridden, what proxies should be created, how aspects should be implemented, what parameters should be set with specific values, etc. An outline of the *Smartwea er* proposal is shown in Figure 2.

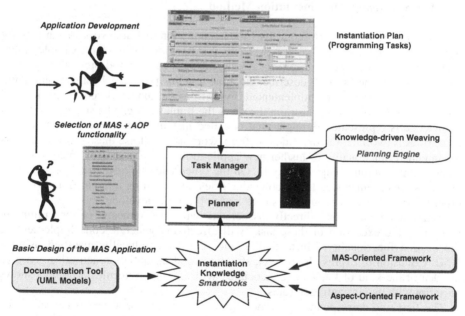

Fig. 2. Assisting instantiation of aspect-based MAS frameworks using *Smartwea er*

The main components of the *Smartwea er* environment are the following:

- **A Documentation Tool.** Framework users utilizes this module to specify the basic design of his/her MAS application.
- **A Corpus of Framework Documentation.** This documentation is written by framework developers for both a MAS framework and an AOP framework, and it is internally represented as instantiation rules in Prolog format.
- **A Functionality Collector.** This module helps the user select the MAS-AOP functionality items required for the application currently being developed. This

functionality is actually the one provided by the underlying frameworks, documented as explained above.

- **A Planning Engine.** It uses least commitment planning techniques to build instantiation plans. Any generated plan will have also associated a number of programming tasks.
- **A Task Manager.** This component keeps track of the tasks involved in instantiation plans.

Documentation knowledge about MAS and AOP frameworks is described through a predefined format of rules following the *Smartbooks* documentation method. Indeed, *Smartwea er* can be seen as an extension of this method that additionally incorporates aspects models. In the next sub-section, we shortly   describe the *Smartbooks* method and the corresponding planning engine.

3.1 The *Smartbooks* Documentation Method

The *Smartbooks* method 16 conceives the instantiation of frameworks as an activity based on a well-defined number of basic instantiation tasks, for example, class specialization or method overwriting, among others. The method prescribes that the framework designer should describe the functionality provided by the framework, how this functionality is implemented by different framework components, and provide rules to somehow constraint the ways the framework can be specialized. This knowledge is represented through what is called *instantiation rules*. The purpose of these rules is twofold. On one side, the framework user will use these rules to express the intended functionality of his/her new application, so the user is oriented to define what his application is supposed to do. On the other side, the *Smartbooks* engine will take these requirements and the knowledge rules documenting a target framework, in order to guide the user through the process of application development.

Instantiation rules are directly associated with the concept of programming activities. The execution of these tasks will effectively generate code implementing the desired functionality. Instantiation rules can be graphically specified using a UML extension to express framework structures and instantiation activities. To give an idea of the kind of knowledge associated with instantiation rules, Figure 3 shows an script with two instantiation rules.

The first rule corresponds to the definition of a proxy for aspect behavior in the *AM* framework, while the second rule corresponds to the definition of a simple agent in the *Bubble* framework. According to the first rule, the *AM* 's developers state that in order to have a functional proxy for a component, the proxy class should implement the *unctionalPro yI* interface and wrap the component. More precisely, the rule prescribes that four tasks should be carried out by the user, namely: an *ImplementInterface* task to produce a subclass of *unctionalPro yI* , a   *efine ariable* task to add a *my omponent* attribute to the proxy, a   *efineMethod* task in charge of overriding a functional method of the component (to incorporate aspect behavior), and finally, an   *ptional efineMethod* task if any update to the constructor is required. The second rule, on the other hand, specifies how to create an agent using a default implementation. The user needs just to extend the *Agent* class, and then completes the *initiali e* and *run* methods.

```
Rule: DefineFunctionalProxy
      Input: [ComponentProxy, Component, Method ]
      Output: []
      Preconditions: definedClass(ComponentProxy), definedClass(Component),
                     not(definedMethod(Component, Method)), proxyOption('composition')
      Postconditions: definedMethod(ComponentProxy, Method), wrapped(ComponentProxy, Component)
      Body:
          do implementInterface(ComponentProxy, 'FunctionalProxyIF')
          do defineVariable(ComponentProxy, 'myComponent')
          do defineMethod(ComponentProxy, Method, 'It should call Method in Component')
          do optionalUpdateMethod(ComponentProxy, 'new')

Rule: defineAgent
      Input: [ConcreteAgent]
      Output: []
      Preconditions: definedClass('Agent'), not(definedClass(ConcreteAgent)),
                     not(definedMethod(ConcreteAgent, run)), agentOption( default )
      Postconditions: definedClass(ConcreteAgent, Agent), definedMethod(ConcreteAgent, run),
      Body:
          do createClass(ConcreteAgent, 'Agent')
          do defineMethod(ConcreteAgent, 'run', 'It should execute agent tasks')
          do optionalUpdateMethod(ConcreteAgent, 'initialize')
```

Fig. 3. Instantiation rules for the frameworks *AM* and *Bubble*

Note that the focus of the *Smartbooks* approach is the automation of the activities dictated by framework documentation, rather than how this documentation is obtained. As framework documentation, either automated or not, is usually hard to come by framework developers, good-quality documentation is ultimately up to developers' experience.

To support the framework instantiation process, we have developed as prior work an experimental tool 16 , now called *Hint*. For the sake of simplicity, we just comment on the most relevant components of the *Hint* architecture for this paper, namely: the Task Manager and the Planning Engine (refer to Figure 2). A more complete description of the tool can be found elsewhere 8, 16 . The Task Manager is responsible for coordinating tasks, so that they may be executed, interrupted in order to work on other tasks, or even cancelled at any time. The Planning Engine takes a list of functional requirements (written as instantiation rules), and then elaborates a list of required instantiation tasks based on the core knowledge provided by the framework designer. During the planning phase, the engine uses a P P-like algorithm called *PHint*. It follows the least-commitment principle 18 , that is, it produces a partially ordered sequence of tasks, delaying decisions as much as possible. This flexibility allows the framework user to choose different alternatives of task execution when they are really needed.

4 Applying Smart Guidance on an Application Example

In order to better understand the *Smartwea er* approach, this section describes a case-study based on a workflow application 7 , and explains each of the phases developers should go through to implement the application using the *Smartwea er* environment The functionality required for this example can be informally described as follows. The application defines a workflow model for structured documents, with different users having access to these documents. Users can play different roles (e.g., supervisor, editor, or auditor), and each role has set its own permissions to operate on the documents. During its lifecycle, a document typically goes through a number of predefined states, e.g. edition, approval and publishing. Initially, the document is empty, waiting for edition. As the editor adds information to the document following certain standards, the document is sent to the auditor for approval. If the auditor considers the document contents relevant to the system, it is marked as ready for distribution. If so, every user potentially interested in this type of documents is notified about the event. If not, the document is sent back to the edition phase for revision. However, the auditor may reject the document if defective. In addition, a supervisor can review documents at any time and decide about their status. After certain period of time, some documents may become useless or require modifications. In such cases, a new version of the document is generated. As a result, the old version of the document is no longer available. Old documents are temporary stored as items pending of deletion, until they are finally removed from the system. For simplicity, we suppose a supervisor can read, write or check documents, an editor is only allowed to read or write some documents, and an auditor can read or check other documents.

This workflow is actually part of the *In uality* system, and it was originally implemented on top of the multi-agent infrastructure provided by *Bubble* This design helped to simplify the representation and flexible configuration of documents, roles and activities, thus reducing development efforts. Table 1 summarizes the main components of the resulting implementation.

4.1 Introducing the *Smartweaver* Assistance

This section takes the development of the same workflow application, but this time based on the *Smartwea er* approach. To apply smart guidance on a given application, it is necessary to accomplish four main activities. Firstly, we need to create some documentation books of support technology, that is a *Smartbooks* representation of particular approaches for multi-agent systems and aspects. Then, we should proceed with the design of the target application. After that, we are required to add mapping rules to effectively generate a weaving plan. Finally, all these things are put to work together so that the tool can suggest a series of programming tasks producing the desired MAS-AOP functionality. Figure 4 shows a roadmap of these activities

For the case-study, we have identified the aspects given in Table 2. From a multi-agent viewpoint, these aspects are strongly connected to agency features. For example, concurrency is typically required to provide agent autonomy, authorization may affect both communication and mobility issues, event mechanisms are generally relevant to support interaction protocols and update of mental states in reaction to environmental changes. Moreover, these aspects have also influence on the quality attributes of the final system. Therefore, managing the composition of these aspects in MAS frameworks as cleanly as possible, can significantly favor qualities such as reusability, ease of understanding and maintainability 11, 12 .

---

[2] Some details of the workflow application have been modified or simplified for clarity reasons, and also due to academic-industrial confidentiality agreements.

Table 1. Basic workflow implementation using *Bubble*

Component	Description
Workflow	Instead of having a centralized workflow engine, every particular workflow instance (or process) associated with a document is represented as a container agent.
	The workflow instance agent encapsulates the knowledge related to the structure of the particular workflow and related to creating the other corresponding agents and associated tasks that will implement the workflow.
	Workflow instances are generated by means of a Petri-net-based graphical editor. The editor produces a specification of the network that is used to configure the specific workflow instance.
Activity	Each activity within the workflow instance is represented as a single agent. Activity agents listen to events generated by the execution of previous activities, and react when these events arrive.
	Tasks associated with activity nodes of the workflow will produce messages directed (through a blackboard component) to the specific role or participant in charge of executing such activity.
Document	Each type of document has an associated workflow. A document is modeled as a simple agent, which sends/receives events according to different transitions.

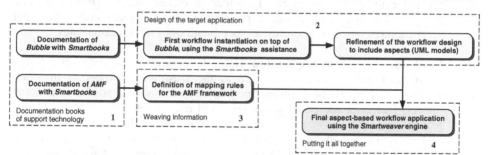

Fig. 4. Activities required to apply smart assistance on the workflow application

Table 2. Aspects for the workflow application

Aspect	Description
Concurrency	It mainly deals with synchronization and scheduling issues, by controlling the access to a given document of many potential readings or writings coming from different user sessions. It should consider mechanisms to lock/unlock documents and mechanisms to determine who is the next reader/writer when a document is available (unlocked).
Authorization	It refers to security policies regarding document handling, so that only authorized users can access to certain document contents.
Logging	It is in charge of keeping track of activity on the documents after some abnormal situation involving security issues has occurred in the system. Typically, any unsuccessful authorization should dynamically activate the logging aspect to register user actions from that point on.
Event Handling	Event mechanisms are frequently used in the *Bubble* architecture with notification purposes. For instance, an event may have information about the next activity to execute or about changes in certain document properties. As a result, the system behavior is strongly influenced by the policies in charge of managing event flow within the system

4.1.1 Building Documentation Books of Support Technology. At the beginning, the approach requires the definition of the *Smartbooks* knowledge documenting a given framework implementation. If we take the *AM* framework, its services should be represented in terms of instantiation rules. For example, developers may include rules documenting functionality items such as the definition of aspects, joinpoints, after/before advice, functionality proxies or weaving policies. Likewise, documentation for the *Bubble* framework should be provided. In this case, functionality items may refer to the specification of different types of agents, activation of tasks, sensor filtering policies or event handling in containers, among others. The *Smartwea er* tool stores all this documentation for further usage.

Note that framework developers arbitrarily fixes the terms used to document the framework functionality. Within the *Smartbooks* method, it is assumed that the documentation provided is correct, so that we do not care neither about the relevancy/consistency of the documentation nor how it is acquired by framework developers.

As a comment, both the *AM* and *Bubble* frameworks are mostly composed of abstract classes and interfaces, so they can be though more as a programming model than a component-based framework. This feature makes the *Smartbooks* method particularly useful, because we can express many agent model constraints, not completely captured by code structures, as specifications of instantiation rules.

4.1.2 Designing the Target Application. Here, developers should define the design of the core workflow components as well as the crosscutting properties affecting components' functionality. In a similar line that 2 , we have extended conventional UML models including additional stereotypes and relationships to support different AOP features. Figure 5 shows a class diagram with some of the classes involved in the workflow application and its associated aspects[3]. For instance, the design defines advice of the *W oncurrency* aspect for the *W ocument* class, and also exposes the conditional activation of the *W Logging* aspect as a result of evaluating the *W Authori ation* aspect.

Note that in order to specify which aspects crosscut the workflow application, developer have to previously sketch out the main workflow classes as instantiation of the *Bubble* framework. In the general case, developers can incrementally specify portions of aspect diagrams and define particular properties regarding before/after crosscutting, aspect priorities or conditional activation, among others. These descriptions may be complemented with more detailed views documenting aspect behavior. For brevity, we omit the details about the UML notation. Please refer to 8 to get more information.

4.1.3 Adding Weaving Information. During this phase, developers provide more details about their previous aspect diagrams. That is, they should specify the ways crosscutting relationships and aspect tasks should be translated into programming constructs according to the aspect support available in the environment. Aspect

---

[3] Aspects are represented as special stereotyped classes defining attributes and operations, and also incorporating stereotyped advice operations. Besides, special relationships between aspects and normal classes (e.g., crosscutting) or relationships between aspects (e.g. conditional activation) are modeled.

diagrams usually include special tasks, which correspond with activities that developers should carry out in order to tune specific details of the aspect-based application. These tasks indicate how abstract weaving specifications are mapped to a particular aspect implementation (an AOP framework in our example), which has been previously documented in terms of instantiation rules during phase 1 (section 4.1.1).

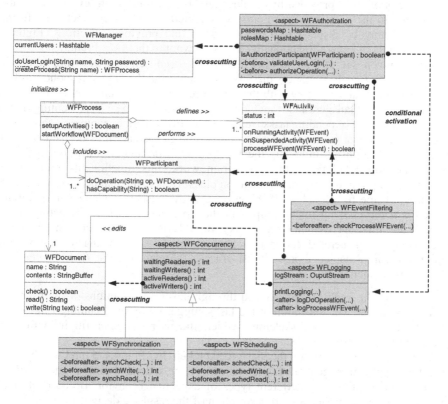

Fig. 5. Aspect diagram for the workflow application

The code template of Figure 6 illustrates (partially) how the *AM* framework would implement before/after advice and conditional activation of aspects with programming tasks, according to the design given in Figure 5. More specifically, the diagram shows a number of implementation details for the crosscutting relationships *W Autori ation-W Participant* and *W Logging-W Participant* respectively. To do this, a proxy called *W ParticipantPro y* has to be defined, as prescribed by the corresponding instantiation rule of Figure 3 . Furthermore, the diagram describes a possible way of implementing the conditional activation of *W Authori ation* on *W Logging* In this case, the advised method of *W ParticipantPro y* is updated in order to reflect this activation policy in the pre-activation/post-activation phases of the moderator. Note that not everything can be expressed in terms of tasks. Some framework constraints are just documented by means of warning messages.

4.1.4 Putting it all Together. Once aspect models have been defined using the Documentation Tool, it is possible to translate them to rules expressing the functionality required by the final application. Then, this basic functionality is enriched with information collected by the Functionality Collector. This module is in charge of interacting with the user to get a more accurate description of the application requirements. For example, when running the Functionality Collector, it starts presenting the user the initial available functionality, based on the instantiation knowledge previously provided by the designer. Firstly, only high-level functionality is presented to the user. As some items are selected, other options including further information may be displayed so he/she can refine previous selections. Figure 7 shows a sample of general functionality items relevant to the *AM* Framework.

Once a given set of functionality items has been selected, the tool internally generates a set of goals to express these requirements and the engine responds with an implementation plan according with these requirements. This plan is presented to the user by the Task Manager, and it includes a set of waiting tasks (representing design decisions) and a set of pending tasks (representing framework instantiation activities).

To exemplify this guidance, let's consider some of the activities derived from the crosscutting relationship involving the *W Authori ation* and *W Participant* classes. As we mentioned before, in the *AM* framework, this functionality requires the definition of a proxy to wrap the application class. Hence, the planner asks the user to provide the name for this class. If the class already exists, the planner may initially check for a sub-classing relationship, and then presents a task for selecting which methods are to be overwritten by the proxy. In addition, a task for creating the target subclass may be generated during the checking process. Following the template of Figure 6, Figure 8 depicts a possible list of tasks (shown from the *TaskManager*) for the described functionality.

At the end, the application is shaped through several interactions of the user with the Task Manager. The execution of the tasks suggested by the Planning Engine will generate a number of code skeletons, which the user can later fill in with more specific implementation details.

In our case, according to the design sketched by Figures 5 and 6, the final workflow application generated with *Smartwea er* extended the original *Bubble*-based implementation with different types of aspectual behavior. Because of space limitations, we just provide a short description of the resulting design:

- Synchronization and scheduling aspects for the methods *read*, *write* and *check* of class *W ocument*. This was done using a document proxy.
- A logging aspect affecting the method *processE ent* of class *W Acti ity* and the method *do peration* of class *W Participant* This was again implemented by means of functionality proxies.
- An authorization aspect for the *do peration* method of class *W Acti ity* This aspect also affected the functionality of the classes *WorkflowManager* and *W Participant*. If any failure in the authorization process is detected, the corresponding activity proxy dynamically activates the logging aspect on class *W Participant*
- An event-filtering aspect giving advice to the method *processE ent* of class *W Acti ity*. This aspect was introduced in order to customize the predefined event policies prescribed by *Bubble* for this kind of agents.

```
DefinePointcut(WFParticipant, WFParticipantProxy, WFAuthorization) :-
  DefineFunctionalProxy(WFParticipant, WFParticipantProxy, 'doOperation(...)','inheritance')
  UpdateMethod(WFParticipantProxy, 'configureAspects(...)'),
  Warning('Method configureAspects() should create aspects using the create(...) method
  AspectFactory and then aspects should be registered with the moderator using the
  method in AspectModerator'),
  UpdateMethod(WFParticipantProxy,
  Warning('Method doOperation(...) should call preActivation(...) in Aspect Moderator and
  postActivation(...) in the same class, to evaluate its associated
```

```
class WFParticipantProxy extends WFParticipant implements FunctionalProxyIF {
  // Constructor
  WFParticipantProxy(String name) { ... }
  protected void configureAspects() {
    // Aspect creation via AMF factory
    WFAuthorization opauth;
    opauth = AspectFactory().create("doOperation","authorization");
    WFLogging oplogging = AspectFactory().create("doOperation","logging");
    ...
    // Registration with the Aspect Moderator
    AspectModerator().register("doOperation","authorization",0,BEFORE,opauth);
    ...
  }
  public boolean doOperation(String op, WFDocument doc) {
    int pre = AspectModerator().preActivation("doOperation","read",...);
    if (pre == RESUME) {
      boolean result = this.doOperation(op,doc);
      AspectModerator().postActivation("doOperation","read",...);
      return (result);
    }
    if (pre == ERROR) {
      this.plugAspect("doOperation","logging",2,AFTER, ...);
      AspectModerator().postActivation("doOperation","read",...);
      return (false);
    }
    return (false);
  }
  ...
} // End class WFParticipantProxy

class WFLogging implements AspectIF
{ ... }

class DoOperationLogging extends WFLogging {
  protected void print(...) { ... }
  public int postaction(Object args) {
    this.print(...);
  }
  ...
} // End class DoOperationLogging
```

```
DefineConditionalActivation(WFAuthorization,
WFLogging, WFParticipantProxy) :-
UpdateMethod(WFParticipantProxy,
 'doOperation(...)'),
Warning('Method doOperation(...) should
first its corresponding parent method, and
evaluate preActivation(...) and postActivation(...)
in Aspect Moderator . Upon return, the method
should also request the activation of
conditional aspect to the
```

```
DefineAfterAdvice(WFLogging) :-
  DefineClass(WFLogging),
  ImplementInterface(WFLogging, 'AspectIF'),
  DefineClass('DoOperationLogging',WFLogging),

  Warning('Method postaction(...) in class
  doOperationLogging should invoke method
  somewhere').
```

Fig. 6. Mapping generic aspect functionality to programming tasks of the *AM* framework.

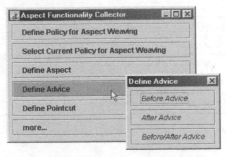

Fig. 7. Functionality items suggested by the Functionality Collector

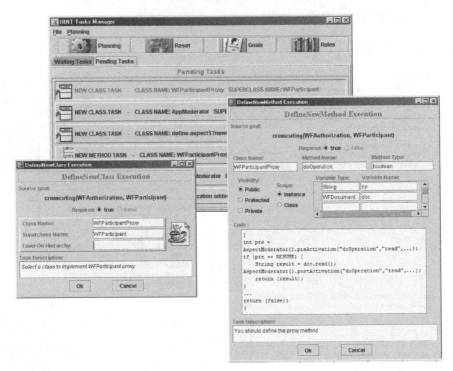

Fig. 8. A class-refinement and method-creation tasks proposed by the Task Manager

5 Conclusions and Future Work

This work describes an approach for assisting the developing of aspect-based MAS applications. The concept of *smartwea ing* proposes essentially an earlier incorporation of aspects in agent models, so that designers are able to combine both object and aspect models, reuse parts of these models, and also provide different strategies to map generic model structures to specific implementations (AOP approaches). The benefits of the mapping from aspect design to implementation are twofold, as it is recognized in 2 . First, from a design perspective, traceability of aspect models is maintained at the programming phase, making design changes easier to incorporate into code. Second, from the programming perspective, the abstraction level of aspects is raised by explicitly considering aspect programming at the design phase.

A novel aspect of this work is the use of planning techniques to generate sequences of programming tasks to guide a developer to implement applications on top of frameworks. In particular, we present an application of these ideas to multi-agent and aspect-oriented frameworks, expressing typical agency properties in terms of aspects. This approach represents a significant advantage in terms of automation levels and separation of concerns, over more passive development environments. As future work, we have started to explore how to make the *Smartbooks* support more suitable for MAS development, so that we could provide specific guidance for engineering standard agency properties in MAS applications.

Finally, we believe that, although a more rigorous and complete specification of the *Smartwea er* approach is still subject of research, the results obtained have been encouraging enough to evidence that use of artificial-intelligence techniques integrated with CASE tools can open new challenges in the software engineering field, and also promote more systematic MAS practices.

References

1. Chauhan. D. *afMas A a a-based Agent ramework for Multi-Agent Systems e elopment and Implementation*. PhD. Thesis. ECECS Department, University of Cincinnati, 1997.
2. Clarke, S. *esigning eusable Patterns of rosscutting Beha ior with omposition Patterns*. Workshop on Advanced Techniques for Separation of Concerns. OOPSLA'00, Minneapolis, USA. October 2000.
3. Constantinides C., Bader A., Elrad T., Fayad M. *esigning an Aspect- riented ramework*. Computing Surveys 32(1es):41. 2000.
4. Demazeau, Y., Müller, J. (eds.). *ecentrali ed AI* – Proceedings of the First European Workshop on Modeling Autonomous Agents in a Multi-Agent World (MAAMAW'89). Elsevier Science B.V. Amsterdam, Netherlands. 1990
5. Douence, R., Motelet, O., and Südholt, M. *A formal definition of crosscuts*. Proceedings of the 3rd International Conference on Reflection, LNCS 2192, September 2001.
6. Diaz Pace, A. *An Empirical Study of Separation of oncerns Approaches*. Master Dissertation, Faculty of Sciences, UNICEN University. March 2001.
7. Diaz Pace, A. and Campo M. *e eloping b ect-oriented uality rameworks using Proto-frameworks*. Software Practice and Experience, 32:1–7, July 2002.
8. Diaz Pace, A., Campo, M. and Trilnik, F. S*martwea er Aspect- riented e elopment using the Smartbooks Approach*. Proceedings ASSE 2002, 31 JAIIO (Jornadas Argentinas de Informatica e Investigacion Operativa), Santa Fe, Argentina. 2002.
9. Elrad, T., Filman, R., and Bader, E (eds). *Theme Section on Aspect-oriented Programming* Communications of the ACM, Vol. 44, No. 10. 2001.
10. Fayad M., Schmidt D., Johnson R. *Building Application rameworks b ect- riented oundations of ramework esign*. Wiley Eds. 1999
11. Garcia, A., Silva, V., Chavez, C., and Lucena, C. *Engineering Multi-Agent Systems with Aspects and Patterns*. Journal of the Brazilian Computer Society, Special Issue on Software Engineering and Databases, August 2002.

12. Garcia, A., Lucena, C., and Cowan, C. *Agents in b ect- riented Software Engineering.* Software: Practice and Experience, Elsevier, 2003. (accepted, to appear)
13. Jennings, N. *Agent-oriented Software Engineering.* Proceedings of MAMAW'99, Valencia, Spain. June 1999.
14. Kendall, E., Krishna, P., Pathak, C., and Suresh, C. *A ramework for Agent Systems* In Implementing Application Frameworks: Object-Oriented Frameworks at Work. M. Fayad, D. Schmidt, and R. Johnson Eds. Wiley & Sons. 1999
15. Murphy, G., Walker, R., and Baniassad, E. *E aluating Emerging Software e elopment Technologies Lessons Learned from E aluating Aspect-oriented Programming.* In IEEE Transactions on Software Engineering 25, 4, 1999.
16. Ortigosa A., Campo M, and Moriyon, R. *Towards Agent- riented Assistance for ramework Instantiation.* Proceedings of OOPSLA 2000, October 2000.
17. Parnas, D. *n the criteria to be used in decomposing systems into modules.* Communications of the ACM, 15(12):1053–1058, December 1972.
18. Weld D. *An Introduction to Least ommitment Planning.* AI Magazine, Summer/Fall 1994.
19. Zunino, A. and Amandi, A. *Building Multi-Agent Systems rom eusable Software omponents* Proceedings 3rd Workshop in Distributed Artificial Intelligence and Multi-Agent Systems (3WDAIMAS), IBERAMIA 2000. Ed.: Luis Otavio Alvares. Atibaia, São Paulo, Brazil, November 19–22, 2000.

Dynamic and Adaptive Replication for Large-Scale Reliable Multi-agent Systems

Zahia Guessoum, Jean-Pierre Briot, Olivier Marin, Athmane Hamel, and Pierre Sens

OASIS and SRC teams, LIP6, Université Pierre et Marie Curie (Paris 6)
8 rue du Capitaine Scott, 75015 Paris, France
{Zahia.Guessoum,Jean-Pierre.Briot,Olivier.Marin,Pierre.Sens}@lip6.fr
hamel@poleia/lip6.fr
http://www-src.lip6.fr/darx/

Abstract. In order to make large-scale multi-agent systems reliable, we propose an adaptive application of replication strategies. Critical agents are replicated to avoid failures. As criticality of agents may evolve during the course of computation and problem solving, we need to dynamically and automatically adapt the number of replicas of agents, in order to maximize their reliability and availability based on available resources. We are studying an approach and mechanisms for evaluating the criticality of a given agent (based on application-level semantic information, e.g. messages intention, and also system-level statistical information, e.g., communication load) and for deciding what strategy to apply (e.g., active or passive replication) and how to parameterize it (e.g., number of replicas).

1 Introduction

A multi-agent system is a set of autonomous and interactive entities called agents [1]. Recent real-life applications (e.g., intensive care monitoring, air traffic control and process control) are often distributed at large scale and must run continuously without any interruption. As distributed systems, multi-agent systems are exposed to possibility of failure of their hardware and/or software components. The failure of one component can often evolve into the failure of the whole system. To make these large-scale systems reliable, an obvious solution is the introduction of redundancy: duplication (replication) of the critical components.

Replication mechanisms have been successfully applied to various distributed applications [10], e.g. data-bases. But in most cases, replication is decided by the programmer and applied statically, before the application starts. This works fine because the criticality of components (e.g., main servers) may be well identified and remains stable during the application session.

Opposite to that, in the case of dynamic and adaptive multi-agent applications, the criticality of agents may evolve dynamically during the course of computation. Moreover, the available resources are often limited. Thus, simultaneous replication of all the components of a large-scale system is not feasible.

A. Garcia et al. (Eds.): SELMAS 2002, LNCS 2603, pp. 182–198, 2003.

Our idea is thus to **automatically** and **dynamically** apply replication mechanisms **where** (to which agents) and **when** it is most needed. In this paper, we will introduce our approach to this objective and the software architecture to help at building reliable multi-agent systems.

This paper is organized as follows: Section 2 presents fault tolerance concepts and replication principles. Section 3 introduces a new approach of dynamic and adaptive control of replication. Section 4 presents the DarX framework that we developed to replicate agents. This framework introduces novel features for dynamic control of replication. Section 5 describes our approach to compute agent criticality in order to guide replication. Section 6 describes the implementation of this solution and our preliminary experiments.

2   Requirements and Techniques for Fault-Tolerance

2.1   A First and Simple Example

We consider the example of a distributed multi-agent system that helps at scheduling meetings. Each user has a personal assistant agent which manages his calendar. This agent interacts with:

- the user to receive his meeting requests and the associated information (a title, a description, possible dates, participants, priority, etc.),
- the other agents of the system to schedule meetings.

If the assistant agent of one important participant (initiator or prime participant) in a meeting fails (e.g., his machine crashes), this may disorganize the whole process. As the application is very dynamic - new meeting negotiations start and complete dynamically and simultaneously - decision for replication should be done automatically and dynamically.

2.2   Principles of Replication

Replication of data and/or computation is an effective way to achieve fault tolerance in distributed systems. A replicated software component is defined as a software component that possesses a representation on two or more hosts [9]. There are two main types of replication protocols:

- active replication, in which all replicas process concurrently all input messages,
- passive replication, in which only one of the replicas processes all input messages and periodically transmits its current state to the other replicas in order to maintain consistency.

Active replication strategies provide fast recovery but lead to a high overhead. If the degree of replication is n, the n replicas are activated simultaneously to produce one result.

Passive replication minimizes processor utilization by activating redundant replicas only in case of failures. That is: if the active replica is found to be faulty, a new replica is elected among the set of passive ones and the execution is restarted from the last saved state. This technique requires less CPU resources than the active approach but it needs a checkpoint management which remains expensive in processing time and space.

2.3 Limits of Current Replication Techniques

Many toolkits (e.g., [9] and [19]) include replication facilities to build reliable applications. However, most of them are not quite suitable for implementing large-scale, adaptive replication mechanisms. For example, although the strategy can be modified in the course of the computation, no indication is given as to which new strategy ought to be applied; moreover, such a change must have been devised by the application developer before runtime. Besides, as each group structure is left to be designed by the user, the task of conceiving a large-scale software appears tremendously complex.

Therefore we designed a specific and novel framework for replication, named DarX (see details in Section 4), which allows dynamic replication and dynamic adaptation of the replication policy (e.g., passive to active, changing the number of replicas). Moreover, DarX has been designed to easily integrate various agent architectures, and the mechanisms that ensure dependability are kept as transparent as possible to the application.

3   Towards Dynamic Replication and Adaptive Control

Several solutions have been proposed to replicate distributed systems. These solutions are often used by the designer to replicate the system components before run time. The number of replicas and the replication strategy are explicitly and statically defined by the designer before run time. However, these solutions are not suitable to multi-agent systems. The solution we propose is mainly characterized by dynamic replication and adaptive control.

3.1   Dynamic Replication

The two replication strategies (active and passive) can be used to replicate agents. Active replication provides a fast recovery delay. So, it is dedicated to applications with real-time constraints. Moreover, passive replication provides a low overhead under failure but it does not provide short recovery delays. So, the choice of the most suitable strategy relies on the environment context. Active replication must be chosen when the failure rate becomes too high or when the application has real-time constraints. Otherwise, passive replication is most suitable.

In most multi-agent applications, the environment context is very dynamic.

So, the choice of the replication strategy of each component, which relies on a part of this environment, must be determined dynamically and adapted to the environment changes.

Moreover, a multi-agent system component which can be very critical at a moment can loose its criticality later. If we consider the replication cost which is very high, the number of replicas of these components must be therefore dynamically updated.

Thus, the solution we propose allows to dynamically adapt the number of replicas and the replication strategy. This solution is provided by the framework DarX (see Section 4).

3.2 Adaptive Control

DarX provides the needed adaptive mechanisms to replicate agents and to modify the replication strategy. Meanwhile, we cannot always replicate all the agents of the system because the available resources are usually limited. In the given example (Section 2.1), we can consider more than 100 assistant agents and resources that do not allow to duplicate more than 60 agents. The problem therefore is to determine the most critical agents and then the needed number of replicas of these agents.

We distinguish two cases: 1) the agent's criticality is static and 2) the agent's criticality is dynamic. In the first case, multi-agent systems have often static organization structures, static behaviors of agents, and a small number of agents. Critical agents can be therefore identified by the designer and can be replicated by the programmer before run time.

In the second case, multi-agent systems may have dynamic organization structures, dynamic behaviors of agents, and a large number of agents. So, the agents criticality cannot be determined before run time. The agent criticality can be therefore based on these dynamic organizational structures. The problem is how to determine dynamically these structures to evaluate the agent criticality?

Thus, we propose a new approach for observing the domain agents and evaluating dynamically their criticality. This approach is based on two kinds of information: semantic-level information and system-level information (see Section 5).

4 DarX: A Framework for Dynamic Replication

DarX is a framework to design reliable distributed applications which include a set of distributed communicating entities (agents). Each agent can be replicated an unlimited number of times and with different replication strategies (passive and active). Note that we are working on the integration of other replication strategies in DarX, including quorum-based strategies [2]. However, this paper does not address the design of particular strategies, but describes the infrastructure that will enable to switch to the most suitable dependability protocol. The number of replicas may be adapted dynamically. Also, and this is a novel feature, the replication strategy is reified such as one may dynamically change the replication strategy.

4.1   System Model

We consider a distributed system consisting of a finite set of n processes (or agents) $\Pi = \{p_1, p_2, \ldots, p_n\}$ that are spread throughout a network. These processes communicate only by sending and receiving messages.

Processes can fail by crashing only, and this crash is permanent. Our algorithm does not need synchronized clocks, but local clocks must not drift with respect to real time. They must measure time intervals accurately.

We consider the model of partial synchrony proposed by Chandra and Toueg in [3]. This model stipulates that, for every execution, there are bounds on process speeds and on message transmission times. However, these bounds are not known and they hold only after some unknown time.

4.2   DarX Architecture

DarX includes group membership management to dynamically add or remove replicas. It also provides atomic and ordered multi-cast for the replication groups' internal communication. Messages between agents, that is communication external to the group are also logged by each replica, and sequences of messages can be re-emitted for recovery purposes. For portability and compatibility issues, DarX is implemented in Java.

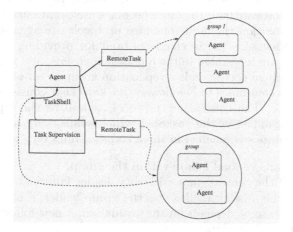

Fig. 1. DarX application architecture

4.3   Agent Replication

A replication group is an opaque entity underlying every application agent. The number of replicas and the internal strategy of a specific agent are totally hidden to the other application agents. Each replication group has exactly one leader which communicates with the other agents. The leader also checks the liveness of each replica and is responsible for reliable broadcasting. In case of failure of a leader, a new one is automatically elected among the set of remaining replicas.

DarX provides global naming. Each agent has a global name which is independent of the current location of its replicas. The underlying system allows to handle the agent's execution and communication. Each agent is itself wrapped into a TaskShell (Figure 1), which acts as a replication group manager and is responsible for delivering received messages to all the members of the replication group, thus preserving the transparency for the supported application. Input messages are intercepted by the TaskShell, enabling message caching. Hence all messages get to be processed in the same order within a replication group.

An agent can communicate with a remote agent, unregarding whether it is a single agent or a replication group, by using a local proxy implemented by the RemoteTask interface. Each RemoteTask references a distinct remote entity considered as its replication group leader. The reliability features are thus brought to agents by an instance of a DarX server (DarxServer) running on every location. Each DarxServer implements the required replication services, backed up by a common global naming/location service.

4.4 Failure of the DarX Server

Assuming that a DARX server will never fail contradicts the very existence of DARX. Indeed, software fault tolerance becomes useless in a zero-failure context. Besides, in our solution the fault tolerance protocols are agent-dependent, and not place-dependent, i.e. the mechanisms built for providing the continuity of the computation are integrated in the replication groups, and not in the servers. For every agent there corresponds a replication group: a set of software entities - replicas - which contains 0 to N followers/backups kept consistent with respect to a single leader. The consistency protocol as well as the replication group information are handled by the TaskShell which wraps every replica. A machine crash - server failure - is handled in three steps within every replication group:

- detection of an eventual failure within the group,
- evaluation of the context: new criticality, leader failure, ...
- recovery: If the missing replica was the group leader, a new one is elected. In the other case, it depends on the evaluation; a new follower/backup may or may not be instantiated.

Obviously, if a leader without any follower/backup fails, then it will not be recovered. This derives from the original assumptions we made: the criticality of an agent evolves during the computation, and there are phases when an agent need not be fault-tolerant.

4.5 Measurements

Our first measurements of DarX are very promising. We evaluated several costs and made comparisons with other systems (see [14]).

In this paper, we just show the cost of sending a message to a replication group using the active replication strategy. Figure 2 presents three configurations with different replication degrees. In the RD-1 configuration, the task is local and not replicated. In the RD-2 (resp. RD-3) configuration, there is one (resp. two) replica(s); the leader being on the sending host and the other replica(s) residing on one (or two) distinct remote host(s).

Measures were obtained using JDK1.1.6 on a set of UltraSparc II 333 MHz linked by a fast Ethernet (100Mb/s).

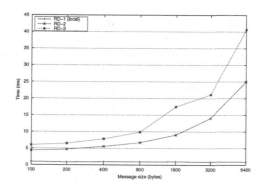

Fig. 2. Communication cost as a function of the replication degree

5   Adaptive Control of Replication

We will now detail our approach for dynamically evaluating criticality of each agent in order to perform dynamic replication where and when best needed.

5.1   Hypothesis and Principles

We want some automatic mechanism for generality reasons. But in order to be efficient, we also need some prior input from the designer of the application. This designer can choose among several approaches of replication: static and dynamic.

In the proposed dynamic approach, the agent criticality relies on two kinds of information:

– System-level information. It will be based on standard measurements (communication load, processing time...). We are currently evaluating their significance to measure the activity of an agent.
– Semantic-level information.

Several aspects may be considered (importance of agents, independence of agents, importance of messages...). We decided to use the concept of role [16][13], because it captures the importance of an agent in an organization, and his dependencies to other agents.

Note that our approach is generic and that it is not related to a specific interaction language or application domain. Also agents can be either reactive or cognitive. We just suppose that they communicate with some agent communication language such as ACL [8] and KQML [7].

5.2 Example

The application designer will manually evaluate criticality of the roles, corresponding to their "importance" in the organization and in the computation.

In the example introduced in section 2.1, we are considering two roles: Initiator and Participant [7]. Their respective weights will be set by the application designer to respectively 0.7 and 0.4 (see Table 1).

Table 1. Examples of roles and their weights

Roles	Weights
Initiator	0.7
Participant	0.4

5.3 Architecture

In order to track the dynamical adoption of roles by agents, we propose a role recognition method. Our approach is based on the observation of the agent execution and their interactions to recognize the roles of each agent and to evaluate his processing activity. This is used to dynamically compute the criticality of an agent.

The basic architecture controlling the replication of agents is shown in Figure 4.

In order to collect the data, we associate an observation module to each DarxServer on each machine (see Section 4.2). This module will collect events and dara (provided by DarxServer). A monitoring agent (called Mi and Mj in Figure 3) is then associated to each agent (the leader of replica group). This monitoring agent realizes the role analysis and activity analysis of the associated agent by considering his sent and received interaction events, and his system data. He then uses the obtained roles and degree of activity to compute the agent criticality.

The next sections describe the role analysis and activity analysis methods that we propose.

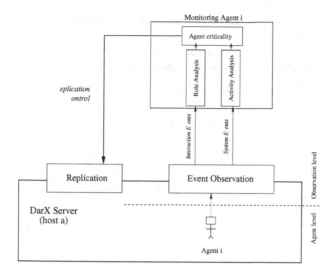

Fig. 3. General architecture for replication control

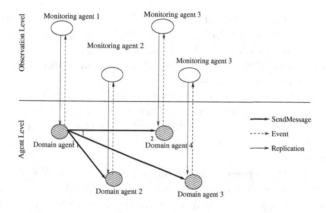

Fig. 4. General architecture for replication control

5.4   Role Analysis

We consider two cases. In the first case, each agent displays explicitly his roles or interaction protocols. The roles of each agent are thus easily deduced from his interaction events. In the second case, agents do not display their roles nor their interaction protocols. The agent roles are deduced from the interaction events by the role analysis module.

In this analysis, attention is focused on the precise ordering of interaction events (exchanged messages). The role module captures and represents the set of interaction events resulting from the domain agent interactions (sent and received messages).

We associate to each agent an entity that analyses the associated interaction events. This analysis determines the roles of the agent. Figure 5 illustrates the various steps of this analysis.

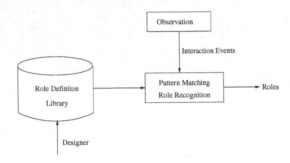

Fig. 5. Roles recognition

To represent the agent interactions, several methods have been proposed such as state machines and Petri nets [5]. For our application, state machines provide a well suitable representation. Each role interaction model is represented by an augmented transition network (ATN) [20]. A transition represents an interaction event (sending or receiving a message).

A library of roles definition is used to recognize the active roles. To facilitate the initialization of this library, we have introduced a role description language. Each role is represented by a set of interaction events. This language is based on a set of operators (similar to those proposed in [13], see Table 2), interaction events and variables.

Interaction events represent the exchanged messages. We distinguish two kinds of interaction events: ReceiveMessage and SendMessage. The attributes of the SendMessage and ReceiveMessage interaction events are similar to the attributes of ACL messages:

- SendMessage(Communicative act, sender, receiver, content, reply-with, ...).
- ReceiveMessage(Communicative act, sender, receiver, content, reply-with, ...).

In order to be able to filter various messages, we introduce the "wild card" character ?. For example, in the interaction event ReceiveMessage ("CFP", "X", "Y", ?), the content is unconstrained. So, this interaction event can match any other interaction event with the communication act CFP, the sender "X", the receiver "Y" and any content.

In the example of scheduling meetings, the assistant agents use the contract net protocol [8] (see Figure 6) to schedule a meeting. The interaction model of the initiator role is deduced from the contract net protocol. It is described in Figure 3.

Table 2. Operators

Operators	Interpretation
A.B	Separate two consecutive events
A|B	Or
A||B	Parallel events
(A)*	O time or more
(A)+	1 time or more
(A)n	n time or more
[A]	Facultative

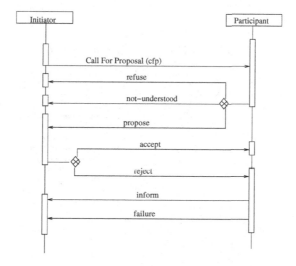

Fig. 6. Contract net protocol

This description represents the different steps (sent and received messages) of the Initiator. It can be interpreted as follows [8].

- A call for proposals message is sent to the participants from the initiator following the FIPA Contract Net protocol.
- The participants reply to the initiator with the proposed meeting times. The form of this message is either a proposal or a refusal.
- The initiator sends accept or reject messages to participants.
- The participants which agree to the proposed meeting inform the initiator that they have completed the request to schedule a meeting (inform).

Figure 7 and Figure 8 show examples of ATN that represent the interaction models of the roles Initiator and Participant described below.

Note that in many cases, roles can be deduced before the end of the associated sequence of interaction events (final state of the associated ATN). In the

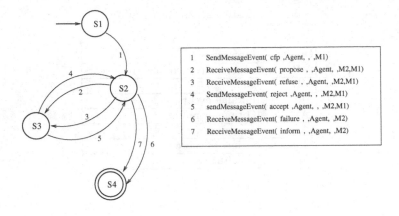

Fig. 7. Machine State for the Initiator

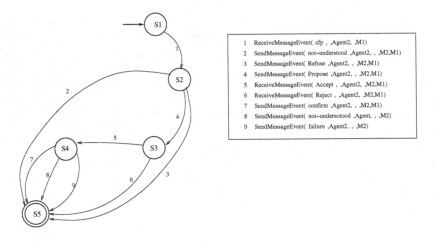

Fig. 8. Machine State for the Participant

scheduling meetings example, the role Initiator may be recognized as soon as the "CFP" message is received, as it is unique to this role.

5.5 Activity Analysis

In multi-agent systems, the internal activity of agents cannot be observed, because it is private. The observation is restricted to events. To evaluate the degree of the agent activity, we use system data that are collected at the system level. We are considering two kinds of mesures: CPU time and communication load. We are currently evaluating the significance of these measures as indicators of agent activity, to be useful to calculate agent criticality.

For an agent $Agent_i$ and a given time interval Δt, these mesures provide:

- The used time of CPU (cp_i),
- The communication load (cl_i).

cp_i and cl_i may be then used to measure the agent degree of activity aw_i as follows:

$$aw_i = (d_1 * cp_i/\Delta t + d_2 * cl_i/CL)/(d_1 + d_2) \tag{1}$$

where:

- CL is the global communication load,
- d_1 and d_2 are weights introduced by the user.

5.6   Agent Criticality

The analysis of events and mesures (system data and interaction events) provides two kinds of information: the roles and the degree of activity of each agent. This information is then processed by the agent's criticality module. The latter relies on a table T (an example is given in table 1) that defines the weights of roles. This table is initialized by the application designer.

The criticality of the agent $Agent_i$ which fulfills the roles r_{i1} to r_{im} is computed as follows:

$$w_i = (a_1 * aggregation(T[r_{ij}]_{j=1,m}) + a_2 * aw_i)/(a1 + a2) \tag{2}$$

Where a_1 and a_2 are the weights given to the two kinds of parameters (roles and degree of activity). They are introduced by the designer.

For each Agent A_i, his criticality w_i is used to compute the number of his replicas.

5.7   Replication

An agent is replicated according to:

- w_i: his criticality,
- W: the sum of the domain agents' criticality,
- rm: the minimum number of replicas which is introduced by the designer,
- Rm: the available resources which define the maximum number of possible simultaneous replicas.

The number of replicas nb_i of $Agent_i$ can be determined as follows:

$$nb_i = rounded(rm + w_i * Rm/W) \tag{3}$$

The numbers of replicas are then used by DarX to update the number of replicas of each agent.

6   Experiments

We made some preliminary experiments using the scenario of agents scheduling their meetings, as introduced in Section 2.1.

Agents take randomly roles of Initiator, choose Participants for scheduling meetings or remain inactive (without any role). Several meetings are scheduled simultaneously. The number of critical agents (which can be either Initiator or Participant) is 60% of the number of agents.

In order to simulate the presence of faults, we implemented a failure simulator randomly stopping the thread of an agent (chosen randomly).

Measures were obtained using a set of Pentium IV/2GHz PCs running linux with JDK1.2 and linked by a fast Ethernet (10Mb/s). We considered 100 agents which are distributed on 10 machines. We run each experiment 10 mn and we introduce 100 faults. We repeated several times the experiments with a variable number of extra resources (number of replicas that can be used).

We consider here the following variables:

$$ReplicationRate = \frac{NumberOfExtraReplicats}{NumberOfAgents} \tag{4}$$

and the rate of simulations which succeeded (i.e., which did not fail):

$$SuccessRate = \frac{NumberOfSuccessfulSimulations}{NumberOfSimulations} \tag{5}$$

Figure 9 shows the success rate as a function of the replication rate.

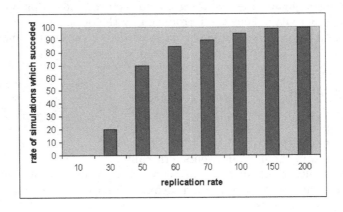

Fig. 9. Rate of succeeded simulations for each rate replication

From these experiments, we found that the number of extra resources should be at least equal to the number of critical agents.

Although preliminary, we believe these results are encouraging. Note that the results are similar for the two replication strategies.

7   Related Work

Several approaches address the multi-faced problem of fault tolerance in multi-agent systems. These approaches can be classified in two main categories. A first category focuses especially on the reliability of an agent within a multi-agent system. This approach handles the serious problems of communication, interaction and coordination of agents with the other agents of the system. The second category addresses the difficulties of making reliable mobile agents which are more exposed to security problems [17]. This second category is beyond the scope of this paper.

Within the family of reactive multi-agent systems, some systems offer high redundancy. A good example is a system based on the metaphor of ant nests. Unfortunately:

- we cannot design any application in term of such reactive multi-agent systems. Basically we do not have yet a good methodology. Moreover, these systems are more suitable for simulations.
- we cannot apply such simple redundancy scheme onto more cognitive multi-agent systems as this would cause inconsistencies between copies of a single agent. We need to control its redundancy.

Some work [4] offers dynamic cloning of specific agents in multi-agent systems. But their motivation is different, the objective is to improve the availability of an agent if it is too congested. The agents considered seem to have only functional tasks (with no changing state) and fault-tolerance aspects are not considered.

S. Hagg introduces sentinels to protect the agents from some undesirable states [12]. Sentinels represent the control structure of their multi-agent system. They need to build models of each agent and monitor communications in order to react to faults. Each sentinel is associated by the designer to one functionality of the multi-agent system. This sentinel handles the different agents which interact to achieve the functionality. The analysis of his believes on the other agents enables the sentinel to detect a fault when it occurs. Adding sentinels to multi-agent systems seems to be a good approach, however the sentinels themselves represent failure points for the multi-agent system. Moreover, the problem solving agents themselves participate in the fault-tolerance process.

A. Fedoruk and R. Deters [6] propose to use proxies to make transparent the use of agent replication, i.e. enabling the replicas of an agent to act as a same entity regarding the other agents. The proxy manages the state of the replicas. All the external and internal communications of the group are redirected to the proxy. However this increases the workload of the proxy which is a quasi central entity. To make it reliable, they propose to build a hierarchy of proxies for each group of replicas. They point out the specific problems of read/write consistency, resource locking also discussed in [18]. This approach lacks flexibility and reusability in particular concerning the replication control. The experiments have been done with FIPA-OS which does not provide any replication mechanism. The replication is therefore realized by the designer before run time.

In distributed computing, many toolkits include replication facilities to build reliable application. However, many of products are not enough flexible to implement an adaptive replication. MetaXa [15] implements in Java active and passive replication in a flexible way. Authors extended Java with a reactive metalevel architecture. Like in DarX, the replication is transparent. However, MetaXa relies on a modified Java interpreter. GARF [9] realizes fault-tolerant Smalltalk machines using active replication. Similar to MetaXa, GARF uses a reflexive architecture and provides different replication strategies. But, it does not provide adaptive mechanism to apply these strategies.

Pre-defined library of replication mechanisms enable more flexibility to be obtained. The users or the system themselves can tailor their own fault tolerance mechanisms to suit their needs by using these replication mechanisms and updating the strategy to the evolution of their environment. Indeed, the system must have the ability to observe the agents to determine their criticality and to replicate them according to this criticality (see Section 5).

8 Conclusion

Large-scale multi-agent systems are often distributed and must run without any interruption. To make these systems reliable, we proposed a new approach to evaluate dynamically the criticality of agents. This approach is based on the concepts of roles and degree of activity. The agent criticality is then used to replicate agents in order to maximize their reliability and availability based on available resources.

To validate the proposed approach, we realized a fault-tolerant framework (DarX) and we used a multi-agent framework (DIMA [11]) to implement multi-agent systems. The integration of DarX with the multi-agent platform DIMA provides a generic fault-tolerant multi-agent platform. In order to validate this fault-tolerant multi-agent platform, two small applications have been developed (meetings scheduling and crisis management system). They are intended at evaluating our model and architecture viability. The obtained results are interesting and promising. However, more experiments with real-life applications are needed to validate the proposed approach.

References

1. N. A. Avouris and L. Gasser. *Distributed Artificial Intelligence: Theory and Praxis*, chapter Object-Oriented Concurrent Programming and Distributed Artificial Intelligence, pages 81–108. Kluwer Academic Publisher, 1992.
2. F. Belkouch, M. Bui, and L. Chen. Self-stabilizing quorum systems for reliable document access in fully distributed information systems. *Studies in Informatics and Control*, 7(4):311–326, 1998.
3. T.D. Chandra and S. Toueg. Unreliable failure detector for asynchronous distributed systems. In *10 th Annual ACM Symposium on Principles of Distributed Computing*, pages 325–340, 1992.
4. K. Decker, K. Sycara, and M. Williamson. Cloning for intelligent adaptive information agents. In *ATAL'97*, LNAI, pages 63–75. Springer Verlag, 1997.

5. A. El Fallah-Seghrouchni, S. Haddad, and H. Mazouzi. Protocol engineering for multiagent interactions. In *MAAMAW'99*, number 1647 in LNAI, pages 128–135. Springer Verlag, 1999.

6. A. Fedoruk and R. Deters. Improving fault-tolerance by replicating agents. In *AAMAS2002*, Boulogna, Italy, 2002.

7. T. Finin, R. Fritzson, D. McKay, and R. McEntire. KQML as an agent communication language. In *Third international conference on information and knowledge management*. ACM Press, November 1994.

8. FIPA. Specification. part 2, agent communication language, foundation for intelligent physical agents, geneva, switzerland.
http://www.cselt.stet.it/ufv/leonardo/fipa/index.htm, 1997.

9. R. Guerraoui, B. Garbinato, and K. Mazouni. Lessons from designing and implementing *garf*. In *Proceedings Objects Oriented Parallel and Distributed Computations*, volume LNCS 791, pages 238–256, Nottingham, 1989.

10. R. Guerraoui and A. Schiper. Software-based replication for fault tolerance. *IEEE Computer*, 30(4):68–74, April 1997.

11. Z. Guessoum and J.-P. Briot. From active objects to autonomous agents. *IEEE Concurrency*, 7(3):68–76, 1999.

12. S. Hagg. A sentinel approach to fault handling in multi-agent systems. In C. Zhang and D. Lukose, editors, *Multi-Agent Systems, Methodologies and Applications*, number 1286 in LNCS, pages 190–195. Springer Verlag, 1997.

13. N. Jennings M. Wooldridge and D. Kinny. The methodology gaia for agent-oriented analysis and design. *AI*, 10(2):1–27, 1999.

14. O. Marin, P. Sens, J.-P. Briot, and Z. Guessoum. Towards adaptive fault-tolerance for distributed multi-agent systems. In *ERSADS'2001*, pages 195–201, 2001.

15. M.Golm. Metaxa and the future of reflection. In *OOPSLA -Workshop on Reflective Programming in C++ and Java*, pages 238–256. Springer Verlag, 1998.

16. James J. Odell, H. Van Dyke Parunak, and Bernhard Bauer. Representing agent interaction protocols in uml. In Paolo Ciancarini and Michael J. Wooldridge, editors, *Agent-Oriented Software Engineering*, number 1957 in LNCS, pages 121–140. Springer Verlag, 2000.

17. F. De Assis Silva and R. Popescu-Zeletin. An approach for providing mobile agent fault tolerance. In S. N. Maheshwari, editor, *Second International Workshop on Mobile Agents*, number 1477 in LNCS, pages 14–25. Springer Verlag, 1998.

18. L. Silva, V. Batista, and J. Silva. Fault-tolerant execution of mobile agents. In *International Conference on Dependable Systems and Networks*, pages 135–143, 2000.

19. R. van Renesse, K. Birman, and S. Maffeis. Horus: A flexible group communication system. *CACM*, 39(4):76–83, 1996.

20. W. Woods. Transition network grammar for natural language analysis. *Communication of Association of Computing Machinery*, 10(13):591–606, 1970.

Achieving Software Robustness via Large-Scale Multiagent Systems

Michael N. Huhns, Vance T. Holderfield, and Rosa Laura Zavala Gutierrez

University of South Carolina, Department of Computer Science and Engineering,
Columbia, SC 29208, USA
{Huhns, Holderfield, Zavalagu}@engr.sc.edu
http://www.cse.sc.edu/~huhns

Abstract. This paper describes how multiagent systems can be used to achieve robust software, one of the major goals of software engineering. The paper first positions itself within the software engineering domain. It then develops the hypothesis that robust software can be achieved through redundancy, where the redundancy is achieved by agents that have different algorithms but similar responsibilities. The agents are produced by wrapping conventional algorithms with a minimal set of agent capabilities, which we specify. We describe our initial experiments in verifying our hypothesis and present results that show an improvement in robustness due to redundancy. We conclude by speculating on the implications of multiagent-based redundancy for software development.

1 Introduction

Computer systems are now entrusted with control of global telecommunications, electric power distribution, water supplies, airline traffic, weapon systems, and the manufacturing and distribution of goods. Such tasks are typically complex, involve massive amounts of data, affect numerous connected devices, and are subject to the uncertainties of open environments like the Internet. Our society has come to expect uninterrupted service from these systems. Unfortunately, when problems arise, humans are unable to cope with the complexity of the systems and the speed with which they must be repaired. Increasingly, the result is that critical missions are in jeopardy.

To cope with this situation, companies and researchers are investigating self-monitoring and self-healing systems, which detect problems autonomously and continue operating by fixing or bypassing the malfunction [25]. The techniques employed include redundant hardware, error-correction codes, and, most importantly, models of how a system *should* behave, so that the system can recognize when it *mis*behaves.

The most common technique for hardware, redundant components, is inappropriate for software, because having identical copies of a module provides no benefit. Software reliability is thus a more difficult and still unresolved problem [2,3]. The amount of money lost due just to software errors is conservatively estimated at US$40B annually. To produce higher quality software, researchers are

A. Garcia et al. (Eds.): SELMAS 2002, LNCS 2603, pp. 199–215, 2003.
© Springer-Verlag Berlin Heidelberg 2003

trying to define more principled methodologies for software engineering [6]. They are also looking to new technologies, such as multiagent systems, and this leads to a natural interest in combining the latest software engineering methodologies with multiagent systems [22].

There are at least three ways that software engineering intersects multiagent systems:

- Multiagent systems can be used to aid traditional software engineering, such as by agent-based or agent-supplemented CASE tools
- Traditional or new software engineering techniques can be used to build multiagent systems; e.g., UML has proven to be useful for conventional software, so Agent-Based UML and similar efforts are underway to extend it to support the development of agents [23]
- Conventional software can be constructed out of agents, and software engineering can be used in this endeavor.

The focus of this paper is on the last.

2   Background

2.1   Methodologies for MAS Modeling

Software engineering principles applied to multiagent systems have yielded few new modeling techniques, despite many notable efforts. A comprehensive review of agent-oriented methodologies is contained in Iglesias, et al. [13]. Many, such as Agent UML [23] and MAS-CommonKADS [12], are extensions of previous software engineering design processes. Others, such as Gaia [28], were developed specifically for agent modeling. These three have been investigated and applied the most. Other methodologies include the AAII methodology [18], MaSE[7], Tropos [26], Prometheus [24], and ROADMAP [16]. Because agents are useful in such a broad range of applications, software engineering methodologies for multiagent systems should be a combination of efforts. A combination of principles and techniques will generally give a more flexible approach to fit a design team's particular expectations and requirements.

Agent UML (AUML) extends UML, which emphasizes things, relationships between things, and diagrams for grouping things and their relationships, by including agent interaction protocols. An extension to CommonKADS [12] includes notations from several object-oriented modeling techniques (pre-UML), and introduces seven knowledge models to take advantage of agent-oriented design. Gaia was formulated from an organization theory perspective. Its methodology is based on a system model consisting of roles, permissions, responsibilities, protocols, activities, liveness properties, and safety properties.

2.2   Benefits of an Agent-Oriented Approach

Multiagent systems can form the fundamental building blocks for software systems, even if the software systems do not themselves require any agent-like behaviors [15]. When a conventional software system is constructed with agents as its modules, it can exhibit the following characteristics:

- Agent-based modules, because they are active, more closely represent real-world things, which are the subjects of many applications
- Modules can hold beliefs about the world, especially about themselves and others; if their behavior is consistent with their beliefs, then their behavior will be more predictable and reliable
- Modules can negotiate with each other, enter into social commitments to collaborate, and can change their mind about their results
- Modules can *volunteer* to be part of a software system.

The benefits of building software out of agents are [5,11]

1. Agents enable dynamic composibility, where the components of a system can be unknown until runtime
2. Agents allow interaction abstractions, where interactions can be unknown until runtime
3. Because agents can be added to a system one-at-a-time, software can continue to be customized over its lifetime, even potentially by end-users
4. Because agents can represent multiple viewpoints and can use different decision procedures, they can produce more robust systems. The essence of multiple viewpoints and multiple decision procedures is redundancy, which is the basis for error detection and correction.

2.3   Bugs, Errors, and Redundancy

Hardware robustness is typically characterized in terms of faults and failures; equivalently, software robustness is typically characterized in terms of bugs and errors. Faults and bugs are flaws in a system, whereas errors and failures are the consequences of encountering the flaws during the operation or execution of the system. The flaws may be either transient or omnipresent. The general aspects of dealing with flaws are the same for both hardware and software: (1) predict their occurrence, (2) prevent their occurrence, (3) estimate their severity, (4) discover them, (5) repair or remove them, and (6) mitigate or exploit them.

Fault and bug estimation uses statistical techniques to predict how many flaws might be in a system and how severe their effects might be. For example, when Windows XP was released by Microsoft, it was estimated that it still contained 60,000 bugs, based on the rate at which its bugs were being discovered. Bug prevention is dependent on good software engineering techniques and processes. Good development and run-time tools can aid in bug discovery, bug repair is knowledge-intensive, and mitigation depends on redundancy.

Indeed, redundancy is the basis for most forms of robustness. It can be provided by replication of hardware, software, and information, and by repetition of communication messages. For years, NASA has made its satellites more robust by duplicating critical subsystems. If a hardware subsystem fails, there is an identical replacement ready to begin operating. The space shuttle has quadruple redundancy, and will not be launched without all copies functioning. However, software redundancy has to be provided in a different way. Identical software subsystems will fail in identical ways, so extra copies do not provide any benefit.

Moreover, code cannot be added arbitrarily to a software system, just as steel cannot be added arbitrarily to a bridge. Bridges are made stronger by adding beams that are not identical to ones already there, but that have equivalent functionality. This turns out to be the basis for robustness in software systems as well: there must be software components with equivalent functionality, so that if one fails to perform properly, another can provide what is needed. The challenge is to design the software system so that it can accommodate the additional components and take advantage of the redundant functionality.

We hypothesize that agents are a convenient level of granularity at which to add redundancy and that the software environment that takes advantage of them is akin to a society of such agents, where there can be multiple agents filling each societal role [10]. Agents by design know how to deal with other agents, so they can accommodate additional or alternative agents naturally. They also typically are able to negotiate over and reconcile different viewpoints.

Fundamentally, the amount of redundancy required is well specified by information and coding theory. Assume each software module in a system can behave either correctly or incorrectly (the basis for unit testing as used by most software development organizations) and is independent of the other modules (so they do not suffer from the same faults). Then two modules with the same intended functionality are sufficient to detect an error in one of them, and three modules are sufficient to correct the incorrect behavior (by voting, or choosing the best two-out-of-three). This is how parity bits work in code words. Unlike parity bits, and unlike bricks and steel bridge beams, however, the software modules cannot be identical, or else they would not be able to correct each other's errors.

If we want a system to provide n functionalities robustly, we must introduce $m \times n$ agents, so that there will be m ways of producing each functionality. Each group of m agents must understand how to detect and correct inconsistencies in each other's behavior. If we consider an agent's behavior to be either correct or incorrect (binary), then, based on a notion of Hamming distance for error-correcting codes, $4m$ agents can detect $m - 1$ errors in their behavior and can correct $(m - 1)/2$ errors.

Fundamentally, redundancy must be balanced with complexity, which is determined by the number and size of the components chosen for building a system. That is, adding more components increases redundancy, but also increases the complexity of the system. This is just another form of the common software engineering problem of choosing the proper size of the modules used to implement a system. Smaller modules are simpler, but their interactions are more complicated because there are more modules.

An agent-based system can cope with a growing application domain by increasing the number of agents, each agent's capability, the computational resources available to each agent, or the infrastructure services needed by the agents to make them more productive. That is, either the agents or their interactions can be enhanced, but to maintain the same degree of redundancy n, they would have to be enhanced by a factor of n.

To underscore the importance being given to redundancy and robustness, several initiatives are underway around the world to investigate them. IBM has a major initiative to develop autonomic computing—"a systemic view of computing modeled after the self-regulating autonomic nervous system." Systems that can run themselves incorporate many biological characteristics, such as self-healing (redundancy), adaptability to changing environments (reconfigurability), identity (awareness of their own resources), and immunity (automatic defense against viruses). An autonomic computing system will adhere to self-healing, not by "cellular regrowth," but by making use of redundant elements to act as replenishment parts. By taking advantage of redundant services located around the world, a better range of services can be provided for customers in business transactions.

For example, IBM's Tivoli Risk Manager monitors a network's health, protects it against attack, and heals it in the event of attack. Among its autonomic features is a monitoring function referred to as the "heartbeat" that tracks so-called "keepalive" messages from third party security products and gives administrators an early warning about failures in their security infrastructure. If a connection is lost, the heartbeat monitor issues an alert to the Risk Manager to take action or notify a human operator.

Exemplifying extreme redundancy in hardware, HP Labs has built a massively parallel computer, the Teramac, with 220,000 known defects, but it still yields correct results. As long as there is sufficient communication bandwidth to find and use healthy resources, it can tolerate the defects. Allowing so many defects enables the computer to be built cheaply.

The National Science Foundation has launched the Infrastructure for Resilient Internet Systems (IRIS) project, which is a five-year initiative to produce a robust, decentralized, and secure Internet infrastructure. The infrastructure will be developed using distributed hash table (DHT) technology, which can prevent all the data in a network from becoming vulnerable if one server crashes. Rather than centralizing the data in a single server, each server contains a partial list of the data's storage location; the challenge lies in developing a lookup algorithm that can locate data using the fewest possible steps. IRIS grew out of rising worries of the Internet's susceptibility to failure and attacks from viruses, worms, and possibly cyberterrorists.

2.4 N-Version Programming

N-version programming [8,20], also called dissimilar software and design diversity, is a technique for achieving robustness first considered in the 1970's. It consists of N disparate and separately developed implementations of the same functionality. Although it has been used to produce several robust systems, it has had limited applicability, because (1) N independent implementations have N times the cost, (2) N implementations based on the same flawed specification might still result in a flawed system, (3) the resultant system might have N

times the maintenance cost (e.g., each change to the specification will have to be made in all N implementations), and (4) the N versions must be combined without introducing additional errors. Our work addresses this last problem.

2.5 Transaction Checkpointing, Rollback, and Recovery

Database systems have exploited the idea of transactions for maintaining the consistency of their data. A transaction is an atomic unit of processing that moves a database from one consistent state to another. Consistent transactions are achievable for databases because the types of processing done are very regular and limited.

Applying this idea to general software execution requires that the state of a software system be saved periodically (a checkpoint) so that the system can return to that state if an error occurs. The system then returns to that state and processes other transactions or alternative software modules, known as recovery blocks [1,17,27]. This is depicted in Figure 1.

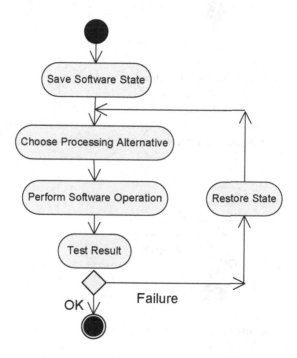

Fig. 1. A transaction (recovery block) approach to correcting for the occurrence of errors in a software system

There are two ways of returning to a previous state: (1) reloading a saved image of the system before the recently failed computation, or (2) rolling back, i.e., reversing and undoing, each step of the failed computation [4]. Both of the ways suffer from major difficulties:

1. The state of a software system might be very large, necessitating the saving of very large images
2. Many operations cannot be undone, such as those that have side-effects. Examples of these are sending a message, which cannot be un-sent, and spending resources, which cannot be un-spent. Rollback is successful in database systems, because most database operations do not have side-effects.

2.6 Compensation

Because of this, compensation is often a better alternative for software systems. As in database systems, it is often better to perform a compensating action, rather than save a checkpoint of a system with a large state. Figure 2 depicts the architecture of a robust software system that relies on compensation of failed operations.

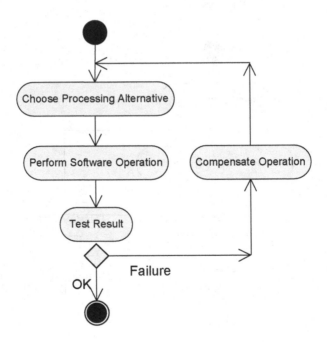

Fig. 2. An architecture for software robustness based on compensating operations

3   Architecture and Process

Suppose there are a number of sorting algorithms available. Each might have strengths, weaknesses, and possibly errors. One might work only for integers, while another might be slower but be able to sort strings as well. How can the algorithms be combined so that the strengths of each are exploited and the weaknesses or flaws of each are covered? In solving this in a general way, we hypothesize that the end result is an "agentizing" of each algorithm.

3.1   Architectural Approaches

A centralized approach, as shown in Figure 3, would use an omniscient preprocessing algorithm to receive the data to be sorted and would choose the best algorithm to perform the sorting. Each module's characteristics would have to be encoded into the central unit. The central unit could use a simplistic algorithm for determining best, based on known facts about each of the modules. The difficulties with this approach are (1) the preprocessing algorithm might be flawed and (2) its maintenance is difficult as new algorithms are added and existing algorithms become unavailable. Also, only one module at-a-time executes, there is low CPU usage, and results are taken as-is when completed.

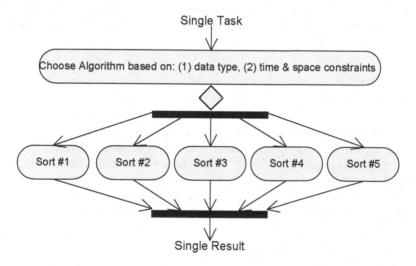

Fig. 3. Centralized architecture for combining N versions of a sorting algorithm into a single, more robust system for sorting, where a preprocessing algorithm chooses which sorting algorithm will execute

An improvement might be a postprocessing algorithm, as shown in Figure 4, that receives the results of all sorting algorithms and chooses the best result to be the output. Results have to be compared and voted on in order to determine the best. This approach is also centralized and suffers from a waste of CPU resources, because all algorithms work on the data. However, due to the comparison of outcomes, it is likely to produce better results.

A combination of the pre- and postprocessing centralized systems could also be used. Since criteria are known about each module, a subgroup could be selected to perform the desired task based on known factors such as speed, time,

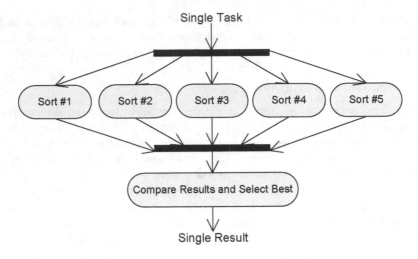

Fig. 4. Centralized architecture for combining N versions of a sorting algorithm into a single, more robust system for sorting, where a postprocessing algorithm chooses one result to be the output

and space. This subgroup would then have its results compared to determine the best results as above.

A fourth approach is a distributed solution, where the algorithms jointly decide which one(s) should perform the sorting, and if there is more than one qualified algorithm, they jointly decide on the best result. Conventional algorithms do not typically have such a distributed decision-making ability, so in this paper we investigate whether there is a generic capability that can be added to an algorithm to enable it to participate in distributed decision-making. We also show that the result has the characteristics of a software agent.

3.2   Multiagent System Approach

Moving the administrative responsibilities from the central intelligent unit and distributing those responsibilities into the different modules creates a multiagent system. An agent in this system would have to know about itself: what it needs, what it can accomplish, and how. Before accepting a task, it would have to believe it could accomplish the task. Specifically, each agent must know

- Something about its own algorithm, such as its time and space complexity, its input data structures, and its output data structures
- Something about other agents, such as their time and space complexity and reliability
- How to negotiate
- How to communicate
- How to compare results
- How to manage reputations and trust.

A transformation from the three conventional systems to an agent system would entail moving the responsibilities from a central unit, either a preprocessor, post-processor, or combination, to the individual agents.

An agent system transformed from a conventional system based on a pre-processor approach would have the agents themselves deciding on who would do the assigned task. Since an agent knows about itself, it could choose to submit a bid, which implies an auction environment to determine task assignment. This is an acceptable approach when there are many competing agents, but robustness due to reinforced redundant involvement would be lost.

An auction environment, where agent interactions take place without any dependencies among the agents' abilities, can be represented by Lorge and Solomon's "Model A:"

$$P = 1 - (1 - p)^r$$

where the probability, P, of a group of individuals solving a problem is the probability that the group size r contained at least one individual solver, given the probability, p, of a correct solution by an individual [21]. This representation is based on the agents' being able to detect a correct solution. The result is that a group of agents will outperform an individual on a consistent basis [9].

An agent system transformed from a conventional system based on a cen-tralized postprocessor would entail that each of the agents attempt the task and some type of voting mechanism (either with a voting factor or not) would be set up among the agents. A vote could be based on reputation only (more later) or on a majority rule vote based on a comparison of results. The communication overhead could be significant.

It should be noted that a group can sometimes be wrong, but with a func-tional basis, a group will be correct more often than its most accurate member. Shapley and Grofman give the following example of five weather forecasters pre-dicting whether it will rain or not on a given day. The decision is "yes, it will rain" or "no, it will not rain." The forecasters are given weights in proportion to $log(p_i/(1 - p_i))$, where p_i is the probability of forecaster i making a correct decision. Assigning the following weights to the forecasters: 0.9, 0.9, 0.6, 0.6, and 0.6, yields a group decision correctness probability of 0.927. This is higher than that of any one individual and also of unweighted voting, which has a group probability of 0.877.

The notion of a group is determined by the number of its members, the amount of communication among the members, and the identity of the members. Infrequent communication between individuals indicates casual relationships and not a group. A group can have its own way of identifying each of its members, but the members do not cease to be individuals while in the group, because they still have a personal responsibility to themselves, their own reputation, and their own desires.

Group decision-making is uninteresting for fewer than two members, but there is also a maximum size for a group. Beyond 10 to 15 members, a group becomes an assembly (where members do more waiting around than not) or a mob (where members are out of control) [19].

The comparison of results can be done in several ways. The results can all be compared and a majority of exact outcomes would determine the results that are selected, where each of the agents have an equal chance at having their results selected. (For example, assume that there are four different results: A, B, C, and D. Five agents have result A, while two agents each have results B, C, and D. Therefore, result A is passed on as the accepted result.) This method is fine when there is a clear-cut winner, as above, but in the following case this methodology becomes cloudy. (For another example, assume three agents have result A and three agents have result B, while two agents have result C and D, respectively. A and B have the same number of votes, so an additional procedure must be used to choose between them.) A secondary factor might be information the agent knows about itself, such as whether it completed the task or not, its time and space requirements, and the total number of runtime errors it has produced in the past.

4   Initial Experiments

We collected a number of sorting algorithms, each written by a different person and therefore having different input and output signatures and performance characteristics. We converted each algorithm into a sorting agent composed of the algorithm without any modifications and a wrapper for that algorithm. The wrapper knows nothing about the inner workings of its associated algorithm. It has knowledge only about the external characteristics of its algorithm, such as the data type(s) it can sort, the data type it produces, its time complexity, and its space complexity. The sorting algorithms were written in Java and the wrappers in JADE [14].

Figure 5 is the AUML diagram of the protocol used. The sorting system begins by a notification sent to the Initiator agent about data to be sorted, which notifies the sorting agents. Upon receiving data to be sorted, each agent determines whether or not it can sort it successfully (based on the type of the data and its own knowledge of what types it can sort). If the agent believes it can sort the data, it broadcasts an INFORM message to every other agent specifying its intention, along with a measure of performance for its algorithm (based on time and space complexity).

The decision of which agent (i.e., algorithm) to choose among those that are capable of sorting the input data is made in a distributed manner: upon receiving the INFORM messages from other agents, each agent compares its own performance measure against those received in the messages. If the agent has the best performance measure, it will run its algorithm and send the results back to the system. If it does not have the best performance measure, it will do nothing. Also, once they receive the data to be sorted from the system, the agents will wait for INFORM messages for only a limited amount of time; this avoids waiting infinitely long for messages from agents that either have problems sending a message or are not able to sort the data.

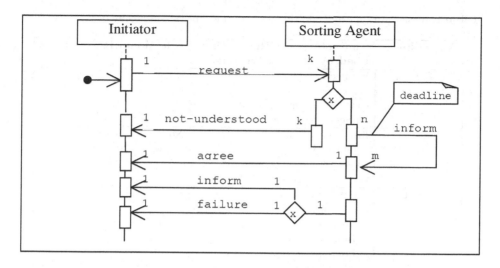

Fig. 5. AUML diagram of the agents' interactions

As can be seen, the current implementation of the wrappers is a preprocessing approach. Agents themselves decide on who will do the task placed before them. Even with the simplicity of the current implementation, results showing improvement in robustness due to redundancy were obtained. As a group, the agents sort data better than any one of them alone.

Table 1 summarizes the algorithms collected and information about them. The Additional Restrictions column shows restrictions not used by the default Wrapper to determine whether the agent can sort the data. Nevertheless, it is possible to cope with these cases by providing an implementation of a WrapperRestrictions interface, which only has one method that takes as input the data to be sorted and returns a Boolean value indicating whether the sorting algorithm can sort the data. This provides a way of customizing the wrapper for algorithms that need additional considerations, resulting in better performance for the whole system.

Finally, Table 2 provides a summary of the initial tests performed with the system. For the first set of inputs all the algorithms but RadixSort were appropriate. C.A.R Hoare's Quick Sort algortihm was selected because it had the best performance. For the second set of inputs only the QuickSort algorithm was selectable, because it was the only one that could handle strings. In the runs it was selected only when appropriate. For the third set of inputs RadixSort was selected. For the last set of inputs only the QuickSort algorithm could be selected because it was the only one that could handle reals.

As a group, the agents sorted data better than any one of them alone. Both C.A.R Hoare's Quick Sort and HeapSort algorithms could not handle inputs 2 and 3. The RadixSort algorithm could handle only one of the data sets. Finally, although the QuickSort algorithm was able to handle all the inputs, it did not have the best performance.

Table 1. Input data type and additional restrictions for the sorting algorithms available

Algorithm	Characteristics/Restrictions Used by Default Wrapper	Additional Restrictions
C.A.R Hoare's Quick Sort	Input data type: int array (positive and negative numbers accepted)	None
HeapSort	Input data type: int array (positive and negative numbers accepted)	None
QuickSort	Input data type: Byte array Short array Integer array Long array Float array Double array String array Char array	None
RadixSort	Input data type: int array	Only 10 inputs accepted

Table 2. Initial results for wrapping sorting algorithms with agents

Data Input	Algorithm Selected	Data Output	Comments
12, 45, 3, 2, 56	C.A.R Hoare's Quick Sort	2, 3, 12, 45, 56	
ann, john, sue, marie	QuickSort	ann, john, marie, sue	Only this algorithm could handle strings
9, 8, 7, 4, 3, 2, 12, 4, 5, 10	RadixSort	2, 3, 4, 4, 5, 7, 8, 9, 10, 12	Best performance but only worked for 10 inputs
3.54, 90, 23.4, 3.55, 60, 60.1	QuickSort	3.54, 3.55, 23.4, 60, 60.1, 90	Only this algorithm could handle reals

5   Group Decision Making

The system sends data to be sorted to the group of sorting agents. For simplicity, we assume that no matter what kind of data is sent, there is at least one agent that can sort the data. Each agent receives the data, decides whether it can sort the data, and broadcasts its decision. This first step will then determine the subgroup size. Because at least one agent can sort the data, the group size will range from 1 to N, where N is the total number of sorting agents in the group.

When only one agent indicates it can sort the data, the decision is trivial. When there is more than one agent with the ability to sort a data input, then a decision strategy must be put to use to determine which output to accept.

A voting strategy is considered for our experiments. There are three basic voting incentives: the data, reputation, or secondary factors. If the strategy involves the data, then direct comparisons need to be made about the data. An agent could compare another agent's result, which was positive, with its own. An array could be used to tabulate the results for each agent based on whether there is an exact match with itself or not.

For example, assuming only sortAgents 1, 2, 4, and 6 are capable of sorting the data, the array for sortAgent1 could be as follows:

$$compare = Array(sortAgent2 => yes, sortAgent4 => no, sortAgent6 => yes)$$

Counting itself, sortAgent1 would receive three positives and one negative.

Comparisons could also be normalized according to the amount of similarity between different agent's results. Comparison could have a direct relationship between exact locations, a relationship between substrings, and/or a relationship between the number of location matches or exact substrings.

CPU usage could be reduced if the result (yes or no) of a comparison is calculated only once, instead of by both agents. Logic could also aid in a reduction of CPU usage. If an agent A agrees with an agent B exactly, and agent A also agrees with agent C exactly, then agent B and agent C also agree. The sortAgent with the highest percentage of positives is selected. A tie can have two possibilities: (1) when the agents in the tie are a perfect match, then it does not matter which is chosen, or (2) when the agents are not a perfect match, then deciding is a problem.

If the strategy involves reputation, then a single sortAgent's vote is just its reputation factor; the result would be determined based on this factor alone. A tie here is a problem. Note that a reputation can be computed by many different means: e.g., neural nets, Bayesian networks, expert systems, or a simple normality based on successes. Reputation requires feedback for the system, either internally among the agents or externally from a user.

Secondary factors, such as what the agent knows about itself, can affect a sortAgent's vote. Completion of the task has to be taken into consideration. Time and space constraints and runtime errors encountered during execution could be sorted in relative order of importance. A high number of runtime errors could affect a vote; a long delay or large space requirements could also affect a vote. A formula based on its time and space constraints and any runtime errors could be formed and used. A tie could be broken by hierarchically organizing each mitigating factor as above.

Combinations of these three basic voting incentives could be used. First, a formula based on secondary factors would be used (since the presence of runtime errors is a very important fact); second, the data comparison would be made; and finally, a normalized reputation factor based on past successes in a group would be used. For example:

```
decisionVote =  a * Completed? +
                b * number of runtime errors +
                c * time used +
                d * space used +
                e * exact comparisons +
                f * reputation (if there is one)
```

Variables a, b, c, d are secondary factors, variable e is a data factor, and variable f is a reputation variable. The "best" algorithm is determined by

$$Performance \times Flexibility \times Reliability$$

where *Performance* is a function of time and space complexity, *Flexibility* is a function of how broad a range of input and output data structures the algorithm can handle, and *Reliability* is a measure of how well the algorithm can avoid runtime errors and exceptions.

6   Conclusion: Challenges and Implications for Developers

Producing robust software has never been easy, and the approach recommended here would have major effects on the way that developers construct software systems:

- It is difficult enough to write one algorithm to solve a problem, let alone n algorithms. However, algorithms, in the form of agents, are easier to reuse than when coded conventionally and easier to add to an existing system, because agents are designed to interact with an arbitrary number of other agents.
- Agent organizational specifications need to be developed to take full advantage of redundancy.
- Agents will need to understand how to detect and correct inconsistencies in each other's behavior, without a fixed leader or centralized controller.
- There are problems when the agents either represent or use nonrenewable resources, such as CPU cycles, power, and bandwidth, because they will use it n times as fast.
- Although error-free code will always be important, developers will spend more time on algorithm development and less on debugging, because different algorithms will likely have errors in different places and can cover for each other.
- In some organizations, software development is competitive in that several people might write an algorithm to yield a given functionality, and the "best" algorithm will be selected. Under the approach suggested here, all algorithms would be selected.

Ultimately, the production of robust software will require that we understand the relationship between

- the social world as represented by humans and their physical environment, and
- the social world as represented by agents and other automated systems.

Acknowledgements. The US National Science Foundation supported this work under grant number IIS-0083362.

References

1. Anderson, T. and R. Kerr: "Recovery blocks in action: A system supporting high reliability." *Proc. 2nd International Conference on Software Engineering*, October 13–15, 1976, San Francisco, CA, p.447–457.
2. Avizienis, Algirdas: "Fault-Tolerant Systems." *IEEE Transactions on Computers*, 25(12), pp. 1304–1312, 1976.
3. Avizienis, Algirdas: "Toward Systematic Design of Fault-Tolerant Systems." *IEEE Computer*, 30(4), pp. 51–58, 1997.
4. Chandy, K.N. and C. V. Ramamoorthy: "Rollback and recovery strategies for computer programs." *IEEE Transactions on Computers*, June 1972, pp. 59–65.
5. Coelho, Helder, Luis Antunes, and Luis Moniz: "On Agent Design Rationale." In *Proceedings of the XI Simposio Brasileiro de Inteligencia Artificial (SBIA)*, Fortaleza (Brasil), October 17–21, 1994, pp. 43–58.
6. Cox, Brad J.: Planning the Software Industrial Revolution. *IEEE Software,* (Nov. 1990) 25–33.
7. DeLoach, S.: "Analysis and Design using MaSe and agentTool." In *Proc. 12th Midwest Artificial Intelligence and Cognitive Science Conference (MAICS 2001)*, 2001.
8. Eckhardt, D.E., and L.D. Lee: "A Theoretical Basis for the Analysis of Multiversion Software Subject to Coincident Errors." *IEEE Transactions on Software Engineering*, SE-11(12), pp. 1511–1517, 1985.
9. Hasling, John: *Group Discussion and Decision Making,* Thomas Y. Crowell Company, Inc. (1975).
10. Holderfield, Vance T. and Michael N. Huhns: "A Foundational Analysis of Software Robustness Using Redundant Agent Collaboration." In *Proceedings International Workshop on Agent Technology and Software Engineering*, Erfurt, Germany, October 2002.
11. Huhns, Michael N.: "Interaction-Oriented Programming." In *Agent-Oriented Software Engineering,* Paulo Ciancarini and Michael Wooldridge, editors, Springer Verlag, Lecture Notes in AI, Volume 1957, Berlin, pp. 29–44 (2001).
12. Iglesias, C. A., M. Garijo, J. C. Gonzales, and R. Velasco: "Analysis and Design of Multi-Agent Systems using MAS-CommonKADS." In *Proc. AAAI'97 Workshop on agent Theories, Architectures and Languages*, Providence, USA, 1997.
13. C. Iglesias, M. Garijo, and J. Gonzalez: "A survey of agent-oriented methodologies." In J. Muller, M. P. Singh, and A. S. Rao, editors, *Proc. 5th International Workshop on Intelligent Agents V: Agent Theories, Architectures, and Languages (ATAL-98)*. Springer-Verlag: Heidelberg, Germany, 1999.
14. *JADE: Java Agent Development Environment,* http://sharon.cselt.it/projects/jade.
15. Jennings, Nick R.: "On Agent-Based Software Engineering." *Artificial Intelligence,* 117(2) 277–296 (2000).
16. Juan, T., A. Pearce, and L. Sterling: "Extending the Gaia Methodology for Complex Open Systems." In *Proceedings of the 2002 Autonomous Agents and Multi-Agent Systems*, Bologna, Italy, July 2002.

17. Kim, K.H. and Howard O. Welch, "Distributed Execution of Recovery Blocks: An Approach for Uniform Treatment of Hardware and Software Faults in Real-Time Applications." *IEEE Transactions on Computers*, 38(5), May 1989, pp. 626–636.

18. Kinny, David and Michael Georgeff: "Modelling and Design of Multi-Agent Systems." In J.P. Muller, M.J. Wooldridge, and N.R. Jennings, eds., *Intelligent Agents III—Proc. Third International Workshop on Agent Theories, Architectures, and Languages*, Springer-Verlag, Berlin, 1997, pp. 1–20.

19. Light, Donald, Suzanne Keller, and Craig Calhoun: *Sociology* Alfred A. Knopf/New York (1989).

20. Littlewood, Bev, Peter Popov, and Lorenzo Strigini: "Modelling software design diversity—a review." *ACM Computing Surveys*, 33(2), June 2001, pp. 177–208.

21. Lorge, I. and H. Solomon: "Two models of group behavior in the solution of Eureka-type problems." *Psychometrika* (1955).

22. Nwana, Hyacinth S. and Michael Wooldridge: "Software Agent Technologies." *BT Technology Journal*, 14(4):68–78 (1996).

23. Odell, J., H. Van Dyke Parunak, and Bernhard Bauer: "Extending UML for Agents." In *Proceedings of the Agent-Oriented Information Systems Workshop*, Gerd Wagner, Yves Lesperance, and Eric Yu eds., Austin, TX, 2000.

24. Padgham, L. and M. Winikoff: "Prometheus: A Methodology for Developing Intelligent Agents." In *Proc. Third International Workshop on Agent-Oriented Software Engineering*, July, 2002, Bologna, Italy.

25. Paulson, Linda Dailey: "Computer System, Heal Thyself." *IEEE Computer*, (August 2002) 20–22.

26. Perini, A., P. Bresciani, F. Giunchiglia, P. Giorgini, and J. Mylopoulos: "A knowledge level software engineering methodology for agent oriented programming." In *Proceedings of Autonomous Agents*, Montreal CA, 2001.

27. Randell, Brian and Jie Xu: "The Evolution of the Recovery Block Concept." In *Software Fault Tolerance*, M. Lyu, Ed., Trends in Software, pp.1–22, J. Wiley, 1994.

28. Wooldridge, M., N. R. Jennings, and D. Kinny: "The Gaia Methodology for Agent-Oriented Analysis and Design." *Journal of Autonomous Agents and Multi-Agent Systems*, 2000.

What Can Cellular Automata Tell Us about the Behavior of Large Multi-agent Systems?

Franco Zambonelli[1], Marco Mamei[1], and Andrea Roli[2]

[1]Dipartimento di Scienze e Metodi dell'Ingegneria – Università di Modena e Reggio Emilia
Via Allegri 13 – 42100 Reggio Emilia – ITALY
{franco.zambonelli, mamei.marco}@unimo.it

[2]Dipartimento di Elettronica Informatica e Sistemistica, Università di Bologna
Viale Risorgimento 2 - 40136 Bologna - ITALY
aroli@deis.unibo.it

Abstract. This paper describes the behavior observed in a class of cellular automata that we have defined as "dissipative", i.e., cellular automata for which the external environment can somehow inject "energy" to dynamically influence the evolution of the automata. In this class of cellular automata, we have observed that stable macro-level global structures emerge from local interactions among cells. Since dissipative cellular automata express characteristics strongly resembling those of open multi-agent systems, we expect that similar sorts of macro-level behaviors are likely to emerge in multi-agent systems and need to be studied, controlled, and possibly fruitfully exploited. A preliminary set of experiments reporting two ways of indirectly controlling the behavior of dissipative cellular automata are reported and discussed w.r.t. the possibility of applying similar sort of indirect control on large multi-agent systems.

1 Introduction

The Internet will soon get populated by multitudes of agents and multi-agent systems. For this reason, it is of dramatic important both to predict prior to their deployment how such multi-agent systems will behave and to control their behavior during execution. It has been recently discovered that the Internet and the Web (as well as Gnutella) have evolved and behave in rather peculiar and unexpected way, strongly impacting on performance and reachability of information [1, 2, 21]. Thus, we think that researchers in the area of multi-agent systems should learn from this, and should ask themselves whether similar situations may occur for large multi-agent systems.

In this context, this paper discusses some experiments that we have performed on a new class of cellular automata that we have defined as *dissipati e cellular automata* (DCA). DCA differ from traditional cellular automata [3, 26, 27] in two characteristics: while traditional cellular automata are composed of cells that interact with each other in a synchronous way and that are influenced in their evolution only by the internal state of the automata themselves, dissipative ones are asynchronous and open. First, cells in the DCA update their status independently of each other, in an autonomous way. Second, the automata live embodied in an environment that can directly influence the internal behavior of the automata, as in

A. Garcia et al. (Eds.): SELMAS 2002, LNCS 2603, pp. 216–231, 2003.

open systems. In other words, DCA can be considered as a minimalist open agent system 8, 12, 30 and, as that, their dynamic behavior is likely to provide useful insight into the behavior of real-world open agent systems.

DCA exhibit peculiar and interesting behavior, as the experiments reported in this paper show. During the dynamic execution of the DCA, stable macro-level spatial structures emerge from local interactions among cells, a behavior that does not emerge when the cellular automaton is synchronous and closed (i.e., when the state of a cell is not influenced by the environment). On this basis, the paper argues that similar sort of macro-level behaviors are likely to emerge as soon as multi-agent systems (or likes) will start populating the Internet and our physical spaces, environments which are both characterized by their own processes and by intrinsic and unpredictable dynamics. Such behaviors are likely to dramatically influence the overall behavior of our networks at a very large scale. This may require new models, methodologies, and tools, explicitly taking into account the environmental dynamics, and exploiting it during software design and development either defensively, to control its effects on the system, or constructively, as an additional design dimension.

On this basis, the paper also shortly describes two different methodologies that we have tried to apply in order to indirectly control emergent behaviors in DCA (i.e., to control which pattern, among the several possible ones, to make emerge in a DCA). Finally, the paper discusses how similar sorts of indirect control can possibly be applied to large multi-agent systems.

The following of this paper is organized as follows. Section 2 introduces cellular automata. Section 3 introduces DCA and describes the emergent behaviors observed in the experiments. Section 4 discusses the strict relations between DCA and multi-agent system. Section 5 introduces the two methodologies to control DCA behaviors. Section 6 discusses related works and Section 7concludes the paper.

2   Cellular Automata

Cellular Automata (CA) are regular lattices of cells, each one being a finite-state automaton. According to simple dynamics, cells update their state depending on a (typically simple) state transition function of their state and of the state of neighboring cells. The scientific interest on CA comes primarily from the fact that, despite the simplicity of local rules, they can show complex global behaviors.

Formally, a CA is statically defined by a quadruple

$$A   (S   d   f),$$

where S is the finite set of possible states a cell can assume, d is the dimension of the automaton,   is the neighborhood structure, and f is the *local transition rule*. The automaton structure is a d-dimensional discrete grid L Z^d, where Z is the set of integers. Each cell is identified with an array of d components i $(i_1,...,i_d) \in L$ which represent the coordinates of the cell in the grid. It is generally assumed that the grid is infinite, either not limited or closed to a d-dimensional torus. The state of a cell is expressed as a variable   whose domain is defined by S; and the ordered list of cell states defines the CA *global* state   . The neighborhood structure   defines which cells influence any cell.   is defined as a function $:L \rightarrow \wp(L)$ which maps a cell to a set of cells. The neighborhood structure is regular and isotropic, i.e.,   has the same definition for every cell. Usually,   is a subset of the group of translations in L. Finally, the *local transition rule* is a function $f:S \rightarrow S$ which maps a configuration of states in a neighborhood to a state. The transition rule defines the future state of a cell depending on the state of its neighbors (and, possibly, the state of the cell itself). f is typically the same for each cell (uniform CA).

Fig. 1. State of a cyclic attractor in a synchronous CA – RULE A

Fig. 2. A fixed point attractor in an asynchronous CA – RULE A

While the above defined quadruple A specifies the   static   characteristics of an automaton, the complete description of a CA requires the definition of its *dynamics*, i.e., of the dynamics ruling the update of the state of the CA cells. The usual definition of CA is with *synchronous dynamics*: cells update their state in parallel at each time step. However, synchronous dynamics is hardly representative of real-world phenomena, making it not suited for the modeling and the simulation of those phenomena involving a population of autonomous interacting elements, for which asynchronous dynamics have to be introduced. In the experiments presented in this paper, CA have an asynchronous dynamics 11, 14 : at each time, one cell has a uniform probability of rate λ_a to autonomously wake-up and update its state.

The behavior of a CA under synchronous and asynchronous dynamics can be very different 22, 26, 27 . As an example, let us consider a 2-states CA (S 1 where cells are said to be dead or alive, respectively), the Moore neighborhood structure (the neighbors of a cell are the 8 one defining a 3x3 square around the cell itself) and the following transition rule (RULE A):

f =   {a died cell gets alive iff it has 2 neighbors alive; a living cells lives iff it has 1 or 2 neighbors alive}

Once a synchronous CA starts to evolve from an initial random situation, the states of all cells synchronously change accordingly to the above rule, and after a transitory eventually reaches the final cyclic attractor of which one of the composing global states is shown in Figure 1. Figure 2 shows the same CA having evolved accordingly to asynchronous dynamics: the CA usually reaches a fixed-point attractor that its synchronous counterpart has never been observed to be able to reach

3   Dissipative Cellular Automata

3.1   Description

CA studied so far are closed systems, as they do not take into account the interaction between the CA and an environment. Instead, the new class of CA that we have studied is, in addition to asynchronous, open , in the sense that the dynamic behavior of the CA can be influenced by the external environment. From an operative point of view, the openness of the CA implies that some cells can be forced from the external environment to change their state, independently of the cell having evaluated its state and independently of the transition function (Figure 3).

By considering a thermodynamic perspective, one can consider this manifestation of the external environment in terms of energy flows: forcing a cell to change its state can be considered as a manifestation of energy flowing into the system and influencing it 18 . This similarity with thermodynamic systems made us call this kind of CA as dissipative cellular automata (DCA), in that the DCA consumes external energy to reach a final (regular, as shown in the following) configuration.

From a more formal point of view, a DCA can be considered as:

- •*A   S   d   f*
- • asynchronous dynamics (with uniform distribution of rate λ_a);
- • a perturbation action $\varphi(\alpha, D)$.

where A is the quadruple defining a CA, the dynamics is the one already discussed in Subsection 3.1, and the perturbation action φ is a transition function which acts concurrently with f and can change the state of any of the CA cells to a given state α with some probabilistic distribution D, independently of the current state of the cells and of their neighbors. Specifically, in our experiments with V 0,1 , α 1 and D is a uniform distribution of rate λ_e.

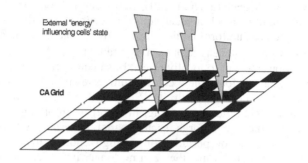

Fig. 3. Dissipative cellular automata

3.2   Emergent Behaviors

The behavior exhibited by DCA is dramatically different from both their synchronous and closed asynchronous counterparts. In general, when the degree of perturbation (determined by λ_e) is high enough to effectively perturb the internal dynamic of the DCA (determined by the rate of cell updates λ_a) but it is still not prevailing over it so as to make the behavior of the DCA almost random (what happens when λ_e is comparable to λ_a), peculiar patterns emerge. The interested reader can refer to the page http://polaris.ing.unimo.it/DCA/ to repeat the experiments on-line.

We have observed that the perturbation on the cells induced by the external – while keeping the system out of equilibrium and making impossible for it to reach any equilibrium situation – makes the DCA develop large scale regular spatial structures. Such structures exhibit long-range correlation between the state of the cells, emerged despite the strictly local and asynchronous transition rules, and breaks the spatial symmetry of the final state. In addition, such structures are stable, despite the continuous perturbing effects of the external environment.

As an example, Figure 4 shows a pattern emerged from a DCA, both exhibiting stable macro-level spatial structures. For this DCA, the transition rules and the neighborhood structure are the same of the CA described in Section 2: the presence of global-scale patterns – breaking the spatial symmetry of the automata – is evident. As another example, Figure 5 shows a typical pattern emerged for a DCA with a neighborhood structure made up of 12 neighbors (all cells having a maximum distance of 2 from the cell itself) and with the following transition rule (RULE B):

f *a died cell gets ali e iff it has   neighbors ali e a li ing cells li es iff it has   or*
neighbors ali e

Again it is possible to see large-symmetry breaking patterns emerge, extending to a larger scale than the local patterns emerging under asynchronous but closed regime (Figure 6).

The phenomenon underlying the behavior of DCA are very similar of the ones determining the emergence of large-scale structures in dissipative systems 18 , e.g., in Bénard's cells, where, the temperature gradient between the two plates is substituted by the ratio λ_e/λ_a. When this ratio is small, expressing small perturbations, each autonomous component (a DCA cell), acting asynchronously accordingly to strictly local rules, tend to reach a local equilibrium (or a strictly local dynamics), which reflects in a global uniform equilibrium of the whole system. When the ratio λ_e/λ_a ratio increases, the system is kept in a substantial out-of-equilibrium situation, resulting in continuous attempt to locally re-establish equilibrium. This typically ends up with cell groups having found new equilibrium states more robust with regard to the perturbation (or compatible with it). Such stable local patterns start soon dominating and influencing the surrounding, in a sort of enforcing feedback, until a globally coordinated (i.e., with large scale spatial patterns) and stable situation emerges. When the degree of perturbation is high enough to avoid local stable situations to persist for enough time, they can no longer influence the whole systems, and the situation becomes turbulent: spatial patterns disappear and the DCA dynamics becomes highly disordered. Deatiled quantitative analysis are in progress.

4   Multi Agent Systems vs. DCA

There are three characteristics which are typical of distributed multi-agent systems (and that are more and more characterizing all types of software systems) that are reflected in DCA: autonomy of agents, locality in interactions, situatedness in an open and dynamic environment.

Agents are autonomous entities 12 , in that their execution is not subject to a global flow of control. Instead, the execution of an agent in a multi-agent system may proceed asynchronously, and the agent's state transition occur accordingly to local internal timings. This is actually what happens, because of the adopted dynamics, in DCA: each state transition in a DCA cell is driven by an internal clock, which is independent from the clock – and the state transitions – of the other DCA cells.

Agents typically execute in the context of a multi-agent organization, and most of the interactions of an agent (causing internal state transitions) occur in the context of that organization 8, 30 . Such abstract concept of locality often reflects also in an actual – physical – locality. In fact, for the sake of scalability and efficiency, multi-agent organizations typically execute in a spatially bounded distributed domain, and wide-area – inter-organizations – interactions are limited as much as possible, and sometimes enabled by making agents move from site to site 6 . In DCA, a cell interacts with (that is, can check the state of) only a limited number of other cells in its neighborhood.

Agents are situated entities that live dipped in an environment, whether a computational one, e.g., a Web site, or a physical one, e.g., a room or a manufacturing unit to be controlled. The agent is typically influenced in its execution (i.e., in its state transitions) by what it senses in the environment. In this sense, agents and multi-agent

Fig. 4. A Behavior evolved in a DCA – RULE A

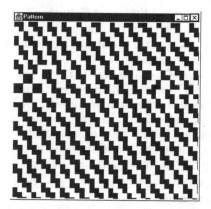

Fig. 5. A behavior evolved in a DCA – RULE B

Fig. 6. A stabilized situation in an asynchronous closed CA – RULE B

systems are "open systems": the global evolution of a multi-agent system may be influenced by the environment in which it lives 20 . And, in most of the cases, the environment possesses a dynamics that is not controllable or foreseeable. For instance, the computational resources, the data, the services, as well as the other agents to be found on a given Web site cannot be predicted and they are likely to change in time. Analogously, the temperature and lightening condition in a room that an agent is devoted to control may vary dynamically for a number of reasons that cannot be predicted. This sort of openness is the same that we can find in DCA, where the perturbation of the environment, changing the internal state of a cell, can make us consider the cell as situated in an environment whose characteristics dynamically change in an unpredictable way.

Given the above similarities, and given that the characteristics leading to the observed DCA behaviors are present in most of today's multi-agent systems there are very good reason to presume that similar strange behaviors will be observed as soon a agents will start populating the Internet and our physical environments.

4.1   Defending from Undesired Emergent Behaviors

The reported experiments open up the possibility that a multi-agent system immersed in a open and dynamic environment may exhibit behaviors very different from the ones it was programmed for. Of course, this is not desirable and may cause highly damaging effects 20 . For instance, in the case of agent-based Internet pricing systems, and despite theoretical equilibrium results, environmental dynamics can make macro-level spatial patterns emerge, leading to great price differences in different sites of the planet. In the case of cooperative agent-based information retrieval, this may cause a large amount of available information to be left out from the search, while making the remaining part over-accessed.

Accordingly, we think that a re-thinking of the methodologies currently adopted for the design, development, and maintenance of multi-agent systems is required to avoid such situations to occur, or at least to be able to predict and control them. By now, software systems are designed in a mechanical way, component by component, so as to exhibit a specific, deterministic behavior. Such approach immediately fails when a large number of autonomous components are involved. Modern multi-agent systems researches recognize this problem, and have gone farther, by approaching the study of multi-agent systems in more systemic, macro-level, terms 12 . The next challenge is to approach the study of multi-agent systems by making the environment and its dynamics play a central role. In other words, one should design a system so as to make it exhibit, under a wide range of environmental conditions, the desired global behavior, disregarding if necessary the full understanding of the behavior of its components, and rather trying to understand the behavior of the system as a whole depending on the environmental conditions. Possibly, a software system should be designed so as to be able to re-adapt itself dynamically and make its internal dynamics contrast the environmental one.

As a consequence of the macro-level approach and of the primary role of environmental dynamics, multi-agent systems will be no longer tested with the goal of finding errors in them (or in their components), but they will be rather tested with regard to their capability of behaving as needed as a whole, independently of the exact behavior of its component 30 , and under the environmental conditions in which the system is expected to operate when released. It is also important to note that, in most of the cases, a newly deployed software system will execute in an environment where other systems already executes. Thus, the new software system will impact on the environmental condition of the pre-existing systems and, by executing, on their environmental dynamics. Thus, designing and testing a system will not only be devoted to make a software system useful, but also to guarantee that it will not be dangerous to other systems.

4.2   Exploiting Useful Emergent Behaviors

Clarifying the dynamic influences between multi-agent systems and their environments can make environmental dynamics become an additional design dimension, rather that an enemy to fight.

As a very trivial application example, directly inspired from the visual appearance of the DCA patterns, one could think at "intelligent paintings". Paintings can be made up of active, radio-enabled, micro-components (or micro-agents), able change their colors according to local transition rules, and making it possible to change the color patterns via simple radio-commands perturbing the transition rules and causing a global change in the pattern of a wall 29 . As another example, the possibility of making global patterns emerge from a system relying on local interactions could be exploited so as to enforce global coordination in a wide-area multi-agent system with very low efforts.

More generally, one could think at exploiting the environmental dynamics to control and influence a multi-agent system from "outside the loop" 24 , that is, without intervening on the system itself. In a world of continuous computations, where decentralized software systems are always running and cannot be stopped (this is already the case for Internet services and for embedded sensors) changing, maintaining and updating systems by stopping and re-installing them is not the best solution, and it could not be always feasible. Instead, given the availability of proper models and tools, one could envision the possibility of influencing the system without stopping it, simply forcing specific environmental dynamics changing the global behavior of the system so as to make it exhibit the required behavior.

5   Methodologies to Control DCA Behavior

Form the previous discussion, it turns out that it would be of fundamental importance to have the possibility of controlling emergent behaviors in DCA. In fact, by considering again the relations with agent-based distributed computing, having the possibility of controlling emergent behavior may open up the doors to both defending from the emergence of undesirable behaviors and exploiting useful behaviors by making them emerge as needed.

However, due to the characteristics of such systems (large number of components, large-scale distribution, autonomy of components) one cannot think at imposing behavior via direct control on all its components. Instead, such control must be as much distributed and decentralized as possible, and can rely only on he possibility of controlling a few components of the systems, without making any assumption on the possibility of controlling all components and their dynamic interactions.

To this end, we experienced two complimentary way of controlling DCA behaviors, both having lead to successful, and rather surprising, results.

5.1   Rule-Based Control

The *rule-based* methodology we have experienced amount at changing the rules determining state transitions in cells. With respect to multi-agent systems, such rule changes would translate in injecting in the agents of a multi-agent system (e.g., via mobile code technologies) some new working parameters and activities. In the DCA, to make a desired pattern emerge, the rule as to change so as to make (some of the) cells recognize that the cells in the neighborhood are in the right configuration, i.e., in a configuration that approaches the configuration that would be required for the required pattern to emerge.

Among a variety of possible rule modifications, we have found that such rule modification should not be too strict, e.g,, a cell should lives *if and only if* its neighborhood is in one of the possible configurations that would have assumed in the presence of the desired pattern. For such strict rules, all cells in the automata quickly die. Instead, we have found out that such rules modifications have to be very weak and, counter-intuitively, should enable a cell to get to life and live in a wider range of configuration than the unmodified rule allow. For instance, given the generic rule:

f =   *{a died cell gets alive iff it has between D_1 and D_2 neighbors alive; a living cells lives iff it has between L_1 and L_2 neighbors alive}*

The simple modified rule **mf** that enables a specific pattern to emerge is in the form:

mf =   *{rule f **OR** a cell must live and get alive as soon as the there are alive neighbor cells in one of the correct configuration w.r.t. the desired patterns}*

which can re-phrased as follows: a cell must follows the normal transition rules, however, independently of that, and independently on the number of alive and died cells, a cell must get to life whenever in the neighborhood there are alive cells in the right position.

Applying the **mf** rule, we have been able to make any desired pattern emerge from any initial configuration from a DCA, independently of the chosen f rule and independently of the dimension of the DCA grid. OF course, such configuration emerges only in the presence of a correct range of value for the λ_c/λ_a ratio. For instance, we have been able to make the pattern of Figure 7 emerge from a DCA by applying the modified *rule B*, a pattern that emerged only very rarely (about 0,01   of the cases) in previous experiments.

Fig. 7. Rule-based methodology: a rare pattern whose emergence can be controlled

Fig. 8. Generalization-based methodology: a local pattern imposed on a portion of a DCA grid.

Of course, for a control methodology to be applicable to large distributed multi-agent systems, it must not assume the capability of influencing the behavior of all the agents of the system. For this reason, we have tested the rule-based methodology also by modifying the rule only in a sub-set of the DCA cells. Such experiences have been very satisfying, in that the rule-based enables to make the desired pattern emerge even when only a very low percentage (down to 30) of the cells apply the modified rules.

5.2   Generalization-Based Control

The generalization-based methodology starts from totally different considerations, and gets its inspiration from Hopfield's work on neural networks 9 . It is known that Hopfield's networks can generalize a pattern from imposition of a partial pattern. Should DCA exhibit such generalization property, controlling them would imply initializing a localized sub-set of the DCA cells in accord to the desired patterns (see Figure 8), and then let the DCA evolve by making the global pattern spontaneously emerge from the local imposition. In the case of a multi-agent system, such methodology would require the possibility of controlling the activities of a local cluster of agents, and then let this locally imposed control diffuse to the whole multi-agent system.

At the beginning, we were not really convinced of DCA possessing such generalization property. Instead, rather surprisingly, we found out that, for a few rules we have experienced, such methodology worked well: for a desired global rule to emerge of a 40x40 DCA grid, we had to initialize a local portion of about 20   of the global grid size. In the case of a multi-agent system, this means for instance that controlling the initial state of cluster of a few hundred agents may be enough to influence a multi-agent system of several thousands.

Further experiments have to be performed to analyze in better detail such generalization properties, and to quantify their capability of working in larger grids and for larger sets of rules.

6   Related Work

This papers is strictly related both to the research area of cellular automata and to the research area of multi-agent systems. Both threads of work are discussed in the following of this section.

6.1   Cellular Automata

CA has been extensively studied in the scientific literature 26, 27 , with either a specific interest on the very properties of CA, or an interest in the exploitation of CA for simulation purposes, or both.

Apart from those threads of studies mainly interested in CA as complex dynamical systems 3, 26 , a well-developed and assessed thread of studies relates to the analysis of the computational properties of CA as turing-equivalent machines and as random generators 23, 27 . Strictly related, studies in the so called cellular programming area aim at exploiting the emergent behaviors of non-uniform CA where each cell can have its own local transition function (possibly determined assigned by means of an evolutionary algorithm) for the sake of image recognition, combinatorial optimization problems and evolvable hardware 23 . However, in most of the above studies, CA are considered as synchronous and closed systems, for the sake of achieving determinism and predictability in CA's behavior (and, thus, in the performed experiments). Even the omni-comprehensive book of S. Wolfram 27 strictly limits to synchronous and closed cellular automata. Some works exist recognizing the peculiar and interesting computational behaviors exhibited by asynchronous model 11, 14, 22 , they still missed in identifying the strong influences that the "openness" of the system and the perturbation of the environment can have on the behavior of the CA and on its dynamics. Possibly, our investigations on perturbed CA may lead to further useful application of cellular-based computational approaches.

In the area of simulation 3 , CA have been and are still widely exploited for the simulation of biophysical processes and socio-economical phenomena. However, simulation of biophysical processes with classical CA is typically made by considering, in most of the cases, closed systems. As already outlined (Section 3.4), a few recent works rooted in the area of macroecology and biogeography 28 recognize that the patterns of species diffusion in a landscape may strongly depends, other than on internal processes of interactions between species, on the effects and dynamics of external disturbances. As a consequence of these findings, effective simulations via cellular automata require the introduction of factors of disturbances in the evolution of the CA, thus making this CA assimilable to perturbed CA 28 . More generally, we believe that the CA model we have introduced could put simulation researches forward, by providing a suitable general-purpose framework for the simulation of biophysical and social systems, other than of bio-geographical ones. For instance, on the side of socio-economical processes, simulations with classical CA are viable only under the assumption of that the actors of the simulation, i.e., the CA cells, have perfect knowledge of their own and of their neighbors' states, and have full control over their own state. Unfortunately, these hypotheses are rarely fulfilled in real-world society and markets. Our approach can be effectively used to model the influence of a dynamic environment and the presence of noise in the process (i.e., limiting both knowledge and control over local states).

Strictly related to the works on CA are those researches on boolean networks 13 and, more recently, on small-world networks 25 . Form a broad perspective, both boolean and small-world networks can be considered as sorts of non-uniform CA with a topology of interconnection that can be described as an undirected graph, typically not regular. These types of networks have found several interesting applications in modeling biological (e.g., genetic) and social (e.g., acquaintance) networks and their dynamics. Still, as in the case of CA, researches related to the influence of a perturbing environment on network dynamics is missing.

Studies on stochastic cellular automata 3 (i.e., CA in which transition rules are made somehow probabilistic) have shown that non-determinism in cell updates may lead to global scale spatial patterns emerge. We are conscious that non-determinism can be considered as a sort of openness and that, therefore, stochastic automata strongly resembles perturbed CA in their global dynamics. Still, the explicit identification of non-determinism as a sort of openness to the environmental dynamics and of its relations to agent-based computing is missing. To the best of our knowledge, the only work that identifies the potential relations between stochastic automata and distributed computing systems is described in 4 . As discussed in Section 4, the authors correctly identifies that global scale behavior emerging in stochastic CA can potentially be used as a tool for globally coordinating the behavior of multi-agent systems. Still, the authors experience with mono-dimensional CA, thus missing the spatial expressiveness that instead emerges in out two-dimensions. Moreover, the lack of modeling environmental dynamics let the authors miss the potential dangers of such emergent behaviors.

6.2   Multi-agent Systems

In the computer science community, the specific area in which the problem of emergent behaviors has always been given more attention is the area of multi-agent systems. This is mainly due to the fact that multi-agent system, being agents autonomous and situated by definitions, thus prone to exhibit unexpected emergent behaviors.

Since the origins of distributed artificial intelligence and of multi-agent systems researches, a large amount of studies have shown that system in which autonomous components interact with each other in a network, and change their status accordingly to the outcomes of these interactions, can make peculiar global behaviors – whether useful or damaging – emerge 10. Recent examples of these studies may be found in the area of computational markets 7 and of computational ecosystems 8. However, most of these studies focused on the internal dynamics of the system, without taking into account the perturbation of the environment.

Studies in the area of artificial social laws 17 show that global rules constraining the behavior of all the agents in a group can notably influence the dynamic behavior of the group. Analogously, studies adopting an organizational metaphor for the design of multi-agent systems 6, 15, 30, shows that the definition of global environmental rules to which all agents must obey is very useful toward the effective control of the global multi-agent system behavior. For all the above approaches, the basic intuition is that agents, for the very fact of living in an environment (i.e., a society or an organization) are not fully autonomous but, instead, their actions can be constrained by the environment, the same as the state of the cells in DCA can be changed by the perturbation function. However, the above studies exploit such kind of environmental abstractions constructively during the design process, and assume having full control over the environment behavior. Still, these researches typically misses in identifying that agents may live in dynamic environment, where the rules governing their execution and their interactions can change during the evolution of the multi-agent systems and can influence their behavior in unpredictable (or simply uncontrollable way).

The importance of the environmental abstraction and of its dynamic in the global behavior of the system is properly attributed in the study and implementation of ant-based multi-agent systems 5, 15, 19. In these systems, very simple agents can indirectly interact with each other in a local way, by putting synthetic pheromones in the environment and by sensing pheromones concentration in a spatially bounded portion of the environment. The environment, by its side, affects interactions with its own dynamics, causing pheromones evaporation or diffusion. Such very simple models may be characterized by self-organization and emergent phenomena that can be useful to achieve difficult goals (swarm intelligence): finding shortest paths, clustering data, etc. The similarities between ant-based multi-agent systems and perturbed CA are strong: they both exploit asynchronous components affected in their execution by the environmental dynamics, and both evolve to low-entropy global states 15 where long-range correlations are established, generally by means of positive feedback. However, till now, ant-based systems researches have focused on the possibility of "designing" the environment and its dynamics to constructively exploit it, and few researchers focused on the perturbing effects that uncontrollable environmental dynamic can have on the global behavior of a system 20.

7   Conclusions and Future Works

Large-scale spatial patterns, not observed under closed regime, emerge in open DCA. Since distributed multi-agent systems exhibits all of the characteristics of DCA (autonomy of components and openness) similar sort of structures are likely to make their appearance as soon as agents will start populating the Internet. This requires methodologies, and tools, to predict and control emergent behaviors in large multi-agent systems, and enabling to either exploit emergent behaviors as an additional design dimension, or to prevent undesirable behaviors.

The experiments reported in this paper – and the two methodologies proposed to control emergent behaviors – are indeed preliminary. First, since real multi-agent systems are characterized by agents of different types (unlike DCA, in which all cells have the same rules) and that can also sometimes communicate to "distant" agents (unlike DCA, where all interactions are strictly local), we are planning to extend our experiments to evaluate the behavior of DCA with non-uniform transition rules and non-strictly local interactions. In addition, we are trying to better formalize the concepts of "openness" and of "perturbation", and to characterize and measure the degree of perturbation and the degree of order of the emergent patterns. Finally, we are trying to define effective models for controlling emergent behaviors in large-scale multi-agent systems, with a key focus on mobility of components 15 . The main goal is to make our experiments more and more approximate to the characteristics of agent-based distributed and mobile scenarios and, eventually, to end up with a more realistic simulations.

Acknowledgements. Work supported by the Italian MURST in the project "MUSI UE – Infrastructure for   oS in Web Multimedia Services with Heterogeneous Access".

References

1.   R. Albert, H. Jeong, A. Barabasi, "Diameter of the World Wide Web", Nature, 401:130–131, 9 Sept. 1999.
2.   R. Albert, H. Jeong, A. Barabasi, "Error and Attack Tolerance of Complex Networks", Nature, 406:378–382, 27 July 2000.
3.   Y. Bar-Yam, Dynamics of Complex systems. Addison-Wesley, 1997.
4.   T. D. Barfoot, G. M. T. D'Eleuterio, "Multiagent Coordination by Stochastic Cellular Automata", Proceeding of the Joint International Conference on Artificial Intelligence, Seattle (WA), Aug. 2001.
5.   E. Bonabeau, M. Dorigo, G. Theraulaz, Swarm Intelligence. From Natural to Artificial Systems, Santa Fe Institute – Studies in the Science of Complexity. Oxford University Press, 1999.
6.   G. Cabri, L. Leonardi, F. Zambonelli, "Engineering Mobile Agent Applications via Context-Dependent Coordination", IEEE Transactions on Software Engineering, 28(11), Nov. 2002.
7.   C. V. Goldman, S. Kraus, O. Shehory, "Equilibria Strategies for Selecting Sellers and Satisfying Buyers", Proc. of the 5th International Workshop on Cooperative Information Agents, LNAI, No. 2182, pp. 166–177, Sept. 2001.

8. R. Gustavsson, M. Fredriksson, "Coordination and Control in Computational Ecosystems: A Vision of the Future", in Coordination of Internet Agents, A. Omicini al (Eds.), Springer Verlag, pp. 443–469, 2001.

9. J.J. Hopfield, "Neural Networks and Physical Systems with Emergent Collective Computational Abilities", Proc. of the National Academy of Science, 79:2554–2558, 1982.

10. B. A. Hubermann, T. Hogg, "The Emergence of Computational Ecosystems", in SFI Studies in the Science of Complexity, Vol. V, Addison-Wesley, 1993.

11. T. E. Ingerson, R. L. Buvel, "Structure in Asynchronous Cellular Automata", Physica D, 10:59–68, 1984.

12. N. R. Jennings, "On Agent-Based Software Engineering", Artificial Intelligence, 117(2), 2000.

13. S. A. Kauffman, The origins of order, Oxford University Press, New York, 1993.

14. E. D. Lumer, G. Nicolis, "Synchronous Versus Asynchronous Dynamics in Spatially Distributed Systems", Physica D, 71:440–452, 1994.

15. M. Mamei, M. Mahan, "Engineering Mobility in Large Multi-agent Systems", 2003in this volume.

16. M. Mamei, L. Leonardi, F. Zambonelli, "Co-Fields: Towards a Unifying Model for Swarm Intelligence", 3rd International Workshop on Engineering Societies in the Agents' World, Madrid (E), Sept. 2002.

17. Y. Moses, M. Tenneholtz, "Artificial Social Systems", Computers and Artificial Intelligence, 14(3):533–562, 1995.

18. G. Nicolis, I. Prigogine, Exploring Complexity: an Introduction, W. H. Freeman, 1989.

19. V. Parunak, "Go to the Ant: Engineering Principles from Natural Agent Systems", Annals of Operations Research, 75:69–101, 1997.

20. V. Parunak, S. Bruekner, J. Sauter, "ERIM's Approach to Fine-Grained Agents", NASA/JPL Workshop on Radical Agent Concepts, Greenbelt (MD), 2002.

21. M. Ripeani, A. Iamnitchi, I. Foster, "Mapping the Gnutella Network", IEEE Internet Computing, 6(1):50–57, Jan.-Feb. 2002.

22. B. Schönfisch, A. De Roos, "Synchronous and Asynchronous Updating in Cellular Automata", BioSystems, 51(3):123–143, 1999.

23. M. Sipper. "The Emergence of Cellular Computing". IEEE Computer, 37(7), July 1999.

24. D. Tennenhouse, "Proactive Computing", Communications of the ACM, May 2000.

25. D. Watts, Small Worlds : The Dynamics of Networks between Order and Randomness, Princeton University Press (Princeton, NJ), 1999.

26. S. Wolfram, Cellular Automata and Complexity. Addison-Wesley, 1994.

27. S. Wolfram, A New Kind of Science, Wolfram Media Inc. 2002.

28. J. T. Wootton, "Local Interactions Predict Large-scale Patterns in Empirically Derived Cellular Automata", Nature, 413: 841:844, 25 Oct. 2001.

29. F. Zambonelli, M. Mamei, "The Cloak of Invisibility: Challenges and Applications", IEEE Pervasive Computing, 1(4):63–72, Oct.-Dec. 2002.

30. F. Zambonelli, N. R. Jennings, M. J. Wooldridge, "Organizational Abstractions for the Analysis and Design of Multi-agent Systems, 1st Workshop on Agent-Oriented Software Engineering, LNCS No. 1957, Jan. 2001.

The RETSINA MAS, a Case Study

Katia Sycara, Joseph A. Giampapa, Brent Langley, and Massimo Paolucci

The Robotics Institute, Carnegie Mellon University,
5000 Forbes Ave,
Pittsburgh, PA 15213–3890, (U.S.A.)
{katia,garof,blangley,paolucci}@cs.cmu.edu
http://www.cs.cmu.edu/~{katia,garof,blangley,paolucci,softagents}

Abstract. In this paper we identify challenges that confront the large-scale multi-agent system (LMAS) designer, and claim that these challenges can be successfully addressed by agent-based software engineering (ABSE), which we consider to be distinct from object-oriented software engineering for multi-agent systems (OOSE for MAS) in its consideration of agent *goal*, *role*, *context* and *attitude* as first class objects. We show how we have discovered these principles through our experiences in developing the RETSINA multi-agent system, in implementing specific test applications, and in the derivation of three distinct architectures that help guide and describe the designs of our systems: the *individual agent* architecture, the *functional* architecture, and the *infrastructure* architecture.

1 Introduction

As information technologies become accessible to more and more people and as commercial and government organizations are challenged to scale their services to larger market shares and wider user communities while minimizing or reducing their costs in doing so, there is an increased demand for software applications to provide the following three features to their human end-users:

1. richer application end-to-end functionalities,
2. a reduction of human involvement in "the process" by:
   - reducing information overload,
   - reducing configuration management and system maintenance overheads, and
   - enabling the rapid specification of new, often context-aware tasks, and
3. in the combinatorial use of existing software applications and systems in novel or adaptive ways.

Distributed multi-agent system (MAS) technologies and web services show much promise at satisfying the above desiderata by means of their inherent modularity and ease with which they can be recombined to form new applications. When designing new distributed software systems, however, the above broad requirements and their translations into specific implementations are typically addressed by

A. Garcia et al. (Eds.): SELMAS 2002, LNCS 2603, pp. 232–250, 2003.

partial, complementary and overlapping technologies, and the combination of the three gives rise to significant software engineering challenges. Some of the challenges that may arise are: determining the components that the MAS application should contain, organizing the components of the MAS, determining the assumptions that one needs to make in order to implement a MAS application, and if using multiple components off the shelf (COTS), how can their compatibilities with each other, or the degree of effort involved in making them interoperate with each other, be estimated? In this paper we further identify other challenges, and claim that they can be successfully addressed by agent-based software engineering (ABSE). We consider ABSE to be distinct from object-oriented software engineering for multi-agent systems (OOSE for MAS) in its consideration of agent *goal, role, context* and *attitude* as first class objects. We show how we have discovered these principles through our experiences in developing the RETSINA multi-agent system, in implementing specific test applications, and in the derivation of three distinct architectures that help guide and describe the designs of our systems: the *individual agent* architecture, the *functional* architecture, and the *infrastructure* architecture.

The goal of the design of the RETSINA multi-agent system is to have a positive impact in any combination of the following three areas: (1) to augment a human end user's information-based perceptual capabilities by reducing information overload and providing context-relevant information, (2) to qualitatively and quantitatively improve the range of actions and activities in which the end user can engage, and (3) to enhance the means — typically through the context-aware use of devices, as is done in pervasive and ubiquitous computing — by which humans may perceive the world or by which humans may effect their decisions within it.

The RETSINA MAS is based on the assumption that it will be operating in an open world. The networked environment in which an agent is operating is *open*, or without bounds, it is *dynamic* in nature from the perspective of network topologies, agent capabilities and agent locations, and the networked environment is *uncertain*, that is, the same agent that provided an answer to an earlier request may not be available when called upon again. In the RETSINA MAS there is also an assumption that often there will be some degree of service or functional replication so that should one agent fail, one or many other agents and service providers can be found to substitute for the failed agent. And finally, there is the assumption that many of RETSINA agent behaviors can port to physical robots and produce meaningful results in the physical robotic world.

The RETSINA definition of multi-agent systems is driven by our vision that multi-agent societies should be populated by heterogeneous agents that autonomously organize their own social structures. Our thinking of MAS infrastructure is guided by the desire to enable the flexible design, building and operation of such societies. We consider MAS infrastructure to be the domain independent and reusable substratum on which MAS systems, services, and components live, communicate, interact and interoperate; the infrastructure should support agents and facilitate their social interactions with each other rather than impose it.

One important consequence is that to achieve heterogeneity the MAS infrastructure should minimize the assumptions that it makes on the agents that populate it, therefore, we make a very strong distinction between the MAS *infrastructure* and the *agent* architecture. We believe that to achieve heterogeneity the MAS infrastructure should not dictate what kind of computational architecture agents have, rather it is up to the agents to find the best way to use the infrastructure to their advantage. Ultimately, the only assumption we make on the architecture of an agent is the awareness of the existence of the MAS infrastructure and of its components, and how to use those components to enable the agent to be part of a multi-agent society, i.e to be socially aware.

The definition of MAS infrastructure that we put forward does not impose any biases with respect to the social structure and coordination regimes of the agents. Indeed, we do not have a "coordinator" component that makes sure that the agents behave socially in a coherent way. Rather we claim that the social structure and coordination regimes should emerge from the behavior of the agents rather than being imposed by the MAS infrastructure. We claim that the MAS infrastructure should be general enough to facilitate any coordination scheme such as team behavior [33,13], negotiation [17], Contract Nets [27] and auction protocols [8], etc. We feel that a coordination regime as well as social norms [2] are not part of the infrastructure but are particular to the design of a given MAS application society, and are determined by the requirements of the task that the agents are performing. Multi-agent social structure and coordination mechanisms result as applications of the MAS infrastructure rather than being mandated by the infrastructure per se.

The rest of the paper is structured as follows. We begin with a review of the challenges of software engineering for large-scale MASs, and our characterizatoin of agent-based software engineering in Section 2. Section 3 presents a brief description of the three RETSINA architectures. Section 4 discusses some of our lessons learned. We conclude in Section 5.

2   Challenges of SELMAS

The report from the SELMAS workshop [10] lists many challenges, perspectives, and unanswered questions about the nature of large-scale multi-agent systems (LMASs) and agent-based software engineering (ABSE): *how does one define a MAS, what are the central issues to be addressed when designing one*, and *is there* really *a difference between ABSE and object-oriented software engineering for MASs?* As strong proponents of ABSE as a unique software engineering paradigm, we would like to briefly discuss what we view as some of the challenges of MAS and LMAS construction, how we characterize ABSE, and what are some of the consequences of these characterizations.

2.1   The Recognized Challenges

Multi-agent systems operate in an open, unbounded world and thus have imposed upon them the requirements that they must be context-aware — aware of how the environment conditions the interactions that the agents can engage in. MAS openness also refers to the actual, implemented agent system, itself. Even if an initial MAS design begins with a limited number of agents, new agents or newer versions of agents will most likely be added to the original MAS at a later date as requirements for the system change, and new features and functions are requested. Because of this openness, there is no single point of resource allocation, synchronization, or failure recovery. The environment is also dynamic and changing, which challenges any software engineering paradigms that require the explicit enumeration of objects and relationships among objects in the environment. The MAS distributed computing environment is uncertain, a characteristic that justifies concerns for partial failure recovery [35]. In distributed computing, where there is no centralized point of control, the failure of any one computation, communication link or network node can render the distributed execution state of the MAS application inconsistent, and the resulting inconsistency may be difficult to identify and thus difficult to remedy. As the number of agents participating in MAS applications increases, the dimensionality of the above concerns becomes combinatorial, and challenges human perception of control and predictability of the system. And, there are different types of heterogeneities that multi-agent systems must address, unpredictably, during their life cycle. Some of the heterogeneities that we have identified and try to accommodate within the RETSINA system are the following:

Communications Heterogeneity. Considerations include how many different communications interfaces can or should the agent use for effecting its communications with its peers (e.g. IR, radio, wire, etc.), and what are the available underlying network protocols that will be used.

Coordination Heterogeneity. There are multiple coordination techniques [28] such as capability-based coordination [30], team-oriented coordination [14,33], the Contract Net Protocol [27], auction-based coordination schemes [8,34], and others, which depend primarily on the task that needs to be performed, and the coordination attitude of an agent (e.g. cooperative, self-interested, antagonistic, etc.).

Environmental Heterogeneity. The operating environment can range from the network operating environment, in which considerations focus on how well network protocols are performing (e.g. throughput, transport reliability, network connection permanence, etc.), to the computational environment in which software capabilities change, to physical and terrain environments of agent-augmented hardware and robots.

Functional Heterogeneity. This is the identification of agent roles in terms of the services or functions that they contribute to a multi-agent system, and is the focus of the Functional Architecture, described in Section 3.2.

Security Heterogeneity. In RETSINA, security is viewed as being parameterized by the application [36], in addition to encryption of communications and authentication of component identities. Some examples of differences in security models are evaluations of trust per individual agent vs. trust of agents running on a trusted platform, and digital rights management for MAS-aided information fusion, aggregation and sharing.

Semantic Heterogeneity. The chief focus of any multi-agent system, this heterogeneity expresses the issue that any two interoperating agents must be certain when using a vocabulary of terms, or translations thereof, that they are using the same concepts with the same relevant inferences of relations as the other communicating agent.

Systems Heterogeneity. This heterogeneity is derived from differences of devices and hardware, operating systems, implementation language and execution environment (e.g. within a virtual machine or not), etc., and from the proliferation of versions of all of the above.

Despite these challenges, we believe that practical and non-trivial LMASs can be implemented and executed reliably, by recognizing some important characterizations of ABSE.

2.2   Agent-Based Software Engineering

Our claim is that the engineering principles that motivate a robust and reliable MAS design are those that consider an agent to be defined by its goal, role, context, and attitude. We consider these to be first class objects in the ABSE paradigm, and contend that by not treating these four characteristics as first class objects, object-oriented software engineering founders in its abilities to properly model and predict MAS and LMAS behaviors. We describe these principles as follows.

Goal. A *goal* provides the motivation for an agent to perform any activity at all. It constrains the behaviors of individual agents during their interactions with each other, and enables inferencing and predictability of individual agent behavior as well as of the emergent behavior of an entire MAS, itself. We assume that all agents have at least the implicit goals of wanting to announce their existence to the multi-agent community through the advertisements of their capabilities. Another implicit goal that agents may have is the desire to maintain the reliability of their services, which results in them seeking alternative planning and execution strategies should one route to goal completion fail or be perceived to be unlikely.

An agent's goals sometimes might not be completely consistent and place the agent in a dilemma: the agent then must evaluate the tradeoffs involved in pursuing one or another of its goals. For example, an information agent might have the two goals of finding the most current stock information and of acquiring information for free or as cheaply as possible. During its execution, the agent may discover that the free or inexpensive information providing sites respond poorly, or do not provide current information. The agent might need to consider a pay-per-query site that charges for every query, but guarantees a rapid response with the latest data. The agent must evaluate and choose which of the goals it will attempt to achieve.

Role. The notion of *role* is confused by the multiple connotations that it has in human languages. We characterize it as a mesh of agent relationships, including authority relationships, that exist within a given context. Authority relationships are important for deriving an agent's range of actions when performing tasks that were delegated to it by a human, and for reasoning about information access and divulgence rights. An agent's role within a given context may change. Roles allow inferences to be made about how an agent will interact with a group of other agents, or about how it will achieve its goals. A characterization of *role* for team coordination, defined in terms of goal, authority, and some contextual indicators, is provided in [14].

Context. A *context* establishes the conditions by which an agent's roles, and sometimes goals, can be defined. We do not believe that it is possible to enumerate all the types of contexts in which an agent may be situated, but it is important for an agent to have the ability to recognize when its context has changed. When an agent realizes that it is in a new context, it may need to acquire a new set of roles. Somehow, the agent must be able to determine if the new roles form relationships with roles from other contexts in which the agent belongs, and if so how do the roles from one context impact the decisions and actions of the agent in another context. Consider the example of an agent that provides financial portfolio management advice to an investor, but which also should try to sell certain stock to increase the value of that stock's individual shares. The agent has two distinct roles derived from the two contexts in which it may operate: trusted advisor and interested seller. If the role of the interested seller translates into the context in which the agent is advising, then its role as trusted advisor will be doubted. If the role of seller does not translate to the context of advisor, unless explicitly requested by the client, then the agent as adviser will be trusted by the client.

Attitude. The *attitude* of an agent is: its positive or negative disposition to provide reliable and trustworthy services, degree of being deceptive or forthright, the degree to which it will allow its actions to be verified, and its degree of cooperativeness, which can range from altruistic, to self-interested, to being competitive. Most agent systems begin with an implicit assumption about the degree of cooperativeness of their agents.

Not all of the above four characteristics need to be significantly present in a MAS application at the same time. Just as all non-distributed software applications will have varying degrees of functional and dynamic behaviors [22], agents will have varying degrees of: motivation by goal, identity by role, awareness of its context, and dispositions to behave with certain attitudes.

2.3   Consequences

One of the consequences of our characterizations of agent-based software engineering is that agents have grounds by which to make inferences about new priorities and consequences as the open, uncertain, and dynamic agent environment changes. That is, the power of inference enables an agent to be adaptable to its changing environment. Another consequence of our ABSE characterizations is that one of the desiderata of software engineering, *predictability* of MAS behavior, changes from two perspectives. From the agent perspective, the agent is now *empowered to infer* its own range of actions, perceptions, and expectations for achieving its multiple goals, given: its multiple roles in multiple contexts, its attitudes, and the types of heterogeneities that are in its environment. From the perspective of the MAS observer — which may be another agent, as well — the range of actions and behaviors in which the agent may engage can vary greatly based on the unpredictable contexts, the roles of the agents within those contexts, etc., and therefore ABSE predictability estimates should be performed in terms of ample tolerances rather than in terms of precise specifications with narrow tolerances. Thus, when designing a MAS, an engineer is no longer specifying exactly how an agent will behave, but establishing the bounds and tolerances, or an envelope of acceptable behaviors, by which agents may plan their actions, and by which observers may judge a MAS' behaviors.

The other principle consequences that we will discuss in this paper are the ways in which we translate our ABSE principles into the RETSINA MAS. One of the first derivations of these principles was to adopt a goal-driven hierarchical task network (HTN) deliberative planning system as the general planning architecture for a RETSINA individual agent. By doing so, we could enable agents to plan and replan subtasks and umbrella tasks for achieving their goals. One of the ways in which we tested this scheme was to have a goal-driven, HTN planning agent participate in multiple simultaneous auctions, with different protocols, to achieve the goal of acquiring an object at the "globally" lowest possible price [8].

Another way in which we translate our ABSE principles into reliable implementations is the way in which we use the nature of hierarchical task networks to provide parallel means for composing services, monitoring the execution of distributed computations and fusing the resulting data and control flow as the concurrent computations finish, and automatically determining rollback segments should distributed computations fail partially. We hope that how this happens will be clearer as the reader continues into the next section.

3   The Three RETSINA Architectures

The following three sections provide abstract architectural descriptions that, combined, address many of the heterogeneities listed in Section 2 and that conform to the software engineering principles mentioned in section 2.2. They are the architecture of an individual agent, the functional architecture of a society of RETSINA agents, and the infrastructure architecture that provides the most practical guidance in the systems integration of agent components and technologies.

3.1   The RETSINA Individual Agent Architecture

The *RETSINA Individual Agent Architecture* [29,1,7] is illustrated by Figure 1. This agent architecture implements hierarchical task network (HTN) planning, scheduling and execution monitoring [21] in three parallel execution threads, while a fourth thread, the *Communicator* [23], provides the means by which the agent communicates with the networked world. The Communicator provides a level of abstraction that insulates the components from issues of agent communication language (ACL), communication session management, the location of

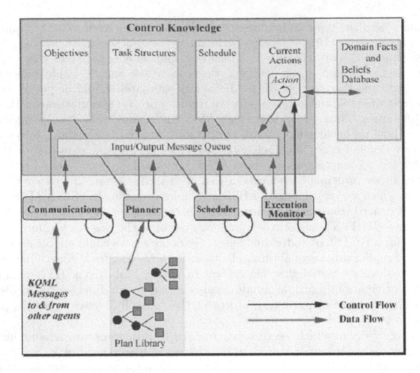

Fig. 1. Schematic diagram of the RETSINA Agent Architecture.

agent services, the logging and visualization of agent messages and state information, and the communication transport being used (e.g. infrared, telephone, base band, etc.). The *HTN Planner* thread receives HTN plan *objectives* from the Communicator, extracts the information and instructions contained therein (e.g. an information request, which becomes a current goal of the recipient agent), and attempts to apply the extracted data to all the plans in its plan library. Plan actions are partially *enabled* as the data is applied to them, and once all actions of a plan are completely enabled, they are scheduled by the *Scheduler*. The Scheduler maintains the enabled actions in a priority queue, and works with the *Execution Monitor*, which actually executes the enabled actions, monitors the execution, and handles failures. The coordination among the three planning modules is done in such a way that high-priority actions can interrupt those being executed by the Execution Monitor, if those being executed are of a lower priority.

3.2   The RETSINA Functional Architecture

The RETSINA multi-agent system is a collection of heterogeneous software entities that collaborate with each other to provide a result or a service to other software entities or to an end user. Individual agents within that collection have roles which represent their commitment to achieving — or participating in an

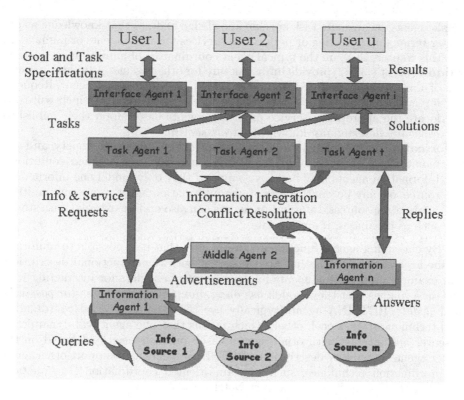

Fig. 2. The RETSINA Functional Architecture

activity that will achieve — a team goal. Describing agent roles in achieving that goal is easily done by considering the functional contributions that an agent makes, and by focusing on the requester of that contribution (e.g. its anticipated permanence or its frequency of requests) to determine the range of communicative behaviors the service provider agent should support.

The RETSINA Functional Architecture [29] is illustrated by Figure 2, which categorizes agents as belonging to any of four agent types:

Interface agents present agent results to the user, or solicit input from the user. In addition, they could learn from user actions [3]. Interface agents typically represent specific modes of input or output, such as a *VoiceRecognition* agent or a *SpeechGeneration* agent, or can interact with *device agents*[1] to determine the proper way to display information given a device's display characteristics, or to retrieve input from a user. Interface agent behaviors can also be associated with *task agents*.

---

[1] Device agents are a type of information agent that represent systems information about devices to a MAS. Some RETSINA device agents that have been written are for PDAs (e.g. PalmPilots and iPAQs), and WAP-enabled cell phones.

Task agents encapsulate task-specific knowledge and use that knowledge as the criterion for requesting or performing services for other agents or humans. In this respect, they are the typical agent coordinators of a multi-agent system.

Middle agents [38,12] provide infrastructure for other agents. A typical instance of a middle agent is the *Matchmaker* [30,31], or *Yellow Pages* agent. Requesting agents submit a *capability* request to the Matchmaker, which will then locate the appropriate service-providing agents based upon their published *capability descriptions*, known as *advertisements*.

Information agents model the information world to the agent society, and can monitor any data- or event-producing source for user-supplied conditions. Information agents may be *single source* if they only model one information source, or may be *multi-source* if one information agent represents multiple information sources. Information agents can also update external data stores, such as databases, if appropriate.

By classifying agents functionally, we believe that it is possible to uniformly define agent behaviors [7] that are consistent with their functional description. For example, information agents implement four behaviors for interacting with the data sources that they model: *ask once, monitor actively, monitor passively,* and *update*. RETSINA agents typically use the capability-based coordination [28] technique to task each other, which means that one agent will dynamically discover and interact with other agents based on their need and based on the other agents' capability descriptions. RETSINA agents also support other forms of coordination techniques, such as team-oriented coordination [14], auction-based coordination [8], and Contract Net Protocol.

3.3   The RETSINA Infrastructure Architecture

Agents in a MAS are expected to coordinate by exchanging services and information, to be able to follow complex negotiation protocols, to construct models of each other and shared models of their tasks and world, to agree on commitments, and to perform other socially complex operations. In order to interact robustly, agents need an infrastructure of services that enable them to, for example, find each other in open, ever changing and uncertain environments, to communicate, and to warrant that the proper security constraints are satisfied, etc. In addition, agents need conventions, such as Agent Communication Languages (ACLs), conversational policies and ontologies that define the meaning of the terms agents use to provide the basis for achieving semantic interoperability and agreement with each other. Moreover, agents need to share knowledge of how to use the infrastructure, ACLs, and protocols. In this section we analyze some of the requirements of the MAS infrastructure as it emerged from our experiences with the RETSINA MAS. The reader is referred to [32] for a more detailed explanation.

Figure 3, which describes the organizational architecture of RETSINA, represents the abstract dependencies of the upper layers of infrastructure modules on the lower layers, for each of the two columns[2]. The figure is organized to

---

[2] For the sake of clarity, this diagram is a simplification of our own intuitions and some details are not accurately represented. For example, the placement of the security

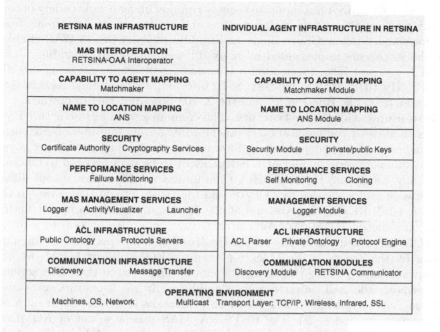

Fig. 3. The RETSINA MAS Infrastructure and Individual Agent Infrastructure

show, in the left column, the organization of the MAS , and in the right column, how the overall architecture of the MAS is reflected in the internal modules of an individual agent so that it may interact with the infrastructure components. While the diagram shows the settings adopted by the RETSINA MAS, we believe that every MAS implements, in whole or in part, implicitly or explicitly, the modules described by the diagram, thus our belief that every MAS can ultimately be mapped to this diagram. Note that we do not impose the requirement or expectation that every agent must have modules that support each of the infrastructure components: an agent implementation may include some modules and not others. Nor does the infrastructure dictate how these modules are implemented or how they should interact with each other. Rather, as has been our experiences, the infrastructure serves as a reference to guide in understanding and placing different information technologies in an architecturally sound manner, and in informing the ways in which interoperability may be achieved between systems of differing MAS architectures [12]. In the paragraphs that follow we briefly describe the layers of the left column, from the bottom, up.

Operating Environment. The operating environment may force a decision about programming language, communication protocols, network bandwidth and

---

level should either span or be a component of multiple layers to imply that security is a feature of the whole MAS. Similarly, *performance services* are also a feature of *capability to agent mapping*.

persistence. RETSINA has supported agents running under a wide variety of conditions, such as: different operating systems and versions thereof, spanning from Windows and WindowsCE, to Linux, to Sun OS, to Palm OS, to WAP-enabled cell phones; agents implemented in many different languages including: Java, C and C++, and Lisp, to mention a few; and agents communicating directly in: TCP/IP, UDP, HTTP, wireless, SSL, infrared, across mobile sockets [18], low-power radio like BlueTooth[3], and the X-10[4] powerline carrier protocol.

Communication Infrastructure. The communication infrastructure layer defines an abstract communication channel for intra-agent information exchange. It should be medium-independent to allow agents to communicate on any physical transmission medium, and ACL independent to be parametrized to function under any condition. The RETSINA Communicator [23] makes use of different network protocols such as TCP/IP and multicast; in addition, through the DARPA Grid, RETSINA makes use of the Jini[5] communication infrastructure based on remote method invocation.

ACL Infrastructure. The ACL infrastructure layer specifies the language spoken by the agents in the MAS, for example KQML [9] or FIPA[6], as well as conversational policies [15,26] agents should adhere to in their interactions. Furthermore, the ACL infrastructure should specify the semantics associated with the language, whether it is based on a mentalistic model [16] or on a social interaction model [25]. The RETSINA MAS uses a subset of KQML as the typical ACL for all the agents in the MAS, but the modular design of the RETSINA Communicator allows agent programmers to easily use other ACLs, such as FIPA, or novel languages that are based on XML [8,4,5].

Management Services. Management services can support the analysis of agent activity to support optimization or debugging in the case of failures, and since the deployment of a MAS requires the deployment of a number of agents, they also should support launching capabilities to minimize the burden of deploying a MAS and to make the management of large MASs scalable for humans. Within the RETSINA MAS infrastructure a number of management tools have been developed to support activity monitoring, visualization and launching [11]. It should also be noted that the infrastructure that supports agent location and discovery also addresses a significant portion of the activities involved in MAS configuration management.

Performance Measurement. The performance measurement layer provides a set of protocols and tools that allow an agent to learn about the trust and reliability of other agents. Agents should also monitor their own behavior to verify that they are meeting their expected requirements. Self monitoring capabilities have led to the implementation within RETSINA of agents that are able to clone themselves [24] when overwhelmed by many tasks delegated to them to increase the likelihood that they can fulfill all their assigned tasks.

Security. We identified two dimensions of security: communication security and infrastructure integrity. Communication security guarantees privacy so that

---

[3] http://www.bluetooth.com/
[4] http://www.x10.org/
[5] http://www.sun.com/jini
[6] Foundation for Intelligent Physical Agents, http://www.fipa.org/.

a message cannot be eavesdropped, authentication so that an agent is certain of its partner's identity, and non-repudiation, which prevents agents from denying that they took part in a transaction. Infrastructure integrity guarantees that no agent can manipulate the information stored in the infrastructure components such as the Agent Name Server or the Matchmaker, and that the contents of a message cannot be changed by an unauthorized agent. RETSINA supports communication security through the use of a Certificate Authority that provides unique public and private keys to agents in the MAS [37]. Infrastructure integrity, has been achieved by strictly controlling the operations an agent can do against the infrastructure components to protect their load and prevent unexpected uses. It has also been studied formally in the way in which it applies to protocols for electronic commerce [36].

Name to Location Mapping and **Capability to Agent Mapping.** The *Name to Location Mapping* module maps an agent identifier (e.g. name) to the specific location where an agent may be found. The *Capability to Agent Mapping* refers to processes of semantic matchmaking [30,31], which were described in Section 3.2. Although, for reasons of space, we cannot elaborate on the many complexities and heterogeneities that are embodied by these layers, these two layers are at the heart of a robust and scalable MAS.

MAS Interoperation. This modules permits multiple agents of different MAS architectures to interoperate with each other despite their architectural differences. As mentioned earlier, interoperability across MAS boundaries is based on the identification and exploitation of similarities between the two agent architectures, across multiple infrastructure levels. Details of the issues involved are provided in [12]. In addition to interoperating with the Open Agent Architecture (OAA) [20] and DARPA Grid [6] MASs, we have also developed interoperators with Jini services.

4   Lessons Learned

Given the breadth and scope of our experiences in developing the RETSINA system and reference architectures, there are many lessons learned, evaluations of our architectures, and metrics that we could discuss. Given limitations of space, we limit our lessons to how we deal with heterogeneity, and how we respond to the three questions which motivated the workshop.

4.1   Dealing with Heterogeneity

One of the lessons learned from designing the RETSINA MAS for the types of heterogeneity listed in Section 2.1 is the confirmation that there are practical merits to designing a MAS for such levels of heterogeneity. The practical merits are: the ease by which components can be combined to achieve better scalability, the achievement of new functionality, and the achievement of novel functional dimensions. The following are some example derivations of MAS functionality that were accommodated by the design of the RETSINA MAS. That is, these software artifacts, listed according to the heterogeneity that they address, were implemented *without* needing to retroactively modify any of the existing RETSINA architecture.

Communications Heterogeneity. Separating the implications of contractual commitment in agent-to-agent requests made it possible to interoperate between any RETSINA and OAA agent when designing the *RETSINA − OAA_InterOperator* [12]. In contrast, the lack of such separation inhibited scalability of agent interoperations between two other agent systems in the same experiments. Also, by using a "loosely coupled" agent message passing scheme as opposed to a "tightly coupled" remote method invocation, RETSINA agents need only "pick and choose" the arguments and parameters that they need or can translate, and can ignore the rest if they are not essential to the computation. Nor is it necessary to modify or have access to an agent's program code to effect new communications between two previously existing agents.

Coordination Heterogeneity. In RETSINA, the coordination model is provided by each individual task agent[7], which employs the most appropriate coordination model for its task. Since task agents can be added and executed as needed, RETSINA allows for a wide variety of agent coordination models to interoperate with each other.

Environmental Heterogeneity. We have describe schemes by which agents that represent physical robot capabilities help determine role assignments of the robots in a variety of heterogeneous team-coordination tasks [13,14]. Our location discovery infrastructure, e.g. local and hierarchical agent name service, local and wide area discovery, and viral agent-to-agent community formation services [19] provide agents with a variety of ways to find each other in different network topologies and administrative domains.

Functional Heterogeneity. A simple extension of device agents to include specific input and output properties of their host device enabled RETSINA interface agents to search for the most appropriate display device for a user in a computer rich environment. Alternatively, if the user has limited display capabilities available, such as limited screen real estate on a WAP-enabled cell phone or PDA, then the RETSINA interface agents would use that device agent-provided information to modify the display of information[8].

Semantic Heterogeneity. In addition to the matchmaking approach to achieving semantic interoperability among agents and services [5,30,31], there are also issues of different implementation-dependent representational schemes, such as those encountered in the translation of RETSINA and OAA advertisements [12].

Systems Heterogeneity. To assist systems administrators in the allocation, configuration, launching and monitoring of MAS applications in a heterogeneous computing environment, we developed RECoMa, the RETSINA Configuration Manager [11]. RECoMa uses the RETSINA infrastructure discovery services, capability-based matchmaker, and device agents that represent

---

[7] See section 3.2.

[8] http://www.cs.cmu.edu/ softagents/mocha.html

the capabilities and resource loads of the heterogeneous computing platforms on which the agents are running, in order to help systems administrators perform their duties.

4.2   Lessons Relevant to the Three Workshop Goals

The report from the SELMAS workshop [10] identified three concerns as the goals of the workshop: (1) to determine the overlap and the integration of agent-based software engineering (ABSE) and object-oriented software engineering for multi-agent systems (OOSE for MAS); (2) to understand the issues in the agent technology that hinder or improve the production of large-scale distributed systems; and (3) to provide a comprehensive overview of software engineering techniques that may successfully be applied to deal with the complexity associated with realistic multi-agent software.

To address the first concern, our perspective is that ABSE focuses MAS design consideration on *what* declaratively defines and motivates the agent system, whereas OOSE for MAS focuses on *how* those motivations will be achieved and implemented. From the RETSINA perspective, the principles of goal, role, context and attitude are motivated by the task, which is represented in the MAS by the task agents. Task agents provide the overall coordination for any ad hoc assembly of agents, so it is fitting that the principles of agent-based software engineering motivate considerations that define their nature. For example, consider how all four first class ABSE principles simultaneously enter into consideration of whether a task agent will need to cooperate as a peer with other task agents and therefore need to define and understand notions of subgoals and roles for itself and peers, while operating in an agent social context of peer-to-peer cooperation with a presumed attitude of mutual trust and desire to collaborate. Such considerations will motivate the need to employ mechanisms of team-oriented plan negotiation, revision and execution monitoring. Contrast these considerations, for example, with those that a task agent might have if it is participating in a competitive auction in which its bidding might be negatively influenced by devious agents.

We perceive OOSE for MAS, on the other hand, as informing the interactions of the components of the individual layers of the RETSINA Infrastructure Architecture, in which the issues of reliability and predictability in the traditional OOSE sense apply to the interactions between the individual agent and the MAS infrastructure as a whole, and vice versa. By mapping OOSE for MAS to this architecture, we feel that we respond directly to the concerns of how to model MAS, what design standard methodologies are appropriate for MAS without misusing the abstractions that they provide, and to the overall question of how ABSE and OOSE for MAS differ.[9]

In response to the second concern, it has been our experience that the issues which hinder agent technology are derived from the many heterogeneities, complexities and views that confront the designer of a large-scale MAS, particularly

---

[9] See the bullet, *How is multi-agent software engineering different from object-oriented software engineering*, in section **8. Workshop Discussions, Lessons Learned and Lines for Future Research** of the workshop report [10].

for open, uncertain and dynamic computing environments. The first step, in a way, is to know when to focus on them, and when to know that many of these heterogeneities and complexities will be addressed automatically by MAS infrastructure. We feel that MAS designers can derive inspiration for identifying their heterogeneities and for estimating how they will be resolved by our discussions and examples in sections 2.1 and 4.1.

MAS designers can benefit from many off-the-shelf technologies, but knowing how to map those technologies to a MAS implementation sometimes imposes significant overheads to MAS designers. Hence, we view MAS infrastructure and agent libraries to interact with that infrastructure, as is present in the RETSINA libraries, and MAS architecture maps such as the RETSINA Infrastructure Architecture, as critical enablers to the scalability of large-scale distributed systems.

Regarding the tacit question of what makes a MAS *large-scale*, we take the position that issues of scale in terms of number of stake holders and numbers of agents need to be evaluated in light of the tasks that motivate the agents' interactions. Based on parallels with human social institutions, tasks are iteratively decomposed into subtasks and large populations into smaller communities until the proper dimensions of task complexity and participants are reached. In other words, issues of interaction complexity of large numbers of agents in complex tasks are often reduced by the human approach to solving the task, so it is difficult to study in the abstract. Those scalability issues that can be studied in absence of specific tasks are those that relate to infrastructure scalability, which often provides services of search, discovery, location, and community formation. And, given mechanisms of formal analysis and protocol simulation systems, these types of analyses are feasible without actually implementing large-scale MASs.

While the papers of the workshop respond collectively to the third workshop goal, we would like to add an observation that was not reflected in the workshop summary but does respond to both the second and the third goals. Namely, by "empowering" agents with the autonomy to pick and choose with which other agents and services they will work, distributed network application designers are "delegating" significant portions of their design and execution overheads to automation. When this happens, the emphasis of design considerations shift appropriately to issues of capability representation, recognition, and understanding, and to the specifications of tolerances by which agents and services will be composed and evaluated. In a few of our test application scenarios we have seen how the enabling of agents to dynamically locate each other across a variety of network topologies and administrative domains significantly reduces the human overhead of managing the execution of non-trivial MASs in a partially redundant, heterogeneous computing environment [11].

5   Conclusions

The contributions of this paper are multiple, from multiple perspectives. First, we identified some high-level challenges that face multi-agent system designers, and identified seven types of heterogeneities that render the challenges more concrete in addition to providing some initial metrics by which MAS architectures can be evaluated. Second, in our belief that agent-based software engineering is distinct from object-oriented software engineering for MASs, we named and described the four principles that should be considered as first class objects in ABSE: goal, role, context and attitude. A key motivation for identifying these objects as *first class* is the generality with which they can determine which MAS features will be needed for a specific MAS application. Third, we were able to describe the three RETSINA architectures, combined, in a way that illustrated their mutually complementary nature, and which also provided an indirect validation and verification of our choice of heterogeneity types. And a fourth contribution is the recognition that through our descriptions of challenges, heterogeneities, and the RETSINA architectures, we were able to respond to the three goals of the workshop, and to observe how MAS infrastructure and design principles also reduce the dimensionality of ABSE preoccupations for MAS designers. Although ABSE is in its infancy and is therefore relatively less articulate of its precepts than traditional and object-oriented software engineering, it certainly has features that make it a unique discipline in its own right, and promising in the guidance that it can offer to the reliability of large-scale multiagent systems.

Acknowledgments. The authors would also like to acknowledge the contributions of past and present members[10] of the Intelligent Software Agents Laboratory at CMU, who provide the many ideas and enthusiasm that make this research possible. This research was sponsored in part by the Office of Naval Research Grant N-00014-96-16-1-1222, by DARPA Grants F30602-98-2-0138 and F30602-00-2-0592, by the Air Force Office of Scientific Research Grant F49620-01-1-0542, by the National Science Foundation Award IIS-0205526, and by National Aeronautics and Space Administration Grant NCC21317.

References

1. D. Brugali and K. Sycara. Agent technology: A new frontier for the development of application frameworks? In M. Fayad, D. Schmidt, and R. Johnson, editors, *Object-Oriented Application Frameworks*. John Wiley, 1998.
2. C. Castelfranchi. Modelling social action for AI agents. *Applied Artificial Intelligence*, 103:157–182, 1998.
3. L. Chen and K. Sycara. WebMate: A personal agent for browsing and searching. In *Proceedings of the Second International Conference on Autonomous Agents and Multi-Agent Systems (ICMAS-98)*, May 1998.
4. DAML-S Coalition. DAML-S: Semantic markup for web service. In *Proceedings of the International Semantic Web Workshop (SWWS-01)*, 2001.
5. DAML-S Coalition. DAML-S: Web service description for the semantic web. In *The First International Semantic Web Conference (ISWC-02)*, 2002.
6. DARPA CoABS Program. Grid web site. http://coabs.globalinfotek.com/, 2000.
7. K. Decker, A. Pannu, K. Sycara, and M. Williamson. Designing behaviors for information agents. In *Proceedings of the First International Conference on Autonomous Agents (Agents 1997)*, February 1997. 0-89791-877-0/97/02.

---

[10] http://www.cs.cmu.edu/~softagents/people.html

8. G. Economou, M. Paolucci, M. Tsvetovat, and K. Sycara. Interaction without commitments: An initial approach. In *Proceedings of the Fifth International Conference on Autonomous Agents (Agents 2001)*, 2001.

9. T. Finin, Y. Labrou, and J. Mayfield. KQML as an agent communication language. In J. Bradshaw, editor, *Software Agents*. MIT Press, Cambridge, 1997.

10. A. F. Garcia and C. J. P. de Lucena. Software engineering for large-scale multi-agent systems SELMAS 2002. *ACM Software Engineering Notes*, 27(5):82–88, September 2002.

11. J. A. Giampapa, O. Juarez-Espinosa, and K. Sycara. Configuration management for multi-agent systems. In *Proceedings of the Fifth International Conference on Autonomous Agents (Agents 2001)*, pages 230–231. Association for Computing Machinery, June 2001. ISBN: 1-58113-326-X.

12. J. A. Giampapa, M. Paolucci, and K. Sycara. Agent interoperation across multagent system boundaries. In *Proceedings of the Fourth International Conference on Autonomous Agents (Agents 2000)*. Association for Computing Machinery, June 2000. ISBN: 1-58113-230-1.

13. J. A. Giampapa and K. Sycara. Conversational case-based planning for agent team coordination. In *Case-Based Reasoning Research and Development: Proceedings of the Fourth International Conference on Case-Based Reasoning (ICCBR 2001)*, volume 2080, pages 189–203, Berlin Heidelberg, July 2001. Springer-Verlag.

14. J. A. Giampapa and K. Sycara. Team-oriented agent coordination in the RETSINA multi-agent system. Technical Report CMU-RI-TR-02-34, The Robotics Institute, Carnegie Mellon University, Pittsburgh, PA, December 2002. Presented at AAMAS 2002 Workshop on Teamwork and Coalition Formation.

15. M. Greaves, H. Holback, and J. Bradshaw. What is a conversation policy? In *Agents-99: Workshop on Specifying and Implementing Conversation Policies*, 1999.

16. M. J. Huber, S. Kumar, P. R. Cohen, and D. R. McGee. A formal semantics for proxy communicative acts. In *Agent Theories, Architectures and Languages (ATAL-01)*, 2001.

17. N. Jennings, K. Sycara, and M. Wooldridge. A roadmap of agent research and development. *Journal of Autonomous Agents and Multi-Agent Systems (JAAMAS)*, 1(1):275–306, 1998.

18. B. Kuntz and K. Rajan. MIGSOCK: Migratable TCP socket in Linux. Master's thesis, Information Networking Institute, Carnegie Mellon University, February 2002. TR 2001-4.

19. B. Langley, M. Paolucci, and K. Sycara. Discovery of infrastructure in multi-agent systems. In *Agents-2001 Workshop on Infrastructure of Agents, MAS and Scalable MAS*, 2001.

20. D. Martin, A. Cheyer, and D. Moran. The open agent architecture: A framework for building distributed software systems. *Applied Artificial Intelligence*, 13(1–2):92–128, 1999.

21. M. Paolucci, O. Shehory, and K. Sycara. Interleaving planning and execution in a multiagent team planning environment. Technical Report CMU-RI-TR-00-01, The Robotics Institute, Carnegie Mellon University, 2000.

22. J. Rumbaugh, M. Blaha, W. Premerlani, F. Eddy, and W. Lorensen. *Object-Oriented Modeling and Design*. Prentice-Hall International, Inc., 1991.

23. O. Shehory and K. Sycara. The RETSINA Communicator. In *Proceedings of the Fourth International Conference on Autonomous Agents (Agents 2000)*, 2000.

24. O. Shehory, K. Sycara, P. Chalasani, and S. Jha. Increasing resource utilization and task performance by agent cloning. In M. S. V. A. Rao and M. Wooldridge, editors, *In Lecture Notes in AI: Intelligent Agents*. Springer Verlag, 1998.

25. M. P. Singh. Agent communication languages: Rethinking the principles. *IEEE-Computer*, 11, 1998.
26. I. Smith, P. Cohen, J. Bradshaw, M. Greaves, and H. Holmback. Designing conversation policies using joint intention theory. In *Proceedings of the Second International Conference on Autonomous Agents and Multi-Agent Systems (ICMAS-98)*. IEEE Press, 1998.
27. R. G. Smith. The contract net protocol: High-level communication and control in a distributed problem solver. *IEEE Transactions on Computers*, 29(12):1104–1113, 1980.
28. K. Sycara. Multiagent systems. *AI Magazine*, 19(2):79–92, Summer 1998.
29. K. Sycara, K. Decker, A. Pannu, M. Williamson, and D. Zeng. Distributed intelligent agents. *IEEE Expert, Intelligent Systems and their Applications*, 11(6):36–45, 1996.
30. K. Sycara, K. Decker, and M. Williamson. Middle-agents for the internet. In *IJCAI-97*, 1997.
31. K. Sycara, M. Klusch, S. Widoff, and J. Lu. Dynamic service matchmaking among agents in open information environments. *Journal ACM SIGMOD Record, A. Ouksel, A. Sheth (Eds.)*, 28(1):47–53, March 1999.
32. K. Sycara, M. Paolucci, M. van Velsen, and J. Giampapa. The RETSINA MAS Infrastructure. *Joint Special Issue of Autonomous Agents and MAS*, 7(1–2), July 2003. forthcoming.
33. M. Tambe. Towards flexible teamwork. *JAIR*, 7:83–124, 1997.
34. M. Tsvetovat, K. Sycara, Y. Chen, and J. Ying. Customer coalitions in the electronic marketplace. In *Proceedings of the Fourth International Conference on Autonomous Agents (Agents 2000)*, June 2000.
35. J. Waldo, G. Wyant, A. Wollrath, and S. Kendall. A note on distributed computing. Technical Report SMLI TR-94-29, Sun Microsystems Laboratories, 1999.
36. H.-C. Wong. *Protecting Individuals' Interests in Electronic Commerce Protocols*. PhD thesis, Computer Science Deptartment, Carnegie Mellon University, 2000. CMU-CS-00-160.
37. H. C. Wong and K. Sycara. Adding security and trust to multi-agent systems. In *Agents-99 Workshop on Deception, Fraud and Trust in Agent Societies*, 1999.
38. H.-C. Wong and K. Sycara. A Taxonomy of Middle-agents for the Internet. In *Proceedings of the International Conference on Autonomous Agents and Multi-Agent Systems (ICMAS-00)*, 2000.

Secure Multi-agent Coordination in a Network Monitoring System*

Anand R. Tripathi, Muralidhar Koka, Sandeep Karanth, Abhijit Pathak, and
Tanvir Ahmed

Department of Computer Science,
University of Minnesota, Minneapolis, U.S.A.
{tripathi, koka, sandeep, apathak, tahmed}@cs.umn.edu

Abstract. We have developed a mobile-agent based network monitoring system. In this system, multiple agents coordinate with each
other to collectively perform network monitoring. This paper deals with
the coordination of multiple agents to achieve monitoring functions
and failed component recovery. We also address the security needs of
our monitoring system, i.e. types of attacks that could be launched
on the system, and our solutions to thwart them. Finally, we present
our experiences with the system and the resource overhead imposed by it.

Keywords: Mobile agents, Network monitoring, Monitoring system security, Multi-agent systems, Cooperating agents, Mobile code.

1 Introduction

One of the important tasks of a system administrator is to monitor networks to
ensure proper system operation and protect system resources from being misused
by intruders or attackers. This typically involves monitoring for inconsistencies
in user activities, resource usage, system configuration, and enforcing security
policies. A large enterprise network typically consists of hundreds of nodes and
resources with varying amount of heterogeneity among them in terms of the
hardware and software used. The difficulties in monitoring these networks led us
to identify the following requirements in a monitoring system. The monitoring
functionalities may need to be changed due to hardware or software reconfigu-
rations, change in administrative policies, and addition of new monitoring tools.
Also, it should be possible to enhance the monitoring system's capabilities in
response to new attacks. This would require the monitoring system to be *dynamically configurable* and *dynamically extensible*. The huge amount of data
generated by various nodes and resources need to be analyzed in real-time to
detect attacks and alter the monitoring system's detection policies. We call this
active monitoring. It is necessary for the monitoring system to be *scalable*, as the

---

* This work was supported by National Science Foundation grants ANI 0087514 and
EIA 9818338.

A. Garcia et al. (Eds.): SELMAS 2002, LNCS 2603, pp. 251–266, 2003.

number of nodes in the network increases. As network monitoring employs different kinds of tools, a monitoring system should be able to integrate such tools easily. Attacks could be launched against the monitoring system itself, hence it should be *secure*. A monitoring system needs to run continuously, so that there is less opportunity for attackers to bypass it. For this, it has to detect the failure of its components and restore them with minimal human intervention. Also, the monitoring system should not hinder the normal operation of the environment in which it is deployed, hence its resource consumption should be within *acceptable limits*.

In our research, a mobile-agent based approach is used because it provides several capabilities such as local monitoring to overcome network latency and reduce network load, asynchronous execution, disconnected and autonomous operations, and dynamic adaptability [1]. A *mobile-agent* represents an object capable of migrating in a network to perform designated tasks at one or more nodes [2,3]. In our monitoring system, mobile-agents are sent to continuously monitor nodes in a network, perform data filtering locally, and notify other system components of any significant events. As mobile-agents are first-class objects, their state and behavior can be altered remotely by invoking methods on them. These features are used for making the mobile-agents dynamically extensible and securely modifiable.

Our agent based architecture is inspired by the paradigm of *cooperative security managers* [4]. In our monitoring system, agents are customized to perform specific functionalities. E.g., we have agents which monitor user activities or check for system files' consistencies at different hosts. These agents can work in isolation to detect local attacks, but their actions need to be coordinated to correlate information from different hosts in real-time to detect network-wide attacks. An example of such a coordination would be to find if an attacker is trying to crack a specific user password across the network.

Most of today's monitoring systems rely on SNMP to collect data from various components [5]. The SNMP model supports low level device management; it does not support abstractions for network-wide monitoring policies. In our approach, SNMP can be integrated as one of the building-blocks for low level device monitoring. Another common approach used in today's monitoring systems is to periodically execute scripts to monitor the status of a component or to process event data. Script based detection procedures tend to be tedious to install, debug, and to modify remotely. In contrast to an object-based approach, scripts offer a lower level of abstraction for remote manipulation. This also has the disadvantage of a coarse-grain protection, as scripts execute with complete privileges of a specific user.

The focus of this paper is on agent coordination for network monitoring and to perform recovery of any failed components in the monitoring system. In the context of security needs of the monitoring system, we present the types of attacks that can be launched against it and the features built into the system to thwart them. The monitoring system is currently deployed in our lab environment, and we present our initial experiences. The contribution of this work is in showing that mobile-agent based monitoring systems are feasible.

The rest of the paper is organized as follows. Section 2 gives an overview of the monitoring system. The coordination paradigms used in the monitoring system are presented in Section 3. Sections 4 discusses the security of the monitoring system. The system's capabilities and our initial experiences in using it are described in Section 5. Sections 6 and 7 discuss related work and conclusions respectively.

2 Overview of the Network Monitoring System

The network monitoring system is implemented using Ajanta [6], a secure Java-based framework for programming with mobile agents. It facilitates creation of agents and their autonomous migration. The Ajanta framework provides *agent servers* for hosting agents. An agent server exercises admission control and provides restricted access of its local resources to an agent based on its credentials. All globally accessible entities are given location-independent names maintained by the Ajanta name service. Every node in the monitoring system runs an agent server to support the installation and migration of agents for event detection, which is done through data collection, filtering, and correlation. Inter-agent communication in the monitoring system is based on the *publish-subscribe* paradigm implemented using RMI.

A *basic event* represents a significant change in the state of an entity being monitored. Higher level *compound events* are derived from these basic events by correlating them. A canonical definition and representation of events, independent of operating system specific details, is used. The event hierarchy is presented in Figure 1. The *SyslogEvent* class represents events generated from the system log files. Its subclass, *ConnectEvent* class represents various kinds of connections to a host.

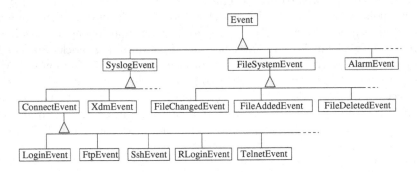

Fig. 1. Event hierarchy (partial)

The events correlated could either be local or remote events occurring in real-time, or they could be past events stored in a data repository. The events are assigned different *alarm levels* based on their severity. E.g., a successful login from a host outside the monitoring domain, is given higher alarm level than from one within the domain. The *alert level* of a host is cumulatively determined by the alarm levels of the events generated either locally or across the network. Some of the detection procedures might be dormant at a host with a low alert level.

The monitoring system has four types of agents: *Monitor, Subscriber, Inspector,* and *Auditor* [7]. A typical monitoring configuration is shown in Figure 2. The *System Management Servers* (SMS), agent servers running on secure hosts, launch and remotely control the agents. A monitor agent collects and filters data from primary data sources such as log files and generates events. These events are forwarded to subscriber agents, which are capable of correlating events and generating compound events. They also store events in local databases or shared ones across the network. A subscriber agent can also do monitoring functions. An inspector agent can travel to different hosts across a network based on an itinerary and performs event detection functions. An auditor agent visits nodes across the network, collects data, makes correlations, and may migrate to other nodes based on the events detected. Depending on the functionality of the agents, they are either single-hop or multi-hop. For example, the monitoring agents are single-hop, but there is nothing in the architecture which prohibits them from being multi-hop agents. The inspector agent is a multi-hop agent as it travels across the network visiting different nodes to collect information.

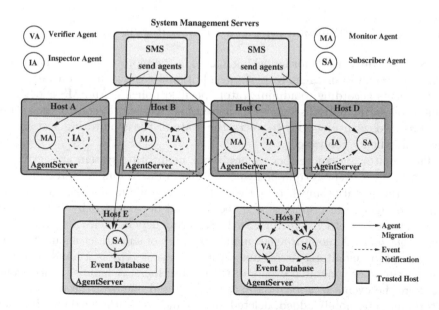

Fig. 2. Monitoring system organization

The system monitors different aspects of a network using data from a wide-range of sources. A host's log files are monitored to detect different types of login connections to a host such as `ssh, ftp,` and `telnet`. The system files are monitored for any changes in their administrator-specified attributes such as modification time, permissions, and contents. A host is also monitored for changes in its configuration such as routing table, and network interfaces. At the process-level, the system monitors for new processes running with root privileges, runaway processes consuming too much of resources, failure of system level services such as termination of daemons, and execution of malicious programs such as packet sniffers and password crackers. Snort [8] is integrated into the monitoring system to detect network-level events, which are correlated with other events such as login events.

3 Agent Coordination

Multiple agents coordinate with each other to collectively perform network monitoring. For cooperation, inter-agent communication can be achieved in two modes. They communicate directly with each other using RMI and indirectly through events stored in shared databases. Agents in our monitoring system coordinate to provide two types of functionalities. Primarily, they coordinate to monitor the network by collecting data, filtering and correlating it. This coordination also involves agents migrating to specific nodes for system-wide monitoring. Secondly, agent coordination is also required to facilitate recovery of failed components.

3.1 Agent Coordination for Network Monitoring

The SMS are responsible for launching agents in the monitoring system and can remotely configure an agent to perform additional tasks. They can *redirect* or *retract* agents according to administrator-specified policies. An SMS is designed to be stateless. It can be disconnected and reconnected later to control the agents. It is provided with functions to query the state of the monitoring system and control it, when reconnected.

The monitor and subscriber agents in our monitoring system are active objects. A monitor agent is equipped with a variety of *detectors* for detecting basic events at the host it is launched to. Event detection could include parsing log files or monitoring system resources. A detector could be triggered by events which were generated by other detectors. Such triggering dependencies are maintained in a *trigger table*. A monitor agent maintains a list of subscriber agents for each of the events it monitors. Associated with each event type is a handler object, which notifies the generated events to their subscribers. A handler object could also store the events in a local database or a shared one over the network. Detectors can be remotely added, deleted, or modified by authorized entities, such as SMS, to enhance monitoring at a host or as part of fault recovery process.

A subscriber agent subscribes to events published by other agents, correlates them, and generates compound events. A subscriber agent may correlate an event generated in real-time with other events generated earlier. The generated events can be stored in a local or a remote database. Subscribers can also perform specialized functions to aid in the recovery of failed components.

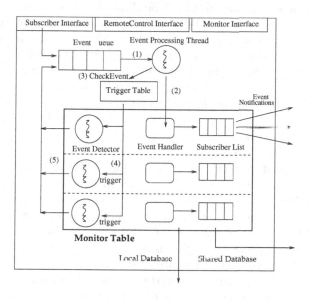

Fig. 3. Architecture for a monitor or subscriber agent

The architecture of a monitor or subscriber agent is shown in Figure 3, which is extended from Ajanta's base *Agent* class and implements the *RemoteControlInterface* and the *MonitorInterface*. The *SubscriberInterface* is only implemented by the subscriber agent. Event detectors, handlers, and subscribers corresponding to an event are registered through the monitor interface. Java reflection and class loading facilities are used to dynamically load these objects for an agent.

Each detector contains a thread, which executes the detection procedure asynchronously with other activities in the agent. All the events generated by the detectors are deposited in the *event queue* to be processed by the agent's *event processing thread* (step 1 in Figure 3). In a subscriber agent, an event received from a remote node is also put in this event queue. The event processing thread waits for an event to arrive in the event queue. On the arrival of an event, it first executes the event's specific handler, and then through the trigger table initiates asynchronous execution of dependent detectors (steps 2, 3, and 4 in Figure 3). The event handlers send the events to all currently registered subscribers. This model facilitates any hierarchical organization for disseminating events.

An inspector agent travels to different hosts in a network, based on a predefined itinerary. The *File Integrity Checker* is implemented in our monitoring

system using inspector agents. It is used to check if system files or other important files have been tampered. It consists of a *file inspector* agent and a stationary
verifier agent, which is a subscriber residing on a secure node. The file inspector
agent visits nodes in the network and records file attributes and content checksum of the specified files, and sends this data to the verifier agent. The verifier
agent is responsible for tallying and correlation. During the initialization round,
the verifier agent stores this data in a database. In subsequent rounds, the verifier agent compares the received data with the stored one. Any inconsistencies
generate *alarm* events such as *FileDeleted*, or *FileModified*, which in turn may
notify the administrator. In order to remain lightweight, the file inspector agent
sends data to the verifier agent from each host before migrating to the next.
A single-hop model could also have been adopted in which the SMS launches a
file inspector agent to each node in the monitoring system. These file inspector
agents reside at the monitored nodes and send data to the verifier agent periodically. The tradeoff between these two models is migration overhead versus
maintaining additional agents.

An auditor agent provides capabilities for active and ad-hoc monitoring.
These agents are of specific use in large networks which are partitioned into
multiple administrative domains. Depending on the events received and correlations deduced, these agents can autonomously migrate to parts of the network,
which need to be monitored with higher degree of alertness. A scenario in which
an auditor agent is used is when there is some suspicious root activity on a host.
i.e., there is either a root login initiated from a node outside the domain, or a
new process with root privileges is started without a corresponding root login.
The auditor agent will migrate to the node in question and can have access to
that node's event history for further processing.

3.2   Agent Coordination for Recovery

To handle failure of system components, our goal is to repair the failed components or have a graceful degradation. The failure modes in the system could
range from agent server failures or host failures to detector failures. In the current
environment, the failure modes we address are described below. Agent servers or
hosts may crash bringing down the entire monitoring mechanism on that particular host. Agent servers could also fail partially. For example, the agent transfer
protocol might fail, but the agents currently residing might continue to function.
The agents themselves could fail. One or more detectors in an agent could fail.

The monitoring system achieves robustness by self-monitoring its components. The publish-subscribe model and dynamic extensibility supported by the
system eliminates the need for additional infrastructure for monitoring the health
of the system. Each monitor and subscriber agent is equipped with an additional
detector for self-monitoring, which periodically generates *heart-beat* events. A
heart-beat event contains the list of detectors which are functioning in an agent.
The frequency of heart-beat events is configurable by the administrator depending on factors such as the load on the host, system configuration of the host,
alertness level of system operation, and network traffic. *Recovery Manager*, a

subscriber agent running on a secure host, subscribes to these events. A timer is enabled for each detector in an agent, with a user-defined timeout interval, which is a multiple of the heart-beat event interval. If the recovery manager does not hear from an agent for a detector before the timer expires, it deduces that the detector has failed. Timeout of all the detectors in an agent implies the failure of an agent. In either case, the recovery manager informs the SMS. In case of detector failure, the SMS installs the detector remotely on the reported agent. For agent failures, the SMS constructs an agent with the original config-uration and dispatches it to the node where the agent failed. If the agent server on that node fails, then the SMS will not be able to dispatch the agent and the administrator is informed of the same.

As the recovery manager itself could fail, multiple recovery managers could be used, with each one monitoring the others. These recovery managers gener-ate multiple detector failure events upon the failure of a detector in an agent. A monotonically increasing configuration Identifier (an integer) is generated at the agent end (monitor or subscriber). This is transmitted to the SMS as part of the failure event by the recovery managers. Installation requests with the same iden-tifier are dropped by the SMS. The configuration identifier is increased whenever there a change in configuration of an agent i.e. failure, addition, or re-installation of a detector. An alternate model for fault detection would be to send an agent to inspect each monitored node in the network and report any failures.

Inspector agents are prone to other types of failures as they travel across the network. In the File Integrity Checker, a configurable timer is started at the launching servers for the file inspector agents, and on timeout a new file inspector agent is launched. If the previous agent comes back it is terminated. Since actions of these inspector agents are idempotent by nature, multiple agents executing do not affect the integrity of the system or the consistency of the data collected. If a host or agent server in the itinerary is down, the file inspector agent automatically chooses the next host on the itinerary and reports its inability to the recovery manager. Status reporting by inspectors and use of *ping-agents*, agents which go to the target host and return to check if the agent transfer protocol is working, give feedback about the sanity of the system. In order to prevent loss of an event, in case if all its subscribers are down, the notion of a *default-subscriber* is built into the system. This subscriber agent is responsible for logging all such events and notifying the SMS about them.

4   Security of the Monitoring System

Some components of the monitoring system, e.g., monitor agents, need to run in an untrusted domain. Hence, it is required that the monitoring system is able to protect itself against attacks, which might disable these components. A report [9] on the current state of intrusion detection systems identified security of the monitoring systems as one of the problems not adequately addressed. In that report, several categories of attacks on monitoring systems have been identified: overload or crashing the system, and subterfuge by insertion or evasion of network data. In this section, we address and present solutions for attacks that can be specifically launched on our mobile-agent based monitoring system. It should be noted that some of the security considerations in our system stem from the capabilities that are supported. For example, as dynamic extensibility is supported, the possibility of an attacker trying to modify the agent remotely needs to be addressed.

Security is an integral part of Ajanta design, and Ajanta provides components for authentication, public key maintenance, access control, host resource protection, and cryptographic services [6,10]. It is assumed that the Ajanta name service is trusted and secure [10] because it is a critical component in our monitoring system. It maintains the mapping between the location-independent names of agents, and agent servers with their network locations, and acts as a repository for their public-key certificates. As the Ajanta name space is hierarchically organized, the name service doesn't allow a user to modify or create entries in another user's name space. The administrator of our monitoring system has privileges to take administrative actions, such as recalling agents, adding or deleting detectors in an agent.

4.1   Security of Agent Servers

The agent servers are assumed to be trusted and secure. An attacker could launch a malicious agent to attack an agent server, to corrupt its data structures. This is prevented as agent servers provide distinct protection domains for execution of agents [10]. Based on an agent's code base and the principal on whose behalf it is acting, agent servers enforce restrictions on an agent's access to local resources, such as disk space, network ports, and files. However, it cannot control low-level resource usage such as the amount of CPU consumed. Hence, an attacker might try to launch a malicious agent which consumes too many host resources. To prevent this, the basic agent server in Ajanta is extended to enforce an admission policy accepting agents coming from *authorized entities* only. The admission policy is implemented as an external unit and users running agent servers can implement their own policies. In our current environment, we support a wide range of admission policies. An agent server may accept agents belonging to a specific user in a particular domain, all users in a domain, only from trusted agent servers or hosts, or based on the agent credentials and the type of agents. For example, an agent server might not accept any inspector agents and agents coming from outside the domain. A policy based on the combination of the above can also be used. Also, an agent server could also impose a limit on the number of agents that it might host at any time from a particular entity.

4.2   Security of Monitor and Subscriber Agents

Every agent is associated with an *owner*, the user on whose behalf an agent is executing. The application which creates the agent is called the *creator*, for example the SMS. The monitor and subscriber agents could be attacked while they are being transfered from the SMS to their hosts to be monitored. This is prevented using a secure Agent Transfer Protocol [10]. A malicious agent cannot tamper other agents executing on an agent server, as each agent is executed in a distinct protection domain by its host agent server. A malicious agent might try to forge its owner's identity, which is prevented in Ajanta, by giving each agent a set of *unforgeable credentials*. An attacker could try to direct an agent away, by migrating or recalling it, from an agent server thereby leaving the host unmonitored. An agent server prevents this by allowing these actions to be performed only by privileged entities such as an agent's owner or creator.

There are a number of ways in which an attacker could exploit the capabilities that are supported in our monitoring system. The attacks and the security mechanisms used to thwart them are presented below. An attacker might try to mount attacks on a monitor or subscriber agent by modifying its behavior, e.g., delete or modify existing detectors or add new detectors which might use too many host resources. An agent enforces policies, as specified by its owner, as to who can modify its behavior.

The subscriber agents subscribe to events generated by other agents. An attacker could also try to subscribe to these events, thereby breaching users' confidentiality. An administrator might want to prevent this because the monitoring system might need to run with higher privileges. For example, access to log files may be given to only those users running the monitoring system. Hence, each monitor agent maintains a list of subscribers, which are valid in accordance with the specified monitoring policies.

A subscriber could also delete itself from the subscription list for an event, when it no longer needs access to that event. The deletion could be in accordance with user-specified monitoring policy. An attacker could try to delete a valid subscriber causing loss of information. Hence, a subscriber could only remove itself from a subscription list. An attacker could try to send events to subscriber agents thereby generating false alarms. To prevent this, every subscriber agent maintains a list of monitor agents from which it can receive events of a specified type.

As dynamic extensibility is one of our main goals, the above policies might need to be modified during system operation. The agents allow these policies to be modified either by the administrators or other authorized users. These policies for monitor or subscriber agents are constructed by the SMS, based on the configuration setup that is used by the administrator. The permission to add, delete or modify detectors is given to users in administrative roles. Permission to subscribe to events is given only to those agents running under the privileges of the trusted users. These attacks exploiting the monitoring system's capabilities are prevented using authenticated inter-agent communication.

As the monitor and inspector agents are executed in untrusted domain, they are not given access to communicate with the database servers. Even though the agent servers are trusted, there is a possibility of them being compromised. Thus, only subscriber agents residing on trusted hosts are given permissions to read and write data to databases.

4.3   Authenticated Inter-agent Communication

The security of the communication between agents depends on the authenticated inter-agent communication. For example, assume agent A_1 on agent server AS_1 wants to make an authenticated RMI on method M_1 on agent A_2 hosted by agent server AS_2. A_2 has an entry in its access control list for M_1, indicating that A_1 can invoke the method. A solution of inter-agent authentication should meet the following requirements:

1. AS_1 should not be able to invoke the RMI on behalf of A_1, if A_1 is not hosted by AS_1.
2. When A_1 makes the RMI call, it should not be able to disguise its hosting server AS_1. This is because the access control policy for M_1 may also depend on who is hosting A_1.
3. If A_1 is successful in making an RMI when it is on AS_1, all further invocations of M_1 should fail if either of A_1 or A_2 migrates.

To minimize the risk posed by a compromised agent server, an agent does not carry a private key with itself. It obtains from its hosting agent server, a temporary public-private key pair, in the form of a certificate signed by the hosting server. Note that an agent has to request for a new set of keys when it migrates from one agent server to another. The Ajanta name server generates a *location-certificate*, which binds an agent to its current hosting agent server. Upon migration of the agent, the name server issues a new certificate.

Each invocation of the RMI requires a ticket identifying the caller, in this example A_1. The authentication is based on an extension of the challenge-response protocol [10]. Upon receiving the ticket, A_2 verifies A_1's credentials, and checks the validity of the location-certificate and the temporary public key certificate issued by AS_1 for A_1. A_1 also makes similar checks for A_2.

As part of this protocol, each agent has to sign a nonce generated by the other, confirming the authenticity of the message. Generating a new ticket, every-time a method needs to be invoked, is inefficient. Hence, an optimization is implemented wherein both the agents agree on the next nonce based on their current nonce values, for example, increase it by an integer k.

As the location-certificate issued by the name service is used by A_2 to check if A_1 is actually residing at AS_1, AS_1 wouldn't be able to make an RMI call on behalf of A_1, if it doesn't host A_1. If A_1 migrates to a third server AS_3, it can try to disguise its hosting server as AS_1. This will be detected when A_2 checks the validity of the location-certificate with the name server.

As we depend on the delegated trust model – by an agent to agent server – there are some limitations in our approach. If an agent server is compromised, it could pass the keys from a valid agent to a malicious agent, assuming it hosts both of them, and the malicious agent can masquerade as a valid agent. However, the masquerading can only continue as long as the valid agent remains on the compromised agent server.

5 System Capabilities and Performance

Our system's open architecture, coupled with its event distribution model allows users to build a comprehensive monitoring system. They can modify a running system securely without causing any disruptions. In this section, the system's potential is illustrated by describing its capabilities and our experiences in using it. The various types of scenarios that are monitored are described below. The hosts are monitored for different types of connections such as ssh, ftp, and telnet. In our network, only certain users, typically the faculty and system staff, have access to more than one account. Hence, we monitor for users switching to different accounts. A user switching to root is considered an event of higher alarm level than a user switching to another user. User switch events are correlated to find if there are any multiple user switches. Login events are correlated network-wide to find out if someone is trying to attack a particular account. For example, if the number of login successes or failures exceed a specified threshold, then it is deduced that a particular account is being attacked. The processes on hosts are monitored to detect runaway processes, e.g., those consuming a high percentage of CPU for a long period of time, and execution of malicious programs such as packet sniffers and password crackers. Failure of system level services such as termination of *ssh* daemons are also detected. The hosts are also monitored for disk usage. Fingerprint information is used to detect any change in configuration of the hosts such as routing tables. The file integrity checker is used to detect changes to system files such as last modification time and permissions. Any changes in system files or fingerprint information are correlated with the root login events.

In our monitoring system, other tools can be easily integrated. An agent can be used as a wrapper to generate events by processing information from these tools, which can be correlated with other events in the network. For example, Snort is used to detect port-scans. A successful user login from a host which did a port-scan earlier, is given a higher alarm level. If the successful login happens to be that of the root, then a system administrator is alerted immediately.

The capability of the monitoring system to process data from diverse sources, enables it to detect events or attacks, even if one of the sources is compromised. For example, if an attacker is successful in attacking a host, e.g., modifying the file permissions of the log file, he/she could delete login traces from the log file. The login detectors would not be able to capture that someone has logged in, but the file integrity checker would capture that the permissions have been modified.

An instance of dynamic extensibility is, if an administrator comes to know of a malicious program, virus or worm, its signature can be added dynamically to all the process monitoring detectors. As part of active monitoring, an administrator could have a policy that in case of a user attempting to switch multiple times to a root account, he may want to monitor all the activities of that particular user across the network. An example of online-monitoring is in case of a multiple login attack on a user account, it will be detected as it happens.

Currently, the monitoring system is deployed on 15 hosts, 4 of which are in the trusted domain. A few of these machines are heavily used. Some of the

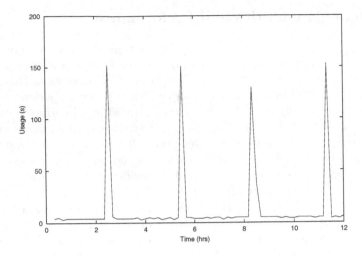

Fig. 4. CPU usage

hosts are primarily used to connect to the network from outside our domain. Figure 4 represents the amount of CPU time consumed in seconds, for a host in the untrusted domain over a 12-hour period, aggregated every 10 minutes. The peaks correspond to the execution of the file integrity checker's inspector agent. On an average, during the non-execution of inspector agents, the agent servers consume less than 1% of the CPU on SunBlade 100 workstations, running on a 502 MHz Sparc processor, and having 512 MB memory. The agent servers consume about 27 MB of memory, whereas a bare-bone JVM uses about 9 MB with default JDK 1.4 settings. The statistics of the file integrity checker system are shown below:

Average statistics per host			
No. of files	File Size (Bytes)	Agent Residency Time	Bytes Sent per file
8830	20757	$\approx$ 8min	175

As can be seen from Figure 4, the inspector agent consumes a significant amount of CPU while calculating the checksum for the specified files. To reduce the inspector agent's effect on host operations, alternate strategies can be implemented. It could be launched when the host is lightly loaded over a period of time or during off-peak hours or on suspicion of malicious activities.

On an average, about 160 to 200 events per host per day are logged to the databases. Filtering of data related to log files at the source results in only about 30% of the collected data generating significant events. As the events are monitored online, the latency of event detection depends on the frequency of the monitoring. The monitoring frequency is configurable, for example, log files are monitored every 20 seconds, and can be adapted depending on the security needs of the host, load on the host, and alertness level in the network.

We have demonstrated the utility of the monitoring system in our lab consisting of 15 hosts. Based on our experiences so far, we expect the system to scale fairly well to a 100 to 150 node environment, which is our target for the next stage. For a large configuration the number of SMS could be increased, with each SMS responsible for monitoring a particular set of nodes. These servers could also communicate with each other to transfer responsibility of agents as and when necessary.

There are some tradeoffs involved in the design of our system. To facilitate active and online monitoring we need to continuously use system resources on each host. Bad policies may aggravate resource consumption. For example, as shown in Figure 4, when the file inspector agent visits a node the CPU consumption on that host is considerable. Good policies are those that let the file inspector agent travel to hosts when the loads on hosts are low or when the hosts are idle. In our design, we do not deal with agent server compromises. But there is a chance that they may be compromised. For example, agent servers listen on specific ports to receive agents, and are vulnerable for attacks. Hence, to limit this vulnerability we run the system with user privileges. The agent servers accept agents based on agent admission policies. However, certain kinds of denial-of-service attacks such as repeated agent transfer requests cannot be prevented.

6   Related Work

AAFID [11] is one of the earliest systems to propose agent mobility in intrusion detection systems. Recent developments in the field of mobile agent technology has motivated several researchers to investigate its application to network management [12,13]. These efforts have mainly focused on code mobility to reduce network traffic. In contrast, our work has focused on building a secure infrastructure to support dynamic extensibility, and active monitoring.

The research in network monitoring, e.g., Emerald [14], and NetSTAT [15], addressed similar problems of scalability and a single point of failure. Similar design goals of configurable and extensible IDSs have been addressed by others [16]. Few systems, Emerald [14] and Bro [17], have addressed security of monitoring systems. Mobile agent based active monitoring utilizes mobile code technology, and incorporates the capabilities of software agents, namely autonomy, dynamic adaptability, and their ability to react and cooperate based on goals. In the area of mobile agent based network monitoring systems, security requirements are different. The security of mobile agent based systems in general have been addressed by several researchers [10,18].

Coordination mechanisms in mobile-agent based applications have mostly been implemented either using message passing or extending Linda, a tuple-space based approach [19,20]. In [20], message sharing using mailbox for mobile-agent coordination is presented. Others have argued that message passing based schemes do not provide enough flexibility for mobile agent coordination and proposed shared-space schemes extending Linda [19]. Our monitoring system utilizes publish-subscribe model of communication to coordinate agents in real time. Correlation of events which depends on past data are supported using databases. Moreover, practical experience demonstrating the capabilities of mobile agents in network monitoring is lacking. Our work has been mainly motivated to address such needs.

7 Conclusions and Future Work

In this paper, we have presented a network monitoring system that has been developed using mobile-agents. The system presented here is dynamically configurable, extensible, and secure. The system actively monitors the network in real-time and supports modification of detection policies in response to events. From our initial experiences, we have found that the system's resource consumption is reasonable. The focus of this paper is on the coordination strategies among agents for network monitoring. We have also identified the types of attacks that could be launched against our system and the features built into the system to thwart them. Our goal is to use this system to monitor our university networks. Furthering this research, we would like to develop agents to facilitate other system administrator's tasks, such as software installation. We plan to extend our system functionalities by monitoring emerging user-level services, smart environments, and collaboration environments.

References

1. Jansen, W., Mell, P., Karygiannis, T., Marks, D.:   Applying Mobile Agents to Intrusion Detection and Response. National Institute of Standards and Technology Interim Report - 6416 (1999)
2. Fuggetta, A., Picco, G.P., Vigna, G.: Understanding Code Mobility. IEEE Transactions on Software Engineering **24** (1998) 342–361
3. Harrison, C.G., Chess, D.M., Kershenbaum, A.: Mobile Agents: Are they a good idea? Technical report, IBM Research Division, T.J.Watson Research Center (1995) Available at URL http://www.research.ibm.com/massdist/mobag.ps.
4. White, G.B., Fisch, E., Pooch, U.: Cooperating Security Managers: A Peer-Based Intrusion Detection System. IEEE Network **10** (1996) 20–23
5. Stallings, W.: SNMP and SNMPv2: the infrastructure for network management. IEEE Communications Magazine **36** (1998) 37–43
6. Tripathi, A., Karnik, N., Vora, M., Ahmed, T., Singh, R.: Mobile Agent Programming in Ajanta. In: Proceedings of the 19th International Conference on Distributed Computing Systems. (1999) 190–197
7. Tripathi, A., Ahmed, T., Pathak, S., Carney, M., Dokas, P.: Paradigms for Mobile Agent-Based Active Monitoring. In: IEEE Network Operations and Management Symposium. (2002) 65–78
8. Roesch, M.: Snort - Lightweight Intrusion Detection for Networks. In: 13th Systems Administration Conference - LISA. (1999)
9. Allen, J., Christie, A., Fithen, W., McHugh, J., Pickel, J., Stoner, E.: State of the practice of intrusion detection technologies. Technical Report CMU/SEI-99-TR-028, Software Engineering Institute, Carnegie Mellon University (2000) Available at URL http://www.sei.cmu.edu/.

10. Karnik, N., Tripathi, A.: Security in the Ajanta Mobile Agent System. Software Practice and Experience **31** (2001) 301–329
11. Balasubramaniyan, J., Garcia-Fernandez, J.O., Isacoff, D., Spafford, E., Zamboni, D.: An Architecture for Intrusion Detection using Autonomous Agents. Technical Report Coast TR 98-05, Department of Computer Sciences, Purdue University (1998)
12. Bellavista, P., Corradi, A., Stefanelli, C.: An Open Secure Mobile Agent Framework for Systems Management. Journal of Network and Systems Management (JNSM) **7** (1999) 323–339
13. Pinheiro, R., Poylisher, A., Caldwell, H.: Mobile Agents for Aggregation of Network Mangagement Data. In: 1st International Symposium on Agent Systems and Applications, and 3rd International Symposium on Mobile Agents. (1999) 130–140
14. Porras, P.A., Neumann, P.G.: EMERALD: Event Monitoring Enabling Responses to Anomalous Live Disturbances. In: Proceedings of the 20th National Information Systems Security Conference. (1997) 353–365
15. Vigna, G., Kemmerer, R.: NetSTAT: A Network-based Intrusion Detection System. Journal of Computer Security **7** (1999) 37–71
16. Vigna, G., Kemmerer, R., Blix, P.: Designing a Web of Highly-Configurable Intrusion Detection Sensors. In Lee, W., Mè, L., Wespi, A., eds.: Proceedings of the 4th International Symposium on Recent Advances in Intrusion Detection (RAID 2001). Volume 2212 of LNCS., Davis, CA, Springer-Verlag (2001) 69–84
17. Paxson, V.: Bro: a system for detecting network intruders in real-time. Computer Networks (Amsterdam, Netherlands: 1999) **31** (1999) 2435–2463
18. Karjoth, G., Lange, D., Oshima, M.: A Security Model for Aglets. IEEE Internet Computing (1997) 68 77
19. Picco, G., Murphy, A., Roman, G.: LIME: Linda meets mobility. In: Proceedings of the 1999 International Conference on Software Engineering. (1999) 368–377
20. Cao, J., Feng, X., Lu, J., Das., S.K.: Research feature - Mailbox-based scheme for mobile agent communications. IEEE Computer **35** (2002) 54–60

Towards Monitored Data Consistency and Business Processing Based on Declarative Software Agents[1]

P.S.C. Alencar, D.D. Cowan, D. Mulholland, and T. Oliveira

School of Computer Science
University of Waterloo
200 University Avenue West, Waterloo, ON N2L 3G1
1-519-8884690
{palencar,dcowan,dwm,toliveira}@csg.uwaterloo.ca

Abstract. Currently Web systems usually involve application and database servers that support user interfaces and static distributed databases. However, applications such as e-commerce require data and service networks that contain many types of active content and dynamic business processes. In this context, a key challenge has been to manage data content and business processes in a flexible way, often in real-time, through operations which augment, refine, interconnect, ensure consistency, and monitor data and processes. In this paper we present an approach to monitor data consistency and business processing based on declarative agents. Because of its declarative nature, the approach facilitates the use, programming and management of such agent-based systems and allows for different distributed database and Web user interface structures to be interoperable. The approach also relates business events to technical events while conveying to the users meaningful business events, and agents that deal with various levels of abstraction of a business object, that can orchestrate and monitor data change and business processing.

Keywords: Software agents, data management, software design, events, data consistency, business process, distributed databases, Web-based user interfaces, monitoring, events, e-business, e-commerce.

1   Introduction

Current Web systems usually involve application and database servers that support user interfaces and static distributed databases 1,2 . These systems involve constant data and process changes such as changes in data presented on Web forms or in data stored in geographically dispersed databases and changes related to business processes.

In addition, software applications such as e-commerce require data and service networks that contain many types of active content and dynamic business processes 3,4 . This new scenario requires data content and business processes to be managed

---

[1] The research described in this paper was supported by the Natural Sciences and Engineering Research Council of Canada (NSERC), the Brazilian National Research Council (CNPq), Human Resources Development Canada (HRDC) and IBM Canada.

A. Garcia et al. (Eds.): SELMAS 2002, LNCS 2603, pp. 267–284, 2003.

in a flexible way through operations that augment, refine, interconnect, ensure consistency, and monitor data and processes.

However, there are still many problems with standard enterprise management systems and event-handling systems that can restrict their solutions 5,6 :

(i)   The infrastructure (i.e., the technical data and processes such as S L stored data and commands) is highly coupled with business processing elements and rules at the code level. The systems do not provide a business view of the enterprise, but a technology-oriented one;

(ii)   The processing environments are largely dependent on specific data sources, individual data formats, database systems or run-rime environments. As a result, there are many interoperability issues to be resolved related to the distributed nature of the data and user interfaces;

(iii)   The events related to changes lack relevant business content in terms of business object information, and thus are related to physical elements, not to business logic elements. Servers and applications (and their commands, such as S L database commands) should be replaced by business logical elements such as "check consistency of two Web forms," "compute online orders income," or "invoke credit card checking;"

(iv)   There is no distinction between the critical business-level processing events and errors related to the software environment. How can we distinguish, for example, errors that affect customer services from the sum of events on downtime or errors in your office-processing environment There is also no path to assist in finding how business information was created from technical events, information that is crucial at the business level for detecting underlying problems;

(v)   The current event systems often do not apply business rules in a network to support distributed event handling based on business and logical areas.

(vi)   Although business objects and rules often relate to multiple data sources and multiple partners that change constantly, events related to changes and status of the data and processes can not be integrated;

(vii)   The tasks or computational actions that cope with changes and monitoring are not related to specific information types and do not contain knowledge about a business-process element or logical group with an individual rule set.

General Goal. In this paper we present an approach to monitoring data consistency and business processing based on declarative software agents 7 . Declarative agent specifications that facilitate the use, programming and management of such agent-based systems allow for different distributed database and Web user interface structures to be interoperable. This declarative approach also relates business events to technical events while conveying to the users business meaningful events, that is agents that can deal with various levels of abstraction of a business object, and that can orchestrate and monitor data change and business processing.

Research Questions. How can we monitor dynamic events related to data consistency and business process in a code independent way How can we manage active data and processes in a flexible way through operations to augment, refine, form interconnections, ensure consistency, and monitor data and processes   How can software agents help manage events at various levels and with various   purposes How can we define events - low-level and high-level (that is, business-related) – and relate them so that we can monitor high-level events independent of the low-level ones   How can we relate a high-level event to its low-level event implementation when necessary (e.g., when we want to trace what were the technical causes of a high-level failure)   How can a multi-agent system be defined that allows the agents to assist each other and orchestrate and monitor data management and business processes

Benefits. The benefits of our approach include:

- Facilitating the use, programming and management of declarative   agent-based systems. The declarative agent specifications help personnel to be able to use, program and manage database and world-wide web content and business processes with reduced knowledge of the technical details of such systems;

- Providing a highly interoperable solution. There is support for disparate database structures (e.g., different forms or database tables) hosted on different, distributed relational database management systems (RDBMS). These features make our solutions highly interoperable;

- Conveying to the users business-meaningful events. Events relate not only to physical elements, but are also related to high-level business objects; the errors and processing status of operations related to a business object can be conveyed to the user based on business logic events even when the events related to these errors involve physical element events that have occurred at the code level;

- Defining the systems in a declarative way that is independent of a specific run-time environment. The software agent declarations are executable in a variety of run-time environments, including synchronous (command-line) execution, web-server driven execution, and asynchronous execution such as the firing of a database trigger or a programmable event;

- Relating business events to technical events. We can trace high-level events to the low-level ones in order to establish a relationship between events related to business logic and events related to the technical issues, such as database and Web form changes;

- Providing agents that deal with various levels of abstraction of a business object. Agents are specialized and can also deal with logical information instead of focusing only on technical and physical elements related to implementation issues;

- Supporting agents that can orchestrate data change management and process monitoring. Some agents can be related to both low-level and high-level data and event declarations and events and can, therefore, be associated with and orchestrate the management of data and business processes in a more organized and flexible way.

Paper Organization. The paper is structured as follows. In Section 2 we give an overview of our approach. In Section 3 we define an instance of our approach that focuses on the problem of consistency and interoperability among distributed databases and Web User interfaces. In Section 4 we briefly describe our current system implementation and applications in which the approach has been applied. In Section 5 we describe related work and, finally, in Section 6 we present our conclusions and future work.

2   Overview of the Approach

The approach is illustrated in Figure 1.

In Figure 1, we illustrate the approach involving: distributed databases (and servers), Web user interfaces (and Web servers), low-level declarative specifications, management (low-level and high-level) events, business objects and rules, high-level specifications, and agents that perceive events at various abstraction levels and orchestrate the management process (e.g., refinement, consistency and monitoring).

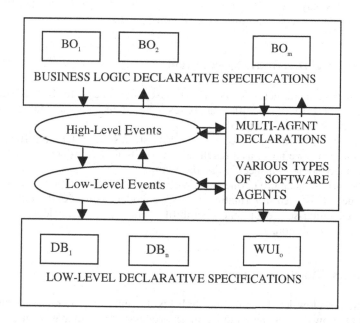

Fig. 1. Multi-agent Approach to Monitored Data Consistency and Business Processing.

In the following text, in order to define our ideas in a more concrete way, we try to illustrate the elements of our approach by focusing on consistency and interoperability problems among distributed databases and Web User interfaces. However, it should be clear that our approach deals with a class of problems that is more general than consistency checking (e.g., problems related to monitoring data changes and business process status).

2.1   Distributed Databases (and Servers)

The distributed databases (DB_1, ...,DB_n) change constantly and should be kept consistent at all times. In most cases changes or additions to data require handling by people or processes within a larger system. Besides having an effect on other data, these changes may also affect business processes related to this data and be subject to business rules that govern the specific data sets.

2.2   Web User Interfaces Servers

In Figure 1, Web user interfaces are denoted by WUI_o. These user interfaces may be defined by forms and other types of user presentation. These distributed user interfaces also need to be kept consistent. Sometimes changes or additions to these forms need to be handled within the context of a larger system. The changes in these Web interfaces may also affect the business processes related to the data forms and be subject to business rules that govern the presented data.

2.3   Low-Level Declarative Specifications

We use metadata to describe each database that needs to be accessed. Meta-information describing specific databases and their relevant tables is defined declaratively using XML and XSL 8,9 .

By defining different databases, which often store similar data in different ways, in a declarative way, we have, as a result, a solution that is interoperable with respect to data and independent of a specific database vendor.

We also use metadata to define each Web user interface component (e.g., a form or a catalogue). This meta-information is also encoded using XML and the resulting solution encompasses data interoperability and is independent of a specific implementation solution.

2.4   Process Monitoring Events

We define both low-level events and high-level events. In general, we want to define events that allow data content and business processes to be managed in a flexible way through agents that augment, refine, interconnect, ensure consistency, and monitor data and business processes. They can be related to the status of data and processes. Events can also be related to time and location.

We also relate high-level to low-level events in order to know, for example, what low-level events somehow led to the occurrence of a high-level event, or what low-level events led to high-level failures in business processing (see Section 3.2.5).

Low-level events relate to technical changes. Low-level events can be defined, for example, to represent changes in a table or a Web form. These events relate to raw information and its changes (e.g., database triggers).

High-level events relate to logical elements, rather than physical ones, and to business-oriented process status monitoring. This monitoring process may be governed by related business rules.

2.5   Business Objects and Rules

A business object is a representation of an active entity in the business domain, including at least its business name and definition, attributes, behavior, relationships and constraints. A business object may represent, for example, a person, a place or concepts such as a domain entity or a user interface 10 . The representation may be in a natural language, a modeling language, or a programming language.

A business rule is a property of a business object, that is, a constraint that governs the behavior, relationships, and attributes of a business object.

2.6   Business Logic Declarative Specifications

These specifications represent the application at a high-level of abstraction. They encode information about the business objects and their associated rules. The specifications are represented using XML tag sets.

2.7   A Diversity of Software Agents

Various software agents are defined for different purposes. Agents perceive events and execute actions that may depend on their internal states, rules or knowledge. Agents may orchestrate actions related to a specific purpose by delegating some of their tasks to specialized agents that can help them. When they orchestrate more complex actions, agents act based on their facts and rules in order to decide when and how to accomplish a certain task. The agents are represented in XML.

Agents can be specialized and can also monitor situations such as the automated processing steps and time constraints related to the processes. They can further process events, generate new events, decide when, where, and how to react, start actions, and generate messages. They can also relate technical events to business logic events.

2.7.1   Database Agents
Database agents are used to connect to one or more databases (interoperability) and perform consistency operations on them. These agents perform tasks such as comparing and copying database content, indexing and harvesting Web content.

2.7.2   Web User Interface Agents
These agents are used to connect one or more Web user interfaces (interoperability) and perform consistency operations among them. They can be used, for example, to check the consistency of two Web catalogs. These agents can perform operations such as comparing and copying the content of Web forms.

2.7.3   Database/Web Agents
These agents are used to connect one or more Web user interfaces to one or more databases (interoperability) and perform consistency operations on them. Operations that these agents can perform include indexing and harvesting Web content, and submitting a series of operations to a world-wide web server as in a POST or GET web form submission.

2.7.4   Synchronous and Asynchronous Agents

These agents can, for example, perform tasks that can be executed synchronously (from a command-line on demand or through a web server) or in response to an asynchronous event such as the firing of a database trigger or a time-based programmable event. In addition, time-out events can be related to the clients, servers, the Web user interfaces or the databases.

2.7.5   Business Logic Agents

These agents are directly related to business objects and associated rules. They are related to events that occur at the business logic level and to logical elements, not to physical elements. They encode expertise in a certain element such as checking product catalog consistency in multiple supplier systems or testing data consistency in regular intervals. However, they can also perform more general tasks such as checking the status of business objects or monitoring process chains.

2.7.6   Orchestration Agents

These agents, which perceive low-level and high-level events, need to interact with other agents, and with low-level and high-level descriptions (e.g., the business-oriented declarations and the Web form and database declarations) in order to execute their actions. Agents that orchestrate[2] the data and process change management needed to recognize events, decide what to do when these events happen, when, how and where to accomplish their tasks, and to whom they can delegate some of their tasks in order to accomplish their goals.

2.8   Interaction among Agents

Because each agent is expert in tasks related to some low-level or high-level elements and events (e.g., a business-process element), agents have to depend on other agents to perform their tasks. An agent in charge of online shopping, for example, may deal with agents in charge of the shopping front end and order entry. An agent that deals with the shopping front may need to deal with agents in charge of tasks such as the product catalog, consistency between catalogs and order creation. An agent that needs to check the consistency of a product catalog in a multiple supplier system needs the help of agents that, for example, compare content, copy data, and agents that execute other low level database operations.

2.9   Multi-agent Declarative Specifications

In our approach multi-agent systems are specified in a declarative way. The declarations are defined with XML tag sets and describe agent features such as beliefs, goals, and plans.

---

[2] Agent orchestration can be seen as a form of agent coordination 7 in which the involved agents relate to different levels of abstraction.

3   An Instance of the Multi-agent Approach

In this section we provide an overview of our approach by focusing on the problem of consistency and interoperability among distributed databases and Web User interfaces, and the relation of this problem to business logic objects.

In the following overview, we will define the events, agents and declarations that are used in the concrete architecture.

3.1   Data Management and Business Processing Events

Low-level events relate to changes in database tables or specific data in the tables. Additions and removal of items may also be monitored through specific events. High-level events in this case relate to the type of consistency that is expected. For example, events can be "product catalog consistency check," "database consistency check," or "database and Web form consistency check."

3.2   Software Agents

In our approach agents and their features are specified in XML. Although we want to take full advantage, in the long run, of the TAO agent representations that we have defined in 11 , our initial agent representations contain beliefs (that we consider as attributes), goals (that we consider as the desired state of the agent), and the agent plans and actions that can be used to accomplish these plans. Our agent schema declaration is shown in Appendix I. In the next subsection we illustrate this declarative specification using database agents as an example.

The agents we specify in the application of our approach include database agents, Web user interface agents, business logic agents and orchestration agents. We also show how high-level events and low-level events are related. Database/ Web agents, which were described in Section 2.7.3, combine the features of database and Web user interface agents, and for this reason, we have not included their declarations. Although we have not provided explicit declarations for synchronous and asynchronous agents, described in Section 2.7.4, we have introduced agents with timeout attributes (Section 3.2.2) and agents that monitor consistency based on time constraints (Section 3.2.4).

3.2.1   Database Agents

The goals assigned to database agents (DBAgent for short) are related to data processing. As a result, their state must reflect characteristics that facilitate reasoning in terms of data accessibility and manipulation. Moreover, the desired state after a goal is attained must reflect the changes, if any, in the underlying DBMS. With this in mind, our DBAgent was designed to incorporate elements such as: connections, data sources, tables and queries, which are represented according to the structure shown in Appendix I.

Consider a database backup system where a DBAgent is responsible for comparing content of tables in order to decide if it is time to perform the backup. First such an agent must have a connection to the database server, which can be represented as a belief given that beliefs represent agent's knowledge about the world (in this case a DB environment). Analyzing the XML code presented in Table 1, the attribute *e pr* specified within the belief named *connection* holds the connection string to a Sybase database called Staff that is located on the local machine.

Table 1. DBAgent's Beliefs Declaration.

```
<beliefs>
    <belief name   connection  expr   127.0.0.1:sybase:Staff ></belief>
    <belief name   timeout  expr   150 ></belief>
</beliefs>
```

The next step is to represent how the comparison goal is achieved. For this purpose we introduce a desired state of the agent; when this desired state becomes true, the goal has been achieved. Table 2 shows that our DBAgent desired state is defined in terms of three possible cases: one stating that the source and destination tables are equal (srcTable E destTable); another stating that they are different (srcTable NE destTable); and the last one (NO), that is our representation of failure to achieve the goal.

Note that in order to represent the desired state cases we can use the belief names and goal parameter names. For example, in Table 2, the parameter named *srcTable* matches the name srcTable present in the *table comparison* desired state cases.

Table 2. DBAgent's Goals Declaration.

```
<goal name   table comparison  desired state   srcTable E   destTable   srcTable NE
   destTable  NO >
    <params>
        <param name   srcTable  value   table1 ></param>
        <param name   destTable  value   table2 ></param>
    </params>
</goal>
```

In this case actions correspond to agents' low-level activities. Table 3 declares an action named *open* that requires a parameter named *srcTable*.

Plans on the other hand, are more complex entities once they coordinate the execution of actions. Thus a plan representation must reflect the sequence in which the actions are executed in the attempt to achieve a goal. In Table 3 the plan called *compare* uses the actions *open,   uery* and *close* during its execution. Another responsibility of this plan is to handle parameter passing among the actions.

Table 3. DBAgent's Plans and Actions Declaration.

```
<action name   open >
    <params>
        <param name   srcTable  value   table1 ></param>
    </params>
</action>
<plan name   compare  actions   open;query;close ></plan>
```

Table 4. WUIAgents Declaration.

```
<AgentDecl>
  <class name  WUIAgent ></class>
  <beliefs>
    <belief name  domain expr  csg.uwaterloo.ca/ ></belief>
    <belief name  timeout expr  150 ></belief>
  </beliefs>
  <goals>
    <goal name  data consistency desired state  srcData E  destData  srcData NE
    destData  NO >
      <params>
        <param name  srcURL  value  url1 ></param>
        <param name  srcData value  d1 ></param>
        <param name  destURL value  url2 ></param>
        <param name  destData value  d2 ></param>
      </params>
    </goal>
    <goal name  form fill desired state  f  NO >
      <params>
        <param name  form value  f ></param>
        <param name  tag value  tag ></param>
        <param name  data value  d ></param>
      </params>
    </goal>
  </goals>
  <actions>
    <action name  get >
      <params>
        <param name  url value  http://csg.uwaterloo.ca/ ></param>
        <param name  form value  demo1.asp ></param>
      </params>
    </action>
    <action name  query >
      <params>
        <param name  url value  http://csg.uwaterloo.ca/ ></param>
        <param name  form value  demo1.asp ></param>
        <param name  tag value  name ></param>
      </params>
    </action>
  </actions>
  <plans>
    <plan name  fill actions  get;query; ></plan>
    <plan name  consist actions  open 1;open 2; query 1 ; query 2 ; test ></plan>
  </plans>
  <relationships></relationships>
</AgentDecl>
```

Web User Interface Agents. Web User Interface agents (WUIAgents for short), deal with WEB documents in order to achieve goals related to form manipulation, data consistency and presentation layout. For that reason such agents' state must be aware of Web aspects like domains, urls and tags in order to perform an activity such as assessing a given webpage. Table 4 illustrates the complete XML declaration of a WUIAgent that is responsible for attaining two goals: Data Consistency and Form Fill.

Data Consistency compares web documents and its state reports if two documents (or parts of them) are equal. The reasoning involved in this goal is based on the parameters that indicate the documents (*src L* and *dest L*) and the regions (*src ata* and *dest ata*) to be compared. Form Fill can fill in the field specified by the *form* and *tag* parameters with the value present in the *data* attribute and then submit it automatically.

3.2.2 Business Logic Agents

Business Logic Agents (BLAgents for short) are directly related to business objects and associated rules. They can use other agents to achieve their goals and their state must reflect the high level constructs that are present the application domain. An example of such an agent can be found in Table 5. The goal *enrollment* is responsible for registering *people* in a webform so that these people can, for example, attend a conference. To do so the BLAgent delegates part of its job to a DBAgent and a WUIAgent. By using this approach the BLAgent can concentrate on issues related to the business logic.

The use of external agents is specified in the control section of the XML representation. Once this is done, agents can be referenced by their names and their goals can be invoked and synchronized as can be seen in the plan named *enroll*. The actions of the *enroll* plan invoke the DBAgent so that the table *people* can be loaded. After that is achieved, the WUIAgent can use the *people* data in order to fill the *enroll asp* form.

Table 5. BLAgent declaration

```
<AgentDecl>
  <class name  BusinessLogicAgent ></class>
  <beliefs>
     <belief name  environment expr  csg.uwaterloo.ca/app ></belief>
     <belief name  timeout expr  150 ></belief>
  </beliefs>
  <goals>
     <goal name  enrollment desired state  people AND enroll  NO >
        <params>
           <param name  people value  tb1 ></param>
           <param name  enroll value  csg.uwaterloo.ca/enroll.asp ></param>
        </params>
     </goal>
  </goals>
  <plans>
     <plan name  enroll actions  DBAgent goal(table  load,people); WUIAgent
        goal(form  fill,people,enroll,  ></plan>
  </plans>
  <relationships>
     <control>
       <agent>DBAgent</agent>
       <agent>WUIAgent</agent>
     </control>
  </relationships>
</AgentDecl>
```

3.2.3   Orchestration Agents

Orchestration Agents (OrchAgents for short), perceive low-level and high-level events, in order to coordinate the agent's environment. An example of such an agent can be obtained by defining an agent that checks table consistency and form consistency at a specific time. According to Table 6, when the DailyCheck event occurs the OrchAgent will perceive it and will achieve the goals of both DBAgent and WUIAgent previously defined in Tables 3 and 4 , respectively.

Table 6. OrchAgent Declaration

```
<AgentDecl>
  <class name   OrchestrationAgent ></class>
  <events>
    <event name   DailyCheck >
      <params>
        <param name   time  value   3:00 ></param>
      </params>
    <event>
  </events>
  <goals>
    <goal name   ScheduledCheck  desired  state   DailyCheck AND DBAgent(srcTable
      E   destTable) AND WUIAgent(srcData E   d2)  NO >
      <params>
        <param name   srcData value   d1 ></param>
        <param name   destData  value    destData ></param>
        <param name   srcTable  value    table1 ></param>
        <param name   destTable  value   table2 ></param>
      </params>
    </goal>
  </goals>
  <relationships>
    <control>
     <agent>DBAgent</agent>
     <agent>WUIAgent</agent>
    </control>
  </relationships>
</AgentDecl>
```

3.2.4   Relating High-Level and Low-Level Events

Our approach allows high-level business events to be related to low-level technical events. Using our agent declarative style, we can define high-level business logic agents that depend on business-related goals and events. For example, a high-level agent in charge of a database consistency check has a goal that depends on several low-level goals such as different table comparisons (e.g., table comparison in Table 2).

We can also define in the high-level agent declarations, a high-level event called "checked database consistency", that occurs when the consistency of the whole database has been established. The occurrence of this high-level event clearly depends on low-level events that occur when each of the individual tables has been compared and found consistent. In other words, only when all the table comparison events occur, can the "checked database consistency" occur.

4   Implementation and Applications

4.1   System Implementation

Our multi-agent system is designed to be easy to use, program and maintain, and yet still offer a rich framework for creating and running software agents for data and process change management.

XSL transformations were defined to create C/C++ programs from XML agent declarations. As well, server side scripts have been set up to compile the C/C++ code into an executable image that can be downloaded back to the client system or saved on the server. The executable program (in Visual C) can be executed by other agents, or run from a command-line, from the web server, as part of a database trigger or in response to some other asynchronous event, such as a timed event.

4.2   Applications

The Computer Systems Group (CSG) at the University of Waterloo recently worked with several community groups in the Regional Municipality of Waterloo in Ontario, Canada to facilitate the presentation of local information throughout the community and beyond.   In the project a web site was created to present a directory of employment support services in the region.   The Waterloo-Wellington Training and Adjustment Board (WWTAB) had contracted with another local agency to contact local employment support agencies and to construct a database with an extensive description of each employment support agency.

WWTAB made the database of employment support agencies available to CSG as part of a community information project and agreed to maintain it.   CSG provided the web site technology, database access services and site hosting facilities.   Several focus groups were held around the community to evaluate the ease with which information could be accessed through the site.   Because direct connectivity from the web server to the remote database has turned out to be too unreliable and slow to provide reasonable responses to web queries, a simple method for synchronizing the database content from WWTAB to the web server was needed.   Both content comparison and copying agents were created in the initial implementation.

On average, approximately one record per week is updated in the WWTAB database of about 400 records.   The agent that was created was intended to synchronize the databases nightly.

Furthermore, WWTAB is one of 23 training and adjustment boards (TABs) in the Province of Ontario that are funded by the Government of Ontario to collect such information.   Partway through the project, the province mandated that all of the local TABs must enter their data into a newly established central Web site for employment support.   The contractor that had created the central database and web site did not permit any direct connections to their database – all local TABs must enter their data into web forms and each employment support agency record would require between 4 and 10 separate form pages to be entered.   In response to this requirement, we have extended the XML/agent technology to include web form submission.   This approach will also be used for ongoing maintenance as database records continue to change.

We are currently experimenting with other features of our agent approach, such as more advanced consistency checking among distributed heterogeneous databases and Web user interfaces.

5   Related Work

5.1   Data Consistency

Data consistency is a critical issue in (distributed) databases and systems involving dispersed distributed databases and Web data 12 . In general, current approaches have focused on consistency issues related to distributed databases at the implementation and network levels and do not consider a hybrid solution based on events and multi-agents 13 .

An approach has been proposed using agents to control database fragments but their focus is on achieving high availability in the face of communication failures and network partitions 14 . Our approach, however, provides a solution that is monitor-oriented in the sense that the consistency is checked as a result of changes indicated by events through various forms of software agents, and the consistency is related to both low-level technical changes and high-level consistency checks related to business objects and their associated rules. The existing solutions often deal with implementation –level consistency problems and do not provide any links to the business logic objects and rules.

In addition, conventional solutions to distributed, shared data consistency, and to maintaining consistency of replicated interdependent data across web distributed sites often use explicit data synchronization messages for consistency and replica management. Our agent-based approach allows the responsibility of consistency management to be assigned to a variety of software agents that work at various levels of abstraction.

5.2   Business Process Monitoring and Event-Based Systems

Various approaches to modeling and implementing business processes 15,16,17 have been proposed. However, the focus of most approaches has been on modeling the processes themselves and not on their relation to agents and events at various levels of abstraction.

The area of business process monitoring addresses issues related to monitoring the status of business process 5 . The justification for this approach is that in e-business environments, automatic interpretation and routing of online information about the status of business process execution will become routine, and messages automatically deriving from inside the company will seamlessly integrate with those from business partners.

Although we share many of the general goals of the process monitoring-based approaches, our approach is directed towards consistency and event notification 6 because we intend to enhance our approach by using techniques based on frameworks we have developed for the extension of the standard Web service architecture with notification and other dynamic features 18 .

Examples of monitoring agents include agents that monitor patients in intensive care units 19 and agents that can be delegated to monitor satellite operations 20 .

Many examples of event-based systems have been provided in the literature. These examples differ in the structure of the events, the way the events are observed, the mechanisms for event subscription, and their overall run-time architecture 6, 21 . In general, these approaches describe implementation infrastructures that do not address the specific features of multi-agent systems.

5.3   Software Agents

There have been several successful implementations and platforms of agent-based systems to support applications such as communities of cooperating robots, Web-based information retrieval, economic system modeling, and group decision-making 22,23 . In contrast with the proposed declarative representations of multi-agent systems 24 , our approach also makes explicit the features and capabilities the agents must posses in order to interact successfully because procedural representations are often difficult to extend to novel domains or characterize formally. However, while their approach focuses on a formalization using propositional linear temporal logic and defines operators to express specific cases such as the achievement of goals, our approach is focuses on declarative representation that are not dependent on a specific formalism such as temporal logic.

6   Conclusions and Future Work

In this paper we have offered a new approach to monitor data consistency and business processing based on declarative software agents. We have provided a general description of the elements of our approach in terms of events, declarative specifications and various kinds of software agents. We have also presented a specific instance of our approach to illustrate some of its representative features, and also described an implementation and applications that have been developed as part of our feasibility studies.

In a broad sense, the orchestration agents we have defined mimic some of the features of dendritic cells in the human immune system. These cells recognize invaders such as bacteria and activate other cells of the immune system that can help them fight the invaders 25 . In our case, as an analogy, orchestration agents recognize specific events and react to them by trying to achieve their goals with the help of other less specialized agents.

As future work, we want to investigate the following issues. We want to improve our agent-based representations by incorporating definitions related to a more general specification approach such as the one we have developed in 11 in order to obtain an enhanced version of our declarative specifications. Some agent and business oriented declarative languages have been proposed in the literature (e.g., 26) but they do not deal with most of the features addressed by our approach.

Although we have considered beliefs as facts (i.e., attributes), we plan to incorporate rules as part of our belief declaration. A challenge will be finding a suitable representation that enables the definition of the interdependency among agent goals, events, roles and beliefs.

We also want to use formal methods to establish certain attributes of the software agents and their interactions. A critical question is "How can we have confidence that the agents that react to change events are preserving the integrity of the applications and the constraints related to the business rules " To accomplish this objective we want to define techniques to transform the declarative representation models into languages such as Prolog and XL (the process algebra language of XMC). We will define model-checking techniques 27,28 to validate the declarative model descriptions using Prolog and a very expressive temporal logic called mu-calculus 29 . We will define techniques to transform the process-based declarative representation into Prolog and XL. We will also define model-checking techniques to validate declarative process-based descriptions using Prolog and mu-calculus. One challenge will be to define properties at the meta-level that have appropriate meaning at the application level.

References

1. Connalen, J., Building Web Applications with UML, Addison-Wesley, 2000.
2. Orfali, R., Hankey, D., Client/Server Programming with Java and Corba, John Wiley, 1998.
3. Yesha, Y., Kou, W., Directions and Trends for E-Commerce Research, Electronic Commerce Technology Trends: Challenges and Opportunities, IBM Press, February 2000.
4. Chen, D., Chung, J., Internet Based Electronic Business Framework and Business to Business Standards, Topics in Electronic Commerce, Second International Symposium (ISEC), Lecture Notes in Computer Science, vol. 2040, pp. 158–169, Springer-Verlag, 2001.
5. Husmann, E., Schmitt, T., Schuler, T., Agents are Watching, Intelligent Enterprise Magazine, online publication, www.intelligententerprise.com/000908/feat2.shtml/ebusiness
6. Rosenblum, D., Wolf, A., A Design Framework for Internet-Scale Event Observation and Notification, SIGSOFT Foundations on Software Engineering (FSE), 1997.
7. Nwana, H.S. Software Agents: An Overview. In: The Knowledge Engineering Review, October/November 1996, Volume 11, Number 3, pages 205–244.
8. Bray, T. et al., Extensible Markup Language (XML) 1.0, W3C Recommendation, http://www.w3.ort/TR.
9. Clark, J., XSL Transformations (XSLT) Specification 1.0, W3C Recommendation, http://www.w3.org/TR.
10. Coad, P. North, D., Mayfield, M., Object Models: Strategies, Patterns, and Applications, Prentice Hall, 1997.
11. Silva, V., Garcia, A., Brandao, A., Chavez, C., Lucena, C., Alencar, P., Taming Agents and Objects in Software Engineering, (this volume, pp. 1–28), 2003.
12. Traiger, I., Gray, J., Galtieri, C., Lindsay, B., Transactions and Consistency in Distributed Database Systems, ACM Transactions on Database Systems, vol. 7, pp. 323–342, 1982.
13. Davidson, S., Garcia-Molina, H., Skeen, D., Consistency in Partitioned Networks, ACM Computer Surveys, vol. 17, no. 3, pp. 341–370, 1985.

14. Garcia-Molina, H., Kogan, B., Achieving High Availability in Distributed Databases, IEEE Transactions on Software Engineering, vol. 14, no. 7, 1988.
15. Osterweil, L.J., Software Processes are Software Too, Proceedings of the Ninth International Conference on Software Engineering (ICSE'87), pp. 2–14, Monterey, California, IEEE Computer Society Press, 1987.
16. Derniame, J.C., Kaba, B.A., Wastell, D. (Eds), Software Process: Principles, Methodology, and Technology, Springer-Verlag LNCS 1500, 1999.
17. Finkelstein, F., Kramer, J., and Nuseibeh, B., (Eds), Software Process Modeling and Technology, Research Studies Press Ltd., 1994.
18. Kalali, B., Alencar, P.S.C. Alencar, Cowan, D.D., WSNF: Designing a Web Service Notification Framework for Web Services, accepted by the International Workshop on Web Services: Research, Standardization, and Deployment, WS-RSD'02, USA, 2002.
19. Hayes-Roth, B., Larsson, J., A Domain-Specific Software Architecture for a Class of Intelligent Patient Monitoring Agents, J. Theoretical and Experimental Artificial Intelligence, 1995.
20. Jones, P., Jacobs, J., Cooperative Problem-Solving in Human-Machine Systems: Theory, Models, and Intelligent Associate Systems, IEE Transactions on Syestems, Man and Cybernetics, 2000.
21. Cugola, G., Di Nitto, E., Fuggetta, A., Exploiting and Event-Based Infrastructure to Develop Complex Distributed Systems, Proceedings of the International Conference on Software Engineering, pp. 261–270, 1998.
22. Hayes, C., Agents in a Nutshell – A Very Brief Introduction, IEEE Transactions on Knowledge and Data Engineering, vol. 11, no. 1, pp. 127–132, 1999.
23. Zincir-Heywood, A., Heywood, M., Chatwin, C., Object-Oriented Design of Digital Library Platforms for Multiagent Environments, IEEE Transactions on Knowledge and Data Engineering, vol. 14, no. 2, pp. 281–295, 2002.
24. Singh, M., Huhns, N., Stephens, L., Declarative Representations of Multiagent Systems, IEEE Transactions on Knowledge and Data Engineering, vol. 5, no. 5, 1993.
25. Banchereau, J., The Long Arm of the Immune System, Scientific American, pp. 55–59, November 2002.
26. FIPA Specification Repository. http://www.fipa.org
27. Clarke, E.M., Grumberg, O., Peled, D., Model Checking, MIT Press, 2000.
28. Clarke, E. M., Emerson, E. A., Sistla, A. P., Automatic Verification of Finite-State Concurrent systems Using Temporal Logic Specifications, ACM TOPLAS 8(2):244–263, April 1986.
29. Ramakrishna, Y. S., Ramakrishna, C. R., Ramakrishna, I. V., Smolka, S. A., Swift, T. W., and Warren, D. S., Efficient Model Checking Using Tabled Resolution, in Grumberg, editor, Computer Aided Verification (CAV'97), LNCS 1243, Haifa, Israel, Springer-Verlag, 1997.

Appendix I

In defining the agents declarations we have followed the DTD 8 shown next.

```
<?xml version='1.0' encoding='UTF-8'?>
<!ELEMENT AgentDecl
(relationships|beliefs|class|goals|plans|actions|events)*>
<!ELEMENT action (params)*>
```

```
<!ATTLIST action
    name CDATA #IMPLIED  >
<!ELEMENT actions (action)*>
<!ELEMENT belief EMPTY>
<!ATTLIST belief
    name CDATA #IMPLIED
    expr CDATA #IMPLIED  >
<!ELEMENT beliefs (belief)*>
<!ELEMENT class EMPTY>
<!ATTLIST class
    name CDATA #IMPLIED  >
<!ELEMENT goal (params)*>
<!ATTLIST goal
    name CDATA #IMPLIED
    desired_state CDATA #IMPLIED  >
<!ELEMENT goals (goal)*>
<!ELEMENT param EMPTY>
<!ATTLIST param
    name CDATA #IMPLIED
    value CDATA #IMPLIED  >
<!ELEMENT params (param)*>
<!ELEMENT plan EMPTY>
<!ATTLIST plan
    name CDATA #IMPLIED
    actions CDATA #IMPLIED  >
<!ELEMENT plans (plan)*>
<!ELEMENT agent (#PCDATA)>
<!ELEMENT control (agent)*>
<!ELEMENT relationships (control)*>
<!ELEMENT event (params)*>
<!ATTLIST event
    name CDATA #IMPLIED  >
<!ELEMENT events (event)*>
```

Author Index